Old Northwest Historical Series
III

ROBERT DINWIDDIE
Lieutenant-governor of Virginia

ROBERT DINWIDDIE

his career in

American Colonial Government and Westward Expansion

by

LOUIS KNOTT KOONTZ

Associate professor of history, University of California at Los Angeles
Author of The Virginia Frontier, 1754-1763

THE ARTHUR H. CLARK COMPANY
Glendale, California, U.S.A.
1941

To
JOHN OLIN KNOTT
For his unceasing encouragement

SPECIAL ACKNOWLEDGMENTS ARE DUE:

To the University of California for a series of research grants
To the Social Science Research Council of New York City for a
grant-in-aid
To the Arthur H. Clark Company for their public service in bringing out this volume
To the Work Projects Administration, Project No. 11864, for research and clerical assistance

Contents

Illustrations

Preface

Two controlling factors have been kept in mind in the writing of this biography: first, that historical accuracy must be the paramount aim; and second, that this study, written exclusively from source materials, is, however, not an editing of correspondence, but a biography. The eighteenth-century flavor has been preserved so far as seems reasonable by a generous use of quotations; but in deference to the undoubted preference of the general reader it has seemed unwise to preserve the original spelling in cases where it would be meaningless to all but specialists, or to retain the excessive use of capital letters, or even to perpetuate the Georgian-age punctuation. Eighteenth-century italics that have no modern significance, as in excerpts from the *Gentlemen's magazine* or from the *Journals of the house of burgesses,* have been omitted. Nor have obvious typographical errors in the documentary material been preserved, since calling attention to them would serve no useful purpose.

Curious contractions of words, such as "y's," "y't," "h'ble," "c't," and equally curious abbreviations, such as "amo." and "aff.," sprinkle the pages of R. A. Brock's two-volume edition of the Dinwiddie correspondence, universally known as the *Dinwiddie papers*. These contractions and abbreviations have long been thought to be an idiosyncrasy of Dinwiddie's. Those historians (and the present writer was once classed among them) who have made sport over these curiosities at Dinwiddie's expense will not have the last laugh; for it is now known that these shortened forms of words were employed only by Dinwiddie's private secretary, William Waller, as a time-saving device – and not by Dinwiddie himself. Waller used the contractions and abbreviations solely in Dinwiddie's letter books – the books in which he kept a draft of all letters to be sent out. He used but few contractions and abbreviations in the actual letters which he copied out in full form for the governor's signature. The letter books eventually were bound in five large folio volumes and have been preserved in the vaults of the Virginia historical society at Richmond. The letter-book drafts of communications serve substantially the same purpose as our modern carbon copies.

I made this discovery about the contractions in 1916 when working in the Draper collection in the Wisconsin state historical society library; comparing a sent-copy (technically called an out-letter) of a communication from Dinwiddie to Lord Loudoun with the letter-book draft of the same communication, the conclusion was inescapable. The long-accepted impression that Dinwiddie regularly used these strange contractions and abbreviations, that in many cases are hardly intelligible, is but another of the misconceptions that have gradually enveloped his personality. Since Brock printed the *Dinwiddie papers* exclusively from Dinwiddie's letter books, the contractions have been perpetuated to this day. Even such historical scholars as Francis Parkman and Herbert L. Osgood – as well as earlier writers like Jared Sparks and Washington Irving – were misled; and considering the great influence of these men, the evil that unwittingly has been done has indeed lived after them. Wherever possible, these now available out-letters have been quoted and cited as the primary source, with Brock's letter-book copies cited as a substantiating source. The present writer has brought together many hundreds of Dinwiddie's letters, as well as a substantial number of his reports and accounts, all of which were unknown to Brock; these are part of the collection now being assembled for a forthcoming volume of supplementary Dinwiddie papers.

No secondary bibliography has been included at the end of this volume for the simple reason that no books on Dinwiddie have been written. No one previously has put together in print more than a few consecutive sentences regarding Robert Dinwiddie. The only qualifications that must be made to this statement are first, R. A. Brock's sixteen-page introduction to his edition of the *Dinwiddie papers* fifty-six years ago; second, Professor T. J. Wertenbaker's brief but appreciative sketch in the *Dictionary of American biography* in 1930; and, third, the chapter on Dinwiddie in my monograph, *The Virginia frontier, 1754-1763,* which the Johns Hopkins Press published in 1925.

It is highly significant that Brock, who was obliged to read all of the Dinwiddie correspondence available at the time, came to a conclusion entirely favorable to the Virginia lieutenant-governor; whatever materials Professor Wertenbaker consulted forced him also to the same conclusion; and certainly the present writer has found no reason to take a different position. This biography grew out of my life-long interest in George Washington. In the course of my investigations, I became more convinced than ever not only that Washington was an important figure at this time, but Dinwiddie also. He simply has been an unknown man because of the black cloud of misconception which has obscured his personality.

Even though there are no lengthy secondary studies

dealing with Dinwiddie, one phase or another of the
critical period in which Dinwiddie lived and wrought
has intrigued the interest of more than one historian.
As a result, many collateral studies in the best traditions
of scholarship are available. For instance, a few biog-
raphies of contemporary characters have been written,
such as Stanley M. Pargellis's *Lord Loudoun,* A. T.
Volwiler's *George Croghan,* and lives of George Washington by Paul Van Dyke, Rupert Hughes, John C.
Fitzpatrick, and now one by N. W. Stephenson and
Waldo H. Dunn. Thomas P. Abernethy's is the best
book on the western lands question. Clarence W. Al-
vord's *Mississippi valley* is supreme in its field. Kenneth
P. Bailey's is the only complete history of the *Ohio company of Virginia;* and it is recent. Hayes Baker-Croth-
ers has written succinctly about the economic conditions
of a segment of eighteenth-century Virginia. Theodore
C. Pease wrote a brilliant 171-page introduction to
his edition of the diplomatic correspondence in the
Anglo-french controversy of 1749-1763. George Louis
Beer's studies of British colonial policy and the old commercial system deserve careful consideration. Herbert
L. Osgood and J. A. Doyle have dealt with the colonies
in general; but their works were published so long ago
that many of the conclusions expressed by both writers
must now be revised in the light of present-day researches. Stimulating, and valuable as broad surveys
within a limited field, are Alfred T. Mahan's sea-power
thesis as applied to the American scene, J. W. Fortes-
cue's study on the British army, and Archer B. Hulbert's
little volumes on historic highways.

Specific data for all or nearly all of the various works
just referred to can now be supplied from, or checked
against, sources available today but generally inaccessi-
ble to the earlier writers, who, however, deserve all the

credit that goes to pioneers in a field. Standing by themselves are the classic volumes by Parkman; yet there now is at hand a vast amount of documentary material, unknown to Parkman, which, for one thing, throws additional light on the French side of the international controversy. Fortunately, copies of practically all this newly-discovered source material are now available in several places in this country – notably in the Library of Congress – thanks chiefly to the technique of microphotography.

Also in a class by itself is Frederick Jackson Turner's epochal essay on the significance of the frontier, which must be the student's first approach to an intelligent understanding of the American colonial westward movement. The appropriate volumes in the three great cooperative histories are valuable. James Truslow Adams's volume, *Provincial society,* should be singled out; its title is a testimony to the change in emphasis in American historical writing. Edward Channing's early volumes are valuable, including his footnotes. The excellent sets that lately have been brought out both by Charles M. Andrews and by Lawrence H. Gipson bear witness to the renaissance of interest in colonial history. One-volume surveys of the whole period are those by Oliver P. Chitwood, Curtis P. Nettels, and Jennings B. Sanders. Enlightening articles on the mid-century era have come and continue to come from the pens of such scholars as Alfred P. James, Philip M. Hamer, and W. Neil Franklin.

In spite of every intention of an author to give credit where credit is due, acknowledgment of all the various types of assistance, cooperation, and encouragement which he receives is extremely difficult. It is impossible. Yet one gladly makes the attempt.

To the University of California I am indebted not

only for a series of research grants but also for space in the university buildings in which to carry on certain parts of the work made possible by the Work Projects Administration of the federal government. It would be ungenerous not to express appreciation of the loyalty, ability, and devotion of the workers who copied and checked materials which came to me in vast quantities in the form of transcripts and photographic reproductions. They rendered far more than perfunctory service. The Library of Congress and the Henry E. Huntington library, among the twenty-odd depositories where I have worked and been greatly aided, should be singled out for special mention. The Social Science Research Council of New York City was good enough to allocate a grant-in-aid for a longer study, many of the by-products of which have gone into this biography.

Of the individuals to whom I am indebted, I can mention only a few. To the late John H. Latané, whose lectures in history were an inspiration to me as an undergraduate student at Washington and Lee university, and later as a graduate student at the Johns Hopkins university, is owed a debt; he was one of the first to catch the vision of Dinwiddie's true stature. Dr. Kenneth P. Bailey, careful student of the colonial period and author of *The Ohio company of Virginia and the westward movement, 1748-1792,* helped prepare and check a large share of the citations to authorities. I owe him much. Many clarifying discussions with Dr. J. O. Knott, Washington, D.C., who early sensed Dinwiddie's true significance, and with Mr. and Mrs. L. H. Schultz, Batavia, New York, all of whom have read portions of the manuscript, place me under lasting obligation to them. I would be justified in dedicating this volume to my wife, considering her unflagging interest in its progress and the fact that every chapter somewhere bears the marks of her discriminating judgment.

Each debt is different. No one was in a position to do for me what Mr. R. B. Dunwoody, collateral namesake of the Virginia governor, eminent portrait-painter as well as businessman, did while I was in London in 1935. For instance, not only did he pilot me to the National Portrait Gallery to view the governor's original portrait, a copy of which he himself had recently painted and then presented at an appropriate ceremony to the state of Virginia, but he secured for me the copy from which came the frontispiece for this volume.

A similar yet special service has been rendered by Sir Campbell Stuart, K.B.E., collateral descendant of the governor. Through Sir Campbell's contacts in England, particularly through his relationship to the London *Times,* he alone was able to secure for me most valuable and hitherto unknown materials for this biography.

To the members of the families in America, in Scotland and in England, who bear directly or indirectly the Dinwiddie name, and who, through correspondence, have done for me what no others were in a position to do, I can but hope that this presentation here of the truth, as I see it, about their distinguished progenitor will be at least some meager return for their cooperation. Would that I might thank each of them by name.

A contribution unlike any other came from the College of William and Mary in the form of an invitation to become visiting professor of colonial history for the fall semester of 1937-1938, with a minimum teaching schedule and ample time for research in the stimulating atmosphere of Robert Dinwiddie's colonial city of Williamsburg.

To the officials of Colonial Williamsburg, inc., much

indeed is owed : manuscripts were copied for me, steno-
graphic service furnished, and the privilege extended to
me to make many personal visits to the restored buildings. Of utmost value for my investigation was the
visible expression in Williamsburg of the Restoration's
creed — "To create accurately and to preserve for all
time the significant portions of one of the most important cities of colonial America."

LOUIS KNOTT KOONTZ

Los Angeles, California
August 1, 1940

By Way of Introduction

Any man would be regarded as distinguished who vitally influenced the early manhood of that American who eventually became the Father of his Country. Or, anyone could lay claim to distinction who had an active part in the Anglo-american westward movement which finally resulted in the dominance of North America by English-speaking people. But where a man has had a notable part both in initiating the youthful George Washington into his career, and has also had quite as notable a part in extending English institutions over that portion of America now known as the "United States," such a man's life and labors cannot forever be ignored by biographers. Hence this account of the career of Robert Dinwiddie.

Dinwiddie has too often been misquoted and therefore misunderstood, misinterpreted, and maligned. These pages, however, do not seek to glorify him. Such a treatment would be equally unhistorical. The purpose is to show him frankly for what he was — the center of a series of events which were fruitful of results beyond the dreams of the men who took part in them. Robert Dinwiddie and the men associated with him, particularly while this Scotsman was lieutenant-governor of the colony of Virginia, naturally could not foresee how their every decision and movement would affect in later years the vast territory which they were then defending and conserving, and which was to be called the "United States of America." In these far-reaching decisions and pivotal movements, Robert Dinwiddie was more often than otherwise the leading spirit. He was not only in the conflict but of it. He was no mere figurehead or an accidental pawn of appointing powers. As his times are now seen in perspective, he was, instead, a man who made history.

Just as the visitor in Rome goes to the hill of the Pincio to get a comprehensive view of the city before making detailed observations, so a highlighted résumé of Robert Dinwiddie's times and accomplishments should prove clarifying to a more detailed study of his life.

Robert Dinwiddie's American career extended over a period of thirty-six years, from 1722 to 1758. There were many factors, some of which tended to promote colonial solidarity and others which tended to promote a spirit of separatism, which should be taken into consideration as the American background against which the administration of any British official in the colonies at this time is to be judged.

Colonial unity was promoted by a number of factors, fewer in number than those which tended to keep the colonies apart, but more significant. Long distance from Europe, rapid growth of population, a common hinterland – with boundless resources and a limitless future, as well as a constantly expanding area of free land correspondingly changed as the frontier was pushed farther westward – are influences that have been easily discernible. In addition, there was the need for a show of solidarity to cope with the occasional threats of the Spanish, the French, and the Indians – separately or in combination. A certain amount of cohesion resulted from a steadily growing opposition to all outside restraint or control, including imperial authority. Finally, an observer, like a colonial traveller, would have found throughout the continental and insular colonies, in spite of notable exceptions, a common language, laws, customs, and institutions, all of which had been derived principally from England.

Disunity was promoted by equally as many factors, even if less virile. A peculiar river system, with its eastward-flowing streams, tended to separate rather than to unite the colonists. A lack of communication and transportation resulted in isolation and provincialism. The several geographic regions were in such contrast as to promote political and economic sectionalism and conflict of interest – for instance, north against south, tidewater against piedmont, and settled area against frontier. Racial antagonisms were accentuated by the influx of non-English peoples, such as the Germans and the Scotch-irish, both of whom were mainly out on the frontiers, and the negroes, who were chiefly in the south. Creedal differences and misunderstandings were a minor, though potential, grievance by reason of the dominance of congregationalism in New England, episcopalianism in Virginia and South Carolina, catholicism in Maryland, quakerism in Pennsylvania, not to speak of methodists, presbyterians, moravians, and other dissenters in all the colonies, but more especially out toward the back country. Ignorance of geography, lack of surveys, and an overlapping of charter grants bred long-standing boundary disputes between almost every colony and its neighbor. The presence in the colonies of crown-appointed governors on the one hand, and of bicameral legislatures with a popularly elected lower house on the other, led inevitably to conflicts of authority, particularly between the governor and the lower house; or, in the case of Maryland and Pennsylvania, between proprietor and assembly, with the governor a kind of pawn in between. Added to these things were the individualistic elements that always gravitate to a new land of supposed opportunity, especially toward the border, where individualism was accentuated. Finally, the colonials, as "heirs of all the past," put into practice in America the long-established English traditions of freedom of speech and of assembly, guarantee from arbitrary taxation, as well as parliamentary control of the purse and popular participation in government. If these things insured the growth of the democratic way of life, they also insured a corresponding growth of the spirit of independence – independence of England and of each other. Thus the American scene was characterized by a series of curious contradictions.

But this period of Dinwiddie's life, 1722-1758, must also be painted upon a European background. During the greater part of this time the western European powers – England, France, Spain, Portugal, Holland, Prussia, and Austria – were involved in either potential or actual warfare with each other. No state in those years was as yet "satisfied." Those powers which possessed extensive holdings in North America were bent not only on retaining what they had but also on adding to them. The powers that had but little wanted more; and the powers which had none were turning hungry eyes upon this land of promise with hopes of finding a foothold here. The eighteenth-century scramble for territory was in full swing when in 1751 Robert Dinwiddie landed here to begin the most important phase of his career as an appointee of the British government.

What may well be styled the Second Hundred Years' war between England and France and their satellites was half over when, in 1722, Dinwiddie originally began his career as an insular colonial administrator in America. It had started, theoretically, at the time of the War of the Palatinate, 1689-1697, with its American counterpart, King William's war, and had ended inconclusively with the Treaty of Ryswick. This was a mere breathing spell, for the War of the Spanish Succession, 1701-1713, broke out almost at once, followed naturally by its American reflection, Queen Anne's war; and again, as before, the Peace of Utrecht, 1713, which closed it, while important, was clearly understood to be but a truce.

During the lull after 1713, which lasted thirty-one years, Dinwiddie held various American posts, on Bermuda, for example, and on the mainland, helping to establish the English mercantilists there, before the skies were again clouded by war. In 1744 the War of the Austrian Succession broke out, and once more America fell in line, as always, with her King George's war. But times changed and eventually she herself took the initiative. The terms at Aix-la-Chapelle in 1748 at the close of this third international and intercolonial preliminary skirmish made little pretense to finality. By this time even the people knew better.

It was immediately thereafter that two series of events took place — one sponsored by the French, the other by the English, and historians even now are by no means agreed as to priority.

The French symbolized their penetration into the upper Ohio territory by burying leaden plates (1749) to cement their claims, and followed this by throwing up a cordon of forts southward from Lake Erie (1753-1754) for the express purpose of intimidating not only the English but the Indians as well. But the English, not to be outdone, had by 1748 already formed the Ohio company, which had been conceived as early as 1745-1746, and whose unconcealed purpose in aid of land expansion and the fur trade was to settle numerous families as quickly as possible on its two-hundred-thousand-acre grant, erecting thereafter such forts as were needed to protect these settlements.

The objective of both nations was the same – the forks of the Ohio river, the "gateway to the west," where the Allegheny and the Monongahela rivers united to form La Belle rivière, and which is now the site of the city of Pittsburgh. This struggle, however, began not in Europe, spreading thereafter to America, as all preceding wars had done, but, contrarily, it began in the colonies and spread eastward until it caught up the great European powers in its flame. Its outbreak in the back country of America signalized the start of the first world war, and had as its inception the shot that killed Jumonville at Indian Rocks in southwestern Pennsylvania on the twenty-eighth of may 1754. This was the beginning of the American French and Indian war.

Two years of undeclared warfare were waged before France and England threw aside subterfuge and recognized in 1756 what had been a *fait accompli* since 1754. The struggle ended in 1763, including the European phase known as the Seven Years' war, when at last was signed what might be called a definitive Peace of Paris.

The vital rôle played by the forks of the Ohio must be clearly kept in mind. This key position was claimed in general by the English, but more especially by the colony of Virginia, whose alleged rights were based upon the terms of two colonial charters – her own and that of her northern neighbor, Pennsylvania. Virginia's second charter of 1609 read: "Two hundred miles north and two hundred miles south of Old Point Comfort, up into the land, west and northwest from sea to sea." Furthermore, Virginia claimed the same forks by virtue of the limitations of Pennsylvania's charter. That charter limited the bounds of the quaker colony to "five degrees west from the Delaware river." But here was the problem: from which great bend of the Delaware did this Pennsylvania claim start, the east or the west? Pennsylvania naturally claimed her five degrees westward should start at the most western bend of the Delaware, which would give her the forks (and which would be her eventual western boundary as a state, when the dispute was finally settled in 1779). Virginia just as naturally contended that Pennsylvania's starting-point should be the most eastern bend of the river; and if Virginia's claim should prevail, then the forks would be lost to Pennsylvania and would undeniably belong to Virginia. Thus, Virginia, the oldest, largest, most central, and most populous of Britain's continental provinces, held good claims to this crucial site in America.

At the moment when the situation was most tense, when any sudden act might precipitate a conflict involving the entire North American continent in a bloody and treacherous war, Robert Dinwiddie arrived to preside over the destinies of his majesty's American colony of Virginia. The Ohio company had just been formed. Dinwiddie became a member of it. George Washington's two half-brothers were members, and he was to become one. Influential Londoners and a sprinkling of other colonials were members. On october 31, 1753 Dinwiddie called upon young George Washington, then only twenty-one years old, to make his way to the French now already south of Lake Erie and warn them that they were on English territory – a procedure which might with equal propriety have been reversed, with the French taking the initiative. But Dinwiddie, backed by his "sea to sea" charter, was the first English governor to act. This charter had been repeated and emphasized for so long that the Virginians were not only fully convinced of its legality but also were prepared to defend their position. This claim, then, left but little of the American continent to the French, who had no such charters, although they had equally good lawyers. The

French declared that since they held the mouths of the two great streams, the St. Lawrence and the Mississippi, they justly laid claim to all the lands drained by them and their tributaries. Their claim left little of the continent to the English. Who had the better claim? And who today would undertake to mediate between them? While, theoretically speaking, no conflict is irrepressible, this French-and-English conflict was the nearest approach to one that any superhuman power, had it been endowed with a set and diabolical purpose, could have devised and thrust between two expanding nations: and Robert Dinwiddie was the man upon whose untried shoulders this imbroglio rested.

Family Background

The name Dinwiddie [1] is old and honorable in Scottish history. It can be dated back at least to the thirteenth century.

In 1296 the name of Alleyn Dinwithie is to be found in the historic "Ragman's Roll." [2] This roster comprised the leaders among the Scots who in that year, and upon terms that did not sacrifice honor, swore allegiance to a stronger leader, Edward I of England. It was at this time that Edward carried back with him from Scotland various of her historic treasures, among them the famous Coronation stone which ever since has remained beneath the Coronation chair in Westminster abbey. This Alleyn Dinwithie is commonly assumed to have been the progenitor of the numerous kinsmen who gave their names to lands that they held, and in some instances still hold, in the Scottish parishes of Apple-

---

[1] Past and present variations of the name abound: Dinwiddie, Dinwiddy, Dinwithie, Dinwoodie, Dinwoody, Dunwoody, Dunwody, Dunwooddy, Dunwiddie, Dumwoodie. One writer in july 1756 even spelled it Dunwhidy! (Loudoun papers, LO 1260 [Huntington library], july 7, 1756). Lord Loudoun, in his Memorandum books now found in the Huntington library, made frequent references to Dinwiddie. He seldom dotted the i's and in one instance apparently contributes a new spelling: Denwedie! (Huntington manuscripts, 1717 [vol. 4], 126).

[2] This notable historical record, once preserved in the Tower of London but at present in the public record office, is sometimes referred to as "Ragman Roll." The set of rolls contains the names of approximately 2000 landholders, subjects of the Scottish king, John Balliol, who acknowledged fealty to the English sovereign. The origin of the word Ragman seems to be shrouded in mystery. See Andrew Lang, *History of Scotland* (Edinburgh and London, 1907-1909), I, 179, 198n. Lang states that "a kind of game of forfeits bore the same name." See also Joseph Bain, ed., *Calendar of documents relating to Scotland preserved in the public record office* (London, 1884), II, xxiv; and for seals see lii and Appendix.

garth, Annandale, and Dumfries. Other kinsmen are widely scattered – from London to Australia – and the United States contains many worthy descendants of this ancient Scottish name.

The early history of the Dinwiddie clan as a whole would seem to be largely a record of feuds and counter-feuds. Yet these conflicts were probably significant of their spirit rather than of any disposition to be insurrectionary. Whatever was the cause or occasion, it is learned from authentic sources [3] that Thomas Dinwiddie, chief of his clan,[4] was killed by the Jardines in Dinwiddie tower in 1503. The Jardines also have been charged with slaying the Laird of Dinwiddie in Edinburgh's streets nine years later. It is further learned that the Laird of Dunwoody (Dinwiddie) and forty-four of his followers were among those Scots who swore allegiance to England in 1547.

Sometime prior to 1690 the branch of the family of Dinwiddie,[5] from which came the subject of this biography, moved to the section near Glasgow, where the descendants were to be found for generations.

Here in 1693, at Germiston,[6] Robert Dinwiddie, fated to be one of Virginia's colonial governors, was born. He came of a family of commercial men. His father, Robert Dinwiddie, was a merchant, born of merchant ancestors for generations. His mother, Eliza-

---

[3] R. A. Brock has discussed the sources of genealogical information available to him in his introduction to *Official records of Robert Dinwiddie, lieutenant-governor of the colony of Virginia, 1751-1758* (Richmond, Virginia, 1883-1884), I, vii-xx (hereafter cited as the *Dinwiddie papers*). Brock was at the time corresponding secretary and librarian of the Virginia historical society, which brought out the two volumes.

[4] The Dinwiddies were of lowland stock.

[5] Brock has an illuminating section in his introduction to the *Dinwiddie papers* (I, xxi-xxviii) on "Dinwiddie of Germiston, near Glasgow, Scotland, a partial genealogy, compiled from the archives of the Merchant's house, Glasgow, family records, etc."

[6] Germiston was a few miles from Glasgow.

beth Cumming,[7] was the daughter of a merchant,
Matthew Cumming, of Cardarroch. From such ances-
try it would be expected that a son would have a liking
for mercantile pursuits and also take business methods
to any public career he might follow. Since mercantile
affairs permeated the atmosphere of his early life, it was
only natural that young Robert should be trained in the
counting-house of his father.

He and his younger brother, Lawrence, formed a
partnership in the Delftfield Pottery company[8] of
Glasgow. This company passed along to descendants[9]
of the family and was not discontinued until the nineteenth century. While engaged in the pottery business,
Robert married Rebecca, the daughter of Reverend
J. Affleck. She must have lived long after her husband's
death, since an entry in the *Scots magazine,* under date
of february 14, 1793, speaks of "Mrs. Dinwiddie,
widow of Robert Dinwiddie Esq., formerly lieutenant-
governor of Virginia." She seems to have been then in
London.

The inclination to church attachment seen in Dinwiddie's marriage and discovered thereafter throughout his entire life is today noted in old Dumfries, Scotland. Here one bearing the name Robert Dinwiddie
was, up to the time of his death not long ago, an elder
in St. Michael's at that place, and, incidentally, wrote
a history of the church.[10]

[7] Sometimes given as Cummings.

[8] The Hon. R. B. Dunwoody, collateral descendant of the colonial executive,
expressed his opinion to me in London, in february 1935, that Dinwiddie had
once engaged in the pottery business. Mr. Dunwoody's opinion has since been
substantiated by information furnished me by Sydney L. Davison, Esq.,
F.R.S.A., curator of The Lady Lever art gallery, Port Sunlight, Cheshire, England, in a letter dated december 29, 1937.

[9] Gilbert, son of Lawrence Dinwiddie, was his successor at the pottery
works.

[10] "Robert Dinwiddie" is still the name of a firm of prominent stationers

The family must have been interested in the cultural side of life as well as the mercantile; at least Robert is known to have attended for a time the University of Glasgow. Perhaps it was the happy memory of those student years, or the attempt to express appreciation for the receipt, later on in life, of an honorary degree from his old alma mater, or both; at any rate Robert Dinwiddie remembered his university in his will.[11]

The details of Dinwiddie's career in Glasgow are not obtainable. Deductions may be made which some would consider strong circumstantial evidence as to his standing, influence, and ability. That his pottery business continued from father to son through the line of Lawrence Dinwiddie, and that Robert himself at twenty-eight years of age was appointed to represent the English government in Bermuda in connection with shipping activities of a governmental character, indicate that the Dinwiddie brothers were not failures in business. On the other hand, there is strong probability that Robert, in connection with his business, had had definite contacts with the colonies of England in America. The government would not have selected a man of little or no experience to represent it in so important a field as the New World, had not that man already shown unusual business ability and loyalty to the government which he came to America to represent.

and printers in Dumfries. Of the Robert Dinwiddie, who became manager and finally principal of the firm in the latter part of the last century, a friend, James McLaren, Esq. (justice of the peace, Surrey), "Beachwood Grove," Sonning Common, Oxfordshire, England, wrote me Christmas day 1937 with deep feeling. Referring to Dinwiddie's character, he said it was not "unworthy to be classed with the greatest . . . He was a man of infinite charm and obvious sincerity, much esteemed in Dumfries . . . When I left Scotland in 1905, he gave me a presentation copy of a book, for which he was largely responsible: the story of Saint Michael's church, Dumfries . . . Dinwiddie was an elder in that church and, I think, clerk to the kirk session."

[11] See note 99.

Collector of Customs

September 1, 1721 was one of the milestones in the life of Robert Dinwiddie, for then it was he really began his American career. This date marks his appointment as Britain's representative on the American island of Bermuda, in charge of admiralty affairs.[12]

The information for these developmental years is only fragmentary. Fortunately, however, the minutes of the commissioners for trade and plantations are now being published. These records of the days of long ago, giving an item here and there of the men who lived and worked in the years when Robert Dinwiddie carried on for his majesty's government on the island of Bermuda, afford us many important hints which prove valuable.

The most remarkable of these scraps of data is one in these minutes which informs us that on september 9, 1722 Colonel John Hope, lieutenant-governor of Bermuda, addressed an inquiry to the board of trade in London, asking "directions how to behave himself in relation to Mr. Dinwiddie's commission . . . there."[13]

Without making more of these stray and detached items than is justified, several inferences are unmistakable. For one thing, we now know that Robert Dinwiddie began his career in America, not in 1751 as lieutenant-governor, as has been ordinarily supposed, nor even in 1727, as R. A. Brock, editor of the *Din-*

---

[12] *Journal of the commissioners for trade and plantations* (November 1718 to december 1722) (London, 1920-——), 386-387.

[13] *Ibid.* (January 1722/3 to december 1728), 18.

widdie papers, supposed – but six years earlier still. He was therefore only twenty-eight when he entered upon his duties in Bermuda.

This extra half-decade of experience in the field of public service, in which he was afterwards to distinguish himself, came to Dinwiddie when he was impressionable. He thus had the advantage of beginning in the formative period of his life to store up observations which would be valuable in the responsible positions he was afterwards to fill.

The particular act or attitude which induced the governor of Bermuda to ask for guidance from his home government as to how to treat the newly-appointed Dinwiddie is left to wide conjecture. Whether the new appointee had shown himself too aggressive, from the governor's point of view, in giving unsolicited advice, or whether in his manner he assumed more than a man of his years should have assumed, we cannot tell. We are not at liberty, however, to read into this item from the old minutes anything prejudicial to Dinwiddie, just as we may not read into them anything which is particularly laudatory as to his zeal and energy. What we can say with confidence is that the young appointee was not only an appointee but a person. He was making his personality felt, so that his superior in office was induced, as the better part of prudence, to ask instructions how best to conduct himself toward this newcomer.

It is also further permissible for us to infer from the absence of any complaint against Robert Dinwiddie or any request for curtailment of his powers or activities on the part of Colonel Hope, that the young man had, either by his poise or knowledge of affairs in business or by that mysterious and undefinable something we call "personality," shown that he was not the average

man who in his early days seeks a job as a stepping-
stone to something higher. If we read this simple
incident in the light of the after-days of Dinwiddie,
we may get a glimpse of those "coming events that cast
their shadows before." In any case, the governor of
Bermuda respectfully asks, without suggesting any
course to pursue or without finding any fault: "How
must I handle myself with relation to this new official?"

There is, however, a sequel to this incident. The
records show that in 1728 this same Colonel Hope,
after Robert Dinwiddie had already, on december 1,
1727, been appointed collector of customs at Bermuda,[14] recommended him for a vacancy in his own
insular upper house, the Bermuda council.[15] This
recommendation was promptly approved by a royal
order in council, under date of march 17, 1730.[16] The
action of Colonel Hope and the approval of the council
join as evidence that Robert Dinwiddie at the age of
thirty-seven was making steady progress in knowledge
and in favor with the officials of the British government in his handling of its affairs in America.[17]

In his Bermuda position he apparently acted in ac-
cordance with a definite policy: as an official of his
government he would be zealous for "his majesty's
rights," and would magnify his office as a direct representative of the crown. Dinwiddie thus went beyond
accepting the minimum authority in his position to the
point of seeking the maximum power. This principle

---

[14] *Dinwiddie papers,* I, viii.

[15] *Journal of the commissioners for trade and plantations* (January 1728/9
to december 1734), 98.

[16] *Ibid.* (January 1728/9 to december 1734), 100.

[17] Dinwiddie, who spent sixteen years in the government service on Bermuda, acquired property there; how much one does not know. Some of it he
kept to his death since a sentence in his will, as of may 2, 1769, reads: "The
messuage I have in Bermuda and which is now used as his majesty's custom
house to my wife for life and at her decease to my two daughters."

may be taken either as an evidence of personal ambition or as the extreme of complete and self-effacing patriotism. It would seem that the man, early in life, had consecrated his business ability to public service for his government, and to it he gave his utmost devotion.

Surveyor-general

Precedent, prerogative, principle, custom, tradition have always been words to reckon with in the English-speaking world. Dinwiddie's day was no exception. They were the key words in his first quarrel, a very human quarrel, with the Virginians – or more accurately, with the Virginia council.

For seventeen years he had been a public servant of his government on the island of Bermuda, not too far from the coast of Virginia. Five of these years he had spent as comptroller of admiralty rights and eleven years as collector of customs. He was now, on april 11, 1738, advanced to the much more responsible appointment of surveyor-general of customs for the southern district of America.[18] "Southern district" was a generous term, even as terms were used in America, since it included all the colonies from Pennsylvania southward, and, apparently, Jamaica and the Bahamas.

The position of surveyor-general of customs by 1738 carried with it, in Dinwiddie's estimation, the right and privilege of the appointee to sit in the upper house of any one of the colonies in the so-called southern district. That precedent seemed to be well established. He had therefore a wide choice of seats, and he chose Virginia – establishing a residence forty-six miles from the capital at Williamsburg [19] – and, as he understood it, a

---

[18] *Dinwiddie papers,* I, viii.

[19] That Dinwiddie did actually establish a home forty-six miles from Williamsburg is evidenced from an enclosure, dated december 21, 1744, from Gooch to the lords of trade. This choice item reports the distance that each member of the upper house lived from the capital: "A list of the present mem-

seat, with all the privileges of membership, in the Virginia council. The man who at this time presided over the colony as chief executive, and thus over the council, was Colonel William Gooch,[20] lieutenant-governor, who had held that post since 1727.

Surveyor-general Dinwiddie chose Virginia in part because she was the largest and most central of the English continental colonies, and in part because of her actual and potential trade advantages. Since he undoubtedly was familiar with the language of her imperial "sea to sea" charter, he anticipated colonial expansion into Virginia's great west and already had dreamed a dream that would metamorphose into reality a decade

bers of his majesty's council in Virginia, with the distances they live from Williamsburg, to which place they never come but when sent for; the general courts and courts of oyer and terminer excepted.

	MILES		MILES
Mr. Diggs	20	Mr. Tayloe	50
Mr. Robinson	45	Mr. Lee	54
Mr. Grymes	30	Mr. Dinwiddie	46
Mr. Custis	in town	Mr. Burwell	10
Mr. Lightfoot	12	Mr. Fairfax	150"

(Gooch to the lords of trade, december 21, 1744, public record office, colonial office, 5/1326, 201-204; library of congress transcript, 80-90 [hereafter cited as P.R.O., C.O., L.C. tr.]). Further evidence of his having been in Virginia in the 1740's is seen in a stray item reprinted in the *Virginia magazine of history and biography*, IV (April 1897), 362: "Robert, son of Robert and Joanna Tucker, was born september 24th 1741 and baptised seven days after by the Reverend Mr. Moses Robinson. The godfathers were Robert Dinwiddie Esquire and Mr. Edward Hack Mosely and the godmothers Mrs.— and Susan Thruston."

20 William Gooch (1681-1751), lieutenant-governor of Virginia from 1727 to 1749, was born at Yarmouth, England. He was early interested in a military career and saw service under Marlborough. Though generally referred to as "colonel"—and even in 1747 having been made a major-general—he is usually thought of as a civilian interested in quiet pursuits, in internal development rather than westward expansion. He was voted a handsome present by the burgesses early in his administration. He was knighted in 1746. When health forced his retirement in 1749, he left for England amid almost universal regret. Between Gooch's departure and the arrival of Robert Dinwiddie, the three presidents of the council, John Robinson, Thomas Lee, and Lewis Burwell, became in turn acting lieutenant-governor.

later with the formation of the Ohio company of 1748.
It is inconceivable that during the years in Bermuda
this inquisitive personality should not have visited Virginia. Further it is not unlikely that he knew Colonel
Thomas Lee [21] of the Virginia council and his sons, as
well as two other prominent tidewater families, the
Washingtons and the Fairfaxes. Two recently discovered letters that were exchanged between Robert Dinwiddie and William Fairfax [22] as far back as 1739,
while both were customs officials in America, fully bear
out this point of view. These communications reveal the
close relationship of the Dinwiddie and Fairfax families. While young George Washington, later to become
a kind of protégé of Dinwiddie, was then, in 1738, but
six years of age, his two older half-brothers, Lawrence [23]
and Augustine,[24] were respectively twenty and eighteen.
Their father had visited London and so had the two
boys. It is more than probable that the father at this
time already knew John Hanbury,[25] the London mer-

---

[21] Thomas Lee (c. 1702-1750) colonial official, acting lieutenant-governor
of Virginia, father of the Ohio company of Virginia, was born at Stratford
in Virginia. He came of progenitors distinguished alike in England and
America. He is known always as colonel. He was long a member of the governor's council, for a time its president, by virtue thereof acting governor
after the departure of Lieutenant-governor Gooch in 1749; and he had been
issued a commission as lieutenant-governor, but died in 1750 before the notifi-
cation reached him in America. He served on important committees and
Indian conferences, and he travelled widely, in order, he declared, to be the
better informed when rendering his comprehensive reports to the crown.
He married Hannah Ludwell, granddaughter of Philip Ludwell, governor
of North Carolina. They had six sons and two daughters. His sons, all of
whom distinguished themselves, were Philip Ludwell, Thomas Ludwell,
Richard Henry, Francis Lightfoot, William, and Arthur.

[22] For William Fairfax (1691-1757), see pages 144-145.

[23] Lawrence Washington, half-brother of George Washington and fourteen
years his senior.

[24] Augustine Washington, half-brother of George Washington and twelve
years his senior.

[25] John Hanbury, a well-to-do London merchant, interested in mid-eight-
eenth-century trading and colonization schemes—including the Ohio company

chant, and Edward Clarke Parish,[26] his friend and Dinwiddie's friend; and if he did – certain results follow.
For Hanbury was the outstanding Londoner who later
joined with Thomas Lee and other colonials in organ-
izing the Ohio company, petitions for which Lee, Hanbury, and their associates were to present to Governor
Gooch of Virginia as early as 1746.

The council of the colony of Virginia in the time of
Dinwiddie was comprised of twelve of presumably the
ablest men in the province. Furthermore, it was a body
within a body; to be exact, it was three bodies in one. In
the council's threefold capacity it participated in three
not necessarily related activities: first, it was a kind of
privy council, and, as such, the governor's advisory
body; second, it was the upper house of a bicameral legislature, common throughout the continental colonies,
and known in Virginia as a general assembly; and finally, this same body of men was also the general court
– the highest court of law in the colony. The council
might thus sit in each of its three capacities on succes-
sive days, weeks, or months, but never simultaneously.
Its functions in each case were theoretically distinct,
however often the distinction became a fiction.

Membership in the council, moreover, was of two
kinds: "in ordinary" and "extraordinary." The "extraordinary" members were additional councillors beyond
the twelve "in ordinary" members. The activity of these
so-called "extraordinary" councillors was rigidly lim-

of Virginia, of which he was one of the organizers. Capel Hanbury, his
brother, was for a time his business partner. His church affiliation was that
of quaker.

26 Edward Clarke Parish, a contemporary and evidently a close friend of
John Hanbury and also of Robert Dinwiddie, upon whose bond he went on
september 7, 1751 when Dinwiddie, newly appointed lieutenant-governor of
Virginia, signed a financial agreement with the Earl of Albemarle, titular
governor. In Dinwiddie's will he bequeathed to the widow of Parish, Mrs.
Elizabeth Parish, and to her two daughters, ten pounds each.

ited to the council's first capacity, that of an advisory body. The "in ordinary" members, on the other hand, were able to sit together on all occasions. In their respective capacities they were thus privileged to participate in all three of the above-mentioned activities of the council. Here then was the crux of the matter: was Dinwiddie to be a full-fledged member "in ordinary," or, was he to be merely a member "extraordinary" and therefore "additional?" A majority of the members of the council apparently took the "extraordinary" view, whereas Dinwiddie, as one would by this time expect him to do, took the "in ordinary" view. A conflict loomed.

Napoleon was once queried as to how he would manage things if the circumstances in a particular case suddenly reversed themselves. "Circumstances?" he shot back, "I make circumstances!" In this respect Dinwiddie reminds one of Napoleon: he too made circumstances. And once he had made them, he held on to them with British tenacity. This first of his two quarrels with the Virginians attested to possession of that quality. It must be remembered that Dinwiddie in 1738 was a man of forty-five, in the prime of life, vigorous in mind and in body. Thus far he had been successful in his claims for proper recognition of the royal prerogative – as with Colonel Hope – and he had no intention now of permitting the slightest infringement upon "his majesty's rights."

The council was ready from the beginning to admit Dinwiddie as an "additional" and "extraordinary" member, and thus as one of the governor's advisors; and if admitted as such he would be allowed to participate in that one phase of the council's activities. For instance, he would be entitled to sit with the other councillors if and when customs duties and related matters were under consideration. This was true inasmuch as he was surveyor-general of customs. Robert Dinwiddie, however, was not a man content to be merely an "observer." He insisted at once that under his new appointment he should be admitted as a member in full standing in Virginia's upper house in order to participate in all three activities of her council.[27] The Virginia council journal for june 9, 1741 tells the story at this point simply and directly:

"The council being informed that Robert Dinwiddie, Esquire, surveyor-general of the customs in the southern district of America attended below to be sworn of the council here, sent their clerk to him to desire him to come in and produce his letter, and be sworn accordingly. And the said Dinwiddie coming in produced only his commission to be surveyor-general aforesaid." Something was missing. Where was Dinwiddie's letter?

But the surveyor-general believed he had a friend at court. ". . . and being askt [by the council] if he [Dinwiddie] had a letter directing his being admitted of the council," the journal continues, "he answered he had given the governor a letter when he first produced his commission to him, and was sworn thereto, not in council, but before the governor. But that by an instruction to the governor he was by virtue of his office to be admitted of the council." This defense put Gooch in a dilemma.

American colonial legislatures, like their prototype in England, already had begun to guard jealously the privilege of admission to membership. The council accordingly decided for the present upon a Fabian policy. They played for time. The journal goes on to record:

27 Dinwiddie to the lords of trade, october 20, 1741, P.R.O., C.O., 5/1321, L.C. tr., 101-104, v.16; *Journal of the commissioners for trade and plantations* (January 1741/2 to december 1749), 2, 8, 9, 16.

"This board being unacquainted with the said letter, and desiring to see the said instruction took time to consider thereof, and the said Dinwiddie withdrew." In fact, it was a long withdrawal for Dinwiddie, since he seems to have made no further appearance before the council from that day in june until october 20.

"Then the council directed their clerk to wait upon Mr. Gooch," the journal continues, "and desire that he would search among his papers for the said letter and for the instruction and to have them ready against tomorrow." [28] The council evidently had not been minded to trust to Dinwiddie's *ex parte* evidence, and they had instructed their own clerk to make for them an independent investigation, including inspection of Governor Gooch's files, and immediately to report his findings; in fact, he was to have them ready "tomorrow." Consequently, the next day, june 10, he was indeed ready — with a report that must have been eminently satisfactory to the council. The journal records: ". . . upon a diligent search neither the said letter nor the instruction could be found; it is the opinion of this board, that if Mr. Dinwiddie can produce any letter or instruction for admitting him of the council, the president may swear him in; but as neither his letter nor the instruction can as yet be found, they cannot advise it at this time." [29]

It was an adroit handling of a difficult case. In fact it was a test case: the councillors felt they were legally entitled to examine the letter upon which Dinwiddie based his demand for admittance. And then, when he was unable to produce the essential piece of paper, they

[28] At a council held at the capitol, june 9, 1741, "Journals of the councils of Virginia in executive session, 1737-1763," in the *Virginia magazine of history and biography*, XV (October 1907), 124.

[29] At a council held at the capitol, june 10, 1741, *ibid.*, XV, 126; cf. Dinwiddie to the lords of trade, october 20, 1741, P.R.O., C.O., 5/1321, L.C. tr., 101-104, V. 16.

took the position that they must for the time being exclude him.

Accordingly, on october 20, 1741, the surveyor-general wrote both in triumph and in protest to the board of trade. Triumphantly he declared: ". . . I waited on the governor of this province, and desired to [be] admitted and sworn of the councell of this collony, which was readily complied with, and was accordingly sworn in." But that triumph had not gone unchallenged; protestingly, he wrote: "The councell immediately after my admission, objected against my being a member of the upper house of the general assembly, or judge of the inferior courts." [30]

He proceeded forthwith to present the board with his case – well bolstered with arguments. He made a dozen allegations: first, he reminded that body that the Virginia council, in barring him from sitting with them as a member of the upper house or judge of the inferior courts, was acting contrary to custom and established procedure. It was discrimination. He added: ". . . all [of] which was [by] virtue of his majesties instructions enjoyed by my predecessors Messrs. Quary,[31] Fitz Williams,[32] and Phinney." [33] His reply, he thought, had been adequate: "I pleaded the precedents of the fore-mentioned gentlemen." Concluding, he said: "[I] did conceive his majesties instruction, directing the surveyor-general to be of the councell, was in generall, to all the benefits enjoyed by the other councellors." Two more times in this same representation he stated that the privilege he was contending for had "been enjoyed by former surveyor-generalls." The council must not violate precedent.

---

[30] *Ibid.*
[31] Robert Quary, at one time secretary of the province of South Carolina.
[32] Richard Fitzwilliams.
[33] George Phenney.

Second, having alleged the Virginia council had violated precedent, he next claimed they did not know their history. Therefore, he begged leave to recapitulate for the board's edification "a short detail of the constitution of this province." He evidently hoped this clinching argument from the early records of the council would gain the board's "interest to support the right of the crown in nominating and appointing additional councellors."

Third, his admission to the council in full standing would serve his majesty as a preventive measure by forestalling the passage of any colonial law that might be in contravention of the mercantilist navigation acts and related legislation. He wrote the board one paragraph, which he was wise enough not to broadcast in Virginia. It would have been tactless, if not fatal, in the present impasse to have done so: "I am of opinion that the design of apointing the surveyor-general to be of the councell, among other things as much as possible, to prevent any laws to pass in this province, that may any ways interferr with the acts of trade, to give his reasons against such laws, and to represent the same home to your lordships." The acts of trade were already anathema to the Virginians, as they were also to the New Englanders, even though most of them had been "neglected" for the past hundred years. Here was one of the irritants leading to revolution. But Dinwiddie did not sense it.

Fourth, his presence there on the council would be a "service . . . to the crown," in guaranteeing both regularity in law enforcement and a proper and legal income for the king's treasury from the customs duties.

Fifth, he argued, by way of skillful warning, that if the privilege of thus sitting in the upper house were allowed to go by default through disuse, the board "will

please to consider whether or not the [government]
service may not suffer by this restraint."

Finally, he insisted on a point that was very clear to
him even if not to the Virginia council. He warned the
board of trade that – whether logically or not – the part
of a surveyor-general's duty having to do with the acts
of trade "he is uncapable of, unless he be admitted to
sitt and vote as a member of the upper house of the general assembly which at present is denied him." If only
an "additional" councillor he felt he would be but a
supernumerary, and his services in support of the trade
laws would be nullified.

A new figure now entered the lists, Edward Clarke
Parish, who was to be Dinwiddie's intermediary. Wrote
the surveyor-general: "Therefore I most humbly entreat your lordships will please to interferr your authority, by granting a letter to my friend Mr. Edward
Clark Parish." Such a letter, he explained, was "to be
forwarded to our governor to restore me to the privi-
ledges enjoyed by my predecessors."

Important as was this communication, and though
prepared the preceding october 20, the message was
neither "received" nor "read" until january 15, 1742.
The original draft of this memorial, on file in the British public record office, is endorsed "VIRGINIA – Letter
from Mr. Dinwiddie ... acquainting to this board complaining that the council immediately after his admission objected against his being a member of the upper
house of the general assembly, or judge of the inferior
courts in that colony. Recd./Read. January 15, 1741/
42." [34] Here is a mute commentary on the uncertainties

---

[34] Double-dating is necessary between the first of january and the twenty-
fifth of march from 1582 to 1752, due to the change in the Gregorian
calendar throughout western Europe and America in 1752. The first of the
year formerly began on march 25.

of communication in that day, the consequences of which were often serious.

The council was now to have its own day in court. Its members lost neither time nor temper. Forthwith they presented to the board of trade their own side of the question: "We . . . find ourselves under a necessity of giving your lordships this trouble, in laying before you the reasons, which induce us to be of opinion, that Mr. Dinwiddie, surveyor-general of his majesty's customs, upon his being sworn a member of the council, had not thereby a right to sit as a judge in the general court . . . at the same time humbly submitting to your lordships consideration, whether by the terms of his appointment, and the naming him a councillour extraordinary, he can have a right to sit and vote as a member of the general assembly."

The council made it plain that from their own standpoint they felt as equally obligated, as good Virginians and good Englishmen, to prevent Dinwiddie from taking his seat as he did in seeking it; they declared they had no alternative but to submit to the board their solemn representations:

". . . We entreat your lordships to interpret with your wonted candor and favour this our representation, as not presuming in the least to oppose or delay the exercise of his majesty's undoubted prerogative but only to lay before you a true state of the case in [the] matter." They called the board's attention to the fundamental character of the dispute and the gravity of the decision its members are called upon to render, "which concerns as well all his majesty's subjects residing in this colony, as our own body in particular." [35]

[35] The council of Virginia to the lords of trade [n.d., c.1741], P.R.O., C.O., 5/1321, L.C. tr.

The council had learned of the contents of Dinwiddie's letter, and, not to be out-maneuvered, their
own representation to the board also appealed to history. They too attempted to refresh the board's memory
as to what had long been the custom, by likewise giving
that board a short résumé of the constitution of the
province.[36]

Ad infinitum!

The upshot of the controversy was that the home government, after carefully considering the opposing arguments, concluded by seating Dinwiddie as a regular
councillor, on a parity with the other members, exactly
as he had prayed them to do.[37]

This should be said for Dinwiddie: while it is true
he had everything to gain and nothing to lose in this
struggle with the council, it is hardly fair thus to explain his action. If his predecessors had enjoyed the
privilege he sought, it was a reflection on him to deny
him the same privilege; if they had sat in council "in
ordinary," in the full plenitude of their powers, it was
unfair to him to be assigned a lesser seat — a discrimination he would never submit to without a battle. Dinwiddie saw also a chance for larger usefulness generally
if he won out; a chance to serve his king the better, if
he could achieve what he honestly believed he was entitled to when he waged this battle.

Once he was admitted to full standing in the council,
he never abused his privilege. He conducted himself
during those succeeding years, while he sat as a member
of Governor Gooch's council, in such a manner as to
make himself the eligible, natural successor to Gooch;

36 *Ibid.* See also Dinwiddie to the lords of trade, october 20, 1741, P.R.O.,
C.O., 5/1321; L.C. tr., 101-104, v. 16.

37 Minutes of the commissioners for trade and plantations, april 27, 1742,
Journal of the commissioners for trade and plantations (January 1741/2 to
december 1749), 40.

in short, he was highly respected by those Virginians who counted most.

On the other side of the contest, that of the councillors, were arrayed localism if not provincialism; suspicion of governmental interference — even revival of long-dormant imperial authority; and a lurking distrust of British officials who were interested in the collection of monies from colonials. Here was suspicion of any outside official who appeared bent upon extending his authority. It was not that Dinwiddie was dangerous; it was that he would, if admitted, be in a position to become dangerous. The Virginia councillors opposed Dinwiddie, not because he was Robert Dinwiddie, not because he was unacceptable personally, but because he represented a tax-gathering, customs-paying system. And customs dues had been systematically "neglected," generally speaking, since beyond the memory of men then living. The Virginians fought him, not because they were professional lawbreakers, but because they believed the customs laws unjust and therefore illegal. As John Stuart Mill once sagely observed: "It is not enough that a law be just; it must be regarded by the people as just."

Those customs matters were vital because they came home directly or indirectly to every colonial Virginian. One is reminded of what Lord Curzon once told a British audience about foreign affairs: "Foreign affairs are the most domestic of all our affairs, for they touch the life, the interest, and the pocket of every member of the community." [38]

---

[38] Paul Scott Mowrer, *Foreign relations of the United States* (American library association, 1927), 9.

Reports on the State of the Colonies

Robert Dinwiddie was the government observer and reporter *par excellence*. His numerous "observations" or "reports" were interspersed through some thirty-five years' transatlantic service for his majesty as an official in Britain's American colonies. Of these documents submitted to the crown, the earliest on record bears the date of 1731, when this rising young Scot was still in his thirties. His first complete report that is available is dated april 29, 1740.[39] Noteworthy indeed is this report since it is by no means limited to Virginia. It is continental in scope and includes valuable data on practically all of the insular American colonies as well as those on the mainland.

As early as march 24, 1731 the journals of the board of trade record that "some observations on the trade to America, offered to the board by Mr. Dinwiddie, collector of the customs at Bermuda, were read."[40] Unfortunately, this particular report, which must have been one of Dinwiddie's earliest, cannot now be located. The last two of his reports, somewhat different in char-

---

[39] This report is concerned not only with the southern colonies but with the northern as well. It is entirely within reason that Dinwiddie had made extended excursions up and down the Atlantic coast during his sixteen years in Bermuda. It is possible, of course, that his report is only a compilation; but it reads as though its author is writing from first-hand knowledge and close-up observation. P.R.O., board of trade plantations general, X, N.45, quoted in William A. Whitehead, *et al.*, eds., *Documents relating to the colonial history of the state of New Jersey* (Newark, 1880-19—), 1st series, VI, 83-91 (hereafter cited as *New Jersey archives*).

[40] *Journal of the commissioners for trade and plantations* (January 1728/9 to december 1734), 187.

acter from the others, were rendered to the home government while he was lieutenant-governor of Virginia. They are dated january 1755 and february 23, 1756 and are almost exclusively concerned with Virginia. They are valuable even though they contain far less statistical but more explanatory material than the preceding reports.

Recently there has been uncovered in England, through the cooperation of Sir Campbell Stuart, a collateral descendant of Dinwiddie, a report dated april 1748. It must have been Dinwiddie's last compilation made while he was surveyor-general, for he resigned the next year. The discovery of this 1748 report fills in an important gap in the series. The list of his reports now known stands as follows: 1731, 1740, 1743, 1748, 1755, and 1756. The two important statistical reports, those of 1740 and of 1743, with which this chapter is largely concerned, were compiled and submitted in the course of his activities as surveyor-general of customs in America.

Dinwiddie's own introduction to the series is told in a straightforward paragraph. It may be taken as a fair presentation of his purpose. Apparently it was upon his own initiative that he prepared many of these reports for his superiors. Their all-embracing character and the careful methods of computation he employed are impressive. To the board of trade on the date abovementioned, april 29, 1740, he wrote:

"MY LORDS: I have been at a great deal of trouble and expense to inform myself of the trade of his majesty's American empire, and the annuall amount of the national produce of each colony or plantation: I give you the following thoughts, observations, and calculations, which is partly from my own knowledge and from the best informations I possibly could get; if it's thought worthy your notice, it will fully answer my hopes." [41]

His opening words to his report three years later to the Duke of Newcastle,[42] then principal secretary of state, contain much the same statements, adding that his information was obtained "during my service in the revenue upwards of twenty years."

The comprehensiveness of his undertaking, so far as geographical extent goes, he indicated thus: "For regularity I shall begin with Barbadoes as the most southerly plantation, and end with the island of Newfoundland." One would like to know just how much of a globe-trotter he had been. Were his data regarding places, people, and products as far north as Newfoundland and as far south as Barbadoes, derived chiefly from his own personal "observations" or were they taken mostly from others whom he refers to as his "best informations?" [43]

As to the character of the 1740 report, he proposed "to make it somewhat regular." His computations fall under a variety of general heads: British and colonial shipping; number of vessels and value of the merchant marine; the amount and value of colonial produce, both insular and continental; the size of each colony's militia, which Dinwiddie calls "fighting men"; the number and value of the slaves on the sugar islands and the value of the equipment on the sugar plantations.[44]

[41] Dinwiddie to the lords of trade, april 29, 1740, *New Jersey archives,* 1st series, VI, 83.

[42] Thomas Pelham, Duke of Newcastle (1693-1768) and brother of Henry Pelham, was prominent in the Walpole cabinet and in British politics for some forty years. As a politician, he is held to have been more cunning than able. His lack of knowledge about the geography of the American colonies has been much deplored.

[43] Dinwiddie to the Duke of Newcastle, august 1743, P.R.O., C.O., 5/5, 200-207b; L.C. tr., 297-307.

[44] Dinwiddie to the lords of trade, april 29, 1740, *New Jersey archives,* 1st series, VI, 83-91.

Since practically the same categories of material are assembled in his report of 1743, it will be of interest, for the sake of comparison, to set down in parallel columns in this chapter some of the outstanding data of the two reports.

Before this is done, attention is called to a third column, arranged for comparison with the first two. This third-column material is derived from a non-Dinwiddie report or, as it was labelled by its author, "memorial." It is in manuscript form, is "humbly submitted to the consideration of his majesty's ministers of state . . . by their most obedient servant, Jas Abercromby," and bears on its cover page the date "may 1752." The date, however, is in a handwriting different from that of the document. This memorial was long thought to have been compiled by or authorized by Major-general James Abercromby,[45] who saw service in America during the French and Indian war.

Apparently some clerk in London had originally filed it among the general's papers – and there it had lain for well over one hundred years. Instead, this enlightening document has recently been found to have been drawn up by the general's contemporary of the same name, James Abercromby,[46] the Virginia agent.

---

[45] James Abercromby or Abercrombie (1706-1781), British army officer, was born of respectable Scot parentage and filled local offices in his native land, but presently followed his predilection for army life. He was early thrown in contact with Lord Loudoun; and upon the latter's selection in 1756 to command the British military forces in America, Abercromby was placed next in command. Arriving in America a month before Lord Loudoun, he was in supreme command—a position he held in 1758 after Loudoun's recall. His great mistake was his assault upon the French stronghold of Ticonderoga in july 1758, when he lost some 2000 men in the action. He was recalled late in 1758, being superseded by General Jeffrey Amherst.

[46] James Abercromby, colonial agent, was born in Scotland, educated in the law, and in due time became judge advocate in the army in 1746. He apparently belonged to the important Abercromby family of County Banff. He had an alert, philosophical mind, travelled to America and for a time lived in the colonies. He was attorney-general of South Carolina from 1735 to 1742. In

Another discovery was made still more recently while studying these revealing statistics – a striking similarity between the data in the Dinwiddie report of 1743, and the data in the statistical section of the Abercromby report compiled a decade later, 1752. To be more specific, the statistical matter in the Abercromby report will be found generally to have been taken verbatim from Robert Dinwiddie's report of 1743.

The significance of the following paragraph in the Abercromby memorial, wherein its writer acknowledges his indebtedness for information to a certain "gentleman . . . long in office, with reputation," now becomes clear. It refers to none other than Robert Dinwiddie. James Abercromby, agent, wrote:

"Allowing the foregoing computations to be pretty near exact, at the time when they were made, viz. 1743, and then given into some of the kings ministers, by a gentleman who had been long in office, with reputation, surveyor-general of the customs, for one of the districts in America, and who is lately for past services, promoted to be lieutenant-governor of Virginia; allowing these computations, I say, to be just, of which, I do not pretend, from my own knowledge to determine. The accessory strength and wealth of these plantations, (exclusive of the property of soil, plantation implements, stock and cash) will at one view stand thus." [47] Aber-

---

1748 Abercromby became agent for the colony of North Carolina, continuing to represent that colony until november 1757. Part of this time he was also the agent of Governor James Glen. Peter Leheup was Abercromby's predecessor; Edward Montague, his successor. Among the most important communications in the Dinwiddie correspondence are the letters that passed between the governor and this agent. The latter's chief weakness was his chirography, even Dinwiddie complaining about vain attempts to decipher his almost illegible writing. He was, however, the personification of the colonial agent at his best. See H. R. McIlwaine and J. P. Kennedy, eds., *Journals of the house of burgesses* (1752-1755; 1756-1758) (Richmond, 1905-1915), 96 (hereafter cited as *Journals of the house of burgesses*).

[47] "An examination of the acts of parliament relative to the trade and the

cromby then proceeded to quote Dinwiddie's statistics.[48]

These reports throw an immense amount of light upon conditions, particularly economic conditions, throughout the colonies, including of course Virginia. And since Dinwiddie, as surveyor-general, had already set up a residence in Virginia, and since he was later to become its governor, especial note will be taken of the data regarding that colony. The following typical excerpts present revealing figures: [49]

COMPARISON OF MILITIA

First are the estimates for the following item, entitled by Dinwiddie "An account of the number of fighting men in each colony and plantation from the years of 16 to 60." Here are a few typical entries:

government of our American colonies . . . by their most obedient servant, Jas Abercromby," may 1752 (hereafter cited as Abercromby memorial). The original is preserved in the Abercromby papers, Huntington library. The identification of this document as belonging to the Virginia agent was made and pointed out to me a few years ago by Prof. Charles M. Andrews of Yale university. The present writer recently discovered the similarity between the data in the two documents and therefore readily identified Abercromby's "gentleman . . . long in office, with reputation," as being Robert Dinwiddie.

48 On april 18, 1752 Dinwiddie as lieutenant-governor of Virginia recommended Abercromby to be the agent in London for himself, for the house of burgesses, and for the council. On april 20 the third reading of the bill occurred and Abercromby was legalized agent. See *Journals of the house of burgesses* (1752-1755; 1756-1758), xvii, 96-97, 99; H. R. McIlwaine, ed., *Legislative journals of the council of colonial Virginia* (Richmond, 1918-1919), II, 1093 (hereafter cited as *Legislative journals of the council of colonial Virginia*); Dinwiddie to Abercromby, july 24 [1754], *Dinwiddie papers*, I, 237. See also *William and Mary college quarterly historical magazine*, 1st series, XXII (1913-1914), 2 (There seems to be a slight anachronism in this article regarding the date of the appointment of James Abercromby as agent).

49 The reports to be compared in the next pages are as follows: Dinwiddie to the lords of trade, april 29, 1740, *New Jersey archives*, 1st series, VI, 83-91; Dinwiddie to the Duke of Newcastle, august 1743, P.R.O., C.O., 5/5, 200-207b; L.C. tr., 297-307; cf. Dinwiddie to Sir Henry Pelham, 1743, Shelburne papers (Clements library, Ann Arbor, Michigan); Abercromby memorial.

COLONY	DINWIDDIE'S REPORTS		ABERCROMBY'S REPORT
	1740	1743	1752
New England } Nova Scotia* }	38,000	61,000	45,000
New York and Jerseys	10,000	18,000	18,000
Virginia	12,000	14,000	14,000
North Carolina	2,000	2,000	13,000
Barbadoes	4,500	8,000	9,000
Bermuda	800	800	800
Jamaica	5,000	6,000	6,000

*Abercromby uses "Massachusetts bay" for his heading.

The totals for all of the twenty or more colonies are also interesting: Dinwiddie's 1740 report has a total of 151,250; the 1743 report gives 222,700; Abercromby's report totals 220,300.

From the standpoint of what Dinwiddie called "fighting men," it is evident that the larger mainland colonies like Massachusetts and Virginia had a considerable advantage over the insular, yet the size of the insular militia is impressive. Jamaica and Barbadoes, for example, were credited with half as many military effectives as a large mainland colony like Virginia. According to the two colonial statisticians, Dinwiddie and Abercromby, Virginia's 14,000 "fighting men" constituted a larger military force than that of any other southern colony. Also it was a larger fighting force than was to be found in any of the smaller northern colonies. Nevertheless, according to these statistics, Virginia's potential popular army was far smaller than that of Massachusetts bay, which might boast as many as 61,000 effectives.

Dinwiddie's estimates for the colonial militia, especially in the mainland colonies, were probably far too conservative. At any rate, about a decade later, according to his report to the board of trade in 1755, he estimated the Virginia militia, on the basis of returns from his four adjutants, as 27,000, and the following year, on the same basis, as 36,000. However, James Abercromby, depending upon Dinwiddie, reported for 1752 substantially the same estimates as did the surveyor-general in his earlier reports of 1740 and 1743.

Comparison of Trading Vessels

Another informing set of comparative figures is what Dinwiddie describes as an "Account of the vessells trading to and from the plantations belonging to Great Britain and Ireland as also those belonging to the British subjects residing in the plantations and employed in their respective trades in the fishery and coasting, distinguished in the two following columns."

COLONY	"Ships belonging to Great Britain trading to and from the plantations and colonies." DINWIDDIE'S REPORTS		"Vessells belonging to the British subjects residing in the plantations and colonies." DINWIDDIE'S REPORTS	
	1740	1743	1740	1743
New England Nova Scotia	20	20	1100	1002
New York and Jerseys	8	10	60	25
Maryland	95	130	60	20
Virginia	120	150	80	50
North Carolina	30	40	25	8
Barbadoes	80	80	20	15
Bermuda			75	75
Jamaica	100	100	30	25

The total of British-owned ships in 1740 is given as 1050, in 1743 as 1421. The total of colonial-owned vessels for 1740 was 2035, for 1743 only 1584. Abercromby relied completely on Dinwiddie in this second category of data. He compiled no separate statistics for each colony but merely repeated the surveyor-general's totals.[50]

[50] There is a slight discrepancy in the totals; the figure of "4" in Din-

Three facts stand out in this section of the reports, namely, the greater comparative importance of Virginia, the decline in colonial-owned shipping, and the complete reliance of Abercromby upon Dinwiddie's compilation.

Virginia's high standing as a commercial colony is evident when one considers the 1050 British-owned vessels trading to the colonies in 1740. Of these Virginia could lay claim to 120, as compared with her nearest rivals, Jamaica with 100 and Maryland with 95. Except for Barbadoes, with 80 craft, the showing of the other provinces is insignificant. Even New England and Nova Scotia combined had only 20 vessels. By 1743 the totals for all the colonies had increased from 1050 to 1421 vessels, a gain of 35 per cent. Virginia, comparatively, more than held her own. Important insular colonies like Jamaica and Barbadoes registered no gain whatever, neither did New England nor Nova Scotia. Virginia, however, increased her number from 120 to 150 vessels, or a gain of 25 per cent, exceeded only slightly by the gain of her neighbor, Maryland.

When one turns to the colonial-owned vessels, it is seen that New England and Nova Scotia, with 1100 sail in 1740 and 1002 in 1743 engaged chiefly in foreign and fishing trade, easily dwarfed all competitors. Nevertheless, Virginia was next highest in the list, more than doubling Jamaica, or Barbadoes, or North Carolina. Again, Maryland was a fairly close competitor, especially in 1740, when she could boast 60 vessels to Virginia's 80.

The most surprising feature of this section of the report, however, was the decline in every colony of home-owned vessels. Virginia's ships declined in number from 80 to 50 (37.5 per cent), which was not so great,

widdie's total of 1584 was evidently mistaken by Abercromby's copyist for a cipher, so that the latter's total reads, instead, 1580.

however, as the decline either for Maryland, from 60 to 20 (66.6 per cent) or for New York and Jerseys, from 60 to 25 (58.3 per cent). Certainly Virginia's falling off was not so great as was that of North Carolina, which dropped from 25 to 8 (68 per cent). New England and Nova Scotia dropped from 1100 craft to 1002. The insular provinces declined relatively less than the mainland. The total decline from 2035 vessels belonging to all colonies in 1740 to 1584 in 1743 (or 22.2 per cent) was a serious setback for colonial-owned shipping.

Negro Slaves

In the third section of his tabulations Dinwiddie listed the negro slaves in the insular colonies at 231,000 in 1740; and the same figure for 1743. Abercromby had no more up-to-date figures for 1752, and he therefore adopted Dinwiddie's figure of 231,000. Abercromby added a note, however, to the effect that "their number of slaves are computed in the islands (vizt.) 231,000; on the continent 150,000; [total] 381,000 slaves." And he followed this statement with an item which, however unfamiliar today, was familiar enough at the time. It read: "Which at £20 a head makes [£]7,720,000 in value."

Both Dinwiddie and Abercromby reckoned that the British continental colonies alone contained about 150,000 slaves. These, valued at £20 each, represented £3,000,000.

Dinwiddie wrote thus of the value of the sugar plantations' equipment:

"My lord, you'll please observe there are 231,000 negroes belonging to and employed in the British sugar colonies which being valued at £20 sterling per head amounts to £4,620,000. The value of their sugar works, mills, stills, worms, horses, cattle, and all other necessarys belonging to a sugar plantation, may justly be valued at one third the amount of the negro slaves, which at that calculation amounts to £1,540,000. Which added together amounts to £6,160,000 and is the value and great expence of the planters, of the sugar plantations, abstract of the soil.

"And also on the main of America, Bermuda, and Providence there is 150,000 negroes, which valued at the above rate amounts to £3,000,000."

Dinwiddie's era believed in mercantilism. He therefore stressed the importance to Britain of the buying power of her colonies. Said he:

"You'll please observe that the supplys from Great Britain to our colonies amounts to £3,615,000 sterling. [The] chief part thereof is the manufactures of Great Britain, East India goods, German linnens. The branch of trade to Guinea and the plantations and wines from Madeira are all included in the forementioned calculation.

"It will naturally give surprize to see the valuableness, growth, increase, and produce of our collonies and plantations in America, considering the time since they were first settled."

There follows in this 1743 report of Dinwiddie's a statement which shows plainly enough that at least this one spokesman for the British people, and presumably for their colonists, appreciated fully the importance of personal liberty, popular institutions, and representative government. Dinwiddie thus expressed himself:

"Next to the blessing of heaven on the industry of the planter and the richness of the soil (particularly in the islands – they are happy in the constitution, in having a power to make laws for their government, which is more than their neighbouring colonies are indulged with."

There was a close commercial relation between the British merchant and his American colonial kinsman, hence the surveyor-general observed:

"Add to that the great credit the merchant has continually supplied them with, which I really believe has been the greatest advantage and help to their present flourishing conditions, which I wish may long continue."

ANNUAL VALUE OF GOODS SHIPPED

In the fourth place, Dinwiddie introduced into his reports of 1740 and 1743 "the annuall amount of the goods shipt from Great Britain and Ireland, to the colonies." He added: "The trade to Guinea and from thence to the plantations included there is more than is wanted for their own consumption, the residue is vended in a trade to the French, Spanish, and Dutch settlements in America."

Here are a few sample entries in this illuminating section of the report:

COLONY	DINWIDDIE'S REPORT, 1743	ABERCROMBY'S REPORT, 1752
New England	[£]600,000	
Massachusetts bay		[£]600,000
New York	150,000	150,000
Jerseys	40,000	40,000
Maryland	150,000	150,000
Virginia	180,000	180,000
North Carolina	40,000	50,000
Barbadoes	300,000	300,000
Bermuda	15,000	15,000
Jamaica	1,200,000	1,200,000

Dinwiddie's 1740 report gives no separate figures but a total of £2,550,000. His 1743 report totals £3,615,000; Abercromby's total is £3,635,000.

The surprising value of the insular colonies' imports from Britain, as compared with the mainland colonies' imports from the mother country, is the important feature of this section of Dinwiddie's reports. When, at a later time, some speculative bargaining over possible exchanges of territory was under discussion among the powers, no wonder Britain was advised by some to part, if it came to the worst, with her mainland colonies before she relinquished her rich sugar insular possessions in America.

It is at once observable from the figures just presented that not only was Jamaica by all odds the most important of the insular colonies but the value of the mother country's shipments to her, £1,200,000, represented exactly one-third of the total value of the imports into all the colonies, £3,615,000. New England was the third highest importer with £600,000; insular Barbadoes was next with £300,000; and Virginia had £180,000. Though second highest among the mainland colonies, she accounted for only a little more than half the value of the imports credited to Barbadoes. Maryland and New York were still farther down the line with £150,-000 each. Finally, it is interesting that Abercromby's figures are identical with Dinwiddie's in eight out of nine items, so that in their totals, exceeding £3,600,000, there is a difference of only £20,000.

VALUE AND VARIETY OF COLONIAL PRODUCE

The report next takes up colonial produce, dealing both with value and variety of articles. Here, even more than in the preceding items, the disparity between the value of the insular possessions and the continental is striking. For example, Barbadoes's products in 1740 were valued at £300,000. This amount was greater than the produce value of any of the following: North Carolina, Maryland, Jerseys, New York, Rhode Island, Connecticut, New Hampshire, South Carolina, Pennsylvania, or even Virginia (£250,000), and exceeded only by New England (Massachusetts) and Nova Scotia (£800,000).

Not only that, but the rate of increase was generally greater on the islands than on the mainland. For example, Barbadoes's products were calculated to have increased £150,000 in value, from £300,000 in 1740 to £450,000 in 1743; and Jamaica's during the same time from £500,000 to £650,000. On the other hand, produce values rose in South Carolina during those three years from £200,000 to £300,000; in North Carolina, from £60,000 to £80,000; in Maryland, from £200,000 to £250,000; and in Virginia, from £250,000 to £380,000.

Virginia, a mainland colony, said Dinwiddie in 1743 – and, of course, Abercromby agreed with him – "produces 35,000 hogsheads tobacco, wheat, Indian corn, flower, bread, pork, deerskins, and furrs [in] large quantitys, lumber and iron amounting to [£]380,000." How different were they from the articles produced in Barbadoes, an insular colony: "communibus annis, 12,000 hogsheads sugar, one-half thereof is improved, 100 hogsheads molasses, 12,000 hogsheads rum, 200,000 pounds cotton, 300,000 pounds ginger, 19,000 pounds aloes, 600 pounds coffee, the whole by estimation in value £450,000." One-half of the sugar, Dinwiddie reported was "improved." The total value of all the produce was held to be £3,745,000 in 1740, and almost double that amount (£6,095,000) in 1743. Most of the entries in this section of the Dinwiddie reports likewise have been taken over word for word and figure for figure by Abercromby in his compilations for 1752. A slight change here and there by the latter accounts for the fact that his total figure of £5,036,000 for the pro-

duce of 1752, represents a variation of only £56,000
from Dinwiddie's total of £4,980,000 (to which he
added £1,115,000, foreign trade, and thus arrived at a
grand total of £6,095,000). This section on colonial
produce is undoubtedly the highlight of Dinwiddie's
two reports.

Here then was a new type of customs official, a new
type of surveyor-general. As a matter of fact, three
kinds of public servants are always in office: first, those
who do less than they ought; second, those who are careful to do only what they have bargained for; and third,
those who magnify their job and do more than they are
paid to do. The last are constantly promoted, rewarded
by greater and greater opportunities and responsibilities, and honored by their countrymen. In this third
classification of officials, history is gradually placing
Robert Dinwiddie. Apparently there was no position
he held that he did not expand, on Bermuda and in
Virginia, discovering new fields where he might exert
his influence to serve his majesty. Whatever the derelic-
tions that were ever at any time charged against Robert
Dinwiddie, they were never those of indolence, indiffer-
ence, or infidelity to his trust. His conflicts with others
throughout his life resulted chiefly from the fact that
he was aggressive, restless with initiative, impatient for
action. Here, as he appears in the voluminous reports
just studied, he is seen as a personification of official
activity.

Dinwiddie versus Lascelles

Robert Dinwiddie has just been studied in the rôle of government statistician; he is now to be seen in his new job of government investigator. While still surveyor-general of customs for the southern district in America – and by virtue thereof also a member of the Virginia council – he was given, sometime prior to january 19, 1743, the special commission of inspector-general of customs.[51] This new appointment armed him with authority to conduct not only a general investigation into insular customs frauds but also a special investigation into the accounts and services of one Edward Lascelles, collector of customs for the island of Barbadoes; of his brother, Henry, former collector; and, to some extent, of Arthur Upton, insular comptroller.[52]

[51] It is clear from Dinwiddie's report of his itinerary, discussed later in the chapter, that he was commissioned inspector-general months earlier than the date assigned by R. A. Brock, who wrote: "Dinwiddie was specially commissioned, august 17, 1743, with the designation of 'inspector-general,' to examine into the duties of the collector of customs of the island of Barbadoes, and in the discharge of this trust, exposed to the English government an enormous defalcation in the revenues there. In 1749 he appears to have resided in London as a merchant, engaged in trade with the colonies" (*Dinwiddie papers*, I, ix). Brock comes to the above conclusion in part from having seen a bill of sale, dated april 3, 1749, to "Robert Dinwiddie, Esqr., of London, merchant, of one-eighth part of the Warren frigate, 300 tons burthen, James Nivin, master, from Andrew Pringle, for the consideration of £193 18s" (*Ibid.*, I, ix, note i).

[52] Dinwiddie seems to have brought charges against Edward Lascelles and Arthur Upton late in 1742 or early in 1743. This is the presumption since one of Dinwiddie's "articles of charge" would appear to have been answered by the collector and the comptroller "in their letter to Mr. Dinwiddie dated at Bridge Town 19th. january 1743." Furthermore, the two accused men say that "on his arrival" Dinwiddie "was informed of the reasons" for the seeming peculiar conditions of the sugar accounts at Bridgetown, Barbadoes (Board

There seem to have been two reasons why Dinwiddie in 1743 reached a decision to press charges of fraud against the Lascelles brothers. First, from about 1720 and for many years afterward – a period during which Dinwiddie himself was for most of the time an official on the island of Bermuda – the conduct on the neighboring island of Barbadoes of the Lascelles brothers, or certainly Henry, had been under suspicion on the part of certain governmental authorities. In the second place, Dinwiddie was convinced that he himself had discovered irregularities not only in the current accounts of Edward, the incumbent collector of customs for the island, but also in the past accounts of Henry himself, whose official relationship with the imperial customs was supposed to have terminated in 1734, when his accounts were closed and his bond surrendered.

The Lascelles brothers appear to have been stormy petrels on Barbadoes for at least twenty-five years. The information to be derived from the minutes of its insular council as well as from those of the board of customs and of the board of trade in London is fragmentary; but these minutes are here set forth, as historical straws in the wind. Three entries in the board journals early in 1720 indicate first that ill-feeling had arisen between Henry Lascelles and the island's governor; and second that when mention of Henry's name had come up before the board it was generally associated with such matters as pirate ships, negro slaves taken from such ships, and money that, from the sale of these apprehended slaves,

of trade memorial relating to the case of Edward Lascelles, july 23, 1746, P.R.O., treasury 1, bundle 320, fo. 159; L.C. tr.). Such a reference must mean either that Dinwiddie had already begun making his inspections on Barbadoes prior to january 19, 1743, or else that he had, while still in England, based his charges against the two customs officials on data that reached him before he set out on his inspection tour of the island in 1743. It is barely possible, of course, that here is another case of double-dating, making the year 1744.

had been placed in his hands for safe-keeping – none too safe, as it was claimed, since he refused to release it.

According to the journal for february 9, 1720, Francis Chamberlain and Francis Sitwell, merchants of London and Barbadoes, set forth in a petition to the board that some negroes had been taken from the petitioners by pirates, "put on board the Charlotte, carried to Barbadoes, there sold, and the money put into Mr. Lascell's hand." Sitwell further alleged he had been "informed of it by letters from the mate of the said ship. That he also had advice from his correspondents in Barbadoes that they had made application for the same, but could not be redressed without an order from the king." [53]

Lascelles, in his defense "memorial" filed before the board on february 16, linked the Barbadoes governor's name with the charges, alleging that the negroes in question had been given to one Captain Culson, and by him delivered, he further declared, to the governor himself.[54] Already, on january 28, the board had questioned him regarding a Spanish sloop that was alleged to have traded there in 1718. He replied that an examination of his papers revealed no mention of any such vessel; therefore, no such thing could have happened, he held, since ". . . no ship or sloop could come there and unload without his knowledge, because they must first make an entry of their loading, or else are seizable." Having cleared his own record, he added, however, that "the governor might have given the Spaniard leave to unload, and he not know it." [55]

That Henry Lascelles viewed such a personal matter as the means of making a living in a vastly different

[53] *Journal of the commissioners for trade and plantations* (November 1718 to december 1722), 144-145.

[54] *Ibid.*, 148.

[55] *Ibid.*, 140.

light from that taken by the president of the council of Barbadoes, Samuel Cox – to put the former's case as fairly as possible – is seen from an informing entry in the British state papers, under date of november 8, 1721. President Samuel Cox, then in London, thus addressed the commissioners for trade and plantations:

"However this shall not discourage me from doing my duty, but I cannot but resent that those very people who are the chief encouragers of it, give me leave, my lords, to assure you that they are none but the great factors who have large consignments and who want the French sugers for their cheapness. But above all Mr. Henry Lascells, collector, who, by being one of the chiefest shippers of sugers to private persons as well as the king, ships the good sugers received for duty to his private correspondents at high prices, and buys French sugers at low rates and ships to the king for duty, which I am ready to prove upon him." [56] This entry throws a ray of light upon Henry Lascelles's commercial activities, his customary business practices, and what at least one government official thought about them.

President Cox made an equally pointed charge against Lascelles in his statement to the board on december 20, 1721. After paying his respects to "the insolent behaviour of the restored members of the council toward me," he turned his remarks to Lascelles and said:

"Mr. Lascells, collector of the customs here, has after seizure discharged and let saile the sloop Spy, one Burrows master, altho' he knew she was under prosecution in his majesty's courts here for breach of the acts of trade, and had on board her when seized severall French sugers, which (she having sailed from this is-

56 Cecil Headlam, *et al.,* eds., *Calendar of state papers, colonial series, America and West Indies* (March 1720 to december 1721) (London, 1860-1919), 484, 486-487.

land without any clearance) had taken in at the French islands, and unloaded great part of, without entry with me, and at the customhouse. How far this gentleman's conduct deserves censure, is humbly submitted." [57]

The story of the Lascelles brothers' commercial career was not new to Dinwiddie. All of these things he was acquainted with, and more, as he made his tours about the islands beginning in 1738 as surveyor-general of customs. But he seems to have played no favorites. In the Henry E. Huntington library is a most interesting letter – the earliest known autograph letter from the pen of Robert Dinwiddie. The letter, dated july 13, 1739, is to William Fairfax, then in Virginia, but who had been collector of customs on Bermuda. Even though Dinwiddie and William Fairfax were friends, Dinwiddie does not hesitate to say, in the course of a friendly letter:

"SIR: This is to inform you of my arivall here last monday, and to desire you will [pl]ease send down the stationary that you received from London, to Hampton that I may divide it among the different offices, at [the] same time let me know what you want, which shall be sent you.

"I am now bound to North Carolina and hope to return in fourteen dayes so shall be glad of a line from you.

"My inspection of the accounts of the Sugar islands reasons me a voyage to England, [so] that [I] am afraid [I] shall not be able to see you this summer. I find in my [instruc]tions that your accounts have not been duely transmitted, you are deficient from midsumer 1734 till Christmas 1735, which I desire you may provide and transmit them [to] me to be carried home.

[57] *Ibid.*, 504-505.

"I had the pleasure of being frequently at your brother Clarks in Barbado's, where I often drank your health. He was in good health when I left th[ere]. I have a letter for you at Ham[pton] [from] him, but not knowing of this conveyance is the reason you have it not enclosed.

> "My respects atends your lady, I am
> > Sir your most humble servant
> > > ROBERT DINWIDDIE

in

York 13th jully 1739" [58]

Fairfax, whose own conscience he declared was clear, promptly replied:

> 28 july, 1739

"SIR: On the 22d instant I received yours of 13, notifying your arrival. I heartily congratulate you thereon. But I am concerned [   ] that your late inspection of the accounts of the Sugar isl[ands] [must be the] occasion of your embarking so soon for London whereby I [am deprived] of the pleasure of your acquaintance for a yet longer time. I ha[d] [inquired] after some vessel that woud take in the two cases and one small box of [   ], the two cases being large and not fit to be risqud [?] where they can't be stowd exposd to any wet, I can't at this time promise when they can be sent unless Mr Ambler coud engage some York tobacco drogher to call for them. I shall not however cease my endeavour.

"I am sorry that in your instructions mention shoud be made of my remissness in not duly sending my accounts to Christmas 1735. I have examin'd my books

---

[58] Dinwiddie to Fairfax, july 13, 1739, Brock collection, Fairfax papers, box 1 (Huntington library). On Dinwiddie's letter is found a draft reply in the handwriting of William Fairfax, under the date of july 28, 1739. These letters are partly torn away as indicated by brackets; insertions are by the author.

FACSIMILE OF DINWIDDIE'S LETTER TO WILLIAM FAIRFAX

[First and last paragraphs only; reduced to about two-thirds size of original]

This is the only known autograph letter of Dinwiddie in America

and therein observe by a N.B. at the foot of each account
by what ship and commander I sent them, also when
their duplicates were sent to Mr Phenney. I have all
moral certainty in my favor, but I shall transcribe them
again and together with them send such [of them] as
I have by me since the demise of our late surveyor-
general. I am glad my brother Clarke in Barbados had
the frequent [pleasure of] your company, and when
I am favord with th' alike [grati]fication, will retaliate
in drinking with you his health.

"Mrs. Fa[irfax] returns your compliments and I am
Sir your most obedient humble servant." [59]

By late 1742 or early 1743, Dinwiddie had reached
a decision as to the activity of the Lascelles brothers
and as to his procedure regarding their activities. Zealous as he was in fact-finding and in laying elaborate
reports before the home government, it is more than
likely that he had informed the lords of the treasury
or the board of trade of his suspicions. At any rate, the
government having given him the requisite authority,
he determined late in 1742 or early 1743 to wage a campaign against such fraudulent practices; he therefore
precipitated the first battle by filing charges against
Henry's brother, Edward Lascelles, and against Arthur
Upton. The matter of chronology at this point has not
been definitely established, but it is quite probable that
the uncovering of these alleged frauds on Barbadoes
began at least as early as when Dinwiddie was still surveyor-general; and if that assumption be true, this ex-
posure of law violation was the move that brought him
the special additional commission as inspector-general.

A true pen picture of the characters of the two opposing men in this bitter legal fight is drawn for us in

[59] Fairfax to Dinwiddie, july 28, 1739, *ibid.*

a communication sent by the plaintiff, Robert Dinwiddie, inspector-general, to the defendant, Edward Lascelles, and dated "inspectors office, march 15th, 1743." Having been suspended from his office by Dinwiddie, Edward Lascelles, like all colonials brought up in the atmosphere of Anglo-saxon law and precedent, had by letter to the inspector-general demanded an immediate public trial. The latter's answer of march 15, just referred to, reflected his usual promptness. He began, "I received yours of this day." Habitually punctual as a letter-writer, he thus wrote Lascelles at once – and with characteristic frankness. He stated that while he had indeed again reviewed the matter in controversy and reflected on his own attitude, he found himself still forced to the same conclusion he had reached before: ". . . I have recollected and lookt over all my observations on your accounts and transactions of your office and I cannot accuse myself with partiallity." Lascelles, in his letter evidently had unloosed an accumulation of spleen against Dinwiddie. The latter, therefore, felt it futile to comment on all of Lascelles's letter and thus multiply warmth, hence he finally declared: "As you seem to write in a passion, I shall not go thorow [through] the whole contents of your letters."

Dinwiddie was the deliberate man always. While he promised that Lascelles eventually would have his day in court, he felt obliged to delay action, hence he added: "Or [nor] can I give you the tryall you desire having no orders by my instructions so to do. But you need not doubt that will hereafter be the case, when your accounts are to be strictly examined and surcharged."

Lascelles had made certain demands in his letter to the inspector-general. He insisted, for one thing, on being given the names of those who had furnished Dinwiddie his data. The latter, however, took the position that this was an unnecessary betrayal of his informants and refused to reveal their identity. Thus: "I have passed my word to the persons that have furnished me with the accounts under your hand, not to make use of their names here, but they will be transmitted with my reports to the commissioners [of trade and plantations]."

Furthermore, in response to the collector's demand for a reversal of the suspension order, he pointed out that he was acting strictly "under instructions." These gave him "power to suspend," the only limitation on his authority being that he must be specific – "suspend [only] upon particular points, appearing against the officers." Dinwiddie assured Lascelles that he would be given justice: "I shall sacredly keep up to my orders and shall endeavour to act consistently and impartialy in the whole transactions of my duty."

What next follows in this revealing letter shows that someone – and the inspector-general declared it was not he – had talked unwisely if not too much. Dinwiddie counter-charged: "I acknowledge it gave me surprize to hear of suspensions, from the town. It was not spread from this but believe from your office. I gave the negative to it, as we both knew it was false." He recognized the futility of letter-writing at this stage of the controversy, hence he told Lascelles that he would "evade going into a paper warr" on the subject, since he himself was not the court of last resort, but instead he declared "the commissioners will be the judges."

The inspector-general closed this vital letter of march 15, 1743 to Edward Lascelles with these words: "On the whole I think I have acted with friendship and honour in giving you the principles on which I shall surcharge your accompts and the reasons for suspending you" – and then added the final touch – "I wish you and family well and am sir your humble servant, Robert Dinwiddie." [60]

Meantime, before Edward's case had reached a conclusion, the name of Henry Lascelles dominates the tangled skein of events. Henry, who, as has been pointed out, was the predecessor of his brother in the office of collector and who was planning to defend Edward when the latter's case came to trial in London, suddenly found that he himself was a defendant in a similar suit brought jointly by the board of customs and Robert Dinwiddie in 1743. Apparently once a peccadillo is discovered and gone into, other and worse sins invariably come to light, implicating more and more people. When Edward's affairs were investigated, Henry's alleged dishonesties appeared to have been discovered simultaneously.

Apparently all had gone well with Henry Lascelles for ten years. At least according to the minutes of the board of customs from as far back as 1733 — march 6, of that year, to be exact — he had stood in the light of a "good and faithful servant." He had settled his accounts as collector and had asked for his bond; the surveyor-general of customs then in office, Charles Dunbar, had added his own word of approval; the report of the comptroller-general, in turn, had been entirely favorable; accordingly the commissioners of the customs, well bolstered with the affirmative findings of all subordinate bodies, had given Henry Lascelles a clean bill of official health. Henry Lascelles apparently had been a model official — according to the records. Nothing remained but for him to take up his bond. Forthwith this was done. According to the rather verbose official statement, "the accounts of the said Mr.

---

60 Dinwiddie to Edward Lascelles, march 15, 1743, P.R.O., treasury 1, bundle 320, fo. 153; L.C. tr.

[Henry] Lascelles were accordingly stated, and closed by the comptroller-general, with the said allowances and Mr Lascelles having upon payment of the balance applyed to the commissioners by letter of the 8th october 1734 to have his bond delivered up. Upon referring the same to [the] comptroller-general, he reported that he had no objection, and the bond was delivered up."

By all persons concerned, save alone the inspector-general, this action seems to have been expected to write *finis* to Henry Lascelles's record as a customs collector in Barbadoes. But he had not reckoned with the keen sense of duty and public trust of Robert Dinwiddie. Back in 1734 when Henry Lascelles was taking his official leave of the customs service, there was at that time, or so it appears from the records, only a perfunctory examination of his accounts. The comptroller-general seems to have contented himself with scrutinizing only the big items, the "principall matters," as he termed them, while the commissioners on their part were concerned chiefly with speeding up the machinery of Henry's leave-taking.

"The commissioners thought it necessary," the record has it, "for the more speedy stating and passing the accounts of this, and all the other collectors of the 4½ per cent, that the method hitherto practiced by the collectors . . . should be admitted."

Time elapsed.

"About nine or ten years afterwards," so goes the same record, "Mr. Lascelles received a letter from the secretary of the board of customs." This letter was one that, undoubtedly, Henry Lascelles felt ought never to have been written; the board of customs, probably on Robert Dinwiddie's information, thought to the contrary.

The board of customs' letter was a serious indictment – nothing less than that of malfeasance in office on the part of Lascelles. He had allegedly short-changed his government, apparently repeatedly and consistently over a ten-year period, on three separate counts: "1st. That he had given short credit for improved or white sugars. 2ly. That he had accounted for Muscov[a]do [i.e., raw] sugars at 12/6 per cent [per hundred] whereas the same were sold from 18/ to 20/ per hundred. And 3. That he had commuted rum and other species at lower prices than they respectively sold for." Here Lascelles was charged with direct violation of the law. If the charge were to be sustained, it was a specific instance of what is commonly held to have been a deplorable general condition in connection with the enforcement of the mercantilist acts of trade, alleged to have been rampant at the time throughout all British possessions: flagrant violation of trust, total disregard for national ethics, a continual mulcting of the government out of its expected income. The board of customs, concerned for the time being only with the fiscal, not the ethical aspects of the case, contented itself with politely asking the surprised Lascelles to make good the deficit. Says the record: "And therefore . . . they had directed him to be surchaged with the difference."

Lascelles decided to fight the charges; especially if he could get many witnesses and many affidavits – some hundreds of them that he counted on, as will be seen later.

Lascelles then proceeded to "answer the first article," regarding giving short credit for white sugar: "The collector absolutely denys that he ever gave short credit for improved, or white sugars, but affirms, that he duely charged himself with the duty on all sugars, under the respective denominations, contained in the entrys, beside this charge is unjust to be made on the collector who is an indoor officer, the landwaiters and searchers only being answerable for an accusation of this sort, whose business it is to attend the shipping, and compare the quality of the sugars."

The former collector next claimed, according to the minutes of the board, that the commissioners of the customs "have been misinformed" with respect to the amount of white sugar produced on Barbadoes, "especially during the time of Mr. Lascelles." He intimated that the "misinformer" was Robert Dinwiddie. He claimed not only that the condition alleged as to white sugar was true of "his own knowledge" but he intended to produce testimony that would support him. Said he, "it will appear by the testimony of the planters and merchants conversant with the state of the island in that period, that not above one-twentieth part of the sugars were improved, and shipped off, and it is well known that Barbadoes Muscovado sugars were and still are of a weaker body, than those of any of the other islands, owing to the land being longer cultivated, and of course more worn out, and in particular about the year 1732, the sugar bakers refused to buy them, because they would not yield in the pans, tho mixt with sugars of a stronger body which induced many of the planters to clay their sugars, who had never attempted it before."

The defendant now produced a "certificate lately given" him and carrying the signatures of "above one hundred eminent planters." This paper was to be proof, according to Lascelles, that as to Dinwiddie's assertions "nothing can be wider from the truth." That Dinwiddie was the moving spirit back of the charges against him is apparent from his language: "Whereas it has been lately asserted by Mr. Dinwiddie, the inspector-general."

The second charge, given above, held that Lascelles had accounted for Muscovado raw sugar "at 12/6 per cent," notwithstanding they were regularly sold at "from 18/ to 20/ per hundred." The former collector's reply was a commentary on the complexities of the bookkeeping then in vogue – "the method in which the accounts were keeped," as he expressed it. Its ramifications almost make one sympathetic toward any official who had to be familiar with this complicated system of accounting. The procedure consisted in "reducing all the other species" to the Muscovado sugar; and this had to be done, it should be noted, "according to their different values." The next step was that the Muscovado, which is to say, raw sugar, must be reduced to money, "at the absolute rate of 12/6 per cent." The defendant next explained that by action of the Barbadoes legislature, Muscovado sugar was really the currency of the island. It was the medium of exchange. It held about the same position on Barbadoes that tobacco did in Virginia. He went into some detail: ". . . by the acts of the assembly, Muscovado sugar was the currency of the country, and a legal tender in all payments, at that standard price, and by the old establishment of the 4½ per cent, and other warrants of the treasury the salarys of the officers are made payable in Muscovado sugar, but tho for the better accounting, by making it a money account Muscovado sugar was reduced to 12/6 per cent, yet the said sugar having always been shipped home in kind, it is the same to the revenue as if the accounts had been kept in hand, and not converted in money."

The third charge against Henry Lascelles had to do with a most important commodity, rum – one of the three articles, along with molasses and negro slaves, that figured in the famous (or infamous) "triangular trade" from the West Indian islands to New England, to the Guinea coast, and back to the West Indian islands. Lascelles was held to have accounted for his supplies of rum, and kindred spirits, at less than the then prevailing market price – meaning, of course, that he had made a handsome profit out of the difference. This charge especially incensed him. He branded it false and groundless. But he himself should have the satisfaction of explaining all this by way of his affidavit: "He averrs that he commuted the dutys of rum, melassoes, and limejuice for money immediately paid down at the market prices that any of them on the days of entry, and those prices were set down upon the entrys and fairly credited in the accounts, without deduction or deminution, the truth of which is notorious to all the officers of the customs and merchants, and others acquainted with the trade in that island to whom Mr. Lascelles appeals (as well as on the aforegoing article about the improving of sugars) against this false and groundless aspersion."

Lascelles concluded his defense against all three charges by denying emphatically that he had been guilty either in act or in motive. Again, through his supporters, let him do his own pleading: "Upon the whole Mr. Lascelles humbly apprehends, that these his answers to the aforegoing charge is sufficient to acquit him of any imputation of injury done by him to the revenue either thro design or neglect."

But there had recently been added to the data before the board a fourth charge against the former collector by way of postscript. By the time the case got to trial Dinwiddie had found what he believed to be an additional charge against the accused man, centering around the word "practice," namely, the very serious accusation that he had "made it a practice to receive money of the planters, and merchants, instead of sugar for the dutys of the 4½ p cent."

Guilt or innocence in connection with such a charge as the above depends in considerable measure upon the definition of "practice." Here follows Henry Lascelles's own denial of wrong-doing: "Mr. Lascelles denys that he made it a practice to take money for the duty. But admits that upon particular occasions he did so, when it was absolutely necessary for the security of the crown and conveniency of the planter etc., it having always been deemed allowable by the act of the assembly granting the duty and according to practice before his time, and Mr. Lascelles farther affirms that this was no loss to the crown, he having always shipped home sugars of the same denominations, and of equall goodness with those which he so commuted." [61]

It is the old, old question of how many separate acts it takes to make a practice; or, in a case where an accumulation of acts is venal, whether each separate act is therefore necessarily venal.

Henry Lascelles then produced the "affidavit of Mr. George Newport and Mr. George Knight, merchants" who stoutly stood up for their fellow islander. Lascelles not only had not insisted on money in place of sugar, they said, but he had often refused it when it was offered; and whenever he did accept money, "they always understood it to be a favour and at the request of the merchant." Even if Lascelles did the thing charged, they added, "it had been a practice for many years before Mr. Lascelles was collector." [62]

---

[61] The report of the commisisoners of customs passing the accounts of Henry Lascelles [probably 1744 or 1745], P.R.O., treasury 1, bundle 320, fo. 143; L.C. tr.

[62] "Extract of the reply of Sr. Robert Davers etc. to Mr. Lascelles answer, and the examination thereon at the board of customs" [n.d.], P.R.O., treasury 1, bundle 320, fo. 13; L.C. tr.

On this charge the records contain this laconic statement by the board of customs to the lords of the treasury: "By any prooffs it does not appear that were
exhibited that Mr. Lascelles had made a practice of
receiving the duty of sugar in mony instead of in kind,
but only on small parcels at the desire of the merchants
to accomodate the trade." [63]

There is an absence of available documentary evidence at this point. The investigation into the case of
Henry Lascelles apparently ceases and the outcome is
shrouded in mystery. So far as Dinwiddie is concerned,
the case tended to bring the indefatigable inspector-
general still more favorably to the attention of his government.

Meantime, evidence was being accumulated in regard to Edward Lascelles. This litigation, as in the
case of Edward's brother, Henry, was also at the instance of the inspector-general. In an odd document
among the treasury papers in the British public record
office, is a long-forgotten entry. According to this record, the commissioners of the customs, on july 23, 1746,
addressed the board of trade as follows:

"May it please your lordships: In our memorial of
the 10th. june last [1746], on the referred petitions of
Messrs. Edward Lascelles and Arthur Upton the collector and comptroller of Barbadoes, we acquainted
your lordships, that Mr. Dinwiddie had charged the
petitioners with breach of several articles of the instructions . . . [of] 1734, and the commission of frauds to
the prejudice of the revenue of four and [one] half per
cent." [64]

[63] Extract of a report by the board of customs to the lords of the treasury
[n.d.], P.R.O., treasury 1, bundle 320, fo. 15; L.C. tr.

[64] The celebrated four and one-half per cent export duty was first enacted
in 1663 by the assembly of Barbadoes, for the purpose of augmenting the
crown's revenue from the island, its passage apparently due to the almost

The next sentence used by the customs officials apparently showed that Dinwiddie had been within his authority in taking action regarding these officials. The commissioners stated "we are of opinion, by what then appeared to us, Mr. Dinwiddie was justified in having suspended the collector and comptroller, supposing what he had alledged against them to be fact." Cautiously they approached the next point. They seem to have learned from their experience with Henry Lascelles – in their too hastily returning him his bond in 1734 – to be more guarded now in their commitments. At any rate, they continue: "As to the frauds to the prejudice of the said revenue, which they were charged with, we could not give any opinion, until Mr. Dinwiddie had produced the original papers he assured us were in his possession and was returned to England to explain several matters relating to the collectors accounts, for which the comptroller-general had certified Mr. Dinwiddie's presence was necessary." [65]

This item from the records of the board of customs indicates that Robert Dinwiddie made the voyage from the West Indies to London late in 1744 apparently to protect himself by presenting his case in person. Further mute evidence is his detailed expense account for the trip. This interesting account is on file among the

hypnotic popularity of the then royal governor, Lord Willoughby. In time the islanders began to protest long and vigorously against this tax but it was not abandoned until the reform era, when parliament by act abolished it in 1838 (John Harding and G. E. J. Gent, *et al.*, comps., *Dominions office and the colonial office list for 1939* [London, 1939], 244; Dinwiddie's memorial, november 25, 1746, P.R.O., treasury 1, bundle 320, fo. 13; L.C. tr. See also G. L. Beer, *Old colonial system, 1660-1754,* I, 178-181, *passim,* citing British museum, Egerton MSS. 2395, f. 383). An interesting contemporary account of Barbadoes and its products has come down from the pen of young George Washington who, with Lawrence, spent four months on the island in 1751-1752 (John C. Fitzpatrick, ed., *Diaries of George Washington, 1748-1799* [New York, 1925], I, 17-36).

[65] Board of trade memorial relating to the case of Edward Lascelles, july 23, 1746, P.R.O., treasury 1, bundle 320, fo. 159; L.C. tr.

treasury papers in the public record office, and is entitled, "The inspection of the four and half per cent and enumerated duties." According to this report of the inspection trip this much-travelled man was in the "Sugar islands, commencing the 17th. august 1743"; he was "at Antigua" on july 14, 1744; then he took passage for Virginia. How long he remained there is not known. Presently he entered his expenses of £50 for "my passage from Virginia to London" – which, by the way, cost him only £10 more than his passage from Antigua to Virginia – a commentary on reduced rates for a long haul.[66] Meantime, from the *Journal of the commissioners for trade and plantations,* it appears that he was back in England and present at a meeting of the board there on wednesday, september 21, 1743.[67] The chronology here is confusing for it is difficult to see how he could have performed this transatlantic legerdemain with himself. At any rate, he must have been back in London early the following year, inasmuch as his report of his tour was filed there on february 13, 1745.[68]

The customs commissioners, going into the minutest details, rehearsed the history of the case for the lords of trade. They related that soon after Dinwiddie's return to England, they had called a meeting of their board. Dinwiddie was asked to attend – as was Henry Lascelles, who was then in London. The complaint however was now against Edward Lascelles, not his brother, Henry. Yet Edward did not appear. Nor did Henry, though he was close at hand. "We . . . gave notice to Mr. Henry Lascelles that he might be present himself

---

[66] Dinwiddie's expense account during his inspection of the customs in the West Indies, february 13, 1745, P.R.O., treasury 1, bundle 320, fo. 154; L.C. tr.

[67] *Journal of the commissioners for trade and plantations* (January 1741/2 to december 1749), 82.

[68] Dinwiddie's expense account, *op. cit.*

to answer to any of the charges brought by Mr. Dinwiddie against Mr. Edward Lascelles," so the record
runs. And then it adds, "but Mr. Lascelles declined
such attendance."

While Henry declined to appear for his brother, the
record states he "delivered in a paper in behalf, of
the said Mr. Edward Lascelles, complaining, that he
[Edward Lascelles] had been denied by Mr. Dinwiddie, an opportunity of being heard on the matter
alledged against him." As has been seen, the inspector-
general, in his letter to Edward Lascelles march 15,
1743, had explained that he had no authority to give a
public hearing in Barbadoes to a suspended official
whose trial was pending in London before the board.
Yet Henry Lascelles, like Edward, stuck to the original
demand – although it was unlikely that the board would
grant it – namely, a change of venue. The curious language reads: ". . . praying that a fair and impartial
enquiry may be made into his conduct and behavior in
the execution of his office, by a publick examination of
witnesses in Barbadoes before the governor and council." Henry Lascelles, therefore, had made the plea
that this trial should be removed from London to America. Such a demand was indicative of a growing sentiment in the colonies that the atmosphere of London was
prejudicial to their interests. Colonials had always re-
belled against going to England for trial; it had been
one of the increasing points of friction with the home
government. In Barbadoes, in this case, the atmosphere
was certain to be more favorable to Henry's brother.
Needless to add, the trial proceeded – in London.

Here intervened what may look like a curious spec-
tacle. Neither the defendant nor his advocate-brother
appeared; someone or something needed to be examined; accordingly, the board proceeded, it is recorded,

"to examine Mr. Dinwiddie." What really occurred was that Dinwiddie's "seven articles of charge" that he had brought against Edward Lascelles were taken up for consideration by the board, article by article. As the board considered them, one by one, they asked for and received Dinwiddie's explanation of the technical points involved in each charge.

The commissioners of the customs resorted to a very effective presentation of the evidence before the lords of trade: "We have caused the said articles of charge, as delivered by Mr. Dinwiddie to be drawn out in one column, and in another column the nature of the proof produced by him to support the same, in a third column the answers of the collector, and in a fourth column" – most important of all – "our observations and opinion on the whole."

At this point is another break in the chain of events; for unluckily, the records that would give us the full story are lacking. What, however, is the "conclusion of the whole matter" – up to this point? The report of the board of customs contains three most enlightening passages bearing on this case. They tell the story better than any interpretation or interpolation.

First, as to Edward Lascelles: "And here we beg leave to represent to your lordships, that the complaints which were made to this board . . . with respect to the practice and method of accounting in those islands, whereby it was strongly suggested, the collectors had defrauded the crown, and made great advantages to themselves, were the foundation for those instructions. And as those instructions appear, by what we have laid before your lordships, to have been essentially if not totally, disregarded by the collector, we cannot think Mr. Lascelles a proper person to be continued in this employment: he having taken upon him to dispence with the instructions, that were prepared with so much attention with regard to the auditors observations, and recommended to him in the strongest manner for his care and execution."

Second, as to Arthur Upton: "With regard to the conduct of Mr. Upton the comptroller, we need trouble your lordships but little, for he ought to have been a cheque on the collector throughout his whole management, and it may be concluded he was privy to all his transactions by having attested his irregular accounts, and therefore an improper person to be any longer continued in that office."

Third, as to Robert Dinwiddie: "With regard to Mr. Dinwiddie's conduct, we think he has shewn more zeal than prudence, and if he had behaved with more temper, the service might have been better performed.

"In our report of the 10th june 1745, we acquainted your lordships, that we thought Mr. Dinwiddie blameable, in giving the collector liberty to commute the duties for cash . . . we think Mr. Dinwiddie blameable in this respect.

"Which is humbly submitted

R. CHANDLER	W. G. WESTBY
J. EVELYN	ROBT. BAYLIS
JOHN HILL	BEAUMT. HOTHAM
	G. VAUGHAN

Customhouse London
23d july 1746" [69]

How like many a modern tax suit this was, for it resulted in a compromise verdict! Dinwiddie thus had been supported on some of the charges; Lascelles on others.

A few more years passed.

Edward Lascelles again figured in the records of the

[69] Board of trade memorial relating to the case of Edward Lascelles, *op. cit.*

board of trade – this time in a more favorable light:
he was recommended to a seat in the Barbadoes council. He was now to have his innings. The minutes of the
board for tuesday, march 18, 1745/6 are given verbatim:

"Tuesday, march 18. Present: Lord Monson, Mr.
Brudenell, Mr. Pitt, Mr. Leveson Gower.

"Read a letter from Sir Thomas Robinson,[70] governor of Barbados, dated the 9th of january, 1745/6,
containing some remarks on the assembly's conduct
with regard to him;[71] promising to transmit his answer to their complaints against him by the first opportunity; and recommending Edward Lascelles, Esquire,
to supply the vacancy in the council, occasioned by the
death of James Dottin, Esquire, eldest member." [72]

It is impossible to pass judgment *ex cathedra* between
the litigants, Lascelles and Dinwiddie. Lascelles had
eventually been appointed a member of the upper house
in the second most important of Britain's West Indian
islands, the island where he lived; Dinwiddie, on the
other hand, was presently to be appointed chief executive of Britain's eldest, largest, and, in some respects,
most important mainland colony.

The history of this case illustrates the ramifications of
a commercial system built upon innumerable laws, acts,
inspections, reports, duties, customs, and collections. It
reveals something of the multifarious problems of a
home government which undertook to administer at
long range certain increasingly unpopular imperial

---

[70] This Sir Thomas Robinson is not to be confused with his contemporary
of the same name who was one of the lords of trade *(q.v.)*.

[71] Whatever the justice of the complaints against Sir Thomas, young
George Washington, who visited Barbadoes with his sick brother, Lawrence,
in 1751, makes a brief reference in his diary to Sir Thomas's "errors" (John
C. Fitzpatrick, ed., *Diaries of George Washington, 1748-1799,* I, 27).

[72] *Journal of the commissioners for trade and plantations* (January 1741/2
to december 1749), 195.

laws for the colonies. Whether or not those laws were unjust is a theoretical matter; the significant fact is that a growing proportion of the colonial people came to regard them as unjust.

The importance of this long-drawn-out suit thus is clear enough: it is an example of the colonial struggle for dominance between two groups, whose politico-economic ideals were not all sordid on the one hand, not all worthy on the other. It is a cross-section of the unreasoning conflict in progress during the next thirty years before that first American civil war, known as the American revolution. On the one side were the forces representing distant British control, a home government's shortsighted mercantilist policy toward colonies, and the spasmodic enforcement of the trade laws made in pursuance thereof; on the other side were the forces representing local autonomy, a highly individualistic homespun attitude toward trade, a propensity for money-getting, and a code of conduct that held it not unethical in matters of trade and customs dues to pay but slight deference to most of the legal distinctions set up by Britain for application in America.

Had this case been more carefully studied by British officials generally and given wide publicity, it might have gone far to convince the British conservatives of the futility of enforcing the acts of trade – and thus to have prevented the enactment of that mass of ill-advised legislation for the colonies which was to occur during the next few decades.

Dinwiddie, in a sense, represents the first of the two groups mentioned; Lascelles, the second. Considering that Britain later lost her continental colonies, to that extent Dinwiddie represented the conservative point of view and the passing order; considering that home rule was finally achieved, to that extent the Lascelles brothers can be regarded as typical at least of one element among those who soon would be called patriots.

In 1749 Dinwiddie resigned from the service.[73] Though he may have spent brief periods of the intervening time, from 1745 to 1749, in Virginia, where he long had had a residence, at the end of eleven years of service he finally gave up his surveyor-generalship and with it, of course, his position on the governor's council in Virginia; furthermore, he wrote that he was leaving Virginia and did not expect to return.[74] Yet he did return, and soon, in 1751. Not only that, but he came back with new honors and still greater authority. In 1749, however, he perhaps was too close to the events of the preceding six years to get the right perspective.

It may be that the Lascelles case had nothing to do with the surveyor-general's resignation. An interesting sequel, however, to this litigation appears in the later Dinwiddie correspondence. A decade after this customs fraud case, Henry Lascelles was again about to oppose his old antagonist in another legal battle, this time as assistant to the Virginia attorney-general, Peyton Randolph, representing the house of burgesses against

---

[73] Corroborative evidence of his having resigned to engage in trade is seen from the bill of sale referred to above (note 51), indicating that Dinwiddie had recently purchased a part ownership in a frigate of 300 tons. This interesting document was furnished Brock by Mrs. M. A. Dinwiddie.

[74] The entry for thursday, april 13, 1749, in the *Journal of the commissioners for trade and plantations* (January 1741/2 to december 1749), 408, is unequivocal:

"Present: Earl of Halifax, Mr. Pitt, Mr. Leveson Gower, Mr. Grenville, Lord Dupplin, Mr. Fane, Sir Thomas Robinson.

"Their lordships having been informed that Peter Randolph, Esquire, had been appointed surveyor-general of his majesty's customs in the southern district of America, in the room of Robert Dinwiddie, Esquire, ordered the draught of a representation to his majesty to be prepared, proposing him to be one of the council of Virginia, in the room of the said Robert Dinwiddie, who attending, informed their lordships that he had no intention of returning to the said colony." See also Order of council, may 2, 1749, P.R.O., C.O., 5/1327, 105; L.C. tr., 61-62.

Dinwiddie in the celebrated pistole fee dispute, but for Lascelles's untimely death. His death called forth a revealing comment in a letter from the governor. Dinwiddie wrote to John Hanbury, march 12, 1754: "Poor Lasselle's death is a fatal loss to the attorney in his negotiations, as I hear that man was to be engaged to solicit his affairs with the ministry. Their motive for this step, I suppose was, believing him to be my enemy, and that he would go great lengths to hurt me. If so, poor people, I pitty their ignorance and narrow, ill-natured spirits." [75]

One of the services of history is, of course, its long-range view of life and its vicissitudes. Could Dinwiddie have been privileged in 1749, the year of his resignation, a glimpse into the future, he would have been heartened by the assurance that in due time his efforts to uphold the law were to be appreciated and himself rewarded; that he was, after all, not leaving Virginia for good, but was within two years' time after his resignation to come back with enhanced prestige to the scene of his earlier diplomatic triumph, a decade before, over Gooch's councillors – coming back justified in all his previous battles for governmental honesty, and as proof thereof rewarded with the governorship of the oldest and largest of Britain's colonies in America.

One fain would know the emotions and sentiments on two particular occasions of these two men – Robert Dinwiddie and Edward Lascelles: of Dinwiddie's, when in 1746 he learned that Edward Lascelles had been rewarded by an appointment to the governor's council in Barbadoes; of Lascelles's, when in 1751 he learned that Robert Dinwiddie had been elevated to the lieutenant-governor's chair in England's imperial colony of Virginia.

---

[75] Dinwiddie to Hanbury, march 12 [1754], *Dinwiddie papers*, I, 103-104.

Governor

On july 4, 1751 Robert Dinwiddie was appointed to the position of lieutenant-governor of his majesty's colony of Virginia in these resounding phrases:

"George the second by the grace of God, king of Great Britain, France, and Ireland, defender of the faith etc. To our trusty and well beloved Robert Dinwiddie Esqr. greetings. We reposing especial trust and confidence in your loyalty, courage, and prudence, do by these presents, constitute and appoint you (in case of the death or absence of our right trusty, and right well-beloved Cousin William Anne Earl of Albemarle, our present lieutenant and governor-general of our colony and dominion of Virginia in America) to be our lieutenant-governor there in the room of Sir William Gooch Bart. To have, hold, exercise, and enjoy the said office of our lieutenant-governor of our said colony and dominion, for and during our pleasure, with all and singular the rights, members, and appurtenances whatsoever to the same belonging; and we do hereby authorize and require you, in such case as aforesaid, to execute and perform all and singular the powers and authorities contained in our commission granted to him, the said William Anne Earl of Albemarle, and according to such instructions as he hath, or shall have, or you shall at any time receive from us and we do hereby command all and singular our officers, ministers, and loving subjects of our said colony and dominion of Virginia, and all others whom it may concern to take due notice hereof, and to give their ready and obedience ac-

cordingly. Given at our court at St. James the fourth
day of july, 1751, in the twenty-fifth year of our reign.
"By his majesty's command
HOLDERNESS." [76]

Immediately upon his appointment Dinwiddie began
setting his house in order for the trip to Virginia, as
witness a news item from London printed by William
Hunter [77] in the *Virginia Gazette*: "Williamsburg, july
18 [1751] – Letters by the Duchess of Queensbury,
from London advise that the Honourable Robert Dinwiddie, Esq. is appointed lieutenant-governor of this
colony, and is preparing to set out for his government." [78] This report without comment may be taken as
testimony that any comment regarding the qualifications of one who was already "so well acquainted" with
Virginia would be superfluous. The new governor
might be welcomed; he already long since had been introduced.

It must be remembered that Dinwiddie and his family were by no means newcomers to the New World.
He had come to Bermuda as early as 1722; his older
daughter had been born there in 1738. His earlier career need not be retold here but it becomes clear what
the city fathers of Williamsburg meant when, in their

---

[76] Holdernesse to Dinwiddie, july 4, 1751, P.R.O., C.O., 234/50, 211-212; L.C.
tr., 231-232; *Virginia gazette,* november 21, 1751, from copy in the library of
Colonial Williamsburg, inc., department of research and education (hereafter
cited as Colonial Williamsburg MSS.).

[77] William Hunter (d. 1761), Virginia printer, is supposed to have been
born at Yorktown. He long had a printshop and a bookstore in Williamsburg.
Besides being a printer of the laws and of books, which may help to account
for his friendship with Benjamin Franklin, he was appointed in 1753 a deputy
postmaster-general, a position which he held until his death. He is best known
as the publisher of the *Virginia gazette,* the first number brought out by him
being dated january 3, 1750/51. He was successor to William Parks who
started the *Gazette* in 1736 (see Rutherfoord Goodwin, *William Parks paper
mill at Williamsburg* [Lexington, Virginia, 1939].

[78] *Virginia gazette,* july 18, 1751 (Colonial Williamsburg MSS.).

address of welcome to Dinwiddie, they referred to him as one who was "so well acquainted with us, our laws, and constitutions." [79] They could not help remembering Dinwiddie's long, and successful, struggle with the governor's council nearly ten years before.

The cream of tidewater aristocracy was on hand on november 20, 1751 to meet the new governor who was to take over the administration of their colony. They went out to "the entrance of the town" to meet him, providing a sharp contrast to his reception a decade before. The clergy were there, represented by their highest colonial official, the bishop of London's commissary, William Dawson, D.D., [80] who was also president of the College of William and Mary. And John Blair, [81] a prominent member of the council, and a nephew of the late Dr. James Blair, [82] was there. As the council was the

[79] Address of the corporate authorities of Williamsburg to Governor Dinwiddie [November 20, 1751], *Dinwiddie papers*, I, 2.

[80] William Dawson (1704-1752) was born in England, educated at Oxford, and came to Virginia in 1729 to teach moral philosophy at the college. He was the second president of the college, 1743-1752. Governor Gooch wrote of him to the bishop of London: ". . . He is well allied here by marrying a niece of the late Sir John Randolph's, one of the best familys in the country; and I make no question, on the first occasion after the commissary's death, will be unanimously elected president of the college, and have his parish" (*Virginia magazine of history and biography*, XXXIII [January 1925], 57).

[81] John Blair (1687-1771), colonial Virginia public official, was educated at the College of William and Mary. He was a burgess from 1734 to 1740 and a member of the council from 1745 to his death; meantime, as president of the council, he was acting lieutenant-governor of the colony on two occasions, between the time when Dinwiddie left, january 12, 1758, until the arrival of Francis Fauquier, june 5, 1758, and from the death of Fauquier, march 3, 1768, to the coming of Botetourt, october 3, 1768. These honors and responsibilities are sufficient evidence of his standing in the colony. His manuscript diary, still preserved in the Virginia historical society, is a simple, direct, unvarnished commentary on the 1750's in Virginia, revealing Blair's diversity of interests, in such things as the rebuilding of the capitol, the filling of parish vacancies, and plans to settle western lands.

[82] Brock obviously is in error when he identifies James Blair, who died in 1743, as one of the officials who went down to York to greet Dinwiddie in 1751 (*Dinwiddie papers*, I, note 1). James Blair (1655-1743), founder of the

upper house of Virginia's bicameral legislature as well as the supreme court of the colony, John Blair was the official representative of a more than ordinarily powerful group in the Old Dominion. The Fairfax, Ludwell, and Nelson families were represented by a spokesman for each of them.

Politics in Dinwiddie's time, in perspective, seem amazingly modern. The diary of John Blair records a typical event: "At the entrance of the town, he [the governor] was complimented by the mayor and aldermen, who (with the gentlemen) were got together to welcome him, and invited him and the council to a dinner they had prepared at Wetherburn's, where we all dined." [83] The *Virginia Gazette* for november 22 reported further: "After meeting the council and qualifying himself by taking the oaths, his honour was invited to an entertainment prepared by the gentlemen of the corporation, and the royal healths drank, under a discharge of cannon. In the evening he returned to York, and is expected back again this day." [84]

The previously-mentioned reception address invited Dinwiddie to continue to be, as "our late Sir William Gooch" was, "our great protector and benefactor." The city officials emphasized that they had "been fortunate in the enjoyment of their kind protection" by preceding

College of William and Mary and president thereof until his death, could not have been at this time the president of the college nor the commissary mentioned in 1751 in John Blair's diary. Reverend William Dawson was at that time president of the college and was the commissary who "went out to meet the governor," as John Blair expressed it. The catalogue (1936-1937) of the College of William and Mary carries this entry: "1743—Dr. James Blair died. Dr. William Dawson elected the second president of the college . . . 1752—Dr. William Dawson died, and Reverend William Stith elected third president of the college."

[83] See also the printed version of this diary in the *William and Mary college quarterly historical magazine*, 1st series, VII (January 1899), 133-153; VIII (July 1899), 1-17.

[84] *Virginia gazette*, november 22, 1751 (Colonial Williamsburg MSS.).

governors, and expressed a hope that under Dinwiddie "we shall still be preserved in our rights and privileges."

"Our rights and privileges" was by no means an empty phrase. It was to be repeated time and again during Dinwiddie's administration by another and larger body, the house of burgesses; and about a quarter of a century later by the lower houses of the legislatures in all the colonies. Those city officials on that november day in 1751 were well aware that their Spanish, Portuguese, and French colonial contemporaries in town and country throughout North as well as South America were enjoying no such "rights and privileges." They had been taught what had occurred at Runnymede, and the pledges that had been extracted of every English king in consequence from that day to then. They knew the long struggle the house of commons had engaged in to gain ascendancy over the upper house. They knew why so many of their forbears had come to America. The English-speaking world since the time of the Magna Charta to the present has kept piling up precedents in government; and in so doing it has treasured the heritage of popular participation in government and popular responsibility. The "corporate authorities of Williamsburg" were but keeping alive tradition and precedent when they emphasized at the outset of the new governor's administration their rights and privileges. Whether the governor would respond with empty complimentary phrases, or with a sincere pledge of faith, he had no alternative but to respond. Theirs was political strategy as well as political philosophy.

That speech by the mayor and his official family did not fall on deaf ears. Dinwiddie, impressed and anxious to say the right thing, pledged himself even beyond what was asked for, in what John Blair's diary styled "a handsome speech." Not only did he promise in general to "do all in my power for the good and prosperity of the collony," but in particular to be mindful of the "rights and privileges of the city of Williamsburg," and thus "on all occasions you may be assured," he told them, "of every thing in my power for the continuance and enlargement of them." [85]

If Dinwiddie in 1751, and during the troubled years immediately ahead, could have looked forward to that january day in 1758, when, about to take ship for England, he would receive the commendation of "good and faithful servant" from the same city fathers, it would have been of great encouragement during the intervening years of trial.[86]

The new executive's first proclamation, in full, was thus reported in the *Virginia Gazette:*

"By the Honourable Robert Dinwiddie, Esq., his majesty's lieutenant-governor, and commander-in-chief of this dominion.

"A PROCLAMATION

"Whereas his most sacred majesty hath by his royal commission, under his signet, and sign manual bearing date the 4th day of july 1751, in the twenty-fifth year of his reign, constituted and appointed me to be lieutenant-governor of this his colony and dominion, and to execute and perform all and singular the powers and authorities contained in his majesty's commission granted to the Right Hon. William Ann Earl of Albemarle,[87] his majesty's lieutenant and governor-general

---

[85] It is interesting to compare this address, which appeared in the *Virginia gazette,* november 28, 1751, with that printed in the *Dinwiddie papers,* I, 3.

[86] Address of the corporation of Williamsburg to Governor Dinwiddie [January 1758], *Dinwiddie papers,* II, 724-725.

[87] William Anne Keppel, second Earl of Albemarle (1702-1754), a titular, or absentee, governor of Virginia, received his second christian name in

of the said colony, in case of the death or during the absence of the said chief governor. Now, to the end that the peace of this his majesty's dominion may be the better secured, and all proceedings at law continued, and that the ordinary course of justice may not be interrupted, I have thought fit, by and with the advice of his majesty's name, to publish and declare that all magistrates and officers, both civil and military, do continue and remain in and singular their powers, authorities, and jurisdictions, until further order be taken therein: hereby requiring them to proceed in the execution of their several duties, and all his majesty's subjects within this colony are to be aiding and assisting to them therein, and to yield all due obedience to this proclamation.

"Given at the council chamber in Williamsburg, this 21st day of november 1751, in the 25th year of his majesty's reign.

"ROBERT DINWIDDIE

"God save the king" [88]

---

honor of the new sovereign, Queen Anne. She is said to have been present at his baptism. His military career, marked by frequent promotions, dated from 1717, when George I made him a captain. In 1743 he rose to lieutenant-general and served creditably on the continent during the War of the Austrian Succession. He participated in the battles of Dettingen, Fontenoy (where he was wounded), Culloden, and (having become a general on august 23, 1746) Vall, july 2, 1747. Meantime, on september 6, 1737, he succeeded George Hamilton, Earl of Orkney, as titular governor of Virginia and held this sinecure until his death. He was rewarded by the additional appointment in 1748 as ambassador to France and served in that capacity until his death in Paris on december 22, 1754. On july 12, 1751, he was made a privy councillor. Commodore Augustus Keppel, whom Dinwiddie mentions, was his second son. Albemarle's portrait long hung in the gallery of William Byrd II at "Westover."

[88] *Virginia gazette,* november 21, 1751 (Colonial Williamsburg MSS.).

Patron of Learning

Speeches and more speeches! The College of William and Mary had no intention of losing its own opportunity to felicitate a new governor — the first chance of the kind in a quarter of a century. Immediately following the greeting extended to him by the city's representatives, therefore, the president and the dozen masters of the college gathered in solemn "convocation" in the Sir Christopher Wren building for the important occasion. (And that building stands today, as nearly like the original as Rockefeller research architects can repair, restore, and reconstruct it.) One can picture not only the colorful gathering of the college authorities, but also the student body of nearly one hundred, including eight Indians from Joshua Fry's Indian school department of the institution.[89] These young tribesmen were housed in old Brafferton hall (also standing and still in use). Present also, as has continued to be the case, were prominent citizens of the city of Williamsburg.

At the appropriate moment, the college officials presented to the new lieutenant-governor what they termed their "humble address." It was couched in as felicitous phrases as the president, Reverend William Dawson,[90] could devise. It would be a good address in any genera-

---

[89] See page 136.

[90] The president of the college at the time of Dinwiddie's coming was not Reverend William Stith, the historian, as Brock records, but Dr. William Dawson (*Dinwiddie papers, I, 3-4n*). The minutes of the early faculty meetings are still preserved among the valued treasures of the college library.

tion. After getting past the customary phrases, they "thankfully acknowledge" their sovereign's "paternal attention to the publick welfare" in that he had been "graciously pleased to appoint" a man "of approved integrity" – a term derived from Dinwiddie's successes in uncovering frauds in the customs service. They saluted the new executive as one who will "set such a pattern to future governors, as may make them prove blessings to succeding generations." A big order for any public official. They would hitch his wagon to a star.

It is noteworthy also that each address to the new governor emphasized the quiet and beneficent administration of the preceding governor. That man, Dinwiddie's predecessor, was the amiable Sir William Gooch. Evidently the several spokesmen who lauded him, while at the same time they welcomed Dinwiddie, were aware that not all comparisons are odious. The college officials, for example, refer to "Sir William Gooch's mild and auspicious government"; yet in the same breath they hasten to assure his successor that they regard him as "qualified to repair the great loss we have lately sustained." [91] Dinwiddie, not to be outdone on such an occasion, responded with a reply that must have been fully up to expectations. The college professors themselves could not have done better. He said:

"It's true, I must appear with great disadvantages in succeeding that worthy gentleman, but his exact principle may have its proper use, and my emulation may be animated, and you probably may see during my administration, that" – Shakespeare to the contrary notwithstanding – "a good man's influence never dies." [92]

The College of William and Mary and Robert Din-

[91] Address of the president and masters of the College of William and Mary to Dinwiddie, *Dinwiddie papers*, I, 4.

[92] Dinwiddie's reply to the address of the president and masters of the College of William and Mary, *ibid.*, I, 5.

widdie chanced to be born in the same year. The president and faculty who felicitated the governor prepared their "humble address," against the background of their own college charter, dated february 8, 1693. This is the cue to the peculiar relationship, with reference to matters ecclesiastical, between the two parties to the agreement. ". . . to the end," ran the terms of that ancient document, "that the church of Virginia may be furnished with a seminary of ministers of the gospel, and that the youth may be piously educated in good letters and manners, and that the Christian faith may be propagated amongst the western Indians." [93]

Church and state were in a sense so closely bound up together in colonial Virginia that not only did the college officials in their address "entertain the pleasing hopes" that they might count upon the governor's "protection to the college," but also his equal solicitude for the "church and clergy." They on their part were able to pledge to him that, "in return for such considerable benefits," he might count upon not only "their constant endeavours" but also upon "their fervent prayers." He was assured of their supplications for an administration "long and prosperous" and for a "succession of able and upright rulers" over the colony. The climax of their devout petitions would be "that irreligion and immorality may be discouraged and suppressed." [94]

It was well known that Dinwiddie had been born in Scotland and under what denominational influence he had been reared. It was expected that since the new appointee had been brought up under the influence of the presbyterian church, he would as a result, in the words

[93] The charter of february 8, 1693 is readily accessible in any current catalogue of the college. It is a document well worth perusal.

[94] For Dinwiddie's instructions (at least the spirit of them) from the crown regarding his responsibility for the clergy in colonial Virginia, see note 177.

of Jonathan Edwards, have "respect for that church."
He did have respect for it. But, since he was appointed
to the executive control of a colony in which the Church
of England was the dominant faith, he felt duty-bound,
as he said, to "support the church, as by law established."

Native son of calvinist Scotland, but now the adopted
son of episcopal England, the new governor never wav-
ered in line of "duty" – a word he seemed to use more
often than any other throughout his career. It was tanta-
mount to a religion with him. He left nothing to be desired by those gentlemen of the Established church
when he replied with these appropriate remarks:

"I am with pleasure engaged and obliged to support
the church, as by law established, and the clergy may
always depend on my countenance and protection, as
long as their lives and conversation is consistent with the
doctrines they profess and are engaged to maintain."
The time would come five years later when certain of
those present or their associates would be held to be
guilty in their "lives and conversation"; they would be
charged with a dereliction from that "duty" so cherished by Dinwiddie; they would incur his wrath; and
there would be worse than weeping and gnashing of
teeth: there would be resignations.

Here is what he did say explicitly regarding the college. It is choice phraseology: "I have always looked
on seminaries of learning with an awful respect and
true regard," he told his college audience, in language
that was as honestly serious as it is now curiously quaint.
"The College of William and Mary is undoubtedly a
very great blessing to Virginia."

Was the governor's declaration mere flattery? Not
likely. The college was the only institution of its kind
in Virginia and almost in America. And it was unique

in many respects.[95] Moreover, the college's "great building," after plans by the celebrated English architect, Sir Christopher Wren, had intermittently been associated with the colonial government – in fact, had housed it; for in this building had been held the sessions of the general assembly of Virginia from 1699 to 1704, or until the completion of the capitol.[96] One governor, Francis Nicholson,[97] had even established his residence in the college.

There is added reason for believing the governor sincere, since it is now known that he himself had attended college. He was an alumnus of the University of Glasgow, an institution that later was to confer upon him the degree of LL.D.; [98] and to its library he was to leave in

[95] A tablet in the arcade of the Sir Christopher Wren building on the college campus lists the thirteen "PRIORITIES OF THE COLLEGE OF WILLIAM AND MARY." It begins with:

"FIRST college in the United States in its antecedents, which go back to the college proposed at Henrico (1619). Second to Harvard university in actual operation."

[96] The 1705 capitol burned in 1747. A second capitol was erected in 1751.

[97] Francis Nicholson (1655-1728), colonial governor of Virginia and, at one time or another, of several other colonies (Massachusetts, Maryland, and South Carolina). He did much to develop Virginia, his chief service being the support given to Dr. James Blair in establishing the College of William and Mary, 1693. Also, he did much for the new capital city, Williamsburg. His name is perpetuated by the two Williamsburg streets, Francis and Nicholson, which flank the wide and stately central thoroughfare known as Duke of Gloucester street.

[98] Edward D. Neill, in his "Notes on American history," in *New England historical and genealogical register,* XXIX (July-september 1875), 298-299, wrote as follows: "He was a native of Glasgow, and a graduate of its university. At a meeting of the college authorities on dec. 20, 1754, 'it was represented by some members of the faculty, that it would be very proper to confer the degree of doctor of laws upon the Honourable Robert Dinwiddie, Esq., governor of Virginia, both as he was an alumnus of this universitie, and a native of this city, and as being a person who, both by high office he bears, does honor to both, and may have occasion to promote their interest. And the faculty unanimously agreed to confer the said degree upon him, *honoris causa,* and appoint a diploma to be immediately expeded *(sic)* for that purpose, to be sent him in a silver box, with the arms of the university engraved upon it.' "

This interesting item of the conferring of the degree upon Dinwiddie was

his will a bequest to the sum of one hundred pounds.[99]

Mixed sentiments undoubtedly accounted for his carefully chosen language before his college audience: to begin with, he was a new governor, and his aim would be to please rather than to alienate. Furthermore, being an educated man, he would naturally feel drawn to an institution of learning, and it was natural he should hope to win its support. Then there was a certain atmosphere of respectability that such support would lend to his administration. From a practical standpoint, moreover, he was talking to a constituency that had political power, for the college was represented in the lower house of the general assembly. Following in the English tradition, it was represented by a burgess – and a burgess might be an important figure in case of a tie, or even of a close vote. Indeed, the college's representative might count for considerably more than one burgess if he were, say, a Peyton Randolph – as, in truth, he was during Dinwiddie's entire administration. This important personage not only represented the College of William and Mary from 1752 to 1758, and the city of Williamsburg before that, but he was also the attorney-general of the colony. Besides, the governor knew that the burgess from a local constituency would be present – always; although absences of other members from sessions were frequent. These were due chiefly to the distance that the one hundred and four members lived from the capital.[100]

---

unearthed for me by my Los Angeles friend, Mr. Harold Slocum, himself an indefatigable searcher after truth. This manuscript has had the benefit of his constructive criticism.

99 Will of Robert Dinwiddie, *Virginia magazine of history and biography,* XIX (July 1911), 282-283.

100 Dinwiddie's report on the state of Virginia, january 1755, P.R.O., C.O., 5/1328, 323-334; L.C. tr., 265-283; *Dinwiddie papers,* I, 383. When more than one source is given in the same footnote, the first citation mentioned is the one used for quotation.

One can be quite certain that the new governor was well aware of the high standing in the colony of both of the presidents that the college had had up to that time: he would do well to have them on his side. Certainly that high standing had been true of Dr. James Blair; not only had he been the leading churchman in the colony but he was also politically a figure of first importance. His prestige extended to England, where he went when occasion demanded. More than one governor had reason to remember an encounter with him. The college's incumbent president was, as has been seen, Reverend William Dawson. First of all, the college head was customarily the bishop of London's "commissary," as that English ecclesiastic's representative in America was called; he was also the titular head of things educational in the Virginia colony. The masters, or as would be said today, the professors, were the intellectual arbiters of the time. They taught aristocracy; they associated with aristocracy; they themselves were aristocracy, of a type.

Following his introductory remarks to the college audience, Dinwiddie interposed a paragraph that will bear re-reading. It was his own conception of a college curriculum. Even today, as an objective, as a statement of educational faith, a fine expression of educational ideals, it sets a standard for any college administration. Dinwiddie would have that curriculum qualify the students, in the right sense of the term, for the service of their country. He thought first of the student body, for he declared:

"The education of the young gentlemen in the different sciences, the examination into their several geniuses, the cultivating their minds with morality, virtue, religion, and honour, so far as to qualify them for the services of their country, is a very great and important

charge which is reposed in you." Well did the College
of William and Mary perform that mission for the Old
Dominion. Many of those who became leaders in the
colony had received their training at the college. For
instance, Thomas Jefferson, in his autobiography, paid
a tribute to Dr. William Small, one of the professors,
who, he declared, "fixed my destinies in life." [101] The
list of prominent men during the later colonial and
early national period who were once students at the
college is noteworthy. The college claims sixteen members of the continental congress, four signers of the
Declaration of Independence, four of the first ten presidents, and numerous lesser luminaries.[102]

Dinwiddie, in the address in question, finally turned
his thoughts to the faculty. Its members must have been
elevated in mind by his commendation as well as by his
challenge, as he continued:

"I congratulate this country in having gentlemen of
your knowledge, capacity, and exemplary life, at the
head of, and in the sole management and direction of
this great and necessary trust. Proceed gentlemen in
your usual endeavours, and I doubt not of a blessing
and success to attend your care in their education."

One particular sentence of the address could not have
fallen on totally deaf ears. It was Dinwiddie's pledge
to the institution — his intellectual oath of office: "And
I shall watch every opportunity wherein I can be of
use or service to the college."

Time would later prove that Dinwiddie did remember to keep his promises to that college audience. One
needs only to turn back again to the charter granted to
"the College of William and Mary, in Virginia" fifty-
eight years before by the Glorious Revolution sov-

[101] Quoted by R. G., Gent [Rutherfoord Goodwin], *Brief and true report
for the traveller concerning Williamsburg in Virginia* (Richmond, 1936), 57.
[102] *Ibid.*, 58-59, for the long and imposing list.

ereigns, and named for them in their honor. It contains highly interesting as well as instructive paragraphs. One of these had to do with the offices of county surveyor and of surveyor-general. For instance, the charter granted to the then governor "Francis Nicholson, William Cole, and the rest of the said trustees, and" — in the characteristic phraseology of that age — "the longest livers or liver of them, and to his or their heirs, the [income to be derived from the] office of surveyor-general of our said colony of Virginia."

The grant in connection with a surveyor-general was elaborate in its details. So much so that if the college had derived from that office an income in proportion to the circumlocutions of the charter provisions in regard to it, the school's financial worries ought to have ended. In short, the colony's office of surveyor-general was, under certain conditions, to be under the control of the college; and, by the college, it was "to be had, held, and executed with all its issues, fees, profits, advantages, conveniences, liberties, places, privileges, and pre-eminences whatsoever, belonging to the said office." [103] This office is not to be confused with the position of surveyor-general of customs that was held by Dinwiddie himself during the decade from 1738 to 1749.

Coupled with the surveyor-general privilege, but shunted to the end of that paragraph, was a more substantial right, namely, the right to nominate and appoint "so many particular surveyors for the particular counties of our colony of Virginia" as the trustees shall "think fit and necessary." By implication, it was later held that this provision included the right to refuse to nominate and appoint, both when the applicant was not actually qualified and also when it seemed politically expedient not to appoint him.

[103] Charter of february 8, 1693.

Brief though the provisions were regarding surveyors, this latter right was to prove to be more productive of income for the college. This specific privilege
was destined also to become of great historic importance, since it was under that authority that the college
on july 20, 1749 appointed young George Washington
to the position of county surveyor for Culpeper county,
his first public office; as it was also later to appoint him
to his last public office, that of chancellor of the college,
1789-1799.

Below is an illustration of how the charter provision
relating to a county surveyor worked out in practice.
About six months after Dinwiddie first addressed the
college, something, possibly new to the governor but
rarely new to any college administration, came to his attention, namely, that the College of William and Mary
was in urgent need of additional income. It occurred to
Dinwiddie, or was suggested to him, that the college's
income from the appointment of county surveyors
might be augmented, the institution's charter having
stipulated that one-sixth of all surveyor's fees should
revert to the college treasury.

On may 6, 1752 the governor wrote to his old friend,
Thomas, sixth Lord Fairfax,[104] a long letter, one half
of which had to do with the college and its financial
problems. Dinwiddie knew that Lord Fairfax had recently come into the possession of an imperial territory
over the Blue Ridge mountains. The thought suggested

---

[104] Thomas (sixth Lord) Fairfax (c.1691-1781), was born in Kent county,
England. He came to America originally for a short stay, 1735-1737, and
permanently in 1747. He resided first on the Potomac, then set up residence
in the Shenandoah valley near what is now Winchester. He threw himself
into the life of his community. He was a justice of the peace for several counties of the Northern Neck; became county lieutenant of Frederick county, and,
as such, the chief reliance of George Washington and Governor Dinwiddie,
both of whom were close in his friendship, in arousing the militia to a defense of their homes during the French and Indian wars.

itself to the resourceful mind of the governor that Lord
Fairfax might remember that every time he appointed a
surveyor he was thereby furthering the cause of education.

Lord Fairfax had a mind of his own; and living in
what was then the exposed frontier, at "Greenway
court" in the Shenandoah valley, he was all but a law
unto himself. This fact some of his neighbors, who dis-
puted his claim to certain lands to the west, were early
to find out. The governor, who appreciated the independent spirit and high social position of his friend,
may have hesitated to force the issue with this land
baron, preferring instead to use tact and diplomacy. He
had known Lord Fairfax either in London or while he,
when surveyor-general of customs, had been a member
of the Virginia council back in the 1740's, or both; but
he had failed, to use his favorite expression, "to keep up
a constant correspondence" with Lord Fairfax. Hence
in addressing him this letter, the new executive first
apologized for not having called upon him personally
or having written him since coming over as lieutenant-
governor; then, after apologizing, hastened to show respect for a man who was but slightly older than he; and
he does it in language that truly is a study in interpretation. His opening paragraph reads:

"My Lord: I intended myself the honour of paying
my due respects to your lordship before this, but have
been prevented by the hurry of business of my first arrival, but I now desire to assure you of the sincerity of
my heart and endeavour on all occasions to testify the
veneration I have for you."

Then Dinwiddie plunged into the real business of his
communication, by quoting as authority for his next
statement the word of a man whom he knew would
carry weight with Lord Fairfax. That man was the

commissary, who of course was also president of the college. Hence he continued:

"Enclosed you have a letter from our commissary in regard to the surveyors of land. The Coledge of William and Mary have a patent of an old date, for the appointing these officers, and" – the reader will note the deference and diplomacy of the writer – "they conceive from that date they have a right to appoint those in your lordship's proprietary." It was not often that any official had presumed to advise Lord Fairfax what might and might not be done in his private domain. It is significant that it was Lord Fairfax who had, full four years before, in 1748, employed young George Washington to assist in surveying his vast acreage in the Shenandoah valley. He had employed Washington as surveyor upwards of a year before the young man was commissioned and licensed by the College of William and Mary, the only institution in Virginia which legally could do so. George Washington records in his diary kept during that surveying tour, when he was but sixteen, that he sometimes made as much as two or three doubloons (possibly as much as $7.00) a day, "when the weather permits." Should some of George Washington's fees for this service have gone to the college? Dinwiddie may have had this in mind when he wrote the above-mentioned letter. It was not, of course, until the following year, 1749, that Washington was appointed by the college to his first public office, that of county surveyor for Culpeper county. The letter to Lord Fairfax continued:

"The perquisites from these officers to the coledge is 1/6 of their receipts." The next sentence, carefully chosen, must be appreciated; the lord of Greenway court was a man who must be handled with gentleman's gloves: "We know your kind and friendly disposition."

Dinwiddie then felt safe in adding: "I doubt not you will countenance them in this their right, which is to be applied towards the support of the only seminary of learning amongst us, and more as many of their other funds proves deficient, or at least much reduced." Whatever the modern connotation of the term "patron of learning," the governor had not forgotten his original promise to the college, namely, to "watch every opportunity wherein I can be of use or service." He concluded his appeal by suggesting appropriate action: "And when your lordship shall think proper to apoint a private surveyor" – it can hardly be otherwise than that by "private surveyor" Dinwiddie had in mind George Washington's recent services in the valley – "that you will please lay your commands on them to account with the coledge for one sixth of their receipts, which [I] shall be glad if this proves agreeable to your own opinion. The commissary says he will always have a due regard to any person recomended to the coledge for their comission." [105]

Lord Fairfax, influenced by this diplomatic, conciliatory, and friendly letter of appeal for college funds, had thereafter, when he needed a surveyor, "a due regard to any person recomended" for their commission by the College of William and Mary. George Washington merely reversed the situation: he was made a surveyor first and commissioned afterward. Interestingly enough, since it was Lord Fairfax who first employed him as a surveyor, and the College of William and Mary which clothed him with legal authority in his first public office, both of them share with Governor Dinwiddie the honor of putting the future first president on this road to opportunity.

This surveying question came up early in Din-

105 Dinwiddie to Fairfax, may 6, 1752, *Dinwiddie papers,* I, 19-21.

widdie's governorship. Not all the records in the Din-widdie-college relationship subsequent to that episode have been preserved. What fragments have been found are significant. One of them is a letter composed by Dinwiddie towards the very close of his term of office in Virginia, before he took ship for England.

It was written september 12, 1757 to the lord bishop of London. An exceedingly long communication, it runs into pages: the important point here is that a large portion of the letter is devoted to a consideration of internal problems at the College of William and Mary. The governor's interest in these matters, some of which drew him into controversy and taxed his energy, already by 1757 depleted from a long illness, was due in great measure to "the just regard" he had declared he would always entertain for "the prosperity of the college." [106] This letter, coming as it does at the end of his administration, coupled with his statements made at the beginning of his residence in Williamsburg as chief executive, is at least acceptable evidence of the faith he kept with the college.

Dinwiddie's ruggedness of character, his regard for culture, and his sociability,[107] must have become well known in Virginia and the Carolinas in the 1740's, during the years that he was surveyor-general of customs and a member of the Virginia council. Prior to his coming over as governor, he had been known in the colony as a man of "approved integrity." His attitude toward such matters as honor, morality, and religion, were well known. The report of all these things would reach by word of mouth, by letter, or by publication in some "gazette" beyond the bounds of Virginia. Apparently, judging by the following, it extended to North Carolina.

---

106 Dinwiddie to the lord bishop of London, september 12, 1757, *ibid.,* II, 698.

107 See for example, note 19.

Gabriel Johnston,[108] wealthy landowner of Edenton, North Carolina, and former governor of the colony, died july 17, 1752, and left his daughter, Penelope, under the guardianship of her cousin, Samuel Johnston, and of Dr. William Cathcart. Mrs. Gabriel Johnston, soon after the death of her husband, married John Rutherford, subsequently one of Carolina's revolutionary heroes. Penelope Johnston was none too happy in the home in which her guardians had placed her and begged to be removed. She apparently had heard of the happy home life in Williamsburg of the Dinwiddie family, including as it did the two daughters, Elizabeth and Rebecca, now in their teens. In response to the young lady's own pleadings, the following letter was written:

"To the Hon. John Rutherford Esq. at Mt. Galland.

"SIR: I desire that you'll take Miss Penelope Johnston under your care and if possible place her at Mr. Dinwiddie's in Williamsburg and if you cannot place her at the governor's I desire that you'll place her in some family of good reputation where she may have the advantages of receiving an education suitable to her birth and fortune. I should not chuse to have her at any other place than Williamsburg as I apprehend she will have the advantages of the best company and education there; you are likewise desired to supply her with all necessities suitable to her rank in a plain but neat and fashionable manner.

"I am your humble and obliged servant,
WM. CATHCART." [109]

---

[108] Gabriel Johnston (1699-1752) colonial lieutenant-governor of North Carolina. His first wife was a widow, Penelope (Galland) Phenney; his daughter by his first wife married John Dawson, son of William Dawson, president of the College of William and Mary.

[109] From an investigation made by Miss Mary F. Goodwin among papers and letters in the private library of Mr. J. G. Wood, Edenton, North Carolina (Colonial Williamsburg MSS.).

Guardians may propose but Cupid disposes. Apparently Miss Penelope Johnston was interested in other things as well as in an education. Within a year of her arrival in Williamsburg, she married John Dawson, son of the college's president. That Governor Dinwiddie did accede to Doctor Cathcart's desire to have his young ward under the governor's supervision and the influence of his home is attested by another paper found in Edenton. This paper is headed "Mr. John Dawson and wife. Account with her father's estate." Some items in the document read as follows:

Sept. 1756	To cash paid by Mr. Watson in Virginia, for her use, to Colonel Hunter [110]	[£]42/13/4
May 1757	Do paid do to Eliz Hawker	32/ 0/0
	To 30 pistoles sent by Colonel Innis [111]	
	To Mr. Dinwiddie for Miss Johnston	38/ 8/0
	To amount of expenses Miss Johnston's education in Williamsburg	83/16/6
	To cash paid Governor Dinwiddie for sundry purchases for Miss Johnston	[£]90
	To cash paid do for Mrs. Hawker	21
	Interest charge of Lidderdale and Co.	6
		117/ 0/0

One comes to the conclusion that whatever may have been Dinwiddie's faults, as charged by certain contemporaries,[112] faults which too many historians have been

---

110 Colonel John Hunter, brother of the printer, William Hunter, was a well-known merchant in Williamsburg. Dinwiddie frequently mentions him in his correspondence.

111 James Innes, army colonel in the French and Indian war, a Scot, and a friend of Governor Dinwiddie. He lived for a time in North Carolina. He had previously served with Lawrence Washington in the Cartagena expedition under Colonel William Gooch, lieutenant-governor of Virginia. There is some difference of opinion as to Innes's capacity as an officer; yet Dinwiddie, who was a good judge of men, even military men, had confidence in Innes. He was for a time governor of Fort Cumberland.

112 See the scurrilous attacks of "Buttonless Browncoat," *et al.*, in the contemporary satire, "Dinwiddianae" (Huntington library).

tempted to repeat,[113] there definitely was another side
to the man: he was highly respected and admired by
those who presumably knew him well. Among those
were persons connected with the college. They had
reason to remember that back in november 1751 he had
declared that "morality, virtue, religion, and honour"
were the fundamentals for public service that the school
must ever cultivate. This successful business man, presently turned government official, was at heart a patron
of learning; his deeds supported his words. He remembered his alma mater in Scotland in his will when he
bequeathed a sum of one hundred pounds for what he
called her "public library"; and during his governorship of Virginia he proved himself a staunch friend of
the College of William and Mary.

---

[113] See note 567 for typical instances where modern historians, repeating
errors long current regarding Robert Dinwiddie, have perpetuated an in-
justice.

Life and Labor in Old Williamsburg

Williamsburg was once reckoned among the eleven "chief cities" of British colonial America. In 1751, Holmes's *Grammarian's geography and astronomy* announced to the world that in the British plantations in America, "the eleven chief towns in order are Rupert's Fort, Annapolis, Boston, York, Burlington, Philadelphia, Annapolis, James-Town, Charles-Town, Williamsburgh, and Savannah." [114]

We have from one George Bickham, in his description of Virginia in 1749, the following detailed account. It gives a very striking picture of what greeted Dinwiddie when in 1751, after several years' absence from Williamsburg, he returned for his seven-years term as chief executive:

"The chief towns in ye whole are James Town and Williamsburg. Though the name of a city be given to the first of these, it does not in the whole contain above 60 or 70 houses, the chief of which are taverns and eating-houses for the conveniency of travellers. Two or three forts and many spacious streets were laid out in the original plan: but fires, revolutions in ye government, ye dispositions of ye Virginians to live on their plantations, and the removal of the courts of justice to Williamsburg, have been ye causes of its present incon-

---

[114] John Holmes, *Grammarian's geography and astronomy, ancient and modern, exemplified in the use of the globes terraqueous and coelestial, etc.* (London, 1751), 120 (quoted in Colonial Williamsburg MSS.). Holmes was the master of the grammar school at Holt in Norfolk.

The first Annapolis referred to in the list is in Nova Scotia.

siderable state. Nor does Williamsburgh thrive better, tho' it has a college, a play-house and other publick buildings, besides the courts; for the private houses are very few. However as it stands in a healthier situation than James City, it bids fairer to grow considerable when society may become fashionable in this province. The college has been once destroyed by fire, but it is now rebuilt, and differs not much in form from Chelsea hospital." [115]

Williamsburg, Virginia, had been the colony's capital since 1699. But it is to the years 1751-1758, the period during which Robert Dinwiddie served as lieutenant-governor of the colony, to which many of the most striking features of the restored colonial city date back. About this time a period of uncertainty as to the permanent location of the colony's government had just been ended by a "vote of confidence" in 1748 on the part of the burgesses, favoring Williamsburg as the capital city as against any other.[116] This gave the city a new lease on life, and expansion followed. Since this city is now in the public eye due to its restoration in recent years, and due also to its associations with the earliest English governmental attempt in colonial America, the story of its rise and decline is of sufficient interest in connection with the story of Dinwiddie's life to call for some detail.

When Dinwiddie arrived in Williamsburg to assume his duties as chief executive, he found a new capitol being erected on the foundations of the first which had been destroyed by fire on january 30, 1747.[117] On

<hr />

115 George Bickham, *Short description of the American colonies belonging to the crown of Great Britain* (London, 1749), 180 (quoted in Colonial Williamsburg MSS.).

116 *Journals of the house of burgesses* (1742-1747; 1748-1749), 244-245.

117 *Pennsylvania gazette,* february 5, 1747, quoted in *Handbook for the exhibition buildings of colonial Williamsburg, inc.* (Williamsburg, 1936), 13

november 1, 1753 the general assembly came together in the new capitol for the first time, having in the meanwhile met in the Sir Christopher Wren building of the College of William and Mary. Dinwiddie took occasion to present at that time his majesty's arms to decorate the capitol.

Here in this new capitol history was made. Within its chambers the legislators were to hear George Washington's report on the French invasion into the Ohio region. They would listen to Dinwiddie's pleas for cooperation in the "common cause," and witness the debates and deliberations which would follow. In this building, George Washington himself would sit as a burgess from Frederick county, when his duties in defending the frontier had come to an end. And along with Raleigh tavern nearby, it would be the arena as well as the forum of those momentous speeches and decisions which took place in the Old Dominion in connection with the American revolution, from the time of Patrick Henry's burning oration and resolution on the Stamp act, may 29, 1765, until december 24, 1779, when the house met here for the last time in Williamsburg. Then the proud capital city of the Old Dominion, rich in history and sentiment, gave way to Richmond.

Even before the capital of the colony was removed from Jamestown to Williamsburg, the governors of the colony had enjoyed no residence commensurate with the dignity of their position. Instructions had been issued to each succeeding governor concerning the building of a house befitting his station. But apparently the assembly and the crown disagreed as to the source of the necessary funds, hence no house had been built. Francis

(hereafter cited as Colonial Williamsburg, inc., *Handbook*); Gooch to the lords of trade, december 5, 1748, P.R.O., C.O., 5/1327, 71; L.C. tr., 43-44; Gooch to the lords of trade, february 17, 1747, P.R.O., C.O., 5/1326, 457; L.C. tr., 281-282.

Nicholson, governor at the time Williamsburg became the colony's capital, had his residence for a while in the great building of the college. He later erected a dwelling of his own near the capitol.[118]

During the governorship of Edward Nott [119] (1706), however, the general assembly was prevailed upon to pass an act to begin the erection of the long-proposed governor's house. Governor Nott, in somewhat disdainful language, had announced to the self-satisfied Virginians:

"I am also by the royal comand to recomend earnestly to your gentlemen of the house of burgesses the building a house fit for the reception of your governor.

"Certainly it is a great dishonour that a colony so considerable which exceeds all others in antiquity should want that accomodation for the person her majesty is pleased to honour with so great a character which almost the meanest under her dominion is provided with.

"I believe some gentlemen here present are sensible what inconveniencys I have and still do labour under upon that account." [120]

This thrust at the pride as well as the sense of dignity of the colony of Virginia seems to have secured the initial move to erect a governor's house in Williamsburg. When Alexander Spotswood [121] assumed his du-

---

118 Colonial Williamsburg, inc., *Handbook*, 68.

119 Edward Nott (d. 1706) governor of Virginia (1705-1706) following Francis Nicholson. He is chiefly remembered for his efforts in behalf of the governor's house, and is the only governor buried in the churchyard of Bruton Parish church.

120 *Journals of the house of burgesses* (1702/3-1705; 1705-1706; 1710-1712), 130.

121 Alexander Spotswood (1676-1740), lieutenant-governor of Virginia from june 23, 1710 to 1722, under the titular governor, George Hamilton, Earl of Orkney. He was throughout his administration interested in promoting the fur trade with the Indians; in explorations westward—of which the famous expedition of the Knights of the Golden Horseshoe was but one of

ties as lieutenant-governor in 1710, the original appropriation of three thousand pounds for this purpose was
exhausted and the work stopped. Spotswood put
through the assembly an act in 1710,[122] and another in
1713,[123] for completing the structure. By 1718 the expenditure for its erection had become so great that the
burgesses, in complaint that the governor was "lavish-
ing away the country's money," soon "began to refer to
the building as the 'palace,'" and "this soon became its
accepted name." [124] The building, however, was formally completed about 1720. In 1724 Reverend Hugh
Jones, in writing of Williamsburg, stated that the "public buildings here of note, are the college, the capitol,
the governor's house, and the church." Of the executive
mansion he wrote as follows:

"The palace, or governor's house, is a magnificent
structure, finished and beautified with gates, fine gar-
dens, offices, walks, a fine canal, orchards, etc., with a
great number of the best arms nicely posited by an in-
genious contrivance of Governor Spotswood's. It likewise has the ornamental addition of a good cupola or
lantern, illuminating most of the town upon birth-
nights . . . These buildings are justly reputed the best

several; in bringing in thrifty immigrants – as he showed when he established
the Germans at Germanna; and in internal development such as the establishment of iron mines, wherein he demonstrated his interest by ownership
and supervision. His administration was punctuated by numerous political
controversies, between the usual parties and over the usual questions, plus
an ecclesiastical dispute regarding the vestries; the last reminding one of the
investiture conflict long before in England. His letters, which were edited in
two volumes by R. A. Brock in 1882-1885, show that he grasped the political
trends of his time as did few of his contemporaries.

[122] R. A. Brock, ed., *Official letters of Alexander Spotswood, governor of
Virginia, 1710-1722* (Richmond, 1882-1885), I, 10n; *Journals of the house
of burgesses* (1702/3-1705; 1705-1706; 1710-1712), 279-280, 282, 285, 290,
295, 298.

[123] *Ibid.* (1712-1714; 1715; 1718; 1720-1722; 1723-1726), XXI, 69-71.

[124] Colonial Williamsburg, inc., *Handbook,* 69. See also the *Journals of the
house of burgesses* (1712-1714; 1715; 1718; 1720-1722; 1723-1726), 213-214.

in all English America, and are exceeded by few of their kind in England." [125]

The palace was later improved by each succeeding governor, the revenue for its repair and improvement being derived from the two-shilling tax levied on each hogshead of tobacco. But Governor Gooch, in 1747, declared the building so "old and decayed" that he insisted it would entail the burden of a yearly repair bill of one hundred pounds. Since the capitol had been burned in 1747, and the governor's house was so badly decayed, Governor Gooch had solemnly counselled the board of trade, in a written report, that the seat of government be moved to some more central location, to the westward — "to a commodious place for commerce upon a navigable river." [126]

The hint or threat implied in Gooch's words brought the question of Williamsburg versus any other site for the colony's capital to a showdown. The result was a vote on democratic principles in the house of burgesses, which resulted in forty for retaining Williamsburg and thirty-eight against.[127] The strong minority good-naturedly succumbed to the winners; and Williamsburg by that vote was to have not only a new capitol erected but the governor's "palace" would henceforth have more attention. This epochal decision, besides the fact that all plans for the earlier campaign in the French and Indian war centered and matured in Williamsburg, breathed new official and unofficial life

[125] Hugh Jones, *Present state of Virginia* (quoted in Colonial Williamsburg, inc., *Handbook,* 69).

[126] Gooch to the lords of trade, june 10, 1747, P.R.O., C.O., 5/1326, 459-462; L.C. tr., 283-286.

[127] Colonial Williamsburg, inc., *Handbook,* 14; *Journals of the house of burgesses* (1742-1747; 1748-1749), 245, records a vote of 42 for and 34 against on april 10, 1747. See also R. G., Gent [Rutherfoord Goodwin], *Brief and true report for the traveller concerning Williamsburg in Virginia,* 61-62.

into the city, already rich in prestige. Hence it was that Dinwiddie's administration as governor of the colony of Virginia saw the renaissance of Williamsburg and its growth as an even more important city than it had been.

At the time of Dinwiddie's arrival in 1751, the governor's palace was undergoing one of its intermittent periods of alterations and repairs, a work of such comprehensive size as to make it impossible for the new governor to take up his residence there. In consequence the assembly was forced to purchase a temporary residence for him, Lady Dinwiddie, and their two young daughters, Elizabeth and Rebecca, and it was not until november 1752, just a year later, that the family was able to move into the palace. Later in his administration another wing was added to the mansion, housing the spacious ballroom and supper-room. If the records left by preceding governors as to the size and magnificence of the entertainment offered by the crown's representative in Virginia are to be taken as a criterion, the new wing was not built before it was needed.[128]

Unquestionably, the wealth, elegance, and culture of the Virginia society of that day was unequalled by any other American colony. There was a certain charm and gaiety here in a society that modelled itself as closely as possible after the court life of London, that was unrestrained either by any such religious frigidity as existed in the New England colonies or by the ever-present fear of Indian invasion which lay heavily on the frontiers of all the provinces.

The king's birthday and other "public times" were celebrated with balls and entertainments and "illuminations" so impressive and elegant, and so costly, that

[128] Burnaby, describing the palace in 1759, refers to it as "the only tolerable good public building." See Charles Campbell, *History of the colony and ancient dominion of Virginia* (Philadelphia, 1860), 502 (Colonial Williamsburg MSS.); Colonial Williamsburg, inc., *Handbook*, 70.

Governor Gooch wrote his brother in 1727 that with "proclaiming his majesty 50 g[uineas], his birthday near 100 g[uineas], Prince Frederick's 20 g[uineas] . . . I have very little reason to expect to make a fortune, or enough to keep me when I grow old, unless my stars are more favorable." Yet with it all, he consoled himself that "the gentlemen and ladies here are perfectly well bred, not an ill dancer in my government." [129]

Dancing, card playing, dining, gambling, and drinking comprised the social life of the time, so much so, that Dinwiddie felt compelled to take note of the last two and warn the Virginians against their excesses. On october 31, 1771, the *Virginia Gazette* published an account of an affair given by Lord Dunmore:

"Last friday being the anniversary of our most gracious sovereign's accession to the throne, his excellency the governor gave a ball and an elegant entertainment at the palace, to a numerous and splendid company of ladies and gentlemen. The Raleigh tavern likewise, by directions of his excellency, was opened for the entertainment of such as might incline to spend the evening there; plenty of liquor was given to the populace; and the city was handsomely illuminated." [130]

Some idea of the sumptuousness of the entertainments given by the various governors may be gained by the record of an inventory taken of Lord Botetourt's cellar after his death, which listed some thirty-two hundred gallons of assorted wines and liquors.

While so far as is known Dinwiddie did not leave any detailed inventory either of publicly-owned or privately-owned furniture and equipment in the palace, his immediate successors did leave such lists, and these may be taken as applicable to Dinwiddie's time also.

129 Gooch to his brother, Colonial Williamsburg, inc., *Handbook,* 74.

130 *Virginia gazette,* october 31, 1771 (quoted in Colonial Williamsburg, inc., *Handbook,* 71).

"The inventories of the privately-owned furniture of Governor Fauquier,[131] Lord Botetourt [132] and Lord Dunmore [133] are . . . available – Botetourt's inventory listing his possessions in minute detail and listing also the rooms in which these furnishings appeared. For example, 'the front parlour' is noted as containing:

 2 leather smoking chairs
 2 card tables, mahogany
 1 walnut writing table
 1 couch mahogany frame covered with checks
 2 small looking glass
   Fry [and] Jefferson's maps of Virginia
   Bowen's and Mitchell's map of North America
 1 pair tongs, shovel, poker, fender, and hearth broom
 11 Chelsea china figures, 2 venetian blinds." [134]

With the coming of Dinwiddie, a novel form of entertainment was introduced with the innovation of theatrical performances. A theater was built near the new capitol and a New York company came down to

[131] Francis Fauquier (1704-1768), was lieutenant-governor of Virginia from january 1758 to his death. He arrived in Virginia june 5, 1758. He served under two holders of the sinecure, the Earl of Loudoun, 1756-1763, and Sir Jeffrey Amherst, 1763-1768, neither of whom set foot in Virginia. He built upon the foundations laid by Dinwiddie, and exerted himself to assist the colonial authorities in bringing victory to the British. He was tactful in his relationship with the house of burgesses, knew when to stand up and when to be conciliatory, and he vies with Governors Gooch and Botetourt as being the most popular governor of the Old Dominion. Fauquier county is named for him. He was a man of cultural attainments, and a political essayist—at least, he published in 1756 one item that ran through several editions.

[132] Norbonne Berkeley, Baron de Botetourt (c.1718-1770), governor of Virginia, 1768-1770. In spite of his misunderstanding with the people almost from the outset, his better qualities are remembered; this attitude is typified by the monument to him, formerly at the capitol but now on the campus of the college. Student rules today require all freshmen, going from the college into the town, to pass Lord Botetourt's monument—the women having to curtsy, the men to doff their freshman caps.

[133] John Murray, Earl of Dunmore (1732-1809), governor of Virginia, 1770-1775.

[134] Colonial Williamsburg, inc., *Handbook*, 71.

celebrate its opening april 24, 1752. The *Virginia Gazette* announced that "on friday, being the twenty-fourth of the instant, will be performed a comedy, called the Constant Couple: or a Trip to the Jubilee ... with entertainment of singing between the acts: likewise a dance, called the Drunken Peasant. To which will be added a farce called the Lying Valet." [135]

More important still in the history of the American theater was an event which took place in 1752 under the sponsorship of Dinwiddie. This was the occasion when the local playhouse became a "regular theatre," and a London troupe was attracted to Williamsburg. On august 21, 1752 the *Virginia Gazette* "desired to inform the publick ... that his honour the governor's permission" had been given to the celebrated actor, Lewis Hallam, to reopen the playhouse, now "with great experience entirely altered ... to a regular theatre, fit for the reception of ladies and gentlemen." Hallam and his "company of comedians, lately from London," made their American debut in the city of Williamsburg with a performance of "The Merchant of Venice (written by Shakespear) and a farce call'd the Anatomist, or Sham Doctor."

With rare courtesy and thoughtfulness the *Gazette* continues: "The ladies are desired to give timely notice to Mr. Hallam, at Mr. Fisher's, for their places in the boxes, and on the day of performance to send their servants early to keep them, in order to prevent trouble and disappointment." [136]

Hallam's success must have been both instantaneous and lasting, for three months later he was called upon by Dinwiddie to aid in entertaining the populace with fireworks in the streets, following a ball at the palace in

---

135 *Virginia gazette*, april 24, 1752 (Colonial Williamsburg MSS.).
136 *Ibid.*, august 21, 1752.

honor of his majesty's birthday. Present at the ball and entertainment were the emperor and empress of the Cherokee nation with their son, the young prince, and "a brilliant appearance of ladies and gentlemen." [137]

But Dinwiddie's period of gay hospitality was short lived. The following year was to usher in a period of fear and uncertainty for Virginians, when not only the mind of the governor but the minds and hearts of his people were occupied with the grim and sobering expectation of war. And war meant not only a struggle with the French for their homeland, but the more terrifying and frightful cry of "Indians!"

Yet, with all the heavy burden of the French and Indian war on his consciousness, Dinwiddie managed to leave the city of Williamsburg unsurpassed by any in the colonies in the fineness and magnificence of its buildings. Already the city was the proud possessor of the only Christopher Wren building in America, and to this was added the princely governor's mansion, enlarged and beautified during his administration, and the now completed capitol whose "political significance extended beyond the borders of the Virginia colony" and whose "architecture was notable in a youthful dominion." Bruton Parish church was enlarged to meet the growing population, an organ loft built, and a wall erected around the churchyard, an important labor in the eyes of those Virginians who still felt, as they did one hundred and forty years earlier, that "men's affairs doe little prosper where God's service is neglected . . ."[138] The public magazine was strengthened and a "high and strong brick wall built around it." The play-

---

[137] *Ibid.,* november 16, 1752. See also R. G., Gent [Rutherfoord Goodwin], *Brief and true report for the traveller concerning Williamsburg in Virginia,* 63.

[138] "Reporte of the manner of proceeding in the general assembly," july 30, 1619, *Journals of the house of burgesses* (1619-1658/59), 4.

house was reopened and under Dinwiddie's influence and patronage became an integral part of the social life of the city.

Altogether, Dinwiddie left Williamsburg in 1758 at the end of his administration a firmly re-established capital and a city which travellers declared contained the finest public buildings in British America. "To the strength and vigor of his administration," a Colonial Williamsburg restoration official has declared, "is due in some measure the enduring place of Williamsburg in Virginia's history." [139]

---

[139] Mrs. Helen Bullock, former curator.

Friends and Quasi-friends

Dinwiddie, having arrived in Virginia november 20, 1751, lost no time in getting his bearings. He hastened by correspondence to revive the old connections he had had nearly ten years before, while almost with the same stroke of his pen he set about establishing new associations. In any age it is wise as a principle to make friends and many of them. Emerson likened them to his books: "I treat my friends as I do my books: I keep them where I can find them." Likewise Dinwiddie.

The new governor could wield a powerful pen. What he may have lacked in literary force, he made up in epistolary volume. Soon after his arrival he swung into action. He kept his private secretary, William Waller,[140] busy. He wrote personally or dictated letters in rapid succession: december 12 to Conrad Weiser,[141] keyman Indian interpreter; the same day to Joshua Fry,[142] prominent Virginia intellectual, map-maker and Indian commissioner-to-be; the next day to Colonel James Patton,[143] a frontiersman slated to be a commissioner; to fellow governors like Samuel Ogle[144] of Mary-

---

[140] William Waller, private secretary to Governor Dinwiddie. As explained in the preface, he employed a system of abbreviations and contractions, such as "y't" for "that" and "h. m'y" for "his majesty," as a time-saving device when he prepared the drafts of Dinwiddie's letter books. Contrary to the general impression among historians, the letters he wrote out for Dinwiddie's signature, and which were dispatched to the governor's correspondents, contained few contractions. The name Waller is perpetuated today in Waller street, Williamsburg.

[141] Dinwiddie to Weiser, december 12, 1751, *Dinwiddie papers*, I, 6-7.

[142] Dinwiddie to Fry, december 12, 1751, *ibid.*, I, 7-9.

[143] Dinwiddie to Patton, december 13, 1751, *ibid.*, I, 9-10.

[144] Dinwiddie to Ogle, december 13, 1751, *ibid.*, I, 11-13.

land, also on the thirteenth; to James Hamilton [145] of
Pennsylvania on the eighteenth; to Colonel Thomas
Cresap,[146] Maryland member of the Ohio company,
january 23, 1752; and to Lord Fairfax,[147] most prominent of the great land proprietors, by may 6. Meantime,
december 13, Dinwiddie had sought out even the ecclesiastical leaders, who now were to learn that a new
hand was at Virginia's helm. He had on that day made
inquiry as to the pastoral needs of churches in Virginia
and finding there was at least one opening, he had sent
a letter to the vestry in question, recommending a rector
to fill their vacancy.[148] These letters reveal the mind
and purpose of a man of action who began character-
istically to "enquire into" every item of the colony's
life to satisfy his insatiable thirst for being informed —
the incentive that probably accounts for a deal of
human progress.

The first of the group of letters, as indicated, was
written to Conrad Weiser.[149] Weiser was a power to be
reckoned with on the frontier. Born in Württemberg,
he belonged to the German stock that had migrated
from the Rhine country about 1710-1712, during Queen
Anne's war, and had found refuge first in New York
and then in Pennsylvania. He was now fifty-five years
of age. Having been brought up in the frontier environ-
ment and early learned the various Indian dialects, he
was ever in demand as an interpreter and was present
at practically all the treaties negotiated by Pennsylvania. Sometimes he was employed even by Pennsyl-

145 Dinwiddie to Hamilton, december 18, 1751, *ibid.*, I, 15-16.

146 Dinwiddie to Cresap, january 23, 1752, *ibid.*, I, 17-19.

147 Dinwiddie to Fairfax, may 6, 1752, *ibid.*, I, 19-21.

148 Dinwiddie to the vestry of St. Anne's parish, Albemarle county, december, 13, 1751, *ibid.*, I, 14-15.

149 Conrad Weiser (1696-1760), Indian interpreter and agent. He early
became adept in the use of the Indian languages, besides being versed in
both English and German.

vania's neighbors. As with all his early correspondents, the governor began by presenting his credentials – to identify himself in his new rôle. He then turned to compliment his correspondent. It was his customary courtesy. He hastened to remind Weiser that "his majesty's council" of Virginia, upon whose advice he was acting, had had "repeated proofs of your abilities and integrity, and ready disposition on all occasions to serve this government." What man, unless already implacably hostile, could under the circumstances resist adding another proof of his "abilities and integrity?"

The forthcoming conference with the Indians was to be held at Logstown on the Ohio, eighteen miles west of present Pittsburgh, in "may next" (1752), the new governor explained. He added: "We shall send commissioners . . . to meet and treat with the Ohio Indians, and . . . desire that you will please to join and assist them." This was the language that was to set in motion the events that led up to the now famous treaty, the object of which was to cement the gains effected at the Lancaster (Pennsylvania) treaty in july 1744. At that earlier meeting, commissioners from Pennsylvania, Maryland, and Virginia had secured from the Six Nations a cession, for the sum of four hundred pounds, of all the lands lying west of the Alleghenies over to the Ohio river. Most colonials felt that the ground thus gained must never be lost.[150]

---

[150] For the Lancaster treaty, see Samuel Hazard, ed., *Minutes of the provincial council of Pennsylvania* (Harrisburg, 1851-1852), IV, 698-737 (hereafter cited as *Pennsylvania colonial records*). See also *Virginia magazine of history and biography*, XIII (October 1905), 141-142; Memorandum on treaty of Lancaster, may 1, 1754, P.R.O., C.O., 5/14, 257; L.C. tr., 231. For the Logstown conference see "The treaty of Logg's Town, 1752," *Virginia magazine of history and biography*, XIII (October 1905), 143-174. As to the territory in question, declared the French: "It is an established fact that the Iroquois have no rights to it." See Minister to Duquesne, may 15, 1752, Archives nationales, ministère des colonies (hereafter cited as Arch. Nat., Col.), series F3, 14:30-32vo.; L.C. tr.

To show appreciation of Weiser's hoped-for services
as an interpreter, Dinwiddie added the promise of
financial reward, for, said he, "I hope nothing will
impede your complyance with our request, and you
may rely on being gratefully and generously rewarded
for your service and trouble." The matter was important. The writer therefore added an urgent "P.S. — We
intreat you'l not refuse going. We [are] depending on
you as an interpreter."

The governor's second letter in the present series was
to Joshua Fry,[151] a Virginian of education and standing,
of equal caliber with Weiser, but a totally different
type of man. Fry, probably related to the John Fry and
the Henry Fry listed among the dead in the well-known
census of 1623, was born in Somersetshire, England.
As early as 1710 he is mentioned as a vestryman and
as a local official in Essex county, Virginia. He was
Oxford trained, and having come to Virginia, gravi-
tated to the College of William and Mary. In 1729 he
became master of its grammar school, and, among other
things, experimented with the teaching of Indians who
were then enrolled in this department of the college.
This close contact with the natives was an education for
Fry himself, and he was to draw much upon this information in the years ahead. In due time his superior
abilities led to his promotion to the chair of mathematics in the college. As early as 1737 he had proposed
to the Virginia assembly the preparation of an adequate
map of Virginia, the surveying of the colony's lands,
and the running of undetermined boundary lines. By
1751 he had joined with Peter Jefferson in preparing
the now celebrated map, universally known as "Fry and
Jefferson's." He served for a time as a burgess and then

---

151 Joshua Fry (c. 1700-1754) was a man of sufficient caliber to win the
esteem and confidence of such men as Governor Dinwiddie, George Washington, and Peter Jefferson, the father of Thomas Jefferson.

as a member of the council; later, march 28, 1745, he was appointed to the highest position in Albemarle, that of county lieutenant. This then, was the professor-surveyor to whom Dinwiddie's second letter was written, inviting him to become a commissioner, along with James Patton and Lunsford Lomax, to the approaching Logstown conference. As usual, the governor did not forget to compliment his correspondent: ". . . their honours [the members of the Virginia council] have been pleased to nominate you and Colonel James Patton as gentlemen the best qualifyed to conduct and execute a business of so great importance." Weiser had been temporarily won to the governor's program; now Fry also.

The governor's third letter, to Colonel James Patton, was penned within twenty-four hours after those just described. Its tenor differed from the others in that it was strictly official in tone and was entitled "instructions to Colonel James Patton." It contained instructions [152] concerning what he was to do at the Logstown conference. One would like to know why Dinwiddie did not write Patton a more cordial letter. If there is any plausible explanation, it probably lies in their differing attitudes toward the Ohio company, a subject discussed in the following chapter. Something of the kind may be gleaned from a letter written by Dinwiddie to Colonel Thomas Cresap [153] of Maryland, janu-

---

[152] Transmitted through Nicholas Walthoe, clerk of the council.

[153] Thomas Cresap (c. 1685-c. 1790), frontiersman, surveyor, trader, land company organizer, known in American colonial history as "Colonel," was born in Yorkshire, England. Coming in his youth to America he settled on the lower Susquehanna, then later farther up the river, and next on the Antietam, in what is now Washington county, Maryland. His moves typified the westward movement. His fourth home was the one which he made famous, and which he located about 1740-1742, far out on what was then the frontier of western Maryland, somewhat above the branches of the Potomac. This home he called Skipton, in memory of the English Skipton, though his stockaded place is usually referred to as Oldtown, sometimes in the records

ary 23, 1752. Unlike Cresap and Dinwiddie, Patton was reported not to have "at heart" the success and prosperity of the Ohio company – possibly his attitude was due to his preference for the land organization that he himself had.[154]

Patton, whose eyes had long been riveted on numerous fine western tracts, had had a colorful background. Born in Newton, Limaddy, Ireland, in 1692, he was a year older than Dinwiddie. He went to sea and in due time rose to be an officer in the royal navy. According to R. A. Brock, he is reported to have crossed the Atlantic "quite twenty-five times, bringing Irish emigrants ('redemptioners,' who served a given time to pay the cost of their transportation) and returning with cargoes of peltries and tobacco." Augusta county, in which he was to receive a one hundred and twenty thousand acre grant of land, "was largely settled through his agency." [155]

This was the Augusta county frontiersman who – so Cresap thought he had discovered – was opposing the Ohio company. Cresap passed his information, or impression, on to Dinwiddie. Cresap had ground for suspicion. That is evident, for instance, from references to the Ohio company in the illuminating John Blair manuscript diary. Blair, in an entry of october 26, refers to "our order for 100,000 acres." On december 12 he set down this item: "Colonel Patton proposes fine land on the waters of Potomack, Delaware, and Susquehanna, as in Virginia, if the western boundary of

---

as Cresap's. With the Delaware Indian, Nemacolin, he blazed the trail that was to become the basis of one of the historic highways of America— Nemacolin's path, Washington's route, Braddock's road, and finally the National road.

154 See James Patton to John Blair, january 1753, Draper manuscripts, 1QQ175-1QQ177 (State historical society of Wisconsin).

155 *Dinwiddie papers*, I, 8n. See also *Virginia magazine of history and biography*, XIII (October 1905), 145n, and XVI (July 1908), 24n.

Maryland and Pennsylvania were run out and settled."
Still another entry discloses the beginnings of friction:
"Approved Greenbriar grant as prior to Ohio company's." The controversy that was to continue through
the years, between the Ohio company on the one hand,
and one after another of several land companies on the
other, and was to subject Virginia to sectional disputes,
was already developing. And it centered about land.
These happenings were relatively new to Dinwiddie,
but he was learning fast. The well-known traveller, Dr.
Thomas Walker,[156] seemed also to be on the other side
of the land company fence. In Blair's diary for december 29 is this item: "Doctor Gilmer [157] promised the
governor the perusal of Doctor Walker's journal [158] of
his travels beyond the mountains." Whatever John
Blair's own position was, he was still able to record,
as an appropriate entry for the last day of the year 1751:
"Invited the governor and family to begin the year with
us tomorrow." [159]

Dinwiddie's letter to Colonel Thomas Cresap, touch-
ing so many different subjects, has already been referred
to. Cresap had sent Dinwiddie a communication suggesting to the new governor that reprisals be taken
against the French for the depredations assertedly done
by them on the Ohio. Cresap was close to the situation

---

156 Thomas Walker (1715-1794), trader, explorer, land company promotor,
soldier, burgess, and physician, was born in King and Queen county, Virginia. He was interested in land schemes from 1748 on. In 1749 he virtually
became the agent of the Loyal Land company whose 800,000 acres had the
approval of at least a part of the Virginia council.

157 "Dr. George Gilmer (d. january 15, 1757) a native of Scotland,
physician, surgeon, and apothecary of Williamsburg, and for some time its
mayor (*Dinwiddie papers,* II, 336n).

158 Thomas Walker's journal is printed in *First explorations of Kentucky*
(Louisville, 1898), edited by J. Stoddard Johnston (Filson club *publications*
no. 13), and in *Annals of southwest Virginia, 1769-1800* (Abingdon, Virginia, 1929), edited by L. P. Summers.

159 John Blair's manuscript diary, preserved in the Virginia historical society.

and had recommended methods immediately at hand to cope with it.

Dinwiddie was interested in the Ohio company and he was interested in frontiersmen. But, more far-seeing than Cresap, he felt obligated to look to more than a temporary redress for the exposed traders and settlers. He foresaw the probably serious consequences of a policy of retaliation on the border. He would later consent to "repell force by force" but only as the last resort. Hence he wrote Cresap in language that some will regard as a model of restraint: "As to making reprisals for the robberies done by the French on the Ohio, it is inconsistent with the laws of nations, while we are in peace with France, and your letter is too general: if you can give a particular account of the different robberies, we must apply to the governor of Canada for redress; upon his refusal, we may proceed in another manner."

All of Dinwiddie's early letters made at least some reference to Indians. He thought Indians. He talked Indians. He wrote Indians. When he arrived as governor he knew something but still too little about Indians. When he left he was well versed in Indian affairs. He seems to have been eager to learn when there was someone competent to teach. When it came to Indian affairs he found his first teacher in this same Colonel Cresap, a man well qualified for the task. In this letter to him, apparently one of the first of the official letters Dinwiddie dictated, he wrote with humility and frankness:

"I shall be glad if you could furnish me with an account of the several nations of Indians, their names and numbers of each separate, viz: their fighting men, women, and children, and your advice how to engage them to the British interest." He confided to Cresap that he hesitated, meantime, to attend any conference with the Indians to discuss a treaty while "confessing ignorance in these affairs."

In his earliest letters to fellow governors, to frontiersmen, and to his military officers, he was obliged to fall back on such vague and meaningless terms as Indians, Ohio Indians, and Six Nations – expressions too general to be of value. Two years later, however, he had learned to use specific Indian names whenever he wrote. And in his communication to Governor James Glen [160] of South Carolina in 1754, he referred to seven different tribes: Catawbas, Cherokees, Creeks, Chickasaws, Chippeways, Ottaways, and Arundocks.[161] But the most convincing commentary of all is that he had addressed a message to his "good and faithful friend Monacatoocha." [162]

[160] James Glen (b. 1701), colonial governor of South Carolina, 1744-1756. He was commissioned as early as december 1738 but did not arrive in America to take office until december 1743. He believed that his colony was the spearhead of imperial advance westward and the natural guardian of the Cherokees. His *Description of South Carolina* was published in London in 1761.

[161] Dinwiddie to Glen, january 29, 1754, P.R.O., C.O., 5/14, 279-282; L.C. tr., 255-258; *Dinwiddie papers,* I, 61-63.

[162] Dinwiddie to Monacatoocha [1754], *ibid.,* I, 57. Monacatoocha (Monakaduto), also known as Scarroyaddy (Scarroyadda), and for a part of the time as Half-king, was an Oneida and Delaware (or Mingo) chief, and thus a member of one of the mixed bands that about 1754 lived near the headwaters of the Ohio. He perforce must divide his allegiance, hence the title Half-king. He served in the Braddock campaign, where his son was killed. This son, along with his mother, had been brought by Monacatoocha to the Winchester conference in september 1753. On sunday, september 16 he had the boy christened. Commissioner William Fairfax and Christopher Gist acted the part of godfathers and named the youngster, then about eleven years of age, Dinwiddie, which seemed to please the parents (P.R.O., C.O., 5/1328, 65; L.C. tr., 69). See also E. B. O'Callaghan and B. Fernow, eds., *Documents relative to the colonial history of the state of New York* (Albany, 1853-1887), VII, 134 (hereafter cited as *New York colonial documents*). He was a dependable ally of the English. He seems at one time to have been given the name of Washington by William Fairfax (See S. M. Hamilton, ed., *Letters to Washington* [Boston, 1898], I, 23). He must not be confused with another Half-king, Tanacharisson.

Unlike such British officials as the tactless Braddock,[163] it was not displeasing to Dinwiddie to have George Washington inform him that he had re-christened the Half-king, Tanacharisson,[164] and given him the name of Dinwiddie. Washington wrote: "I was also informed, that an English name would please the Half-king, which made me presume to give him that [of] your honor, and call him Dinwiddie; interpreted in their language, the head of all." [165] Who first started the rumor that George Washington did not possess a sense of humor?

One paragraph in the governor's letter to Cresap should not be overlooked. This had to do with procuring an interpreter that Virginia could call her own. As noticed above, he was in a pressing, if not desperate, situation when he wrote to Conrad Weiser, the Pennsylvanian, december 12, 1751, and added his quaint postscript. Virginia must be independent in the matter of such indispensable persons as interpreters; hence he interposed in his letter to Cresap: "I shall be glad [if] Mr. Montour [166] will determine to live in Virginia that

---

163 Edward Braddock (1695-1755), army officer. In 1754 he was made commander-in-chief of all his majesty's forces in America. Sailing from England december 21, he arrived at Hampton, Virginia, february 19, 1755.

164 Tanacharisson, a Seneca chief, also known as Half-king because of his divided allegiance. He was a close friend of the English, a shrewd leader, and warrior-adviser to George Washington. It was he who was with Ensign Ward when the French force surprised the English in april 1754, and who counselled Ward to gain time for reinforcements by notifying the French that his instructions and rank did not empower him to capitulate. He claimed personally to have killed Jumonville. One explanation of his enmity toward the French is that he held them responsible for having boiled and then eaten his father. Brock states that he died on october 4, 1754, at Aughquick, Pennsylvania (Dinwiddie papers, I, 148n).

165 Washington to Dinwiddie [June 12, 1754], John C. Fitzpatrick, ed., Writings of George Washington (Washington, 1931-——), I, 80.

166 Andrew Montour, half-breed interpreter, son of the celebrated Madame Montour, herself an interpreter, and an Oneida Indian chief, whose English name was Robert Hunter. Montour was a man of little formal education but highly intelligent and apparently possessed of much hard common sense—an

we may hereafter have an interpreter in our own province on any occasion we may have to do with the Indians; and therefore I desire you will prevail with him to be at your house when the commissioners come to go with the goods to Loggs Town."

Another contact re-established by Dinwiddie within the first six months of his governorship was with a man unique in the annals of colonial America, Thomas, sixth Lord Fairfax, Baron of Cameron. Lord Fairfax was born about 1691, the son of the elder Thomas, fifth Lord Fairfax, and Catherine Culpeper, daughter of Lord Culpeper.[167] Fairfax was about two years senior to Dinwiddie. He studied at Oxford, was a man of culture with inclinations toward writing, and is held by some historians, but denied by others, to have been a contributor to Addison's *Spectator*. This tradition, whether or not true in detail, was probably, as with most traditions, based upon a substratum of truth. Through his mother he came into possession of what has been one of the most publicized sections in America, the so-called "Northern Neck." While technically the term may originally have been limited to the territory within tidewater, and therefore entirely east of the falls line, yet when applied to the Culpeper-Fairfax grant it extended westward through the Shenandoah valley and the South Branch (Potomac) valley to the headspring of the Potomac. It measured upwards of eight million acres. It was on this far-flung inheritance that the holder of the baronial title established a residence

asset of prime importance on the frontier. A part of his pro-English sympathy must have been inherited from his mother. He held a captain's commission in the French and Indian war under Washington, generally commanding Indian scouts.

167 Thomas, Lord Culpeper (1635-1689), colonial governor of Virginia following Sir William Berkeley. The two shillings per hogshead tax on exported tobacco, as the basic fund for the governor's salary, was in his administration definitely placed under royal control.

in 1745 at Greenway court, not far from what was then
Frederick Town, now Winchester, Frederick county,
Virginia, and at the same time that Robert Dinwiddie
made the same move – while surveyor-general of customs for the southern colonies. It was here, close by
Winchester, that Lord Fairfax lived the life of a country gentleman, delighting in entertaining his friends
within the confines of his palatial home; or perchance
with a fox-hunt, a sport much enjoyed among the planters of provincial Virginia. It was here at Greenway
court that George Washington was as a boy a frequent
visitor, and much in the company of this man, when
the latter was not himself a visitor on the Potomac
either at Belvoir or at Mt. Vernon. It was this man
who, more than any other person, save alone Governor
Dinwiddie, was to shape the early trend of George
Washington's life. Co-surveyor with George William
Fairfax [168] of Lord Fairfax's lands, 1747/8,[169] was
George Washington, who was to leave a diary that is
a rare commentary on the men, manners, and highways
of the Virginia frontier.

The actual management of Lord Fairfax's vast estates was entrusted to his cousin, William Fairfax, who
had fixed his residence on the Potomac at Belvoir, on
high land at one of the river's graceful bends, just below
Hunting creek – where now is Mount Vernon. Because
he became county lieutenant of Fairfax county, he is
usually referred to as "colonel." He was long a member of the Virginia council, beginning from 1743, when

[168] George William Fairfax (1725-1787) colonial Virginia surveyor, landowner, member of the house of burgesses, and close friend of George Washington, was born in Nassau, New Providence, Bahama islands. He was the
son of Colonel William and his second wife, Sarah (Walker) Fairfax of
Belvoir.

[169] This is another instance of double-dating, confusing at its best. The
rule is to take the second of two dates, when two are given. The date of this
survey is 1748. The Gregorian calendar was changed in 1752 (See note 34).

he was appointed to succeed Dr. James Blair; as such, and as a friend from the customs service days of the 1730's, he was one of Dinwiddie's staunchest supporters in the upper house. "Colonel" Fairfax had been born in England, the son of Henry Fairfax of Yorkshire. Like his kinsman, Lord Fairfax, he had been well educated, also he had served in the army and been governor of Providence island. Subsequently he had lived in New England. Preferring the climate of Virginia and having the opportunity to become the manager of Lord Fairfax's estates, he had presently established himself below the Potomac in Westmoreland county. Here he remained until he received an additional appointment, that of collector of customs for the South Potomac. This office was secured for him by his relative, Bryan Fairfax, a commissioner of customs during 1723-1728. These facts are pregnant with meaning. Bryan Fairfax very likely knew Robert Dinwiddie in the British admiralty and customs service and on the island of Bermuda during the years mentioned. Furthermore, since William Fairfax was also in the customs service in Virginia at the same time that Robert Dinwiddie was surveyor-general of customs for the southern district of America, he was, in a general way, under Dinwiddie's jurisdiction. In addition, Archibald Cary was at the time collector of customs for the lower James. His daughter, Sally, was the belle who married George William Fairfax, son of William Fairfax of Belvoir. George William was the close friend of George Washington, his nearby neighbor, even though George was seven years his junior. It was George Washington's older half-brother, Lawrence, who married George William's sister, Anne. And Anne's sister, Sarah, married Major John Carlyle, merchant, commissary to Washington's little army, and member of the

Ohio company. These family relationships must be kept in mind throughout this period, since family ties often motivated public policy in old Virginia.[170] Nepotism does not apply. It was but natural that prominent men should turn not marriage to their advantage, but contrarily, advantage toward those who married into their family circle.

This is the background for an appreciation of the position of the man, Lord Fairfax, whom Dinwiddie addressed from Williamsburg, may 6, 1752, beginning with this apology:

"MY LORD: I intended myself the honour of paying my due respects to your lordship before this, but have been prevented by the hurry of business on my first arrival." Then follows a sentiment different, so far as can be ascertained, from any penned by Dinwiddie to any other correspondent while in public office. He spoke from the very depths, and the result of close and honorable association, when he said: ". . . I now desire to assure you of the sincerity of my heart and endeavour on all occasions to testify the veneration I have for you." Only men who have the profoundest regard for each other born of respect, and feel deeply, write to each other in such a vein. Would that someone may find Lord Fairfax's reply!

After a paragraph concerning the right of the College of William and Mary to appoint county surveyors "in your lordship's proprietary," that is, the Northern Neck, the third paragraph brought up a matter that might easily have alienated Lord Fairfax had it not been handled with tact – a trait possessed by Dinwiddie, the Lascelles case and the pistole fee episode apparently

170 *Dinwiddie papers*, I, 20-21n; see Fairfax Harrison, *Proprietors of the Northern Neck, chapters of Culpeper genealogy* (Richmond, 1926) ; John C. Fitzpatrick, ed., *Diaries of George Washington, 1748-1799*, I, 3n.

to the contrary notwithstanding. The matter in question was that of "fines," a moot subject in any era. "Colonel [William] Fairfax was talking with me," continued Dinwiddie, "in regard to the fines laid on different affaires that may come before the courts." Note the courtesy, some would term it diplomacy, of the next sentence: "This is too nice a point for me to give my thoughts on, as your lordship is so nearly concerned in it." Again, he is equally careful and circumspect, feeling his way along with a fine sense of discrimination as he adds: "Give me leave to give my opinion as an indifferent person (but not as a governor). What fines may be laid in the county courts in your proprietary, I cannot determine on, but those at the general court are received by the sherifs and by them paid to the receiver-general and aplicable towards the support and paying to the emergencies of government, and are included in his accounts, swore to, and transmitted home." Having presented the facts, Dinwiddie next stated the conclusion he felt himself forced to take, in language so frank that not even a Lord Fairfax could feel offended: ". . . on which circumstances, I think your lordship has no right, unless you obtain an order from home to him to be accountable for the same to you, I mean those fines that are raised from apeals from the county courts in your proprietary." As a friend he liked Lord Fairfax; as a neighbor he respected him; but as a governor of Virginia, technically responsible for her finances, he was now as insistent upon having the colony enjoy its income from "his majesty's quit rents," as he was later to be regarding pistoles for land patents. His duty, as he saw it, was to collect all fines due the colony. Even when his action crossed Lord Fairfax's path he did not hesitate; he merely was careful to approach his correspondent in language befitting a friend who was at the same time a great landed proprietor. Any irritation on Fairfax's part possibly caused by the above paragraph certainly must have been dissipated by the sentence which followed it: "I hope you will excuse my writing so freely on this subject, which I should not do, but from the opinion I have of your friendship for me."

Lord Fairfax, already mollified, if perchance he had been ruffled, must have been completely disarmed by Dinwiddie's closing paragraph, which should be read in connection with the one at the opening of this remarkable letter: "I shall be glad of the honour of a line from you, and proud of the opportunity, when in person I could have the pleasure of assuring you that I am in great truth,

"Your lordship's most obedient and humble servant."

While Dinwiddie was, at the very outset of his new career, establishing friendly relationships with various private parties, he did not neglect his public contacts. For example, it is known that he wrote letters, also in the middle of december 1751, to two of his fellow governors; and one gathers from the evidence and from inference that he dispatched similar communications to most of the remainder of them in the colonies up and down the coast.

While surveyor-general of customs of the southern department of the colonies, Dinwiddie had come to know some of the governors personally; that fact is apparent from an inspection of the phraseology he used. For instance, he closed his letter of december 13 to Lieutenant-governor Samuel Ogle [171] of Maryland with the following significant and intimate touch: "I tender

[171] Samuel Ogle (d. 1752), colonial governor of Maryland, was born in England. His administration—or three administrations—was punctuated by disputes over tobacco duties, the boundary with Pennsylvania, and proprietary rights; nevertheless, he in the end won over generally the people of Maryland to his position.

my best respects to your lady, Colonel Tasker, and family." Mrs. Ogle was Anne, daughter of Colonel Benjamin Tasker,[172] member of a well-known Maryland family. Following Ogle's death, may 3, 1752, Colonel Tasker was acting governor of Maryland until the arrival of Lieutenant-governor Horatio Sharpe on august 10, 1753.[173] Thus it was that the new Virginia governor knew the Ogles, the Taskers, and probably the Cresaps, and many other distinguished families of Virginia's neighbors. This wide acquaintanceship would serve him well in the years ahead.

Whether Dinwiddie knew the other governors personally, or whether he did not, two parallel threads run through all of his letters to them – a plea for cooperation between colony and colony and a declaration of unquestioned and unquestioning loyalty to "his majesty" and Britain. Since the royal governors owed their places to a single appointive power, this fact was conducive to a common loyalty, to a common binding force among colonial governors generally.

The first two letters to fellow governors were to Samuel Ogle. The second is in tenor much like the first. It probably was written the same day but sent by a different "express" and by a different route, as was a common precaution with correspondence in that day. This second communication begins in a typically Dinwiddie style, one of courteous approach. The next sentence, as amazing in length as in syntax, was in part as follows: "Permit me at the same time to express the sincere pleasure

---

[172] Benjamin Tasker (1690-1768), Marylander, member of the council, 1722-1768, president for twenty-two years, and, therefore, acting governor, following Samuel Ogle and preceding Horatio Sharpe.

[173] *Dinwiddie papers*, I, 11n, 13n. Horatio Sharpe (1718-1790), colonial governor of Maryland, 1753-1769, was born in Yorkshire, England. He is said to have been at one time a captain in the marines and later to have been sent to the West Indies as a lieutenant-colonel but he had seen no active service.

I have the view of in keeping up a correspondance with a gentleman I always retained a very great regard and respect for." In this letter as in succeeding ones to officials, the Virginia governor, whenever he requested aid, made an offer of his own. His immediate objective in this communication to the Maryland governor was to insure his cooperation regarding the coming Logstown conference.

The final letter of this type presented at this point in the Virginia governor's career was a communication he wrote to Governor James Hamilton [174] of Pennsylvania, a few days after the preceding letters just analyzed. James Hamilton held this office from november 23, 1748 to october 3, 1754, and also 1759 to 1763, as well as other offices of trust and distinction in the province until his removal to New York. There he died august 14, 1783. James Hamilton's father was Andrew Hamilton, an eminent lawyer and a native of Scotland, who came to America and settled first on the eastern shore of Virginia, presently removing to Kent county, Maryland. One wishes heartily he might learn whether the Hamiltons and the Dinwiddies were acquainted in Scotland, or whether Robert Dinwiddie and James Hamilton first met in America. Dinwiddie knew Hamilton quite as well as he did Ogle. The present letter first announced his appointment and his arrival in Virginia. Next it expressed a desire for a "frequent correspondence between us" – as one would expect it to do. It informed Hamilton of the nearing Logstown conference and concluded with the postscript that Dinwiddie so often appended, namely, a personal word regarding the two men's mutual friends: "Pray tender my sincere respects

---

174 James Hamilton (1710-1783), son of Andrew Hamilton, the eminent lawyer and attorney for John Peter Zenger, and a member of the provincial council.

to Mr. Allen and his family." [175] The writer seemed never to forget friends, nor his friends' friends, including their ladies.

Meantime, the new executive proceeded to establish another and a different type of contact, and this within the same week which saw that variety of letters to an Indian interpreter, to an Ohio company member, to a local county official, to a landed proprietor, and to two fellow governors – to list only the letters that have been preserved for us; for some, undoubtedly, have been lost. This new contact was with the vestry of St. Anne's parish, Albemarle county. Showing by the letter's phraseology that Dinwiddie himself had taken the initiative, he began: "Gentlemen: I have enquired into the vacancies of church livings, since my arrival." He seems to have desired to be of service not only in the affairs of state but also in things ecclesiastical. His interest in the church was pledged when he first addressed the College of William and Mary and again when he spoke to his first legislature. It was a natural sentiment with him, thoroughly genuine, for it runs through his entire administration. For example, in one of his last letters from America, that of september 12, 1757 to the lord bishop of London, written concerning the same general theme, ecclesiastical problems, this same recurring note is struck. In the latter case, the minister of Hamilton parish in Prince William county had had serious charges brought against him. Said the governor: "The complaint was supported by the vestry and many of the gentlemen of that parish, for monstrous immorality, profane swearing, drunkenness, and very imodest acts."

[175] Dinwiddie to Hamilton, december 18, 1751, *ibid.*, I, 16. William Allen (1704-1780), Philadelphia businessman and eminent lawyer, born of Scotch-irish presbyterian stock, and educated in London. He married a daughter of Andrew Hamilton, celebrated lawyer and defender of John Peter Zenger, and thus was a brother-in-law of James Hamilton, governor of Pennsylvania.

Still, the bishop's commissary, Reverend Thomas Dawson,[176] claiming lack of authority, hesitated to act. But not Dinwiddie. He might have saved himself trouble had he not again felt duty-bound to act. He justified his action under the authority of what he explained was "my 81st instruction [177] from his majesty." He claimed

[176] Thomas Dawson, fourth president (1755-1761) of the College of William and Mary, following Reverend William Stith. It was during his term of office that the college conferred the degree of master of arts upon Benjamin Franklin.

[177] Dinwiddie's instructions have not been found. Presumably they were similar to those issued to the titular governors, Lord Albemarle and his successor, Lord Loudoun. For example, the instructions issued by the lords of trade to Lord Loudoun, and dated march 17, 1756 (P.R.O., C.O., 5/1367, 179-288; L.C. tr., 100-164), begin as follows:

"Instructions for our right trusty and right wellbeloved cousin John Earl of Loudoun, our captain-general and governor-in-chief of our colony and dominion of Virginia in America; and in his absence to our lieutenant-governor or commander-in-chief of our said colony for the time being."

There are one hundred fourteen articles in these instructions, which run to sixty-four typewritten pages. They are amazing in the control they gave to a governor and a lieutenant-governor over matters ecclesiastical. Some of the articles having to do with the church, and undoubtedly similar to those issued to Dinwiddie either when he was commissioned on july 4, 1751, or shortly thereafter (Dinwiddie to lords of trade, august 1751, P.R.O., C.O., 5/1327, 417; L.C. tr., 309-310; Dinwiddie to Halifax, september 10, 1751, P.R.O., C.O., 5/1327, 419-422; L.C. tr., 311), are as follows:

"83.   You are to permit a liberty of conscience to all persons, (except papists), so they be contented with a quiet and peaceable enjoyment of the same, not giving offence or scandal to the government.

"84.   You shall take especial care, that God Almighty be devoutly and duly served throughout your government, the Book of common prayer, as by law established, read on each sunday and holiday, and the blessed sacrament administered according to the rites of the Church of England.

"85.   You shall be careful that the churches already built there be well and orderly kept, and that more be built, as the province shall, by God's blessing, be improved . . .

"86.   You are not to prefer any minister to any ecclesiastical benefice in that our colony without a certificate from the right reverend father in God the lord bishop of London . . . and if any person, preferred already to a benefice, shall appear to you to give scandal, either by his doctrine or manners, you are to use the proper and usual means for the removal of him . . .

"90.   We do further direct that no schoolmaster be henceforth permitted to come from England, and to keep school in the said colony without the licence of the said bishop of London; and that no other person now there or

the parson in question had been "almost guilty of every sin except murder, and this last he had very near perpetrated on his own wife by tying her up by the leggs to the bed post and cutting her in a cruel manner with knives." [178] No wonder he felt justified in writing the bishop of London!

The vestry of St. Anne's parish needed, in Dinwiddie's estimation, a guiding hand. His inquiry upon his arrival into the state of the various parishes brought him a reply, among others, that St. Anne's parish was in need of a rector. The Reverend John Robertson, a zealous anti-presbyterian,[179] had moved from St. Anne's. Dinwiddie wrote a letter sponsoring a new minister: "I have the pleasure and satisfaction of recommending the bearer, the Reverend Mr. John Ramsay, to succeed Mr. Robertson, a gentleman who has brought from England so full testimonials of his capacity and worth, that I the more sincerely recommend him to you, not doubting but he will answer and give you full satis-

---

that shall come from other parts, shall be admitted to keep school in that our said colony of Virginia without your licence first obtained.

"91. And you are to take especial care, that a table of marriages established by the canons of the Church of England be hung up in every orthodox church, and duly observed; and you are to endeavor to get a law passed in the assembly of that colony (if not already done) for the strict observation of the said table.

"92. . . . It is therefore our will and pleasure, that you take due care for the punishment of the forementioned vices, and that you earnestly recommend it to the assembly of Virginia to provide effectual laws for the restraint and punishment of all such of the aforementioned vices, against which no laws are as yet provided . . . And it is our further will and pleasure, that you recommend to the assembly to enter upon proper methods for the erecting and maintaining of schools, in order to the training up of youth to reading and to a necessary knowledge of the principles of religion."

[178] Dinwiddie to the lord bishop of London, september 12, 1757, *Dinwiddie papers*, II, 695-698.

[179] "The Reverend John Robertson in 1752 signed a petition to the house of burgesses for the suppression of the labors of the presbyterian 'apostle' Samuel Davies and others of his sect. *Perry's Virginia church papers*, 383, 414, 427, 446" (*Dinwiddie papers*, I, 15n).

faction, and that he will do everything in his power for
the peace and happiness of the parish." Dinwiddie concluded by assuring the parish that if it would "entertain" the Reverend Ramsay "as your pastor" it would
be "very agreeable to, gentlemen, your most humble
servant." Whether or not Dinwiddie was a good judge
of clergymen, the records at least indicate that Pastor
Ramsay was still officiating for St. Anne's as late as the
summer of 1755.

The clergy have always played an important, sometimes a conspicuous part, in the communities in which
they live. The episcopal clergy of old Virginia were no
exception. The black sheep about whom Dinwiddie
wrote the bishop of London in september 1757 certainly
was not typical of the rank and file of the clergymen.
Their appointment to several parishes in Virginia was
an important matter, and officials vied with each other
in recommending individuals to fill vacant "livings."
For instance, Dinwiddie had arrived, as will be recalled, on november 20. The very next day he found two
of his most prominent Virginians, the president of the
council and the commissary, who was also the president
of the college, instead of spending at least a day in entertaining him, their new governor, and talking generalities, intent, on the contrary, upon sponsoring each his
own candidate for the vacant "living" at Southwark
parish. A rare note in the informing diary of Councillor John Blair under date of november 21, 1751, reads:
"All other business [than buying McKenzie's house]
was, I thought, to be postponed; but Mr. Commissary
[Reverend William Dawson] moved the governor for
his letter of recommendation of Mr Jones to Southwark
parish, which the governor was ready to give in to. But
as I had in my pocket a letter to the governor from Mr.
Menzies for that parish I thought myself obliged to

deliver the letter imediatly, lest it might be quite too late." Dinwiddie was not the only official who took time out to recommend a "pastor" here and another there, with the pious hope that his parishioners would "receive and entertain" him like good churchmen. He was being impressed anew with the intricacies of ecclesiastical administration. But an adept scholar learns rapidly. The urgency which these two men attached to the chance to recommend to the governor a preacher – when Dinwiddie had not yet had time even to bring his family up from York, an event that took place the following day – must have opened the new official's eyes to the importance of the parishes. He, too, began to act.

Within a matter of days, if not hours, thereafter, he himself had "enquired into the vacancies of church livings." Thus it was that on december 13, less than a month after listening to Messrs. Blair and Dawson, Dinwiddie also was recommending a candidate – recommending him so strongly that, as he put it, "I . . . desire you will receive and entertain him."[180] But of such stuff is the kingdom of history.

---

180 Dinwiddie to vestry of St. Anne's parish, december 13, 1751, *Dinwiddie papers*, I, 15. Another instance of the continuance of this practice on the part of Dinwiddie is to be found in notes made by the well-known Bishop Meade from a sermon by a Reverend Mr. Castleman. He represents (William Meade, *Old churches of Virginia, ministers and families* [Philadelphia, 1910], II, 318) the following letter as having been presented by Governor Dinwiddie to the vestry of the parish of Augusta county, november 16, 1752:

"Gentlemen: The Reverend John Jones has been recommended to me by many of good repute and undoubted credit as a worthy and learned divine. As such I recommend him to you, gentlemen, to be your pastor, not doubting but his conduct will be such as will entitle him to your favour by promoting peace and cultivating morality in the parish. Your receiving him to be your pastor will be very agreeable to

"Your very humble servant."

The Ohio Company

Robert Dinwiddie was vitally concerned with the Ohio company of Virginia, the first of the important western land organizations. Yet until recently hardly a beginning had been made in investigating his rôle in that company's affairs. And even though it was primarily the formation of the Ohio company that started a train of events which precipitated the French and Indian war, and thereby the Seven Years' war, nevertheless scarcely anything had been done either on a complete history of the company or a life of Dinwiddie. At last a history of the company is now available.[181]

Heretofore relatively few of the important letters and documents regarding the Ohio company have been known to exist. Investigation has just uncovered or rediscovered, however, significant additional manuscripts. One of them is a communication to the British board of trade from Sir William Gooch, lieutenant-governor of Virginia from 1727 to 1749, and is dated Williamsburg, november 6, 1747. It deserves careful analysis. In it, for one thing, he asked for instructions how to act in an emergency. According to Gooch, his letter to the board was the result of considerable pressure being brought to bear upon him in Virginia. He stated he had been "lately much sollicited" by certain individuals who desired "grants for lands lying on the western side of the great mountains." [182] Ground was being laid for the coming of some expansionist governor.

---

[181] Kenneth P. Bailey, *Ohio company of Virginia and the westward movement, 1748-1792* (Glendale, Calif., the Arthur H. Clark company, 1939).

[182] Gooch to the lords of trade, november 6, 1747, P.R.O., C.O., 5/1326, 547-548; L.C. tr., 349-350.

The date of the formation of the company has commonly been given as 1748. But the date of its incipiency was much earlier. The agitation above referred to, which thus had matured into a concrete proposal by the fall of 1747, had been going on during, instead of after, the four-year King George's war that reached a stalemate in 1748.

Gooch throughout his governorship had approved numerous small grants and favored certain larger ones. For reasons that are at last becoming clear, he restricted himself to generalities when he made reference to the solicitation of what is now known to have been a considerable group of influential men interested in westward expansion. For instance he did not employ the term Ohio company in this or any subsequent writing to the board, so far as is known. Yet that name for the organization must already have been determined upon by 1747.[183]

Even more interesting is the singular fact that in Gooch's request for enlightenment, directed to as important an agency as the board of trade, he did not attempt to identify the Virginia petitioners and their associates, though of course all of them were well known to him – one of them being the most prominent member of his own council. This member was Colonel Thomas Lee, who had been one of the three commissioners to the Lancaster conference with the western Indians in 1744, and who had been associated with practically every important activity in Virginia. He was not even mentioned by the governor. Also in the petitioning group were other prominent men, such as Lawrence and Augustine Washington, both Colonel Thomas and Daniel Cresap, as well as a member of the powerful Fairfax

---

[183] Thomas Lee to the lords of trade, october 18, 1749, P.R.O., C.O., 5/1327, 195-200; L.C. tr., 147-150.

family, George William Fairfax. George William was
the son of another member of Gooch's council, Colonel
William Fairfax. Not only these, but the company's
roster, which reads like a colonial Virginia honor roll,
boasted another man soon to become a member of
Gooch's council, Thomas Nelson. Yet Gooch curiously
referred to men of that standing in his colony merely
as "several persons in partnership." This point is emphasized for this reason: it was the next year, 1748, that
a friend of Thomas Lee and of Robert Dinwiddie, John
Hanbury of London, on behalf of himself and his associates there and in America, presented a similar petition
to the English government. In contrast with Gooch,
Hanbury in his document named names. The personnel
of the petitioning group,[184] as he noted it in the record,
included not only himself, a well-known English merchant, but also a considerable list of officials in Virginia
and in her neighbor colonies, men whose family names
were well known in England.

Robert Dinwiddie, of Virginia and London, surveyor-general of customs, and a member of Governor
Gooch's council, was a close friend of Hanbury's. Sympathetic from the beginning with the objectives of the
new land venture, he presently became a full-fledged
member. But such a roster did not impress Gooch – for
he was not sympathetic with the venture.

There was still another important phrase in the governor's cryptic letter to the home government that has
been overlooked and which must be challenged. When
the governor reported the location of the desired grant
he stated vaguely that it was on the other side of the
mountains, "where we have already two counties well
peopled." Presumably he would leave the impression
that any encouragement to migration out to the frontier

---

[184] Petition of John Hanbury [1748], P.R.O., C.O., 5/1327, 53-57; L.C. tr., 31-35.

would be superfluous. He had reference to Augusta and Frederick counties. Yet the former of these included the territory of half a dozen of the present states of the union west of the Alleghenies and north of the Ohio. Though its inhabitants were spoken of at the time as residing "on the waters of Mississippi river, in the county of Augusta," [185] the statement by Gooch that the county was "well peopled" is certainly subject to challenge. As late as 1756 the population of Augusta county, based upon its tithables, was reported by Dinwiddie to the board of trade to be only 9092 whites and 80 blacks, and Frederick county as 8692 whites and 680 blacks. Even the third frontier county, Hampshire, had but 2232 whites and 24 blacks. The three counties totaled only 20,800 persons. The United States bureau of the census defines the American frontier line as that area where the density of population is two to six persons per square mile. It is evident therefore that the bulk of Augusta county, however "well peopled" it may have seemed to the governor when he considered the Ohio company's petition, was out beyond even the frontier line.

Gooch's november 6 statement, comprehensive as it was delphic, contained still another noteworthy reference. It had gone on to declare that the unnamed several persons in partnership desired to carry on "a more extensive skin-trade with the several nations of Indians, who are willing to enter into commerce with us." He admitted that he himself was sufficiently persuaded that the granting of the petition would "in the course of a few years be productive of many national advantages." Yet he held, and stated definitely that his council concurred with him in holding it, that "we ought not to

185 W. W. Hening, ed., *Statutes of Virginia at large* (Richmond, 1819-1823), VI, 258 (hereafter cited as Hening's *Statutes*).

comply therewith till his majesty's permission was first obtained." He, like Governor Hope of Bermuda back in 1722, uncertain in the contingency facing him, was asking for directions out of his dilemma.

On december 17, 1747 the board of trade received Gooch's inquiry of november 6. It was read the same day. On january 19, 1748 they wrote Gooch their reply, saying that they "desire to know what difficulties" he has been under in granting, or rather in not granting, the lands requested. This reply of the board was received by Gooch on june 5, and on june 16 he sent back his answer from Williamsburg.[186] This was received in London by the board on august 15 and read the next day. Gooch's answer stated that the "only objection" he originally had had to the petitioners' request was his apprehension that the granting of lands in the west "might possibly give umbrage to the French." He then added, deliberately: "Which made the council and me think it advisable to wait for his majesty's pleasure and directions." Precisely what Gooch meant to imply here is not clear. Whether or not he had brought up the Ohio company proposal formally before his council is difficult to determine; likewise, what position each of them took on it, if he did.

A brief analysis of the council, as then constituted, may throw some light where light would be welcome – for Gooch's remarkable statement about his council involved Dinwiddie, a member thereof. Seldom if ever were the later colonial governors of Virginia able to secure at any one time at Williamsburg the attendance of all twelve members of their council. These absences were due chiefly to the great distance most of them lived from the capital. Therefore it is unlikely that Gooch

[186] Gooch to the lords of trade, june 16, 1748, P.R.O., C.O., 5/1327, 7-10; L.C. tr., 7-8.

meant he had presented the Ohio matter to a formal session of his advisors. He probably meant that he had consulted them informally and that he had found the sentiment – ONLY OF THOSE WHOM HE HAD BEEN ABLE TO CONSULT – generally against the Ohio lands petitioners.

That conclusion is reached today, since a poll of the council membership reveals that he certainly did not mean to imply that he had the unanimous support of all twelve of the members. For example, he could not have spoken for – even for the proxy vote of – Robert Dinwiddie, who, though still a member, was probably then in London. He did not resign until the spring of 1749. Had he been consulted there by letter or had he been in Virginia, undoubtedly he would have stood up for the petitioners.

Neither could Gooch have meant that he had the support of another member of his council, Colonel Thomas Lee, inasmuch as Lee himself was, as the governor of course knew, one of the petitioning group that he had styled "persons in partnership." [187]

The lords of trade received from Williamsburg on august 15, 1748, and on the sixteenth read, Gooch's "only objection" letter, dated june 16. The board found nothing in Gooch's letter, not even his one objection, to warrant holding up the Virginians' western lands petition. Therefore, two weeks later, september 2, they endorsed the petition and at once forwarded it to the privy council for additional authoritative approval. On november 24 the privy council sent their approval to the lords of trade. This was received by the board on decem-

---

[187] *Legislative journals of the council of colonial Virginia*, II, 1019-1056, *passim*, give the other ten members of Gooch's council at this time as Colonel John Custis, Lewis Burwell, John Blair, Dr. William Dawson, John Tayloe, John Grymes, Philip Lightfoot, William Nelson, John Robinson, and William Fairfax.

ber 8 and promptly read. Less than a week later, december 13, the board transmitted to the privy council
committee a lengthy favorable report which was accompanied by the authorized instructions to Gooch in Virginia.[188]

It is impossible that Dinwiddie should not have been
informed of all these Gooch-council-board-privy coun-
cil-Hanbury negotiations. For one thing, he had often
during the 1740's sat on that Virginia council with Lee,
he knew the Fairfaxes and the Washingtons, and whenever in London he kept in close contact with Ohio company member John Hanbury; for it was Hanbury who
was to go his bond when he later came to bargain with
titular Governor Albemarle about his "moiety" salary
in august 1751. Again, Dinwiddie undoubtedly was being kept advised of the progress of the Ohio company
proposal because there was an extraordinary amount of
letter-writing taking place. The Washingtons were
nearly or quite as prolific in corresponding as was Dinwiddie. Lawrence Washington had been in communication with Hanbury, and with Dinwiddie before the
latter became governor, regarding his favorite scheme
of settling German immigrants in the over-mountain
west. The chief trouble was that his newcomers were
not members of the Church of England. They balked
at the provincial law requiring them to support by parish taxes what to them was an alien church. Washington was anxious to have the Germans exempted from
this clerical handicap.[189] Dinwiddie significantly wrote
back to him: "It gave me pleasure, that the Dutch

---

[188] Commissioners for trade and plantations considering Gooch's letter,
february 23, 1748, P.R.O., C.O., 5/1327, 1; L.C. tr., 1-2; Order of the lords of
the committee of council, november 24, 1748, P.R.O., C.O., 5/1327, 21; L.C. tr.,
13-14; Lords of trade to the privy council, december 13, 1748, P.R.O., C.O.,
5/1327, 61-64; L.C. tr., 37-41.

[189] Jared Sparks, ed., *Writings of George Washington* (Boston, 1834-1837),
II, 481.

wanted fifty thousand acres of the land granted to the
Ohio company, and I observe what you write about
their own clergyman, and your endeavour to have them
freed from paying the Church of England. I fear this
will be a difficult task to get over; and at present the
parliament is so busy with public affairs, and the ministry in course engaged, that we must wait some time
before we can reply; but be assured of my utmost endeavours therein." [190]

Dinwiddie, though then in England, was already
working closely with the moving spirits in the Ohio
company. That he would use what he termed his "utmost endeavours" was no idle promise on his part.
When, later on, in august 1751, through the courtesy of
his patron, the Earl of Halifax,[191] he was given an advance opportunity to peruse his instructions as governor,
one of the three recommendations he immediately made
to the board of trade was a warning against any discrimination because of creed out on the Virginia frontier. That frontier, he pointed out, "has been less zealously attached to the Established church." He solemnly
counselled that the Church of England's "restriction
might be taken off these poor people." If this "very great
discouragement to forreign protestants setling on the
western parts of Virginia" were removed, he predicted
that it "would probably soon render the frontier of
Virginia as defensible, if not so populous, as a greater
latitude does that of Pensylvania." [192]

Late in 1748, Hanbury, on behalf of his associates,

---

190 *Ibid.*, II, 482.

191 George Montagu Dunk, second Earl of Halifax (1716-1771), son of
George Montagu. He attended Eton and Trinity college, Cambridge. He became earl on his father's death in 1739. In 1748 he was made president of the
board of trade and took great interest in colonial affairs, particularly those
relating to navigation and trade.

192 Dinwiddie to the lords of trade, august 1751, P.R.O., C.O., 5/1327, 417;
L.C. tr., 309-310.

had presented a longer if not stronger petition to the king than the draught of a petition which Lee and the members in Virginia and Maryland had attempted to bring before the king via Governor Gooch. This fact is known, since on january 11 an order in council referred this Hanbury petition to the lords of the committee of council. The privy council committee took almost immediate action. Their move is on record and is dated Whitehall, february 9, 1749.[193] It is the key document in this Ohio series, taken in conjunction with the consolidated document that finally emanated from the home government on march 16, 1749. On that day was issued by the lords of committee a favorable report on the petition. His majesty approved at once, on the advice of the privy council. Immediately was issued the combined memorable order in council directing the Duke of Bedford,[194] secretary of state, at last to draft for the Ohio company the definitive instruction to Gooch "for his majestys royal signature." [195] March 16 was a day to be remembered by the company. Indeed this order in council was to become one of the epochal documents in colonial American history. It begins:

"Additional instruction . . . for Sir William Gooch . . . empowering him to make a grant or grants to John Hanbury, Thomas Lee, and others their associates, of two hundred thousand acres of land . . . on . . . the Ohio . . . within the colony of Virginia." Thus, by the terms of this specific grant, and by the terms of

---

[193] Order of the lords of the committee of council referring the petition of Hanbury to the lords of trade, february 9, 1749, P.R.O., C.O., 5/1327, 51-70; L.C. tr., 27-29.

[194] John Russell, fourth Duke of Bedford (1710-1771), was long in public life. He was secretary of state for the southern department from february 12, 1748 to june 13, 1751, when he gave way to Newcastle.

[195] Order in council approving the draught of an additional instruction prepared by the lords of trade, march 16, 1749, P.R.O., C.O., 5/1327, 93-96; L.C. tr., 57-58.

her own charter, and by the terms of Pennsylvania's, Virginia considered she had ample authority for her acts in the near west. It is vital that there be no misapprehension on this point.

There were four important considerations detailed in the grant; and in each of these Robert Dinwiddie was to be very much concerned in the years ahead. In less formal language they were: first, that the initial grant of two hundred thousand acres was to be confined to Virginia territory, west of the Alleghenies and roughly from the forks of the Ohio, where Pittsburgh, Pennsylvania, now stands, southwestward along the south and east side of the Ohio river to the Kanawha river; second, that this area was to be occupied by actual settlers; third, that a fort was to be erected and garrisoned to protect such settlers; and finally, that once these three pledges had been fulfilled, the governor was authorized to reward their faithful performance by making a further grant of three hundred thousand acres in adjacent territory.

Summed up, the members of the company stated they desired mainly to do two things: first, settle loyal British subjects in the back country about the Ohio as a kind of buffer state against the French encroachments; and second, promote a trade in skins and furs with the Six Nations and other friendly Indians, "westward of the . . . mountains" which would "greatly promote the consumption of our own British manufactures, enlarge our commerce, increase our shipping and navigation, and extend your majestys empire in America." [196]

The petitioners had determined to go outside the colony, if necessary, to get the immigrants required to populate this buffer state. Tidewater and piedmont Virginians were settling up the region but not rapidly

[196] Petition of John Hanbury [1748], P.R.O., C.O., 5/1327, 53-57; L.C. tr., 31-35.

enough, even though Gooch thought it already "well peopled." The Ohio company petition had stated that the design back of their request was, with regard to the Ohio region, "in order to settle the same with strangers." By these "strangers" they meant chiefly Pennsylvania Dutch. Gradually there had developed, in interested quarters, the sentiment for a "proper encouragement to foreign protestants." John Hanbury, the quaker, was for it; so were Thomas Lee and Lawrence Washington, Virginia parish members in good standing in the Established church; so was Robert Dinwiddie, presbyterian; and so were the people and their burgesses, for Hening's *Statutes* for this period is sprinkled with laws made in pursuance thereof.

Another caution the board had finally urged upon the governor had to do with "his majesty's income." That matter too had at first been overlooked. The quit rents, they now instructed him, must not fail to be collected. This land rent matter was destined, in the years ahead, to create most serious problems for Robert Dinwiddie.

Finally, the board dealt with the matter of building a fort to protect settlers in the granted area: ". . . as it is not likely that any number of inhabitants will be induced to settle beyond the great mountains unless they are sure of protection there." But Dinwiddie would be equal to the occasion: he would dispatch one Captain William Trent to build the fort; and one George Washington to protect Captain Trent.

As compared with his successor's attitude, or the attitude of his successor's successor, the westward movement apparently meant less to Gooch — either as a Virginia matter, or, as Dinwiddie later called it, a "national matter." It was a difference in point of view. For example, in Gooch's reports on Virginia to the board of trade he consistently reported the Cherokee Indians as "within the bounds of Carolina." [197] They actually were not, certainly not all of them; whereas Gooch's successor, Dinwiddie, displaying again the difference in point of view, never did so report them.[198] Neither did the interim lieutenant-governor, Colonel Lee.[199] Neither did John Mitchell in his contemporary account.[200] As a governor Gooch was interested primarily in internal development rather than in expansion to the west, either for Virginia or for Britain. He, for instance, had taken stock in an iron mine;[201] Dinwiddie put his faith in the Ohio company.

Did Dinwiddie have the interest of the Ohio company, as he later expressed it, "much at heart" because of his long-established residence in Virginia in the 1740's near Williamsburg, or because he became eventually the colony's chief executive, or because of his membership in the new Ohio company venture? Apparently neither Gooch, nor Lee, nor Dinwiddie regarded such land company activities as unethical or as incompatible with the business of governing. Colonial motives were as mixed then as they ever had been, or were to be. Government officials in those days held their positions but still retained their interest – not in oil and steel and newspapers – but in lands and mines and furs. A dual loyalty did not seem inconsistent.

197 Gooch to the lords of trade, august 22, 1743, P.R.O., C.O., 5/1326, 25-38; L.C. tr., 19-40; december 21, 1744, P.R.O., C.O., 5/1326, 205-218; L.C. tr., 91-112; june 10, 1747, P.R.O., C.O., 5/1327, 465-486; L.C. tr., 287-309; [n.d.] 1749, P.R.O., C.O., 5/1327, 167-178; L.C. tr., 115-135.

198 Dinwiddie to the lords of trade, january 1755, P.R.O., C.O., 5/1328, 323-334; L.C. tr., 265-283; *Dinwiddie papers,* I, 386-390; february 23, 1756, P.R.O., C.O., 5/1328, 427-442; L.C. tr., 347-361; *Dinwiddie papers,* II, 342-343.

199 Lee to the lords of trade, september 29, 1750, P.R.O., C.O., 5/1327, 231-246; L.C. tr., 171-185.

200 Mitchell to the lords of trade, april 14, 1752, P.R.O., C.O., 5/1327, 429-440; L.C. tr., 315-338.

201 Colonial Williamsburg MSS.

Whatever may be the conviction about four years or eight years, most persons regard two years as too short a term for any executive to carry out his policies. Ironically, just at this state of affairs in Virginia history when continuity of policy was so essential — and not alone for the Ohio company's sake — the colony was destined to have as many as five different resident executives between the first of august 1749 and the last of november 1751. Reference is to Gooch, who left for England in august 1749; and to his three successors, as presidents of the council: John Robinson,[202] Thomas Lee, and Lewis Burwell,[203] and, of course, Robert Dinwiddie. And as a fateful coincidence, the company was almost as unfortunate in this respect as was the colony; for Lee, as leading spirit, soon died in november 1750 — before his commission as lieutenant-governor reached him. Lawrence Washington, who succeeded to the presidency of the company, shortly followed him to the grave, in 1752. Lucky indeed, therefore, was it for the Ohio company that the new governor, Dinwiddie, now a member, declared he had the matter of its success so much on his mind.

During the time that he was acting governor Colonel Lee showed amazing energy. As president both of the company and of the colony he now got action — authority

---

[202] John Robinson, son of John and Catherine (Beverley) Robinson, was a man of importance in his day. He became a member of Governor Gooch's council, while his son, John Robinson, sitting in the house of burgesses, was soon to become its speaker, as well as treasurer of the colony. John sr. was a member of the council at the time that body strove to prevent Robert Dinwiddie, then surveyor-general, from sitting therein as a member "in ordinary." Whatever the cause, John jr. was destined to oppose at many a turn this same man when he became governor; and the latter responded by opposing his control of two offices of trust.

[203] Dinwiddie to the lords of trade, march 20, 1756, P.R.O., C.O., 5/1328, 463-467; L.C. tr., 375-378; *Dinwiddie papers*, II, 374; see also John Blair's diary, printed in part in *William and Mary college quarterly historical magazine*, 1st series, VIII (July 1899), 3.

for which he had waited more than two years. Meanwhile, he felt precious time had been lost. For example, he warned the lords of trade in his first comprehensive report to them, dated at Williamsburg, october 18, 1749, that the western Indians had recently been aroused by the French to "such a spirit of jealousy" that only by an urgent treaty and timely presents could anything be done with them. He added significantly, and maybe almost bitterly: "This was not the case when the Ohio company petitioned." [204]

But it was not alone the growing ill-feeling among the Indians that was threatening the Ohio company. Something else was just as damaging, even if less insidious: the dispute between Pennsylvania and Virginia as to jurisdiction over the Ohio forks region. The Pennsylvanians claimed down to the thirty-ninth degree of latitude, Lee pointed out. If allowed, this claim would have given them all of the present western and southwestern Pennsylvania. He declared it would take from Virginia "a considerable quantity of land" and prevent the Ohio company from making settlements with any certainty.

By the time of Dinwiddie's coming, what with Lee in his grave, and Lawrence Washington ill, the Ohio company's matters, not to speak of Virginia's, were in an uncertain state. Dinwiddie acted at once. His first sentence on record, quoted in part above, regarding the Ohio company occurred in the body of a letter the governor wrote two months after his arrival in Virginia to a western Maryland member of the company, Colonel Thomas Cresap: "I have the success and prosperity of the Ohio company much at heart, tho' I have not a line from any concerned since my arrival, but this from you."

<hr>

204 Thomas Lee to the lords of trade, october 18, 1749, P.R.O., C.O., 5/1327, 195-200; L.C. tr., 147-150. For Lee's death on november 14, 1750, see *William and Mary college quarterly historical magazine*, 1st series, VII (January 1899), 303.

Phrasing his thoughts in his own individual way, which his secretary Waller's punctuation and spelling were to match, he continued this cryptic but important letter: "There is a cargo for the concerned come in the ship with me, it now lies at Colonel Hunter's, the severity of the weather prevented his sending the goods to Colonel Mason." Evidently John Hanbury, in London, now armed with authority, had lost no time at his end of the line; Lee's urgently-needed Indian presents and other company supplies had now begun to cross the Atlantic and were about to filter in to the back country. The governor's letter continued: "I am surprized at what you write, that Patton, or any other person should obstruct that company's making a settlement on Ohio, but shall take care that it shall be strongly urged to the Indians." Confirmed optimist that Dinwiddie always was, he added: "and [I] doubt not of success." [205]

In Cresap's estimation, Patton had been one of those who had attempted to obstruct the Ohio company's operations. As a matter of fact Patton was not interested in obstructing the Ohio company but was instead merely concerned wih protecting his own grant.[206] It is apparent that Dinwiddie regarded the Ohio company's shipment as an urgent matter, something of utmost importance. Proceed at once without delay to handle the Ohio company matter was the substance of Dinwiddie's order to Colonel Patton, as transmitted to him on december 13, 1751 [207] by Nicholas Walthoe, clerk of the Virginia council. Cresap's charge against Patton, if indeed there was one, either could not have been well grounded, or else Patton's subsequent services overbalanced in the governor's mind any charges against him.

[205] Dinwiddie to Cresap, january 23, 1752, *Dinwiddie papers*, I, 17-18.

[206] James Patton to John Blair, january 1753, Draper manuscripts 1QQ175-1QQ177.

[207] Instructions to Patton, december 13, 1751, *Dinwiddie papers*, I, 9-10.

That any such charges were without real foundation, later events would lead one to believe. The evidence is Dinwiddie's letter to Patton, written to him four years later, just before he was killed by Indians. It is dated july 8, 1755. The whole communication betokens the confidence of Dinwiddie in his county lieutenant of Augusta county. For example, he gave Patton liberty to write a certain letter "in my name." Furthermore, he gave him wide discretionary power when he advised him that "any money you may advance . . . shall be duly paid you." [208] Blanket privileges like that customarily go only to the most trusted individuals. At the close of this long communication Dinwiddie signed it, as he did his letters to but few men, "your friend." Either it must have turned out that Patton and Dinwiddie did not allow their official relationships with their respective land grants to affect the personal regard each had for the other, or else both men put service for the colony ahead of service for a private or semi-private land company. Notwithstanding the degree to which Dinwiddie did have the Ohio company at heart, the evidence forces one to the conclusion that with him, loyalty to the crown and to Virginia outweighed every other consideration.

[208] Dinwiddie to Patton, july 8, 1755, *ibid.*, II, 92-94.

First Address to the Assembly

Dinwiddie's first address to his legislature, delivered shortly after his arrival, may be said to constitute his inaugural address, his declaration of principles, his platform. The general assembly of colonial Virginia was made up, as will be recalled, of twelve members of the "upper" house, the council, and one hundred and four members of the "lower" house, usually known as the house of burgesses. He had, therefore, the colony's elite as his auditors.

Dinwiddie stood now before the combined legislative houses of Virginia in a serious mood. This was a grave and important moment not only to him but to the peace and well-being of the colony, for in these, his first official utterances, would lie the theme of his governorship. "Gentlemen of the council, Mr. Speaker, and gentlemen of the house of burgesses," he began in the stately language of the eighteenth century, "his majesty having been graciously pleased to honour me with his commission, to be lieutenant-governor, and commander-in-chief, of this his dominion of Virginia . . ."

Thus disposing of the formalities which custom seemed to require, the new governor struck his stride and began to stress his favorite principle, cooperation. He included himself in the assembly as he suggested that "we . . . jointly consider" the colony's best interests. But the power to consider and then to legislate, like the general welfare clause in the American federal constitution, was definitely limited, as Dinwiddie explained. "We can go no farther," he said, than "what we are impowered to do."

He was conscious of his new responsibility. It would follow then that he was eager to convince his audience of his sincerity in desiring to help in "promoting his majesty's interest, and the prosperity of this colony." Therefore he said frankly: "I have so just a sense of the importance of the trust devolved upon me, and solicitude to discharge the same with honour, as wholly prevents my attention to those arts, by which, persons conscious of great abilities, or familiar to command by long habit, are enabled to grace a public character."

"This solicitude," continued Dinwiddie, graciously, "is increased by the virtues of my predecessor." There is no doubt but that Sir William Gooch, who served immediately preceding Dinwiddie, was for the most part both loved and respected by the Virginians. Dinwiddie had known Gooch well and spoke from a close acquaintanceship with his predecessor. In consequence, the truth about Sir William Gooch was as pleasant to relate as it was to hear. Whatever qualities Dinwiddie lacked he would attempt to counterbalance by assiduous attention to the public good. Hence: "But tho' my ambition be disappointed by the example I follow, yet emulation will be animated; if less eminent, I may be more useful by a steady attention to the good of this dominion."

The new executive now pledged himself to certain high objectives which would affect the moral, religious, social, and governmental life of the colony. He declared: ". . . my constant care shall be to support the Church of England." [209] As he had prepared that line of his address, he must have reflected on Lawrence

---

[209] *Journals of the house of burgesses* (1752-1755; 1756-1758), 4; *Dinwiddie papers*, I, 24.

Washington's letter to him not long before, in which Washington had deplored the church's rigid insistence upon parish taxes from non-participating German "members," potential settlers in the Lee-Washington-Ohio company project then forming in his mind.[210] It was a kind of taxation without representation. Dinwiddie had informed Lawrence Washington he shared his feelings.[211] And he had so declared himself to the lords of trade in august 1751.[212] But now it was different. He had taken the oath as governor. He was a new official. Though brought up in presbyterian Scotland, he promised his "constant care" for the interests of the Church of England, an institution that now, for an individual who placed loyalty high in the category of virtues, took on for him a new significance because it was, as he added, "by law established." And then he continued, emphasizing the other things that would be under his constant care: "To encourage virtue, piety, loyalty to his sacred majesty, and with the utmost of my power, to discourage vice and immorality."

Letter-writer that he was and continued to be, he went on to say: "It shall further be my inclination and endeavour, to cultivate those virtues of a social nature" – significant language that seems hitherto to have been overlooked – "by keeping up a good and harmonious correspondence with you, in a private as well as a public capacity."

Judging by the record of his days in Virginia before and during his governorship, those were not meant to be idle words. Sociable by nature, as he seems to have been, he patronized the theater, took an interest in young

---

[210] Jared Sparks, ed., *Writings of George Washington*, II, 481.

[211] *Ibid.*, II, 482.

[212] Dinwiddie to the lords of trade, august 1751, P.R.O., C.O., 5/1327, 417; L.C. tr., 309-310.

people, interspersed even his official letters with items of personal interest to his correspondents, and enjoyed an unusually happy home life.

If Dinwiddie be permitted to speak for himself, "to cultivate those virtues of a social nature" is precisely what he had been accustomed to do during the eight years he had already lived, perhaps intermittently, in Virginia as a government official. His words and subsequent actions would indicate that he spoke from sincere conviction, for he unhesitatingly admits: "It was with great joy I landed here, invested with power of doing good to a people, among whom I had formerly mingled in scenes of domestic felicity, and experienced the endearing reciprocations of friendship." If it be true that only those who naturally show friendship, inspire friendship in return, we may find here another gleam of light on the new governor's character. And on the public attitude toward him.

On the principle that a good name is rather to be chosen than great riches, he declared to the assembly that he could "without regret, resign all pretensions to eminence or distinction," because, he explained, "other acquisitions are in my power" which are the "reward of virtue." He told them that "my affection for you, gentlemen, will be now gratified by frequent opportunities of expressing my zeal for the good of this colony (now my country,) which will be a spring of pleasure in my breast."

He went on to lay emphasis upon the "most ardent benevolence," or, as might be said today, forgiveness and broadmindedness on their part, and the "most inviolable fidelity" on his own part. Yet these were, if taken alone, "frequently insufficient" to attain their ends – a people happy under good government. But the burgesses and he must never overlook one skulking

enemy, he warned, which is ever lurking round about to
undermine or strike in the back. That was the arch foe
Dinwiddie identified as "error." It was his solemn conclusion that "error has perhaps produced as many public calamities as indolence, avarice, or ambition." He
did not regard himself as infallible but showed a willingness to take advice – then as always the mark of a
great mind – when he declared: "I shall therefore, gentlemen of the council, always receive your advice with
pleasure; and gentlemen of the house of burgesses, I
shall rely with confidence on your assistance."

Turning now to the members of the lower house, he
addressed them more particularly. He declared to them,
in phrases filled with devotion and expressed with a
charm of diction, that he had been impatient to call
them together so soon after his arrival that both they
and he might "concur in the gracious design of his
majesty, and to express my duty and gratitude to him
in the most acceptable manner." As for himself he assured them that the manner most acceptable to him, as
well as to the king, would be "by becoming an instrument of happiness to my fellow-subjects."

On the theory, doubtless, that idle burgesses, like idle
hands, tend to mischief, he admonished them that "the
legislature should always be busy." Here follows, in
his address, in language worthy of emulation, a list of
items that were calculated to keep them busy. Said he:
"There are grievances to redress, irregularities to reform, defects to supply, and exuberances to cut off."
Significantly, he placed the redressing of grievances
first in the category.

Amplifying his argument with phrases that suggest
the preamble to the American constitution, he continued: "I . . . most earnestly recommend to you the
prosecution of this great work with diligence and expe-

dition. Consider what bills may be proper and necessary, for promoting the public quiet, and common interest, by more effectually securing property, encouraging and extending commerce, establishing the peace, safety, and regularity of an equitable and well ordered government." In the "attainment of these desirable purposes," he pledged the legislators he would assist them "to the utmost of my power." He followed up that promise with an assurance to them that they could "expect from me, every concession in your favor." That voluntary commitment lost none of its force, even though Dinwiddie hastened to insert a proviso. With a colonial governor's dual loyalty, he felt impelled to add one limitation, namely: ". . . of which my instructions will admit."

Climaxing his formal appearance before the two houses, he particularized regarding two major issues selected for stressing at this initial meeting. Putting his finger directly on one of the long-standing "grievances to redress," he declared: "I shall be glad if you can find some method to prevent delays in the courts of justice, so very inconvenient to the people, and so much complained of in Britain, as well as here." Dinwiddie would presently, in his several addresses to the grand jury, have more to say regarding the struggle in Virginia, as in Britain, to insure "equal justice under law." What he stood for reminds one of the philosophy of Comte, who once expressed himself: "Not man as he is, but man as he would be, is a right royal fellow indeed."

But the ideal of justice Dinwiddie referred to for the white man was coupled in his very next sentence with a high code of morality toward the red man. However original may have been the language he employed in his recommendation, no one could mistake its meaning when he said: "There is one thing I recommend to your particular regard, and that is the cultivating a good correspondence with the neighbouring nations of Indians." With a philosophy highly modern, like a prophet sounding out his clarion warning, he went on: "It is better they should love us, than that they should fear us; and one of the two is absolutely necessary." Relentless logic. The governor then followed his recommendation with an explanation of his philosophy behind it when he observed: "Fear is a slavish passion, and the mind is always struggling to throw it off. On the contrary, love and amity are propagated by acts of kindness, the very exercise of which is delight."

During almost a decade that he had been Gooch's councillor, he had been storing up information about the "neighbouring nations of Indians" and the importance of an Indian alliance, upon which, as governor, he was to draw heavily. He had foreseen that in the years immediately ahead the Indians were often to play a decisive rôle, holding the balance of power between and among their great white invaders. Even before he became governor, and as soon as he was given an advance opportunity while still in England to study his instructions, his prior experience in America made him ready and eager with recommendations. One of these to the lords of trade, as early as august 1751, had to do with Indians: an urgent plea for cultivating cordial relations with the native peoples. It will be remembered that there, in that pronouncement of policy, he had said: "The cultivating a good understanding with the Indians ought to be the daily care of every governor on the American continent, and is of the last importance to Virginia."

Dinwiddie had urged "a good correspondence" with the tribes. He cited examples of the practical advantages that would follow from the adoption of such a concilia-

tory policy: "The mind is happy under their influence;
and their influence for that reason, is continually gaining new strength: so that our European neighbours, who
are settled to the southward and northward of us, would
never be able to inflame the Indians against us, if the
advantage of mutual bounty, gratitude, and public faith,
opposed their attempts." [213] During the years when he
had sat on the Virginia council, Dinwiddie had become
familiar with the complexities of the French-english
impasse in the back country. Only on the basis of the
information and impressions that he had already stored
up before he became governor, was he in a position,
immediately upon his arrival in november 1751, to make
his charges against "our European neighbours . . . to
the southward and northward." He felt he was justified
in so doing because "they have been long endeavouring
to spirit up the Indians that are in amity with us, to the
breach of their faith, with a view to possess, and settle
the interior parts of America, the back of our frontier
settlements to the westward. Your own good sense will
soon discover, what bad consequences such settlements
would be of to us, and our posterity."

Dinwiddie's "settlements to the westward" probably
meant to him chiefly the adjacent west, a section that
was then all-important. He was practical enough not
to declaim about the areas known later as the middle

[213] *Journals of the house of burgesses* (1752-1755; 1756-1758), 5; *Dinwiddie papers,* I, 26. By november 9, 1756 he felt obliged to write home to
Henry Fox: "The Indians are a most inconstant and unfixed sett of mortals,
and laying aside all treaties, promises, and engagements, are always ready
to join with the strongest side, and then no longer than they have success"
(P.R.O., C.O., 5/17, 733-736; L.C. tr., 573-577; *Dinwiddie papers,* II, 539). For
a typical French attitude toward the Indian, his alleged sovereignty over the
land, see French minister's ten-page letter to Duquesne, may 15, 1752 (Arch.
Nat., Col., series F3, 14: 30-32vo.; L.C. tr.). A passage in Villier's journal
of the june campaign of 1754 illustrates the weight the Indians carried: that
officer changed his tactics before Fort Necessity when "the Indians had announced their departure within two days" (Arch. Nat., Col., series F3, 14:
52-60; L.C. tr.).

and the far west, since it was the immediate west of Augusta county that must first be settled and controlled. But he referred time and again to Virginia's "sea to sea" claims and in his reports to the lords of trade he pointed out that Virginia included even the "island of California." Those things all show unmistakably that when he made his formal statements to the home government, he had no intention of permitting the English world, and the French as well, to forget the vast American stretches "to the westward." Acting on the well-known principle of suggestion, he would make it impossible for the people's representatives not to measure up to the faith reposed in them. His appeal closed thus:

"I further sincerely recommend to you, gentlemen, that both in your public, and private capacities, you will diffuse a spirit of benevolence, and unanimity, which are the vital principles of public and private happiness. By such conduct you will approve yourselves good christians, and good subjects; you will then render my administration honourable and easy; you will enjoy the prayers, and blessings, of the whole colony; you will deserve the paternal affection of his majesty; and you will be intitled to the favour of Almighty God, who, that we might consider each other as brethren, has not disdained to be called the Father of us all."

Whatever it was that furnished the impulse, the burgesses on their part, at the close of that first session, did two rather extraordinary things. They presented Dinwiddie with a purse of five hundred pounds as a token of their esteem;[214] and in addition they approved the christening of the newly-created western county by the name of Dinwiddie.[215]

---

[214] *Journals of the house of burgesses* (1752-1755; 1756-1758), 96, 99. Culpeper and Gooch were among Dinwiddie's predecessors who also had been given a present of £500.

[215] *Journals of the house of burgesses* (1752-1755; 1756-1758), xvii.

But the council and the house had no intention of allowing the governor to outdo them in felicitations. They rose to the occasion. Not only did they hasten to assure him that they were his majesty's faithful, loyal, and dutiful subjects, but they returned him their thanks for his "affectionate speech" at the opening of the session.

No special significance probably should be attached to the council's "hearty and unfeigned" thanks as against the "cordial" thanks of the burgesses.[216] It would be only later, after the rise of a temporary misunderstanding between Dinwiddie and certain members of the lower house, that persons would re-read into those words a meaning their authors could not at the time have intended.

The list of those leaders in Virginia who were to be Dinwiddie's advisers, among some of whom he had once sat as a fellow councillor, is full of interest. For example, the president of the council was Lewis Burwell, of whom Dinwiddie later wrote that he "has never come to council since my arrival; nay, I have not seen him." [217] Next was John Blair, nephew of the late councillor, founder of the College of William and Mary, and commissary, Dr. James Blair. Third was William Fairfax, cousin of Lord Fairfax and lord of Belvoir on the Potomac, neighbor, close friend, and relative by marriage with the Washingtons, and usually styled "colonel." Then there was William Nelson, of the well-known Virginia family. Prominent among the members was William Dawson, D.D., commissary to the lord

---

216 *Legislative journals of the council of colonial Virginia*, II, 1060-1061; *Journals of the house of burgesses* (1752-1755; 1756-1758), 8; *Dinwiddie papers*, I, 27-29.

217 Dinwiddie to Abercromby, march 20, 1756, *Dinwiddie papers*, II, 377. See also Dinwiddie to the lords of trade, march 20, 1756, P.R.O., C.O., 5/1328, 463-467; L.C. tr., 375-378; *Dinwiddie papers*, II, 374.

bishop of London since the death of Dr. James Blair in
1743, and also president of the college. He had been
recommended to the council upon the death of Captain
Dandridge and was appointed. John Lewis, another
member, had been recommended twice by Gooch. He
had first been recommended on august 30, 1744 upon
the death of William Byrd II, and was officially appointed on january 14, 1748, following the death of John
Tayloe. The seventh member was Thomas Nelson,[218]
who had been appointed by the privy council on january 11, 1748 after the death of Philip Lightfoot.
Thomas Nelson had been one of those to go down to
York in november 1751 to welcome Dinwiddie back to
Virginia. Philip Ludwell Grymes was another councillor. Gooch had put his name forward in a letter to
the board on december 5, 1748 as successor to John
Grymes and on march 16, 1749 he was officially ap-
pointed. There was Colonel William Byrd, III [219] of
Westover. Richard Corbin [220] was next. In 1749 he took

[218] Thomas Nelson (1738-1789), was a member of the prominent Virginia
Nelson family, brother of William Nelson, secretary, and member of the governor's council.

[219] William Byrd, III (1728-1777), usually known as Colonel William Byrd
of Westover, from the name of the ancestral home on the James river. Following in the Westover tradition, he became a member of the Virginia council,
colonel of the second Virginia regiment, and at one time a special commissioner to the Cherokee and Catawba Indians. William Byrd II (1674-1744)
had been born into prominence. After completing his education in England,
he returned to Virginia and threw himself into colonial activities. He led in
worsting Lieutenant-governor Alexander Spotswood in a bitter controversy
over the collection of quit rents. His private library and art gallery at Westover were probably unexcelled in America. He was one of the commissioners
for running the boundary between Virginia and North Carolina in 1728.
Furthermore, like many of his eighteenth-century associates, he was interested in expansion westward. The first William Byrd (1652-1704) had been
a plantation owner, shipper, Indian trader, member of the council, and a
man of importance in colonial affairs. It was he who selected the site upon
which his son would later erect the mansion known as "Westover."

[220] Richard Corbin (c. 1708-c. 1783) of Laneville, King and Queen county,
long a member and apparently for a time president of the governor's council,

the late John Robinson's place. He was to become the
staunch friend of George Washington. William Beverley [221] had served since 1750 in place of the indisposed
Colonel John Custis. Finally, there was Peter Randolph, reserved here for special mention.

He is usually referred to as Colonel Peter Randolph
of Chatsworth, Henrico county. His father was William, grandson of the immigrant, William Randolph,
of so-called "Turkey island." Peter was the first cousin
of Peyton Randolph, attorney-general.[222] Peter had
been a member of the lower house and was now a member of Dinwiddie's council by virtue of his being successor to Dinwiddie in the position of surveyor-general
of customs for the southern department in America.[223]
He was highly regarded by the governor. Whatever the
differences that may have arisen later between Peyton

and receiver-general of Virginia. He was a county lieutenant of Essex county,
hence his title of colonel. He was a friend of George Washington and favored
his appointment as lieutenant-colonel in 1754. Contrary to belief he was also
friendly with the governor, who even after the expiration of his office and
his return to London kept up a friendly correspondence.

221 William Beverley (d.1756), burgess, councillor, lawyer, was a grandson
of the Robert Beverley who first supported and then opposed Governor William Berkeley, and son of the historian, Robert Beverley, and his wife, Ursula
Byrd, daughter of William Byrd I.

222 Peyton Randolph (c. 1721-1775), son of Sir John Randolph, was born
and reared in Williamsburg, Virginia, but educated in England. At various
times he represented either the city, or the College of William and Mary, in
the house of burgesses. He carried out during his busy lifetime in Virginia
the best traditions of the family. Able as well as popular, he became burgess, attorney-general, speaker of the house of burgesses in 1766 upon the
death of John Robinson, chairman of the Virginia committee of correspondence, and first president of the continental congress (1774, 1775) (see also the
excellent sketch in the *Dictionary of American biography*). Brock states that
"the nominal salary of the attorney-general was £70 from the revenues of
the colony and £70 from the crown" (*Dinwiddie papers,* I, 72n). Peyton Randolph married Elizabeth, daughter of Colonel Benjamin Harrison. There
were no children, and his estate eventually went to his nephew, Edmund
Randolph.

223 Representation to his majesty, april 14, 1749, P.R.O., C.O., 5/1366, 447;
L.C. tr., 225-226; Order of council, may 2, 1749, P.R.O., C.O., 5/1327, 105; L.C. tr.,
61-62.

Randolph and Dinwiddie because the former represented the burgesses in England in their pistole fee controversy, they do not seem to have affected the cordial
relations between Colonel Peter and the governor. For
example, Dinwiddie wrote to Sir Thomas Robinson in
England on november 24, 1755 that he had "prevailed"
with the colonel to accept the appointment with William Byrd to serve as one of the two commissioners to
the Catawbas and Cherokees in december of that year.
But the significant thing about Randolph's career at this
time is that it was he who was appointed by the British
board of trade, and very possibly on Dinwiddie's own
recommendation, to succeed him as surveyor-general
of customs in 1749. Almost or quite as significant here
is the fact that Randolph was now able to profit by the
precedent that Dinwiddie had established, or re-established. It seems that Randolph, as surveyor-general of
customs, was at once accepted, both by the governor and
the councillors without a murmur, as a regular member
"in ordinary" of the upper house, entitled thereby to all
the rights and privileges of that body. The acquiescence
of the members of the council in Randolph's appointment to sit among them was due primarily to the recent
re-setting up of the precedent by Robert Dinwiddie
rather than to the fact that genial Colonel Randolph was
not aggressive Robert Dinwiddie.[224]

Present in this first council of Dinwiddie's were at
least four (John Blair, William Dawson, William Fairfax, and William Nelson) who were members of that
council ten years before and who then had opposed his
sitting among them. Now, however, all joined in thank-
ing King George II for their new governor, as they said:

[224] *Journal of the commissioners for trade and plantations* (January 1741/2
to december 1749), 408, 436; Representation to his majesty, april 14, 1749,
P.R.O., C.O., 5/1366, 447; L.C. tr., 225-226; Order of council, may 2, 1749,
P.R.O., C.O., 5/1327, 105; L.C. tr., 61-62.

"The appointment of you, sir, to preside over us (who formerly lived among us, and are well acquainted with the laws, and constitution of our country) is a circumstance, that, in a more particular manner, demands our acknowledgements."

What the "genuine marks of a good ruler" were, the council now proceeded to set forth in its own responsive address. In view of Dinwiddie's emphasis upon law, order, and justice, as well as his later controversy with various "subordinate officers," the following words are full of meaning: "To preserve the order of society, to protect the innocent, and administer justice impartially; to be circumspect, and watchful that all the subordinate officers of government act in their several stations with a comendable fidelity, are the characteristics, the genuine marks of a good ruler." They were confident that Dinwiddie would be "ever studious in the pursuit of these principles," in which case "the present generation will more imediately feel the effects of [the wisdom of] your administration." They hoped his rule would be wise. They solemnly voiced their encouragement to that kind of an administration by philosophically declaring that "the beneficial consequences of it, will be transmitted to generations that are yet unborn." Such a sentiment must have struck a responsive chord with Dinwiddie, for he later declared, when speaking to the grand jury: "A good man's deeds never die." Never did parties to an agreement mean better or start out more auspiciously. It would have taken a major disaster to upset permanently such a relationship. It never happened.

But Dinwiddie had not spoken merely in generalities; the Indian was a practical consideration, and he had talked of Indians. Either he had aroused the council to the importance of the question, or he had voiced a common attitude, or both, for the council's reference to Indians is the only specific item mentioned by them in their response: "We are truly sensible of the benefits that must arise to the British interest, by cultivating a friendship with the Indian nations; the importance of it is well known, and cannot fail to claim our attention, and to merit our regard." [225]

Dinwiddie was right in putting his finger on the Indian question at the very first meeting with his new legislature. It was the greatest single factor, sea power alone excepted, that would tip the scales one way or the other — for the French or for the English. It was one of the most statesmanlike moves of Dinwiddie's entire governorship that he, in season and out of season, would turn the spotlight of public opinion upon the importance of the Indian and his alliances with the English. At the very start of his administration he went to school himself and learned the names and locations of the tribes, their "fighting men," and their tribal connections. He wrote scores of letters to Indian chiefs, calling them by name; he sent messages to tribes, that he erroneously called "nations," far and near; he called conference after conference to deal with them. He "prevailed" on Colonel Peter Randolph and William Byrd to help keep bright the string of friendship with the Catawbas and the Cherokees. He insisted soon after his arrival in Virginia that Virginia have her own Indian interpreter. A staggering amount in pounds sterling would be represented by the thousands of items of Indian goods that Dinwiddie during his term of office caused to be shipped to America and distributed to the natives.

Leaving the council and their address, we turn to the burgesses, generally regarded as the more sensitive

[225] *Legislative journals of the council of colonial Virginia,* II, 1060; *Dinwiddie papers,* I, 27-28.

barometer of public opinion. Equally deferential and equally cooperative were the burgesses in their own proffer of support when they made their response. In several important particulars, however, the burgesses' address was different. One difference explains the early origin of the oft-used name, Old Dominion. For example, they referred to his majesty's province of Virginia as "this his most antient colony," a priority of which even colonial Virginians were definitely conscious. They stressed it. Throughout the colonial period, Virginians emphasized that fact, just as they and their governors constantly called attention to the colony's "sea to sea" claims – expressions contemporary with the times and by no means originated by later historians.

Noteworthy also was their reference to the appointment of Dinwiddie as "a person of such approved abilities and integrity to preside over us" – an expression borrowed from the college's "humble address" with which the new governor had only recently been felicitated by Dr. William Dawson.

The burgesses then added: "With hearts full of sincerity, we congratulate your honour, upon your safe arrival, with your family, amongst us." We are not surprised therefore that Dinwiddie promised that first assembly that he would try to "cultivate those virtues of a social nature," for those were the virtues that had largely accounted for his popularity in the Old Dominion while a member of Gooch's council. That such undoubtedly was the case is evident from the burgesses' concluding compliment: "When we reflect on those social virtues, with which your honour hath formerly distinguished yourself amongst us, we cannot but promise ourselves every pleasing prospect of an equitable and well ordered government." [226]

---

[226] *Journals of the house of burgesses* (1752-1755; 1756-1758), 8-9; *Dinwiddie papers,* I, 28.

If Dinwidddie, later on, temporarily lost his popularity, particularly with some of the burgesses, it must have been that he determined to be true first of all to his majesty and to Virginia, "now my country," as he called it, and then, and then only, to court what is generally termed popular acclaim.

Enter: George Washington

If one of the eighteenth-century signs of greatness in an individual was to leave for posterity a voluminous correspondence, then Robert Dinwiddie possessed this earmark, for he was an inveterate letter-writer. His correspondents ranged through the whole gamut of personal friends, colonial agents, fellow governors, military officials, merchants in London, his patron Lord Halifax, the British board of trade, and young George Washington. The opportunity he sought to try his sword never came. What success might have been his will of course never now be known. But he wielded a mighty pen.

From the very outset he crowded his days with the carrying on of what he denominated a "constant correspondence." However, his outpouring of letters was due in part to the fact that his aggressiveness, his executive ability, and his encyclopaedic knowledge of colonial affairs had long been known and appreciated by the British board of trade. Because of these things and because of the importance of the forks of the Ohio to Virginia, the colonies, and Britain, early in his administration he was made in many cases the medium of the board's communications with the various royal governors in America.

Even before Dinwiddie's arrival in America he proceeded, as has been noticed, to inform the board in august 1751 [227] of the state of affairs on the Ohio. On

[227] Dinwiddie to the lords of trade, august 1751, P.R.O., C.O., 5/1327, 417; L.C. tr., 309-310.

january 20, 1752, shortly after his arrival here, he went even further to emphasize the "many irregularities, even murders and robberies" in the same area.[228]

By december 10, 1752 [229] and june 16, 1753,[230] matters had reached the point where he practically memorialized the board of trade on the alarming conditions in that region. Six weeks elapsed before the latter communication reached the authorities in England. Yet so convincing was his representation that the officials promptly rose to the occasion and, by august 10, had issued an order in council. This order backed up Dinwiddie not only with "thirty cannon of four pounders" and all the accessories for what was to become two years of eighteenth-century "undeclared warfare," but with unlimited moral support as well.[231] Thus it was that the new governor was able to report to his second house of burgesses that "I also received letters to all his majesty's governors on this continent, with orders to dispatch the same to them immediately." [232]

Among the governor's contemporaries to whom he wrote most frequently was Lieutenant-governor Horatio Sharpe of Maryland. Sharpe arrived at his new post august 10, 1753. Amenities had to be preserved. On his own initiative Dinwiddie "dispatched letters" to the several governors up and down the coast, informing them of his arrival and inviting that "constant correspondence" for which he must have been celebrated even in his own day. In Sharpe's case the difference seems

228 Dinwiddie to the lords of trade, january 20, 1752, P.R.O., C.O., 5/1327, 453-454; L.C. tr., 347-349.

229 Dinwiddie to the lords of trade, december 10, 1752, P.R.O., C.O., 5/1327, 531-536; L.C. tr., 415-424.

230 Dinwiddie to the lords of trade, june 16, 1753, P.R.O., C.O., 5/1327, 637-642; L.C. tr., 529-538.

231 Order in council, august 10, 1753, P.R.O., C.O., 5/1328, 1-8; L.C. tr., 1-6.

232 *Journals of the house of burgesses* (1752-1755; 1756-1758), 104; *Dinwiddie papers,* I, 39-40.

to have been that Dinwiddie did not wait for the Maryland governor to notify him, instead he himself made the first move. A governor had to be welcomed into the fraternity of governors, for colonial governors were bound to each other by far closer ties than the state governors later on were to be. Since the magnificent distances in colonial America banned official calls in person, resort was had to letter-writing. And letter-writing thus became first a necessity and then an art in the eighteenth-century western world.

His first letter to the new Maryland governor apparently has not been preserved. In what seems to have been his second, penned september 3, 1753, he invited Sharpe to a frequent exchange of views by letter on mutually important colonial problems. The tenor of the first communication must have been very similar to the second. Time was to prove that this reiterated invitation of september 3 was as genuine as it was frank: "I . . . desire to repeat my sincere desire to keep up a constant correspondence with you, and when any thing occurs relating to these colonies, I shall keep you duely advised thereof." [233]

More significant even than the character of the foregoing invitation was the fact that in Dinwiddie's next letter to Sharpe, dated november 24, 1753, he informed him that he had sent a "person of distinction" to the commander of the French forces on the Ohio river. Dinwiddie's messenger was to ask him, in language that could not be mistaken, why he had invaded his majesty's colonial dominions. Dinwiddie assured the Maryland governor that as soon as the messenger had returned, he would tell him of his reception. The young man in question, already at twenty-one a "person of distinction"

[233] Dinwiddie to Sharpe, september 3, 1753, William Hand Browne, ed., *Archives of Maryland* (Baltimore, 1883–), VI (*Correspondence of Governor Horatio Sharpe*, I), 4-5 (hereafter cited as *Maryland archives*).

in Virginia, was destined to be weighted down with
"distinctions" of every character from the hands of his
countrymen before his death at Mount Vernon in 1799.
This unusual phrase, "person of distinction," may have
far more significance than is apparent on the surface.[234]
Dinwiddie of course could not foresee the future, but
his judgment as to his man was destined to link his own
name [235] with that of his young ward and thus by this
act, more than by any other in his life, he also achieved
"distinction."

Among the most pressing subjects of the "constant
correspondence" that Dinwiddie hoped to keep up with
Governor Sharpe, was the question of colonial defense
and offense, including military affairs in general and Indian relations in particular. With Dinwiddie an Indian
was in every French woodpile.

The Virginia governor was facing weighty problems

234 Dr. Max Farrand, director of research at the Huntington library, has
declared that the word "distinction" has long enjoyed a unique place in
English thought; it remains even today in England, in the best intellectual
circles, the quality most sought in preferment.

235 Washington's first preferment at the hands of Dinwiddie occurred
november 6, 1752: he was made adjutant of the southern district (but presently was transferred to the northern). The position carried with it the
rank of major, the lowest rank he ever held. His duties included exercising
the militia from time to time. Through Lawrence Washington, who of course
knew Dinwiddie well, young George must have met the governor very
soon after the latter's arrival in Virginia in 1751. George may even have
met him while Dinwiddie was a member of Governor Gooch's council. An
entry in George Washington's diary of his trip to Barbadoes with Lawrence
in 1751-1752 is most instructive. George returned to Virginia in january 1752
ahead of his brother. The very first step he took upon arriving was to go
directly to the governor:

"1752, january [26th] . . . got to the mouth of York river about 11 p.m.
and was met by a pilot boat.

". . . Hired . . . Williamsburg . . . Letters to the gover [Dinwiddie] . . .
had just gone to greensprin. . . dinner as I got to ye great . . . polis; upon
his return (which . . . at night) I waited upon and wa[s] received graceously
he enquired kindly after the health of my brother and invited me to stay
and dine . . . " (John C. Fitzpatrick, ed., Diaries of George Washington,
1748-1799, I, 35).

and he knew it. Even with many years' experience to guide him, he felt the need of friendly counsel from a kindred mind. Therefore, in the above-mentioned letter to Sharpe, november 24, 1753, he was still more explicit: "I shall be very proud of your advice and assistance in an affair that I think will be of great service to Britain, to the trade of these colonies, and strengthening our western frontiers. . . I shall be glad to know the inclination of your people." The "affair" to which Dinwiddie here alluded was his long-delayed meeting with the Indians at Winchester or Frederick Town, a conference upon which he had banked a great deal. But bitter disappointment was in store.

By the middle of june 1754, the blow had fallen; the "may next" conference was over. On june 18 Dinwiddie wrote to Sir Thomas Robinson, president of the board of trade, his sad report on "my going for Winchester, a town on the frontiers of this dominion." Would Dinwiddie still believe, as he had told his first assembly, that "it is better they should love us, than that they should fear us?" Or was he in the process of being persuaded that it was only the fear of the English rather than love that would be the beginning of Indian wisdom?

Meantime, on august 28, 1753, there was completed in London the preparation of a document that was to go out to America addressed to "our trusty and welbeloved Robert Dinwiddie Esq. our lieutenant-governor of our colony and dominion of Virginia in America." It bore the label: "Given at our court at Kensington the 28th day of august 1753, in the twenty-sixth year of our reign." This document, received in Virginia some weeks later, constituted one of the most important communications that Dinwiddie received during his entire administration. This message was his famous "instructions," about which every schoolboy in America has heard but which seems generally not to have been read in its entirety. It was remarkable "news" indeed; but the striking fact about it is that it was the immediate result of the initiative originally taken, as early as the preceding march and june, by Dinwiddie himself. This point has been overlooked. It is borne out by the preamble to the instructions which begin with: "Whereas you have represented in your letter of the 16th june last." This document throws light on the following vital matters: first, it was evidence of full support of Dinwiddie's pleas on the part of the ministry; second, it cautioned the governor to act strictly on the defensive in the Ohio west and placed him in command of all defensive preparations; third, it provided for the possibility of an offensive if, in his judgment, a military offensive should turn out to be unavoidable – in which case the Virginia governor was to repel "force by force"; and, finally, the instructions, coming through the Earl of Holdernesse, made the Virginia governor the intermediary with the other governors.[236]

The importance of these august 28 instructions is obvious: the responsibility for what followed was Robert Dinwiddie's. The instructions continue by stating that he had "represented" the "utility of building some forts upon the river Ohio, in the western part of our colony of Virginia." Dinwiddie's original representation apparently made no reference to the Ohio company project. Though Dinwiddie may have had that company in mind when he made his plea to the crown on june 16, it would seem that he had also kept before him

236 Holdernesse to Dinwiddie, august 28, 1753, P.R.O., C.O., 5/211, 21-32; L.C. tr., 13-25; P.R.O., C.O., 5/1344, 2-8; L.C. tr., 141-145; Loudoun papers, LO 447A, vols. 1-5, 1-6 (Huntington library). See also Holdernesse to Dinwiddie, august 28, 1753, P.R.O., C.O., 5/211, 51-52; L.C. tr., 43-46; Loudoun papers, LO 449A & B (Huntington library).

the larger conception of "our colony and dominion of Virginia."

His reason for urging the "utility," as the lords understood it from him, of building forts on the Ohio was "for the security and protection of our subjects, and of the Indians in alliance with us." If the ostensible reason was also the real reason, then the governor's motives as given were plausible enough; and one is warranted only by the most exceptional circumstances in impugning a man's motives. Hence, says the crown, "we have thought fit, with the advice of our privy council, to approve, that proper forts should be erected on the said river." This was looked upon as a non-aggressive move, hence the use of the added phrase, "for the defence . . . of the inhabitants."

However, there was inserted another phrase that is full of meaning: not only were these fortifications to be built for the protection of the frontiersmen but it is specifically stated in these instructions that they are to be "at the charge of the inhabitants of our said colony, agreable to your proposal." Apparently he had proposed to the board at the outset something resembling a pay-as-you-go plan. Besides, there was precedent: the terms of the Ohio company petition may easily have suggested this procedure since it was substantially the condition upon which that company was to gain protection, namely, by erecting its own forts. The governor desired to do something for Virginia and the mother country; as one who was vitally concerned in the new Ohio company it would be perfectly understandable if he felt his objectives could be the more quickly achieved by utilizing the agency of that organization.

Directions were given that "thirty cannon of four pounders, with a full proportion of stores," be forthwith put aboard ship and consigned to Dinwiddie in

Virginia. The artillery was to be matched by infantry.
Hence, ran the instructions, "lest you should meet with
any unexpected difficulties or obstructions"—which
Dinwiddie did meet—"in carrying on the said works,
our farther will and pleasure is, that you should forthwith cause the whole, or such part of our militia of our
province of Virginia . . . to be drawn forth and armed,
as you may judge necessary for our service." Virginia
thus was to be placed in a position of more adequate
defense, a defense that easily could be converted into
offense, and full discretionary power regarding such
a measure was placed in the hands of the new governor.
A responsibility indeed.

Next the crown attempted to anticipate the emergency that might be created in case this fort-building
program were interrupted: "You are first to represent
our undoubted right to such parts of the said river Ohio,
as are within the limits of our province of Virginia, or
any other [of] our province or provinces in America,
and to require the peaceable departure of any such Europeans, or Indians." It is noteworthy that the crown's
explicit orders were first of all to use every precaution-
ary measure to prevent an open rupture among the
European powers.

But the governor was provided with emergency authority, the natural recourse in case all so-called "peaceable" measures should fail. He was accordingly advised:
". . . but, if, notwithstanding such peaceable representations, they should still persist in endeavouring to obstruct the execution of these our orders, our will and
pleasure is, that you should repell force by force." That
language could not be misunderstood.

The officials went on to make it clear that they have
had information—now known to have come from Dinwiddie himself—"of a number of Europeans, not our

subjects, being assembled in an hostile manner upon the
river Ohio, intending, by force of arms, to erect certain
forts on the said river, within our territory, contrary
to our peace, and the dignity of our crown; we do hereby strictly enjoin you, to make diligent enquiry into the
truth of this information; and, if you shall find, that any
number of persons, whether Indians or Europeans, shall
presume to erect any fort or forts within the limits of our
province of Virginia, you" – and they unquestionably
mean Dinwiddie – "are to take appropriate measures."

Any military action ordered by him was, thus, to be
based upon two conditions: first, the receipt of definite
information that armed forces (not merely traders or
coureurs de bois) presumably intended to erect forts on
the Ohio; and second, that Dinwiddie would not, even
then, jump to a precipitate conclusion but would thoroughly investigate the basis of such a report, in order to
have ample justification for whatever action he finally
took. Considering the fact that three preliminary wars
had just been fought between England and France, considering the rudimentary state of international law, and
considering the intense nationalism of the age, one is
hardly prepared for the kind of conciliatory measures
that the crown of Great Britain thus recommended to
Robert Dinwiddie. He was explicitly cautioned to proceed one step at a time: after he had ordered the alleged
intruders peaceably to move out, then and only then,
were drastic measures to be taken; if they still persisted
in their menace, then British restraint, heretofore
couched in a posture of respectful defense, is suddenly
to be transmuted into an active, dynamic offense. And
not only that, but Dinwiddie at this point is given no
discretion in the premises. His instructions at this point
do not equivocate. They read: ". . . and if, notwithstanding your admonition, they do still endeavour to

carry on any such unlawful and unjustifiable designs, we do hereby strictly charge and command you, to drive them off by force of arms; in the execution of which, all our officers, civil and military, within the limits of your government, are to be aiding and assisting to the utmost of their abilities. G[eorge] R[ex]." [237]

The above analysis of this document demonstrates the restraint that Britain was endeavoring to exercise. Here were two great nations, England and France, with their satellites, nicely poised in the scales; the slightest blunder, the minutest overt act, might easily become a cause of war, or, in the language of diplomacy, a *casus belli*. The board of trade and the crown reposed remarkable confidence in this their "welbeloved Robert Dinwiddie, Esq." when they gave him wide latitude in the exercise of his judgment. Finally, it was in obedience to those memorable instructions that he had received on august 28, 1753, which he himself originally had inspired – and all but wrote – that he had sent a "person of distinction" to the French on the Ohio. [238]

---

237 Instructions for Dinwiddie, august 28, 1753, P.R.O., C.O., 5/211, 33-42; L.C. tr. 21-25.

238 Thus contrary to prevalent belief, it was Dinwiddie's knowledge of the situation in the Ohio country and his determination that representations must be made to the alleged aggressors there, that led him to dispatch George Washington with a warning to the French, and not the reverse. Washington's report of january 16 to the governor was important in that it corroborated what the governor already knew and was evidence to the crown that he had carried out his instructions "to require the peaceable departure of such Europeans." As a matter of fact before Dinwiddie dispatched George Washington to the French, october 31, 1753, he had sent William Trent to the west on an earlier reconnoitering expedition. The governor's matured impressions of the French and Indian advance in the Ohio west had now been confirmed, for he had added proof from Trent's journal, which covered from june to september 1753, that not only were the Indians in a bad mood but the French intended a major offensive toward the forks in the spring. It is thus Trent's report, which clearly set the train of events in motion. See Trent to Dinwiddie, august 11, 1753, Etting collection of "Ohio company papers" (Pennsylvania historical society), I, 1753-1755; Trent's account of his proceedings with the Six Nations, november 17, 1753, P.R.O., C.O., 5/1328, 27-44; L.C. tr., 15-40.

The Pistole Fee Dispute

When Dinwiddie took office he found awaiting him on his desk about one thousand applications for scattered parcels of land, amounting in all to nearly a million acres, in the sparsely settled region to the westward. He decided to allow the royal seal of official approval to be affixed to each application, or as it was termed, patent, only after payment by each applicant of a small fee amounting to a coin then in circulation, called pistole, and worth about three dollars and fifty cents.[239] Some of the applicants refused to pay, for reasons of their own; Dinwiddie refused to sign, for reasons of his own; the public took sides, for reasons of its own. Meantime, the French and Indians menaced the frontiers – and continued to do so throughout Dinwiddie's governorship.

A biographer, though not a special pleader, must seek to present the essential facts and thus help one to reconstruct actual situations. Dinwiddie had been a merchant. He came of a family of merchants. He did not think that "business methods" were being followed when "custom" permitted persons who were receiving over one hundred acres of land free, to have in addition the Virginia seal affixed free of charge.

But this incident has been the occasion for more misunderstanding regarding Robert Dinwiddie's career as governor of Virginia than any one other single happen-

[239] The Virginia council's approval of the pistole fee, april 22, 1752, P.R.O., C.O., 5/1327, 499; L.C. tr., 387; Dinwiddie to the lords of trade, october 6, 1752, P.R.O., C.O., 5/1327, 497-498; L.C. tr., 383-386; *Dinwiddie papers,* I, 44n.

ing during his stay in America. It would seem now to have been chiefly a matter of misinformation – on the part of too many historians.

The facts, now at last in hand, are as follows: when Dinwiddie came to America in the fall of 1751,[240] the great open spaces in the west just beyond the Blue Ridge, comprising a north-south zigzag frontier region, were filling up rapidly with settlers. Land was as cheap as it was abundant. Under Dinwiddie's predecessor, William Gooch, many thousands of these acres had been opened up to home seekers. For each of these a patent or title to the land had been regularly issued. Dinwiddie's predecessor governors had issued these patents to bona fide settlers, to land speculators, or to both, almost for the asking.[241] Curiously enough this matter of a pistole fee is closely associated with the question of the new governor's salary.

Dinwiddie, it will be recalled, was only a lieutenant-governor, not a governor. The titular governors customarily remained in England where they escaped major responsibility but shared their salary with their overseas lieutenant-governors. The deputy, usually known as the lieutenant-governor, was thus the actual governor on the ground in America, while the titular governor held a job that was a perfect sinecure. Dinwiddie's superior officer and the holder of the sinecure at the time of this account was William Anne Keppel, Earl of Albemarle. He struck a bargain with Dinwiddie as to salary.

Dinwiddie, as the resident and responsible executive of Virginia, with the high-sounding title of "deputy

240 Dinwiddie to the lords of trade, january 20, 1752, P.R.O., C.O., 5/1327, 452-454; L.C. tr., 347-349.

241 The method of taking up lands in Virginia, june 16, 1753, P.R.O., C.O., 5/1327, 671-672; L.C. tr., 561-564.

lieutenant and governor-general," in a bond [242] drawn up on september 7, 1751, agreed to halve what amounted to a rather mythical salary of £6660 with the titular governor, Albemarle. The instrument as executed was witnessed by Dinwiddie's two friends as bondsmen, John Hanbury and Edward Clarke Parish, London merchants.[243] This "moiety," set at £1665 every six months,

---

[242] Bond of Dinwiddie, september 7, 1751, Loudoun papers, LO 310 (Huntington library).

[243] Here follows the quaint, legalistic phraseology of the indenture: "Know all men by these presents, that we Robert Dinwiddie Esq. of London and John Hanburry and Edward Clarke Parish of London merchants are held and firmly bound to the Right Honorable William Anne Earl of Albemarle in the penal sum of £3500, of good and lawfull money of Great Brittain to be paid to the said William Anne Earl of Albemarle or his certain attorney, executors, administrators, or assigns for which payment to be well and faithfully made we bind ourselves and each of us in part and for the whole our and each of our heirs, executors, and administrators firmly by these presents sealed with our seals dated this 7th day of september 1751 and in the 25th year of the reign of our sovereign lord George the Second, by the grace of God king of Great Britain, France, and Ireland, defender of the faith etc. . .

"Whereas his most gracious majesty hath appointed the said William Anne Earl of Albemarle lieutenant and governour-general of his colony and dominion of Virginia and hath also appointed the said Robert Dinwiddie to be deputy lieutenant and governor-general of the said colony and dominion of Virginia in case of the death or absence of the said William Anne Earl of Albemarle during his majestie's pleasure

"And whereas the said Robert Dinwiddie is by his majesties instructions ordered and directed to pay one moiety or half part of the sallary and perquisites arising from the said office of lieutenant and governor-general of the said colony and dominion of Virginia to the said William Anne Earl of Albemarle and whereas in and by certain instruments of writing indented bearing even date herewith made and entered into between the said William Anne Earl of Albemarle of the one part and the above bound Robert Dinwiddie of the other part in order to avoid all disputes that might otherwise happen concerning the division of the said sallary and perquisites, the said Robert Dinwiddie hath covenanted and agreed to pay or cause to be paid to the said William Anne Earl of Albemarle or his assigns on the exchange of London the sum of £1665 of good and lawfull money of Great Brittain at the expiration of every six calendar months for and during all such time as the said William Anne Earl of Albemarle shall continue lieutenant and governor of his majesties said colony and dominion of Virginia and be absent therefrom and the said Robert Dinwiddie shall continue to be deputy lieutenant and governor-general of his majestie's said colony and dominion

or £3330 annually, would represent for either party approximately $15,000 today. If the lieutenant-governor actually received his equal share, then he was of course obliged to raise, in order to cover both parties to the agreement, the amazingly large sum of £6660.[244] But did the lieutenant-governor receive this amount as his share? The likelihood is he did not. He declared to one official in London that he had annually given Albemarle more than the position would admit of and that if he had known the situation better, he never would have accepted it; but he had added, with that loyalty that was characteristic of him, that he was "all submission" to his majesty's decision.[245]

of Virginia under the said William Anne Earl of Albemarle in lieu and in full of the said moiety of the sallary and perquisites arrising from the said office of lieutenant and governor-general of his majesties said colony and dominion of Virginia, the first payment to be due and be paid at the expiration of six kallendar months to be accounted from the day the said Robert Dinwiddie is or shall be sworn into the said office of deputy lieutenant and governor-general of his majesties said colony and dominion of Virginia in the said colony of Virginia. Now the condition of this obligation is such that if the said Robert Dinwiddie do and shall well truely and faithfully observe and perform the said covenant made and entered into with the said William Ann Earl of Albemarle to all intents and purposes according to the true intent and meaning thereof, or if this said Robert Dinwiddie should at any time or times hereafter be deficient in payment of all or any part of the said sum of £1665 to the said William Ann Earl of Albemarle and the said John Hanbury and Edward Clarke Parish or one of them, their, or one of their heirs, executors, or administrators, do and shall make good such payment to the said William Anne Earl of Albemarle within 14 days after notice is given or left in writing at the respective dwelling houses of them the said John Hanbury and Edward Clarke Parish, their executors or administrators, and that as often as any such deficiency or default of payment shall happen. Then this obligation to be void or else to remain in full force effect and virtue

Sealed and signed: Edward Parish, John Hanburry, Robert Dinwiddie
[Endorsed:] BOND: Robert Dinwiddie Esq., John Hanbury, and Edward Clarke Parish, To the Right Honorable William Anne Earl of Albemarle. Dated 7th september 1751."

244 Bond of Dinwiddie, september 7, 1751, Loudoun papers, LO 310 (Huntington library).

245 Dinwiddie to Granville, may 7, 1755, *Dinwiddie papers*, II, 33.

Where was Dinwiddie to get the more than several thousand pounds yearly to send to the Earl of Albemarle? As he reported to the lords of trade, january 1755, and as is well known from the accounts of other governors, the specific appropriation for the salary per annum for the office of governor was only £2000. This amount was raised yearly in Virginia from the tax of two shillings per hogshead on all tobacco exported. It is obvious, therefore, that a lieutenant-governor was expected to add to his income in some method or several methods – frankly, by boosting the "perquisites" – in order to be able to pay his superior £3330 annually. Is it any wonder that when Albemarle died late in 1754, Dinwiddie should write to his agent, James Abercromby, confidentially and therefore candidly: "The death of Lord Albemarle gave me very great concern, and if his majesty should think proper to keep it [the sinecure] open a few years, the salary would reimburse a very great expence I have been at in the publick service these last two years, and if properly considered, will be no very great favour. But I must submit to my fate on that head." [246]

Dinwiddie knew the entire situation in Virginia before he accepted the proffered position and honor, some will argue. Hence, he could not plead that he resorted to this meager pistole fee – one of the perquisites, which he, according to the contract, must share with Albemarle – as a legitimate means of augmenting his salary. The flame was not worth the candle.

But did he know what he was getting into? He says he did not. Furthermore, he presently found the "moiety" of £1665, that he swore to send to the titular governor twice a year, was more than he bargained for. It may well be, indeed, that he was never able himself to share

---

[246] Dinwiddie to Abercromby, march 17, 1755, *ibid.*, II, 3.

fifty-fifty in the nebulous salary. He explained it succinctly, in writing to Earl Granville,[247] may 7, 1755:

"I have account from England that the governor so appointed will reside here; if so, I shall very chearfully submit. The salary of £2000 per annum, is paid here, and not from the treasury at home, and as I have been at an extraordinary expence for this last 18 months, I hope that it will not be thought unreasonable to give me the full salary from the death of Lord Albemarle till his majesty thinks proper to appoint another governor. This will in some measure ease me of the very great expence I have been at, and as the salary is paid out of the funds of this dominion, I hope the allowance I pray will not be objected to. I therefore humbly beg your lordship's interest in this affair. I did agree with Lord Albemarle, and gave more annually than the government will properly admit of, and indeed, if I had known the place as well as I now do, I should have declined coming; however, I am all submission to the pleasure of his majesty. The fatigue, trouble, and anxiety I have had for these two years, I cannot well describe, but I was acting in my duty, and I hope what I have done will meet with approbation at home."

Dinwiddie died a fairly wealthy man, as one concludes from the estate left by his will. He had been a prosperous merchant and shipper, judging from many stray items that here and there have come down. Since

[247] John Carteret, Earl Granville (1690-1763), probably best known as one of the proprietors of North Carolina, his name being perpetuated in Granville and Carteret counties. He took his seat in the house of lords in 1711. Honors came to him beginning with the accession of George I in 1714, for one thing because, due to his knowledge of German, he could converse freely with the king and his Hanoverian favorites. In 1719 he was ambassador to Sweden; 1721-1724, secretary of state for the southern department; and 1742-1744, for the northern department. Meantime, 1724-1730, he was lord lieutenant of Ireland. Beginning june 17, 1751 he was lord president of the privy council.

he probably added little to his fortune during the seven years of his governorship, it would seem to follow that he was already comparatively well off before he returned to America in 1751. According to his will, he distributed as much as £50, £100, and £200 to each of many persons, besides £10,000 to each of his two daughters. Any attempt to collect a pittance of a pistole fee hardly need be explained by historians on the theory that he was financially pressed.[248] Indeed, it appears as though Dinwiddie were much like many a modern fairly well-to-do businessman who accepts a government post, either for the opportunity for public service, or for the honor of it, or both; and knowing full well that he must supplement his salary by drawing upon his own personal reserves.

After the passing of centuries it is just now learned in the course of these researches that Dinwiddie attempted immediately after he was appointed governor, and thus before he came to Virginia in 1751, to get a ruling from the home government on this very matter requiring a charge for signing and sealing patents on lands.

It appears that his good friend on the board of trade, the Earl of Halifax, had, soon after Dinwiddie received his appointment, july 4, 1751, if not actually before that date, been in a position to let the new lieutenant-governor make an advance examination of his instructions. This opportunity produced the following statesmanlike paper, showing that as a result of Dinwiddie's previous stay in America he already had matured opinions on how to handle Indians, combat French policy, mitigate the hardships of dissenters on the frontier, and, most

---

[248] Neither can the pistole fee dispute be explained by claiming that the house wished to economize and to save the people's money. Randolph was voted a salary of £2500. Dinwiddie would have received approximately only £900 for all applications then pending.

important of all in this connection, had prepared a recommendation regarding the disposal of public lands in Virginia:

"In consequence of the indulgence granted me I have carefully perused the copy of my instructions as governor of Virginia – in general, there cannot be any reasonable objection formed against them; but, presuming that it is not forbidden me, I beg leave to submit to your lordships an humble intimation of what may possibly be esteemed no improper addition.

"As disputes have arisen, and may arise, with regard to the governor's fee for signing patents and grants of land, it is extremely desireable that a setled allowance for every 100 acres should be ascertained here, or that it be recommended to the council to setle such fee for that quantity on signing every grant. It would be truly prudent also to restrain the governor and council from granting exorbitant quantities of land to any one person – a practice notoriously injurious to the inhabitants in general."

But for some reason as yet unknown the board in London unfortunately delayed action on the requested instruction. Therefore Dinwiddie called his Virginia council together on the matter less than six months after his arrival. The record of the council states:

"At a council held april 22d 1752
Present: The governor, William Fairfax, John Blair, William Nelson Esq., Thomas Nelson, Philip Grymes, Peter Randolph, William Dawson D.D., John Lewis, Richard Corbine, and Philip Ludwell Esq:[249]

"The governor desiring the opinion and advice of the board, relating to a fee for the seal of the colony affixed

---

[249] Philip Ludwell, son of Philip and Frances (Berkeley) Ludwell, is best known as Colonel Philip Ludwell of Green Spring. His daughter Hannah became the wife of Colonel Thomas Lee, president of the Virginia council.

to patents for land, which he thought he was justly intituled to, and might reasonably insist upon agreeable to the practice of all other governments in America.

"It is thereupon the opinion of the board, that the same is reasonable, and they do advise his honour to demand, and take one pistole, as a fee for the seal to every patent, before signing of the same."

These documents, never before published, place Robert Dinwiddie in a very different light in this pistole fee controversy.

In again pressing the board of trade for a ruling, in his letter to them dated october 6, 1752, a full year before the controversy broke out in Virginia, he called the lords' attention to their failure to give him their advice:

"Before I left London, I applied to your lordships, for your opinion, and signing patents for land, agreeable to the usage, and custom, of all the governors on the continent of America." The lords having been derelict in a clear duty, Dinwiddie had no alternative but to lay the matter before his own council in Virginia – the upper house of the legislature – and they supported him. As he went on to explain: ". . . as I had not the honour of the opinion of the board, on this head, I laid the affair, before the council here." The action taken by the local council is significant: the council "unanimously agreed, that such a fee was just, and reasonable, and therefore gave their opinion, that a pistole, for affixing the seal, and signing each patent for land, was very reasonable. This fee is much less than the neighbouring governors charge, however I am therewith well satisfied and only beg your approbation thereof, by a letter, the minute of council on my asking their advice, and concurrence, in this affair. I enclose to your lordships . . . I am with great deference and submission."

One observation is inescapable: that these sins of omission on the part of the board of trade are a tacit criticism of imperial policy. Here was a new official making repeated requests for advice and counsel. Yet the board of trade never so much as replied to their lieutenant-governor, according to the known records, until the dispute was carried up to them from the burgesses. Then, as presently will be seen, they compromised — by upholding both the burgesses and Dinwiddie.[250] Dinwiddie's request for an advance ruling from the board would be comparable to a court's rendering advisory opinions. The board refused to perform what might seem to have been a natural duty. They preferred to wait until the matter came up before them "in due form" in the course of litigation.

Then came the happy beginnings of the session of the Virginia general assembly of november 1, 1753, with the mutual exchange between the governor and the burgesses of more than the usual felicitations. He had expressed to the house of burgesses "the just and distinguished character the legislature of Virginia bears with the king and his ministry at home." He even told them that he was "thoroughly convinced of your duty and attachment to his majesty's person and government." The members of that lower house, not to be outdone, in both chivalrous expressions and in tokens of loyalty to the crown, responded in kind. "With hearts full of duty and gratitude," they assured his honor the governor of "our inviolable fidelity and affection to his majesty's sacred person and government." [251]

But, as it turned out, all was not to be placid — either

---

250 The lords of trade to Dinwiddie, january 17, 1753, P.R.O., C.O., 5/1366, 6-7; L.C. tr., 4-5.

251 *Journals of the house of burgesses* (1752-1755; 1756-1758), 106; *Dinwiddie papers*, I, 43.

as regards external or internal affairs,[252] for on november 27 the unexpected happened. First the burgesses —
or enough of them to make a majority of the one hundred and four — in a preface to a carefully-worded
address, declaring themselves to be "his majesty's most
dutiful and loyal subjects," expressed surprise at finding
that an "extraordinary fee of a pistole, for signing every
patent for land, and the use of the seal, is demanded by
the clerks in the secretary's office, to countenance which
your honour's name is made use of." To this fee, thus
to be collected, the burgesses expressed strong opposition. In their first inquiry of the governor they kept
themselves in a very respectful frame of mind. They
did not demand anything. They desired only to know
whether the governor had condoned such a move, and
if so, on what authority he acted. They respectfully insisted that their inquiry was only "in discharge of the
trust reposed in us by our country."

The next move obviously was Dinwiddie's. The burgesses had asked a categorical question. He had to reply.
He did. In justification of his position he said: "The
welfare and happiness of Virginia I have very much at
heart, and this great point has been the chief object of
my attention ever since I had the honour to preside
over this dominion." Far from his being influenced in
seeking the fee because of any desire for pecuniary gain,
he stressed the fact that he had "been influenced by no
other motive, and my conduct upon all extraordinary
occasions has been regulated by the advice of the council."

There were two reasons, and only two, that were ever
advanced either by Dinwiddie or by the burgesses, as
to why the governor decided to take the fee. It was

[252] See preceding chapter for a discussion of these affairs.

purely and simply a difference in placing of emphasis. The governor put it on one thing, his opponents on another. He alleged his reason to be that he might protect his majesty's quit rents, now long in arrears on parcels of lands to the west. If this fee augmented his own income, that was incidental. The burgesses emphasized the latter reason exclusively, and by implication charged their governor with no other interest in them save the interest of private gain. Dinwiddie was at this time making rather heavy drains upon the royal treasury in asking for shipments of presents for the Indians, and for munitions for his "defensive" campaign on the Ohio against the French and the Indians. He naturally would feel that if he could augment the royal income in a legitimate way, it would make it the easier to secure from home the grants that he was now being forced to urge upon the crown with increasing frequency. The effect upon his own salary he discounted, though admitting that there would be some advantage to him. A "trifling fee," so far as his personal income went, he termed it, for he was constantly advancing from his own purse much more than "trifling" sums to protect his majesty's rights in the west.[253]

A seemingly trivial matter had now been injected into the sessions of the assembly that had begun so harmoniously. On november 28 Dinwiddie assured the burgesses that he would always "shew a just regard for the sentiments of the house of burgesses, in every thing that properly lyes before them." But that was precisely the point: which matters did lie before them and which did not? Dinwiddie reminded them that their own

---

[253] Dinwiddie to the treasury, december 29, 1753, P.R.O., treasury I, bundle 353, fo. 240; L.C. tr. In this same letter Dinwiddie declared that the petitions against the fee had come from only ". . . six inland counties (not on the frontier of this dominion) out of 48 counties," and "were supported in the house by some hot headed gentlemen."

upper house had unanimously advised him to take the fee complained of; that this authority, together with the rather plenary powers he had received from home, would justify his proceedings throughout. He tried to be conciliatory as he said to them: "I therefore hope you will think with me, that I have not acted in an arbitrary manner, but that I am properly invested with regular power and authority, in demanding the small fee so much complained of."

Notice the gathering clouds, as the burgesses were ready the same day with their reply: "We his majesty's most dutiful and loyal subjects . . . are under the deepest concern, to find by your honour's answer to our address, that the demand of a pistole, as a fee for the use of the public seal, is made by your direction; and that we are under a necessity of making application again to your honour on that occasion."

That was only the crouch before the spring – the language that with gathering frequency and in similar tenor would be heard again and again in the next two decades – for they struck boldly, as they declared:

"We do humbly, but in the strongest terms, represent to your honour, that *it is the undoubted right of the burgesses to enquire into the grievances of the people:* they have constantly exercised this right, and we presume to affirm, that the drawing it into question, in any manner, cannot but be of dangerous consequence to the liberties of his majesty's faithful subjects, and to the constitution of this government.

"The rights of the subject are so secured by law, that they cannot be deprived of the least part of their property, but by their own consent: upon this excellent principle is our constitution founded, and ever since this colony has had the happiness of being under the immediate protection of the crown, the royal declarations

have been, 'that no man's life, member, freehold, or goods, be taken away or harmed, but by established and known laws.'

"But the demand of a pistole, as a fee for the use of the public seal, being not warranted by any known and established law, is, we humbly conceive, an infringement of the rights of the people, and a grievance highly to be complained of." [254]

If bad thus began for Dinwiddie, worse remained — for the burgesses had by no means rested their case. They continued, as they quoted history and precedents: "And that we may vindicate the legality and dutiful manner of our proceedings, we beg leave to acquaint your honour, that upon the first plantation of this colony, under the government of the treasurer and company of adventurers, it was by them ordained, that fifty acres of land, should be granted for every person imported into this colony, without any other fee or consideration than the annual rent of one shilling . . . Lord Howard of Effingham, then governor, *demanded a fee for the use of the seal;* which, upon the representation of the burgesses of Virginia, was . . . declared to be uneasy and burthensome to the colony, and ordered to be discontinued, since which no fee has been demanded from the subjects for affixing the seal to patents for lands, but those given to the secretary by the established laws of this colony."

This admission by the burgesses shows that fees were regularly demanded and regularly paid, as an ordinary procedure. Their contention was that in Dinwiddie's case it was an extraordinary procedure. He did not think so.

The burgesses concluded their argument by solemnly affirming: "These being the terms and conditions upon

---

[254] Present author's italics.

which his majesty, and his royal predecessors have been graciously pleased to grant their lands to the inhabitants of this colony, we humbly conceive they cannot be altered by the advice of the council; and as your honour's insisting on the same, will, in our humble opinion, be an infringement of the rights of the people, a great discouragement to the settling the frontiers of this colony, and a prejudice to his majesty's revenue of quitrents, we think it our indispensable duty to desire that your honour will recede from your demand."

The atmosphere became more tense still as Dinwiddie attempted a few days later, december 4, 1753, to justify his conduct. He answered the burgesses:

"I am not unacquainted with the just privileges of the house of burgesses; in the enjoyment of them, they shall always have my protection. My duty to the king, and my regard for liberty has, and will, on every occasion, influence my conduct.

"As I will never injure the one, I cannot suffer any encroachments on the rights of the other."

Diplomatically the governor stated a vital principle as he continued: "The complaints of the people should be heard, and every just grievance redressed, but their complaints should be well grounded, and the grievances really felt." He proceeded next to draw a distinction, reasonable enough to him and the council, but to the burgesses a distinction without a difference, when he said: "The establishment of the fee complained of, relates solely to the disposal of the king's land, and which, it is conceived, may be deemed a matter of favour from the crown, and not a matter relative to the administration of government; and the fixing thereof was with so much circumspection, that it is my care and concern for the improvement of his majesty's revenue of quit-rents, that prompts me to be more earnest in adhering to my

former opinion, and insisting on that fee, which is confirmed to me by unquestionable authority."

By the nineteenth of december the governor had concluded it was time to bring what he regarded as a fruit-
less session to a close. He had really hoped, he later
admitted, for an order from home directing him to dissolve the assembly, which would have been a far greater
rebuke to them than a mere proroguing from him, but
it did not arrive by the nineteenth. Hence, in language
that is reminiscent of Cromwell when he put an end to
the Rump parliament, Dinwiddie thus addressed the
legislature: "The season of the year being far advanced,
and the business of the assembly concluded, it is necessary to put an end to this session." But before he said,
in effect, "and it is at an end," he administered a brief
lecture as follows: "That zeal for his majesty's service,
that disinterested love of your country, for which you
have been distinguished upon former occasions, has now
in some particulars, not been sufficiently attended to.
The friendship of the Indians is a national concern" —
striking language indeed — "the interest of Great-Britain, the welfare of all his majesty's colonies on this continent, and your own peace and safety are engaged upon
the event of the present measures." And Dinwiddie undoubtedly believed what he said. To him Britain and
the colonies never faced a graver emergency. For a man
of his loyalty to the crown and to imperial expansion,
it was unthinkable that men like the burgesses should
create such a tempest about a "trifling fee" of a pistole.

The assembly the governor had thus addressed contained also his council which had to a man supported
him; therefore, he with propriety did not say more. But
when he the same day addressed the burgesses alone, he
indeed lectured them. He advised them to go back to
their homes and, during the recess, to "cultivate piety

and morality." He reminded them that they had been asked for a proper grant of money in the emergency, that they should have preserved "the friendship of the Indians," and they should have consulted the "real prosperity of your country." These, said he, ". . . should have been the fixed object of your attention."

That was his language before the burgesses, which he himself admitted to Governor Hamilton of Pennsylvania showed some "marks of anger." He closed abruptly with: "I have thought fit to prorogue this assembly to the last thursday in april next, and you are accordingly prorogued." All this is an excellent illustration of the old adage that "man proposes but God disposes"; for little did Dinwiddie dream, when he prorogued that recalcitrant house of burgesses on december 19, 1753, that events were so closely in the offing that would force his hand and thus oblige him to bring those same burgesses before him as early as february 14.

But on february 14, 1754, Dinwiddie met the combined houses again called together because of a "very great concern." He hastened to urge their counsel and aid on what he considered a matter of first magnitude. Never did Robert Dinwiddie's qualities of statesmanship assert themselves more clearly than on that momentous february 14. For the sake of the crown, the colonies in general, and Virginia in particular, he rose above his personal inclinations and called the burgesses back, in order, as he expressed it, "to have your advice and assistance." [255] They responded to his entreaty. They appropriated ten thousand pounds, for which, though it was only half the amount he hoped to get, he was grateful.

The only regrettable feature about the appropriation

---

[255] *Journals of the house of burgesses* (1752-1755; 1756-1758), 175; Dinwiddie's speech, february 14, 1754, Draper manuscripts, 1JJ17-1JJ20; *Dinwiddie papers*, I, 73.

of ten thousand pounds was the fact that the burgesses
even in their day knew about and made use of the modern device of a "rider," which they attached to an otherwise satisfactory bill. That rider would authorize their
own expenditure of two thousand five hundred pounds,
more than the annual appropriation for governor. They
had pleaded poverty and economy, yet were here setting
aside two thousand five hundred pounds for principle's
sake – to send their own agent, Attorney-general Peyton
Randolph, to England to plead their cause against the
pistole fee.

Dinwiddie unburdened himself to his close friends
like the Earl of Halifax and John Hanbury at once,
and also in his more formal letter to the lords of trade.[256]
His acid comments on the fee continued through the
spring, summer, and into the fall. One notable series of
letters, largely concerned with the obnoxious rider, he
wrote between september 5 and 23 : to Governor Horatio
Sharpe [257] of Maryland, James Hamilton [258] of Pennsylvania, James DeLancey [259] of New York, Lord Fairfax,[260] James Innes,[261] Secretary of State Robinson,[262]

256 Dinwiddie to the lords of trade, march 12, 1754, P.R.O., C.O., 5/1328,
193-196; L.C. tr., 155-158; Dinwiddie papers, I, 98-104.

257 Dinwiddie to Sharpe, september 5, 1754, Maryland archives, VI, 95-98.
See also Dinwiddie papers, I, 303-306.

258 Dinwiddie to Hamilton, september 6, 1754, Pennsylvania colonial records, VI, 163-165; Dinwiddie papers, I, 306-309.

259 Dinwiddie to DeLancey [September, 1754], ibid., I, 309-311. James De-
Lancey (1703-1760), member of the council, chief justice and lieutenant-governor of New York, 1753-1755 and 1757-1760, a son of the Huguenot emi-
grant, Stephen DeLancey, was born in New York City. He was graduated
from Cambridge university, and while in England studied law. He returned
to America in 1729 and rose steadily in the provincial government of New
York. He is also remembered for having presided over the Albany congress
of 1754 and for having been one of the founders of King's college, now
Columbia university.

260 Dinwiddie to Fairfax, september 10 [1754], Dinwiddie papers, I, 312-
313.

261 Dinwiddie to Innes, september 11 [1754], ibid., I, 314-315.

262 Dinwiddie to Robinson, september 23, 1754, P.R.O., C.O., 5/14, 515-518;

George Washington,[263] Andrew Lewis,[264] the board of trade,[265] Earl Granville,[266] Lord Halifax,[267] and of course to James Abercromby,[268] his trusted representative in England.

To the Earl of Halifax he had said in his letter of march 12, 1754: "I am in pain to know the result of our house of burgesses' address to his majesty in regard

L.C. tr., 475-483; *Dinwiddie papers*, I, 322-327. Thomas Robinson (1695-1770), English diplomat who entered the service shortly after leaving Cambridge. He is universally referred to as Sir Thomas Robinson; but he is not to be confused with his contemporary of the same name who was at one time governor of the island of Barbadoes. According to George Washington's diary of 1751-1752, the Sir Thomas Robinson of Barbadoes was none too popular as an administrator during his term of office, 1742-1747 (John C. Fitzpatrick, ed., *Diaries of George Washington, 1748-1799*, I, 27). He was England's representative at the Austrian court, 1730-1748, and plenipotentiary at Aix-la-Chapelle, 1748. A man with wide contacts, years of diplomatic experience, and a knowledge of business, he was well qualified to deal with colonial matters. He was one of the lords of trade, 1748-1749, a member of the privy council in 1750. He was secretary of state for the southern department, march 1754 to november 1755; succeeded by Henry Fox. Robinson was created Baron Grantham in 1761.

[263] Dinwiddie to Washington, september 11, 1754, S. M. Hamilton, ed., *Letters to Washington*, I, 42-45; *Dinwiddie papers*, I, 315-317.

[264] Dinwiddie to Lewis, september 11 [1754], *ibid.*, I, 317-318. Andrew Lewis (1720-1781), frontiersman, fort builder, soldier, seems to have been born in Ulster, Ireland. His parents, John and Margaret (Lynn) Lewis, were probably of Scotch-irish-huguenot stock and he accompanied them to Virginia in the early 1730's. They settled close to what became Staunton. The Lewis family became leaders in the valley of Virginia, and particularly in Augusta county. He attained a captaincy in the Virginia regiment, march 18, 1754. Though he was with Washington at Fort Necessity, with the Braddock forces, and with Forbes, probably his most important service during the French and Indian war, when he held the rank of major, was his cooperation, under George Washington's direction, with Captain Peter Hog in building a cordon of forts along the frontier in 1756. His least successful drive against the Indians was the ill-fated Sandy creek expedition in 1756; his most successful, the battle of Point Pleasant in 1774. He rose in the Revolution to the rank of brigadier-general. He had four brothers, Samuel, Charles, Thomas, and William.

[265] Dinwiddie to the lords of trade, september 23, 1754, P.R.O., C.O., 5/1328, 255-258; L.C. tr., 195-202; *Dinwiddie papers*, I, 327-330.

[266] Dinwiddie to Granville, september 23 [1754], *ibid.*, I, 331-332.

[267] Dinwiddie to Halifax, september 23 [1754], *ibid.*, I, 334-335.

[268] Dinwiddie to Abercromby, september 23 [1754], *ibid.*, I, 339-343.

to the pistole tax, and their extraordinary resolves thereon." And then he added a most interesting commentary: "I am sorry to find them very much in a republican way of thinking, and indeed they do not act in a proper constitutional way, but making encroachments on the prerogative of the crown, which some former governor submitted too much to them" – the age-old conflict of prerogative versus prerogative, the same type of fight that Dinwiddie had had with the Virginia council exactly a decade before.

Dinwiddie felt he was in the right, yet he could not be positive that the case might not go against him. Hence he hastened on april 26 to acknowledge James Abercromby's reassuring letters of january 29, february 18, and 23. He said to Abercromby: "I find that you have gone throw the offices, and that my friends think my case is entirely in my favour, which gives me some satisfaction, but shall remain uneasy till its finally ended." He added frankly: ". . . and I must confess to you, if I had [known] that this affair would have created so much uneasiness to me, and trouble to my friends at home, I would not have taken that fee."

The gossip of the English coffee houses often determined a man's political future. The governor therefore wrote his agent: "I am sorry the affair makes so much noise in coffee houses, etc.; that must be owing to the unjust advertisement [of] the attorney-general's that was in the news paper, for the fee, if established, never would prevent the 50 acres to servants, which will always be granted without that fee, but I know [of] no application on that head since my arrival; for if they did apply, it would be to lands far back, that are not worth taking up in such small quantities, but you know every trifling thing occasions coffee house arguments and disputations. I am easy, as I think I am right, and properly authorized to take that fee." He added with accustomed candor: "I can honestly say, that the fee, when established, was as much to support his majesty's quit-rents as self interest, for it's [a] trifling income."

At this point the figure of that important ubiquitous personage, the attorney-general, re-enters the drama. In the lengthy and informative letter to Abercromby, dated april 26, 1754, the agent had been advised that if he would turn to the current "journals, page 85," he would "find a resolve of an extraordinary nature." The governor explained that the reference was to Peyton Randolph, whom the burgesses proposed to send to London as their own agent "to negotiate the affairs of this colony," at more than ten times what his own agent, Abercromby, received. These resolutions provided that Treasurer John Robinson,[269] who was also speaker, was to pay out this sum from "his majesty's revenue . . . without the concurrence of the other branches of the legislative." He added: "Is not this a notorious encroachment on the prerogatives of the crown, and imediately contrary to my instructions? . . . pray point out this resolve to my council [counsel retained in London by the governor] that they may speak to it and obtain a proper repremand for this insolence." He then inserted a sentence to let Abercromby know that his own

---

[269] John Robinson (1704-1766), son of Councillor John Robinson, became a burgess in 1738, and presently holder of the combined offices of speaker of the house of burgesses and treasurer of the colony. He held office from 1738 to 1766. Dinwiddie opposed combining the holder of the two offices of speaker and treasurer in one person, and made a recommendation to this effect to his successor, Francis Fauquier, and to the board of trade. On Robinson's death, Peyton Randolph became speaker, and Robert Carter Nicholas, treasurer. Robinson was a close friend of George Washington. As Professor T. P. Abernethy points out in his able sketch in the *Dictionary of American biography,* Robinson's own accounts, at his death, were found to be short by some £100,000, though he may not have been guilty of deliberate public fraud. Ironically, Robinson must have been one of the leaders in the house who insisted, in 1753, upon supervising Dinwiddie's handling of public money.

position as agent was jeopardized: "He [Peyton Randolph] has further orders from that wise body to choose an agent at home, who they engage to pay [£]200 per annum out of his majesty's treasury." Dinwiddie declared he hoped all those things would lead to "an order to me" to show them the necessity of acting in a more "constitutional manner."

The impasse had reached the point where the burgesses were seeking direct channels with the king: "I hear our house of burgesses have lately addressed his majesty on their supply of [£]10,000 for the Ohio expedition, a mere trifle considering the service intended." Then followed a cryptic sentence: "A ship from London brings some news that elates the minds of many of my oponents." Everyone was writing in conundrums. Note the plea to Abercromby: "I wish you would write me frequently. You may believe I am uneasy to hear the progress of the affair; they relate a story I do not believe true, therefore, will not mention it to you."

In London in the *Gentleman's magazine* were appearing dispatches from Virginia that obviously were being prepared by a correspondent who was not favorable to the governor. One such, dated Virginia, december 8, reads: "The governor having demanded a tax of a pistole on each patent for land (some thousands of which are now lying in the land office) the assembly addressed him to know by what authority he made such demand, and his answer was, that it was pursuant to his instructions, and by the advice of his council. In a second address they endeavoured to convince him that by their charters no tax could be imposed on them without their own consent; being as free as the people of England: the governor's answer was so little satisfactory, that they voted the demand illegal, arbitrary, and oppressive, and that whoever paid it should be deemed an enemy to their country, and subject to the censure of the house; and an agent will be sent to England to solicit the suppression of it." [270]

To Capel Hanbury [271] the governor wrote on may 10, 1754, and paid his respects to what he denominated "that silly fee of a pistole." He told Hanbury that someone, he presumed Attorney-general Peyton Randolph, had had inserted in the public papers "many reflections and unjust insinuations" against him, saying, for example, that he as governor had laid a "tax" on the people for patents. That had been astute political strategy on Randolph's part, since anyone who opposed a "tax" of any kind could always be sure of a following. Hence, said Dinwiddie: "Surely every thinking man will make a distinction between a fee and a tax."

Farther on in his same letter he reassured both himself and Hanbury that Virginia's land laws have been the most generous of all the colonies: "Where could they [settlers] go to take up land on so easy terms? They come from Pensylvania, where they are in want of land, and quit-rents 4s sterling per 100 acres; if they go to North Carolina, they must pay 3s sterling per 100, and the fees d[ou]ble, so that the whole incerted in your papers are false reflections." The people were always "very easy and well satisfied till an evil spirit entered into a high priest" [Reverend William Stith], [272] who

---

[270] *Gentleman's magazine*, XXIV (December 8, 1754), 94.

[271] Capel Hanbury, London merchant, was a brother of John Hanbury, and for a time in partnership with him (See note 25 on John Hanbury).

[272] William Stith (1707-1755), episcopal clergyman, historian, third president of the College of William and Mary, was born in Virginia, and attended first the College of William and Mary and then Oxford university. His family connections explain much not otherwise clear about his career. His mother, and likewise his wife, was a Randolph. Thus, his mother, Mary, was the daughter of William Randolph of Turkey island; she married John Stith. Their son William Stith married, in 1738, his cousin, Judith, daughter of Thomas Randolph of Tuckahoe. His brother-in-law was William Dawson, D.D., second president of the college and commissary to the bishop of London.

was supported by the powerful Randolph family.

To James Abercromby Dinwiddie disclosed in a letter on may 10 that he had now learned the burgesses had taken another extraordinary step, namely, to set up a committee to supervise the spending of the ten thousand pounds just voted for western defense. The burgesses thought to undermine a measure of Dinwiddie's support, it would seem, by having named to this committee some members of the council; however, that action according to Dinwiddie was "contrary to their consent or approbation." But here Dinwiddie displayed a statesmanship that rises above the politician and mere opportunist. It was an unpalatable dose to have to submit direction of finances to a committee that "takes from me the undoubted right I have of directing the application of the money raised for the defence of the dominion." He explained however, that due to "the emergency of this present affair" in the west, he had given way and agreed to the innovation; and he hoped the circumstances would excuse his receding from his posi-

---

At William Dawson's death in 1752, Stith was elected president of the college (but lived only three years); while Thomas Dawson was selected as the commissary. Stith, however, never became either a member of the governor's council or commissary to the bishop of London (yet acceptably serving local churches in Virginia), though his two predecessors as college presidents, James Blair and William Dawson, had each occupied all three offices. Governor Gooch had recommended William Dawson, even before John Blair's death, to be the latter's successor as commissary; but Dinwiddie never thus recommended Stith—so far as is known. At any rate, when in 1753 Stith threw in his lot with Dinwiddie's opponents in the pistole fee controversy, he apparently broke completely with the governor. From Dinwiddie's strong language in his letter to Abercromby, he apparently held Stith chiefly responsible for certain popular opposition to his policies. Stith's successor in the college presidency was Reverend Thomas Dawson, commissary.

Striking corroborative evidence of these personal antagonisms is to be found in three letters, one from Thomas Dawson and two from Stith, to the lord bishop of London, between september 1, 1752 and april 21, 1753; they have recently been found in the Library of Congress by Herbert L. Ganter and published by Dr. Earl G. Swem in the *William and Mary college quarterly historical magazine,* 2nd series, xx (July 1940), 391-396.

tion. Then he sagely observed, "but necessity has no law."

He wrote the lords of trade the same day, carefully explaining the entire colonial defense situation and how the house had "clogged," as he put it, an otherwise good bill. When he had learned the purpose of that committee, he had at first determined to dissolve the assembly himself, he told the lords; but he had finally concluded to withhold that action "in hopes of an order to dissolve them by proclamation." That would be more effective than his own action as it would show "much more resentment to their actions."[273]

Among the many matters discussed in the may 10 letter, he told Abercromby he hoped it would not be necessary to refer thereafter to the pistole fee. By june 18, however, he was at it again.

On that date he wrote a letter to the Earl of Albemarle,[274] and another letter to Abercromby. He commended Abercromby for the steps he had taken in regard to it, and thought that since "it is in a proper channel," meaning before the king, he could remain "mighty easy on that head." Still, farther on in the letter he urged Abercromby: "I shall desire you to write me fully of the pistole affair." Abercromby was a better lawyer than penman, hence this admonition: "Write more plain, for really some of your letters I cannot well read." [275]

---

[273] Dinwiddie to the lords of trade, may 10, 1754, P.R.O., C.O., 5/1328, 211-214; L.C. tr., 167-172; *Dinwiddie papers*, I, 161.

[274] According to this letter, Dinwiddie had learned that the titular governor, the Earl of Albemarle, favored Dinwiddie's stand on the dispute. Dinwiddie to Albemarle, june 18, 1754, *ibid.*, I, 208.

[275] Dinwiddie to Abercromby, june 18, 1754, *ibid.*, I, 210-211. Dinwiddie was nothing if not frank. On june 6 he assured Abercromby that no other agent would supplant him "while I preside." Scrupulous about promptly answering his own correspondence, he took his agent to task, by continuing, frankly: "You should have wrote to Colonel Corbin about the act to cut off the intail of some lands which he wrote you to negotiate. He is uneasy not to have

The final decision in Dinwiddie's favor was so long delayed that one finds him, as was noted above, writing a long series of letters during september, burdened in considerable measure with vexations growing out of the controversy. To Abercromby he wrote on september 1, 1754 that the august 22 meeting of the assembly had "met with good dispositions to support [the] present expedition, and on thursday, the 29th, they voted [£]20,000, to be raised by a poll tax at two different payments, 2s. to be immediately collected, and 3s. to be raised next july." When the burgesses voted even a poll tax, it was beginning to look as though the pistole fee was about to be forgotten. Uncertain fate was always just around the corner, for the governor was obliged to add: ". . . but yesterday being the 31st of august, a litigous spirit prevailed in the house of burgesses. They have tacked to the above bill, by way of rider, a resolve they entered into the assembly in november last of paying Mr. Randolph [£]2500 for negotiating their affairs in Great Britain." It had not yet come before the Virginia council, he informed Abercromby; and he began to fear even that some of its twelve members might weaken, the pressure being so great: ". . . I fear some of that board are not so consistent as I could wish." Even if they themselves were to approve the bill with its obnoxious rider, which Dinwiddie did not expect them to do, he had, nevertheless, resolved not to sign it. Fortunately for the governor, in the end the council did not yield but unanimously supported his stand.[276]

heard from you . . . You should also have wrote a letter of thanks to the council for the augmentation of your salary. You know people in this part of the world expect returns for favours, and a proper letter is soon wrote."

276 Dinwiddie to Abercromby, september 1, 1754, *ibid.,* I, 298-301. Dinwiddie reminded Abercromby of the burgesses' "Address to his majesty" (Burgesses of Virginia to the king, P.R.O., C.O., 5/1344; L.C. tr., 169-171), and quoted that portion where the lower house stressed "the great poverty of the colony, and the low condition of the public revenue, occasioned by the bad state of

On september 23, 1754, the governor wrote Abercromby that what he had feared and suspected, that the house would attach a rider to the twenty thousand pound bill in order to have Peyton Randolph paid, had actually occurred, but that the council to a man had opposed it. He told Abercromby that if he would take the journal of the house of burgesses and read it through he would understand the reasons why he (Dinwiddie) expected, nevertheless, a reasonable supply to be granted by the house to carry on his expedition. He said: ". . . I thought I had influence enough with them to succeed, but I observe a general infatuation in all the assemblies on this continent" – a significant remark, more crowded with meaning than Dinwiddie could then know, for the year 1775 was but two decades in the future. He went on: ". . . they are seized with a lethargick supineness, not regarding their own safety or the encroachments of the French, they are now left to perpetuate their malicious designs, and I dread [for] our poor frontier settlers this winter; with the few men I have, I am doing all in my power for their protection."

His personal expenditure showed what he himself had advanced. He reported: "I have already paid £1040. 5.3., and a further charge of upwards of [£]300 very soon. I have wrote to the secretary of war, praying for orders to draw for my reimbursement; pray wait on him and know his resolution thereon; for it is hard after my great fatigue, I should lay out of my money, and [I] doubt not he will see the justice of my demand." [277]

By the close of 1754 Dinwiddie knew that the long dispute had finally been decided in his favor. The ac-

our tobacco trade, and a large debt due," ever since 1746 from the expedition against Canada, as well as their "present indigent circumstances."

[277] Dinwiddie to Abercromby, september 23, 1754, *Dinwiddie papers*, I, 339-342.

count of the whole controversy is recapitulated in the acts of the privy council.[278] There is (a) the original petition presented by Dinwiddie; (b) the supporting address of the council of Virginia; (c) the opposing address of the house of burgesses; (d) the order prepared to be issued rejecting the address of the house of burgesses; and (e) a representation from the house of burgesses praying to be justified in having appointed Peyton Randolph to solicit his majesty against the pistole fee for the charge of two thousand five hundred pounds.

By october 25, 1754 the governor could write three optimistic letters to three important correspondents regarding the pistole fee decision. To the lords of trade he stated he was gratified that the decision was in his favor but he was obliged to point out that on some of the most controversial points "your lordships are silent," therefore, he told them he would "defer granting the patents till I have your determination thereon." [279] To Horace Walpole he was "much obliged for the approbation you are pleased to give on my transactions in regard to his majesty's revenue of quit rents." [280] But the most revealing letter is that to his friend, James Abercromby, to whom he wrote that he was "very glad the pistole fee is finished" and that he was "much obliged for the great care you took in that affair." The lords of trade themselves were culpable, their instructions about the fee being too indefinite to be easily apprehended. Dinwiddie, loyal as ever, merely wrote Abercromby that he felt the lords of trade had not been explicit enough, "for

[278] W. L. Grant, James Munro, and Sir Almeric W. Fitzroy, eds., *Acts of the privy council of England, colonial series* (Hereford, 1908- —), IV, 232-235 (hereafter cited as *Acts of the privy council*).

[279] Dinwiddie to the lords of trade, october 25, 1754, P.R.O., C.O., 5/1338, 283-286; L.C. tr., 221-227; *Dinwiddie papers*, I, 363.

[280] Dinwiddie to Walpole, october 25, 1754, *ibid.*, I, 370.

my conduct therein for the future." In the first place, contended Dinwiddie, they forbade the taking a fee for less than one hundred acres, whereas they had had no demand for land under that head for fifty years; secondly, he explained, the board directed that no fee be taken for lands to the "westward of the mountains," with a carelessness about geography that was all too common in the dispatches from the home government, whereas, said Dinwiddie, there are three distinct ranges of mountains and it is impossible to know which of the three the lords had in mind; and finally, the board forbade Dinwiddie to exact any fee for lands taken up prior to april 22, 1752, the date the council of Virginia legalized Dinwiddie's pistole fee procedure. They did not, however, state whether persons who had taken up lands prior to april 22, 1752 were to pay their arrears of quit rents or not. "On this head," declared Dinwiddie, "their lordships are entirely silent, and I am determined, not to seal or sign the patents till I have directions thereon. . . I am much surprized at the board of trade's taciturnity." Then he added: "The appearances on this fee's being established, may appear to some to be venal and lucrative, no doubt. I thought of the perquisite arising, but am perswaded if established some years agone, it would have been a great increase of quit rent revenue, and when on arrival, I found upwards of 900,000 acres not brought to the quit rent rolls, as steward to that revenue, I, in justice to his majesty's revenue, I must stand approved in the steps I took." [281]

"True friendship is the plant of slow growth," George Washington once wrote quaintly but truly in a letter of counsel to his favorite nephew, then a college student in Philadelphia. The old governor, like many another before and after him, would have occasion during his

[281] Dinwiddie to Abercromby, october 23, 1754, *ibid.*, I, 373-374.

governorship to reflect upon the inconstancy of acquaintanceships sometimes mistaken for friendships. Reflecting upon Dinwiddie's arrival as governor, one reads now with special interest what John Blair recorded in his diary back in 1751: "November 22: the governor went back to York yesterday, and returned this evening with his lady and daughters to the attorney's." [282] The attorney in question, who was playing the rôle of host at that time was Peyton Randolph, attorney-general of the colony since 1748. In the interim between Dinwiddie's arrival and the date he could occupy the governor's palace, then undergoing repair, they probably renewed an old acquaintanceship, if not a friendship, dating from the governor's earlier stay in America. On that november day in 1751 little did either man realize, particularly the guest, that it would be barely four years later that the man now his host would become his political thorn in the flesh; that he would be authorized to go to England to plead for the burgesses their pistole fee case against him; and that he would be the instrument of those burgesses who sought to have him rebuked.

A situation with a touch of humor in it, yet a situation that is a test of Dinwiddie's caliber and character is seen in a letter penned about this time. Reference is to Randolph who had failed in his mission against the governor; worse, he was about to lose even his own pay for attempting it; and, worse still, his very position as attorney-general of the colony. The governor rose above any animus he might have felt; to Abercromby, who from London was interceding with him for Randolph, he wrote in the following vein: "I observe what you write of the attorney, as to reinstating him to his office. You must think that some what absurd, from the bad

282 John Blair's manuscript diary, *op. cit.* (Virginia historical society).

treatment I have met with, however, if he answers properly what I have to say to him, I am not inflexible, and he must confess, before this happened, he had [a] greater share of my favour and countenance than any other in the government. My determination on that head must remain till his arrival."

To Dinwiddie's everlasting credit, he did reinstate Randolph. His letter continued: "As to the speaker [John Robinson], he has behaved with great warmth, and ill manners, therefore, what you propose must be suspended for some time. I always was of opinion, that [the combined offices of] speaker of the house, and treasurer were inconsistent, but so I found it, and [it] has been so for many years, and I dreaded to make any innovations on my first arrival, but am determined on calling a new assembly to regulate it for the future in a more constitutional method."

As late as february 24, 1755 echoes of the pistole controversy were being heard, though they grew fainter and fainter. Evidently some persons in London still felt that the Virginia legislature would have voted greater appropriations for the current war chest but for the pistole affair. Dinwiddie denied this alleged condition when he wrote to Abercromby, february 24, 1755. By way of interjection, his letter is a commentary on eighteenth-century delays in correspondence. He said: "I received your letters 29th november and 16th december by General Braddock, who came to my house last night, and the Gibraltar, by which ship I wrote you, being to sail to morrow, straitens me in time." Then he continued: "I am much surprized the pistole fee should still remain in remembrance and [that it is] thought [to be] that [which] prevents our assembly giving assistance to the present expedition." Dinwiddie threw the responsibility back upon the board of trade, where it really belonged, for he went on: ". . . if it had not been in support of the lords of trade approbation thereof, that affair should have been quashed here." [283]

That the pistole fee matter had not been too seriously interfering with the governor's attempts to wring appropriations from the burgesses to retrieve Braddock's loss,[284] is apparent from a sentence in the long letter, july 23, 1755,[285] to Abercromby which reads: "The enclosed news paper will shew you all I could bring them to, which indeed is much more than the neighboring colonies; Maryland and Pensylvania continue obstinate and refractory." [286] Where arose the false impression that the pistole fee paralyzed Virginia's efforts on the frontier except for a brief period, and made it impossible for Dinwiddie to work with his lower house even to the point that he finally was recalled?

The merits of the pistole fee dispute, like other episodes in history, depend upon the factors of time and circumstance: as of the month in which the pistole fee storm broke, Dinwiddie was too unpopular to secure any vote of supplies at all from his recalcitrant burgesses. As of a year later, he was able to report that they had voted ten thousand pounds for the campaign, at his request; by november 1754 twenty thousand pounds more. As of july 1755, another year later, he was able to declare the Virginians had done "much more than the neighboring colonies." [287] And by june 14, 1757 he was in a position triumphantly to write Governor Sharpe: "Our assembly was prorogued last wednesday.

---

283 Dinwiddie to Abercromby, february 24, 1755, *Dinwiddie papers,* I, 511-512.

284 The house was reluctant to grant their money to be used (or, misused) by British imperial officers who were wont to override colonial opinion.

285 Dinwiddie to Abercromby, july 23, 1755, *Dinwiddie papers,* II, 115.

286 The Pennsylvania and Maryland views are discussed in the chapter, "Appeals to fellow governors," and elsewhere.

287 Dinwiddie to Abercromby, july 23, 1755, *Dinwiddie papers,* II, 115.

With great application and interest they have generously granted every thing I desired; – in my speech on
opening the session they have voted an augmentation of
our regiment to 1200 men, and three companies of rangers of 100 men each and £80,000 for their subsistence
etc. they have laid taxes for that service 2/ on each hogshead of tobacco, 2/ on each 100 acres of land, and 4/
poll tax which is thought will be sufficient." Evidently
also there was now no objection to such items as fees
and taxes. The crux of the impasse had been that the
burgesses intended to maintain what they claimed was
a constitutional right to determine when such taxes and
fees should be laid, how much they should be, and who
should authorize them. Especially, was this true, of
course, after they had set up a finance committee to
supervise them.

Dinwiddie continued his optimistic report to Maryland's Governor Sharpe: ". . . these taxes are to continue for five years; and they further voted £3000 for
maintaining and giving presents to Indians that may
come to our assistance." One governor, as his majesty's
appointee, always tried to console or encourage another,
hence Dinwiddie, who now was even able to point to
the burgesses as a body to be emulated, added: "I hope
this will raise a spirit in your people to follow so necessary and useful an example." [288]

The pistole fee ghost seemed at last to have been
buried. Dinwiddie wrote to Lord Walpole on november
9, 1756: "The lords for trade ordered me to sign all
the old patents without fee, or any demand of arears
of quit-rents, saying the people had an equitable right
to their patents, and I conceived his majesty had the
same equitable right to his arears of quit-rents; however,

[288] Dinwiddie to Sharpe, june 14, 1757, *Maryland archives,* IX, 25; *Dinwiddie papers,* II, 639.

in obedience to their orders, I've signed all the old patents, and I think next year they'll be brought to rent-roll and greatly advance that revenue." [289]

To summarize: before the pistole dispute had been settled it had involved a solemn protest and petition, the tacking of a rider on a bill, the imposition of a finance committee reminiscent of house of commons tactics, the selection of an additional colonial agent, and a personal appeal to the crown. Of course, the burgesses knew their history; and as a colonial lower house they regarded themselves as the New World counterpart of the British lower house.

The payment of the paltry sum of three dollars fifty cents, little more than a notary fee today, in return for many broad acres of whole townsites, was opposed by the burgesses – rather, by a majority of them; certainly not by all of them – on "principle." It was the opposition members, then, who spoke of the fee as an "oppressive tax." And as proof that the lower house used the phrase "oppressive tax" as the ostensible reason only, it voted more money in sending Peyton Randolph to England to resist Dinwiddie than the entire amount from the pistole fee would have meant to the governor.

Without conceding that any conflict is necessarily "irrepressible," still, in the light of after-events, here is one of the nearest approaches to such a conflict.

On both sides there was unquestioned loyalty to an ideal; on both sides were men of honor and of devotion to country. The motives of neither can be impugned. Each deserves his meed of praise for standing for his own conception of right. History must be the judge.

Thus ends the story of the ramifications of this land-question episode. It is a story full of charges and coun-ter-charges; of insinuations as to speculation and pecu-

---

289 Dinwiddie to Walpole, november 9, 1756, *ibid.*, II, 542.

lation. Dinwiddie could have died a very wealthy man had he really sought financial gain. He has been criticised, but there is no direct evidence of wrong-doing. A better case can be made out for him than against him. Throughout this long-drawn-out case one is time and again reminded of Warren Hastings's classic utterance when, standing before his accusers, he was charged with enriching himself in India at the expense of the government. The harassed old Virginia governor could have voiced Hastings's own words: "When I consider what were my opportunities, I marvel at my moderation."

"Repell Force by Force"

Following the affair of the pistole fee, relations between Dinwiddie and his house of burgesses were for the moment decidedly cool if not actually strained. He had prorogued them on december 19 "with some marks of anger," as he later confided to Governor Hamilton, and if left to his own inclinations would probably have preferred never to call the same personnel together again.[290]

But things were happening which were beyond his control. In the west the French were taking matters into their own hands, and when George Washington rode into Williamsburg on january 16, 1754 with the news that they were preparing to come down the Ohio river in the spring, with their own forces augmented by Indians, to take over the Ohio country for themselves, Dinwiddie was appalled by the consequences that faced him.[291]

Without the necessary power – which the French leaders had – to command troops and money from his dominion, Dinwiddie was at once forced to the unpleasant task of calling together his house of burgesses. This he did, setting the date for february 14, 1754,[292] hoping,

---

[290] Dinwiddie to Hamilton, march 21, 1754, *Pennsylvania colonial records,* VI, 7-9; *Dinwiddie papers,* I, 118.

[291] Washington's return, february 14, 1754, Draper manuscripts, 1JJ12-1JJ13; John C. Fitzpatrick, ed., *Diaries of George Washington, 1748-1799,* I, 67; Minister to Duquesne, may 15, 1752, Arch. Nat., Col., series F3, 14:30-32vo.; L.C. tr.

[292] *Journals of the house of burgesses* (1752-1755; 1756-1758), 175-177. When Dinwiddie had prorogued the assembly he had set the date for reassembling as the last thursday in april but the serious events on the Ohio forced a change in plans. As Dinwiddie stated to the assembly, february 14,

meanwhile, as he wrote to Lord Fairfax, that "they come in good temper, and see the absolute necessity of making a push at this time, that they will lay a fund to qualify me to send 4 or 500 men more to the Ohio, which with the assistance of our neighbouring colonies and our friendly Indians may make some figure and defeat the designs of the French." [293]

It would be, however, a full month before the burgesses would meet, a month in which the French would be quietly and steadily preparing for the spring advance, but in which the colonies, his own in particular, would be idle. This, Dinwiddie determined, should not be. Happily, he had for moral support, and to insure an atmosphere of legality to the actions he was about to take, the steadfastly faithful council, one of whom was his friend, Colonel William Fairfax of Belvoir. A true regard for their duty, they had told him back in november 1753 during the dark and uncertain days of the pistole fee controversy, "indispensably obliges us, zealously to concur in all such measures as shall be judged most conducive to these salutary ends, and to the support of his majesty's rights, and the interest and security of his subjects in America." [294]

This was all Dinwiddie needed in this national emergency, particularly since he had back of him the authority, as given him through Lord Holdernesse in the now celebrated "instructions" drawn up august 28, 1753,

1754, in his opening speech: "Nothing less than a very important concern, could have induced me to call you together again, after so short a recess; but the dignity of the crown of Great-Britain, the welfare of all the colonies on this continent, and more especially of this dominion, engage me to have your advice and assistance, in an affair of the greatest consequence." See also Draper manuscripts, 1JJ17-1JJ20.

293 Dinwiddie to Lord Fairfax [January 1754], *Dinwiddie papers*, I, 50.

294 *Legislative journals of the council of colonial Virginia*, II, 1098; *Dinwiddie papers*, I, 42. See also the Address of the council to the king, december 29, 1753, P.R.O., C.O., 5/1328, 85-86; L.C. tr., 85-87.

to "prevent . . . any foreigns from making a settlement upon his majesty's land." [295] To the governor's mind, his duty lay clear before him. He could not be sure of the temper of the burgesses even when they came together a month hence; neither could he be certain that, recognizing the seriousness of the situation, they would be willing to raise the necessary men and arms. His past experience had convinced him, rightly or wrongly, that they were not as zealous for their own protection as they should be, an attitude which had called forth taunts from both the French and Indians, and Dinwiddie was not content now to place his complete dependence and that of the colony upon their uncertain vote.

Consequently, he hurriedly wrote Lord Fairfax, in the latter's capacity as county lieutenant of Frederick county, as the most prominent and influential man in Virginia, and as a personal friend. From the lack of explanatory passages in this letter compared to other letters the governor wrote at this time, it would appear that Lord Fairfax had been at Belvoir visiting his cousin, Colonel William Fairfax, a member of Dinwiddie's council, at the time when Washington passed through there from the west en route to Williamsburg with his report to the governor.[296] Considering the fact that Lord Fairfax knew all about young Washington's mission, including the probable date of his return, it would not be strange if that gentleman had deliberately been present when Washington came to Belvoir, so that he might be informed at the earliest possible

[295] Holdernesse to Dinwiddie, august 28, 1753, P.R.O., C.O., 5/1344, 2-8; L.C. tr., 141-145; P.R.O., C.O., 5/211, 21-32; L.C. tr., 13-25; Loudoun papers, LO 447A, vols. 1-5, 1-6 (Huntington library); Instructions with regard to erection of forts on the Ohio, august 28, 1753, P.R.O., C.O., 5/211, 33-42; L.C. tr., 21-25.

[296] John C. Fitzpatrick, ed., Diaries of George Washington, 1748-1799, I, 67.

moment and at first hand what the situation was in the west. Certainly the interests of both himself and his cousin, Colonel William Fairfax, were strongly tied up in the Ohio company, in which case whatever news Washington was bringing to the governor would be of great moment to them.

". . . the French forces on the Ohio," Dinwiddie wrote, "intend [to come] down as far as Logstown early in the spring." And this is exactly what they did, the anticipation of which proved one of the fruits of Dinwiddie's determined and indefatigable efforts to possess himself of any and all information which might or could affect the dominion of which he was governor. No other governor, no other man in all the colonies was so relentless or so tireless in his quest for information; no other person strove with such perseverance to protect and maintain the American colonies for the crown.

He wrote further to Lord Fairfax on the same subject: ". . . I think it is for his majesty's service and the protection of the settlements of this dominion to do all in our power to prevent their building any forts or making any settlements on that river, and more particularly so nigh us as that of the Logstown."

Following this, he declared, "I therefore, with advice of the council, think proper to send immediately out 200 men to protect those already sent by the Ohio company to build a fort, and to resist any attempts on them." Whether the governor by this declaration meant that he proposed to dispatch 200 men to the Ohio because and only because they would support the Ohio company project, or because in his estimation the Ohio company was but the advance guard of the Virginia colony and British interests, is a matter of conjecture. Without impugning his motives, the conclusion is inescapable that he did send George Washington with an armed force

toward the Ohio "to protect those already sent by the
Ohio company," and that it was there his little army
came into conflict with the French already advanced
into that region. It would thus seem at least possible
that protection of the Ohio company interests was directly the occasion, though not the cause, of the outbreak of the French and Indian war. Certainly, Dinwiddie did have the interests of the Ohio company
"much at heart," as he had admitted both to Colonel
Fairfax and to Colonel Thomas Cresap, but it is equally
certain that nothing can be brought forward to prove
that his interest went so far as intentionally to precipitate actual warfare.

The precise steps Dinwiddie now proposed to take in
the emergency he outlined to Lord Fairfax. Major
George Washington had been commissioned to proceed
at once to Frederick and Augusta counties, the former
county being under the lieutenancy of Lord Fairfax
himself, and raise one hundred men, fifty from each
county. Fairfax was therefore respectfully asked "to
direct the militia of Frederick to be drawn out and fifty
men to be enlisted for that service." Furthermore, as a
measure of precaution, the governor asked that the
men's names be taken so that "if they do not voluntarily
enter . . . [it] may be ascertained so as to prevent as
far as we can, of being surprized [disappointed]," after
which they were to be sent to Alexandria to Major Carlyle for arms and provisions. In carefully chosen language, the governor apologized for the trouble he had
put upon so important and great a man as Lord Fairfax,
nevertheless since the latter "was pleased to take the
care of that county," he was requested now "to exert
your authority so that they [the troops] may be at Alexandria by the 20th of next month." [297]

[297] Dinwiddie to Lord Fairfax [January 1754], *Dinwiddie papers*, I, 48-50.

With Frederick county taken care of, Dinwiddie next turned his attention to Augusta county, that far-flung territory whose most western settlers are referred to as being "on the waters of Mississippi, in the county of Augusta." [298] The lieutenant of this county was Colonel James Patton, a man with whom Dinwiddie was not so well acquainted nor on such easy terms of friendship as with the Fairfax family, and Patton consequently was not in such full possession of the facts. It became necessary, therefore, for the governor to write him in detail the events of the preceding months, including Washington's mission to the west and his report thereon.

There was, however, one omission in his letter to Patton which Dinwiddie felt it politic to make. Lord Fairfax either was a member of the Ohio company or was in full sympathy with its membership and purposes, so that in writing him, the governor felt free to state that the two hundred men being raised were to "protect those already sent by the Ohio company to build a fort." With Patton, however, the situation was changed, because Patton was himself interested to some unknown degree in land companies of his own. Certainly, therefore, he might naturally be expected to object – if he learned the Ohio organization was involved – to being obliged to raise troops for the protection of a rival company, irrespective of the actual or supposed national emergency. It was needless to raise questions in Patton's mind as to the extent of involvement of the Ohio company in the matter, therefore Dinwiddie felt justified in omitting all mention of anything pertaining to it, contenting himself with the statement that, agreeable to the council, he felt it necessary "to send out immediately 200 men from the militia to Monongahela to support those that are already there in building a fort."

---

[298] Hening's *Statutes*, VI, 258.

Patton is then directed, without the obsequious language employed in addressing the great Fairfax, to draw out his militia, draft fifty men and send them to Alexandria by the twentieth of february, "if possible with their arms, etc."

The remainder of the governor's letter is just as significant. Hinting as it does of a characteristic in the make-up of the Augusta county lieutenant with which Dinwiddie, far from being sympathetic, is almost curtly admonitory, he warned Patton: "In the meantime you are to be particularly diligent to raise the number mentioned above and deliver them to Mr. Va[n]braam [299] [Washington's lieutenant] to be by him conveyed with all possible dispatch to Alexandria that no delay or disappointment may be attributed to you!" [300] Here is demonstrated once more the importance of studying the context surrounding any debatable, isolated passage in a letter. Thus this letter, if taken alone, or even in conjunction with certain other letters written to James Patton by Dinwiddie (in which the phrases "proceed immediately," or you are to act "without delay," fre-

---

[299] Jacob Van Braam, a Hollander residing in Virginia. He had seen service in the Cartagena expedition, where he had known Lawrence Washington, then a major. The latter may have influenced him to come to Virginia. At any rate, he did come, and presently found himself instructing Lawrence's brother, George, in military drill or in fencing or in both. Toner was one of the first to discover that Van Braam was a mason and that both he and George Washington were present at a meeting of the lodge in Fredericksburg on september 1, 1753. Whatever the reason, when Washington set out on october 31, 1753 to carry Dinwiddie's message to the French in the Ohio region, Van Braam was the man he selected as his French interpreter. Early in 1754 he was again with Washington as a lieutenant in the little army he was gathering with Dinwiddie's authority on the frontier. He was soon promoted to a captaincy. Van Braam and Captain Robert Stobo were retained by the French as hostages at the Fort Necessity capitulation. He was kept prisoner at Montreal until 1760. The burgesses in 1754 omitted him from their thanks to Washington and his men; in their action in 1761, however, they reversed themselves, even to a special purse of £500, and in these things the governor joined the burgesses.

[300] Dinwiddie to Patton, january 1754, *Dinwiddie papers*, I, 50-51.

quently occur), might cause a rather unflattering sidelight to be thrown on the character of one of the most important officers of Dinwiddie's government.

From Patton, Dinwiddie now turned with almost visible relief to one of his oldest and most trusted friends, Colonel William Fairfax of Belvoir, whose interest not only in the safety of the Ohio company but in the safety of the dominion itself was identical with his own. Here was a man to whom he could write fully and freely, whose advice he could count on, and whose cooperation in all matters had never failed him. And as an additional bond, there was their mutual esteem and affection for the young Washington, whom the governor mentioned in his opening remark: "Your favours [letters] by Major Washington gave me much pleasure, as I was in some pain [anxiety] for him" as, not unnaturally, Colonel Fairfax was also during Washington's hazardous mission to the Ohio river country.

Before going any further it must be clearly understood what Dinwiddie's position was in the matter of troops and defense of the colony at this period of Virginia's history. Sometimes the enlisted men definitely refused to march beyond the confines of the colony, a thing which made the ill-defined colonial boundaries both an advantage and a disadvantage. Sometimes – this one, for example – the militia laws were deficient, a condition which Dinwiddie had deplored in his first meeting with the assembly and begged them to remedy. In the actual work of raising any sizable body of troops, his difficulties were twice multiplied since he had to contend not only with the reluctance of the men themselves but the uncertainty of his house of burgesses.

Thus he complained to Colonel Fairfax: "A regiment of volunteers would have been very agreeable to me, but looking into the militia laws there is no pro.

[vision?] for paying them under that denomination, therefore [I] have commissioned Major Washington to enlist 100 men from the militia of Augusta and Frederick and Captain William Trent has my commission to enlist 100 more among the traders . . . these two companies to march directly after [being] raised to protect and assist them in building the fort," this last, of course, referring to the activities of the Ohio company with which Colonel Fairfax is acquainted and obviously in agreement.

The health of Colonel Fairfax at this time, a matter upon which Dinwiddie remarked with some concern and deep regret, was not such that he had any great hopes of being able to attend the forthcoming general assembly at Williamsburg, particularly since it was to meet during the inclement month of february rather than in april, as both had anticipated when they parted in december. Dinwiddie, therefore, had hoped that he would be able to employ his friend's services at home in order that he might not be completely robbed of so valuable an ally, and proceeded to ask the colonel not only to use his good offices in aiding young Washington but to use his influence with Lord Fairfax toward the raising of troops in Frederick county.

"I am heartily fatigued," Dinwiddie admitted in secrecy to his friend. Here is a confession that will be heard from now on both with increasing frequency and increasing intensity. That iron constitution, driven at terrific pace for many decades, was now at sixty-one beginning to show the effects of overexhaustion. He was more "fatigued" than he knew. Not heeding the admonition of nature, he continued his efforts for the good of his dominion and the crown with unabated vigor, until a stroke added its warning. Even then, though he sought relief in retirement, and begged again and again for the board of trade to accept his resignation, he was obliged to continue at his post until the opening of 1758. Where rose the maligning and utterly false rumor that this man, unequalled in our early history in his love for and untiring efforts in behalf of the country of his adoption, was recalled to England in disgrace, one prefers to pass over as not worthy of serious consideration.[301]

He closed this most revealing letter to his friend, Fairfax: "My wife and two girls join me in sincere respects to you and yours."[302]

In all periods of the history of great nations, there have been certain families whose prominence and prestige were such that too great emphasis could not be placed upon them. In later years, this was true of the Washington family, and still later of the Adams, but at this particular time the great Fairfax family stood over and above any other in the colony of Virginia, if not the entire country. As the years of their residence here grew, their importance and influence increased, since by marriage and intermarriage they became allied with other families of lesser importance, raising them by sheer force of the Fairfax name to a position of respect and prominence.

This was true in the case of John Carlyle,[303] a well-

---

301 See note 567, for a few of the many erroneous statements that he was recalled. It is regrettable not that history repeats itself, but that so many writers merely repeat each other.

302 Dinwiddie to Colonel William Fairfax [January 1754], *Dinwiddie papers*, I, 51-52.

303 John Carlyle (1720-1780), usually referred to as Major Carlyle, was a native of Scotland. He came to America about 1740 and by 1744/45 had established himself in the mercantile business at Bellhaven, later Alexandria, Virginia. His shipping and business activities were carried on in partnership with John Dalton. When Alexandria was granted a charter in 1748, John Carlyle was named one of the town's trustees. In 1752/53 he built a commodious stone residence on Fairfax street. The house is still standing. His rise in colonial affairs was marked. On january 26, 1754 Governor Din-

known merchant of Alexandria. Carlyle had married
Sarah Fairfax, the daughter of Colonel William Fairfax, and in so doing had placed himself in the lime-
light which belonged to that clan. (This Sally Fairfax
Carlyle, however, should not be confused with her
brother's wife, Mrs. George William [Sally Cary]
Fairfax.) Carlyle owed the position and his new title as
"commissary of stores and provisions for the supply of
the forces designed for the river Ohio," [304] which Dinwiddie was now about to bestow upon him, to his father-
in-law, Colonel Fairfax. This fact is evidenced by the
governor's letter to the colonel, stating that "agreeable to your recommendation I have with pleasure
appointed Major Carlisle commissary of stores and provisions"; the governor added, as a further proof of the
closeness of their friendship, "as the hurry of the affairs
of the publick prevents my giving him so distinct instructions as are requisite, I therefore recommend him
to consult you in everything for the service of the publick under his care." [305]

This, no doubt, was a flattering deference to Colonel
Fairfax, and Dinwiddie meant that it should be; nevertheless the governor had no intention of taking this compliment to his friend too literally, nor of letting such
an important undertaking progress without his own full
knowledge and instructions.

widdie named him "commissary of provisions and stores," and for a year
he was engaged in furnishing supplies to the frontier forces. He was superseded in december by Charles Dick and Dr. Thomas Walker. In april 1755
he entertained in his home General Braddock and five governors, including
Governor Dinwiddie, when they met to plan assistance to the general in his
campaign. He was married twice, his first wife being Sarah, the daughter of
Colonel William and Sarah (Walker) Fairfax of Belvoir. Upon the death
of his father-in-law in 1758 he was appointed by the king to succeed him
as collector of customs on the Potomac. He and his family were close friends
of the Washington family.

[304] Dinwiddie to Carlyle, january 27, 1754, *Dinwiddie papers*, I, 53.
[305] Dinwiddie to Colonel William Fairfax [January 1754], *ibid.*, I, 52.

Consequently, in his letter to Carlyle, acquainting him with the news of his appointment, he proceeded to go into the details of this assignment with a thoroughness which was completely characteristic. Flour, bread, beef, and pork for five hundred men for six to eight months were to be procured, he wrote him, adding that it was his own understanding that provisions are plentiful in the "back country." If, however, he found after consulting with Colonel Fairfax in regard to quantity, that he could not secure the necessary amounts, he should send an "account of the prices" so that "what may be deficient must be sent from this [place]." Dinwiddie further advised: "I shall send you ten pounders cannon with stores, etc., suitable and 200 small arms to supply the above two companies if wanted, take receipts for what you deliver. The cannon are large and heavy, therefore I think you must order the sloop with them as near to the falls as possible, to make the land carriage short, and from the falls to be carried by water to Wills's creek, from thence to the Ohio."

Furthermore, he charged Carlyle to "read the act of assembly in regard to the militia and on invasions. You will then observe you have authority to press [impress] boats, waggons, carts, horses, etc. and upon this occasion I think it absolutely necessary unless you can hire at reasonable rates." After this and a wealth of other detail, he added, with what seems like unwitting irony, "consult with Colonel Fairfax in every thing." Yet it was not. With his natural Scotch shrewdness he saw at once what waste could and might occur under the direction of an apparently inexperienced man, and furthermore, he understood better than any man of his time how exceedingly important full instructions and explanations were in the inchoate state of colonial affairs in general, and affairs on the frontier in particular.

In his letter to William Trent,[306] which followed, he bore out this policy. To Trent he wrote: "Your letter of the 6th current I received from Major Washington," [307] evidence both that Trent had been in communication with Dinwiddie and that he had been along Washington's route in the latter's return from the forks and had entrusted his letter for the governor to Washington.[308] Dinwiddie went on to explain that from Washington's report and other information received, he found that the French intended to come down the Ohio, erect forts, and take possession of the "lands on that river," a thing which he was trying to "earnestly prevent."

That Trent had made the governor an offer, backed by information which he had apparently gleaned from talking with Washington on his way to Williamsburg from the west, is evident since Dinwiddie wrote: "And as you think you could [words omitted in the record]

306 William Trent (1715-c.1787), a Pennsylvania Indian trader, soldier, local justice, and land speculator, was for a while in the employ of Virginia. He was a captain in the Pennsylvania contingent raised in 1746. He attended numerous Indian councils. The journal he kept in 1752, covering his trip to Logstown and to Pickawillany, has been published. In 1754 he was in the employ of the Ohio company or of Virginia, or both. He has been both excused and censured for being absent from the Ohio company storehouse-fort at the forks in april 1754. In 1758 he was with General John Forbes. Meantime, he carried on his Indian trade. Presently his name was associated with the firm of Simon, Trent, Levy and Franks.

307 Dinwiddie to Trent [January 1754], *Dinwiddie papers,* I, 55.

308 Throughout 1753 Trent had corresponded with Dinwiddie about Indian affairs. He had been sent out early in that year as an English envoy to the Twightwees and on june 16 made his report to the governor (P.R.O., C.O., 5/1327, 709; L.C. tr., 569). On june 28, 1753 he again wrote Dinwiddie, this time expressing his dissatisfaction with frontier conditions and threatening to quit work for Virginia (Etting collection of "Ohio company papers," I, 1753-1755). On august 11, 1753 another letter was sent which advised Dinwiddie that the time was opportune for bringing all of the Indians to the English side by gifts and proper management *(Ibid.).* On november 17 he sent Dinwiddie an account of his dealings with the Six Nations (P.R.O., C.O., 5/1328, 27-44; L.C. tr., 15-40).

this winter, if properly impowered to do so, I therefore inclose you a captain's commission to raise 100 men in Augusta and in the exterior settlements of this dominion and a blank commission for you to choose a suitable lieutenant to co-operate with you."

He and George Washington, each with a force of one hundred men, were to join their two companies, Trent was informed, and march the men out to the Ohio "where a fort is proposed to be built." The language here is sufficiently clear to show that Dinwiddie did not intend to imply future tense when he said "is proposed," but past tense, since the fort in question was already supposed to be in progress at the hands of the Ohio company contingent. This conclusion is made still clearer by his next command: "When you are there you are to protect and assist them in finishing the fort and to be on your guard against any attempts of the French," [309] an order which Trent did not explicitly follow since he was absent from his post at the critical moment when the French appeared, and Ensign Edward Ward's capitulation followed.[310] Undoubtedly one of the things about Trent which commended him to Dinwiddie was the latter's belief that somehow Trent possessed considerable influence over the Indians, hence he added, hopefully: "As you have a good interest with the Indians I doubt not you will prevail with many of them to join you in order to defeat the designs of the French in taking their lands from them by force of arms."

One of Dinwiddie's most consistent policies was that of taking his subordinates into his confidence, certainly to the extent of advising them from time to time of his own activities in their behalf. It had the desirable

---

[309] Dinwiddie to Trent [January 1754], *Dinwiddie papers,* I, 55.

[310] Ensign Ward's deposition, may 7, 1754, P.R.O., C.O., 5/14, 393-396; L.C. tr., 341-345.

effect not only of encouraging them but of making them feel that they were an integral and essential part of the war machine. Thus he informed Trent with flattering solicitude: "The house of burgesses are to meet the 14th of next month, when I hope they will enable me to send out 400 more men early in the spring to your assistance," omitting, diplomatically, to include Major Washington in this consideration. He further explained to Trent that he was writing to the other governors for assistance and believed he would get it; that he already had some artillery from England, ten cannon that "carry four pound shot," that he had "confidence" in him and a "good opinion" of him, and would be glad of his "advice" on the urgent matters then facing Virginia. With such a letter in his hands, what else could Trent do but throw himself wholeheartedly behind the governor's plan?

One more word of advice the governor added: "I have some cannon come in . . . I fear there will be a difficulty in carrying them out — as you are acquainted with the roads, I shall be glad of your advice therein" — a spirit which Braddock in later years would have done well to emulate, but unhappily did not — "and comunicate the same to Major Carlisle," in order that the commissary as well as himself might be kept informed.

William Trent's commission makes interesting reading. It begins thus, in a curiously familiar vein: "Whereas certain persons pretending to be subjects of his most christian majesty the king of France . . ." [311] The use of the word "pretending" was deliberate, since by its noncommittal use all charges or even suggestions that the king of France could possibly have been guilty

[311] Commission of Trent, january 26, 1754, P.R.O., C.O., 5/14, 147-150; L.C. tr., 113-114; *Dinwiddie papers*, I, 56.

of personally ordering these French upon English soil
was adroitly avoided. Furthermore, military acts
against such irresponsible persons found within English borders would be in the nature of punishing frontier renegades and not legally commissioned French
officers and their contingents. These were the nice distinctions both English and French were using. When
presently one comes to the capitulation of Fort Necessity, he will find that then and ever afterward a tempest
had been stirred up over whether or not Washington
meant to admit that he had murdered the French officer, Jumonville, when he signed the terms containing
the words "l'assassinat du Sieur de Jumonville," which
Washington always declared Van Braam translated for
him as "killed." [312]

The "divers outrages and violences on the persons
and goods" of British subjects that Dinwiddie claimed
had been committed were, he held in Trent's commission, "in direct violation and infraction of the treaties
at present subsisting between the two crowns." If this
be true, it would throw the moral responsibility of
"undeclared warfare" upon the heads of the French.
And since Virginia claimed the forks of the Ohio region by reason of the terms not only of her own charter,
but also of the terms of Pennsylvania's charter, "these
acts of hostility and depredations" Dinwiddie held to
have been perpetrated "in that part of his majesty's
dominions which are under my government."

Dinwiddie's realism must be judged by the times in
which he lived. "In order," as he declared, "to the
preservation of the peace and good understanding between the two crowns," he would authorize one, William Trent, to raise a little army to accomplish that

---

[312] John C. Fitzpatrick, ed., *Writings of George Washington*, I, 36n-38n,
88n-89n.

desirable end. George Washington was instructed later to "act on the defensive" but this word does not occur either in Trent's commission or instructions. Trent was "to keep possession of his majesty's lands on the Ohio, and the waters thereof, and to dislodge and drive away, and in case of refusal and resistance to kill and destroy or take prisoners all and every person and persons whatsoever, not subjects of the king of Great Britain who now are or shall hereafter come to settle and take possession of any lands on said river Ohio or on any of the branches or waters thereof" – a sizable task for an army "not exceeding one hundred men" under Trent, with his officer aides "not exceeding one lieutenant and one ensign." [313]

With Trent now lined up on his side, together with Washington, James Patton, and the Fairfax family, the Indians were all that remained to the indefatigable pen of the governor. To the Oneida chief, Monacatoocha, he indited a letter that for Indian form and courtesy stands out well along with similar ones written by those experienced Indian agents, Sir William Johnson,[314] Edmond Atkin,[315] and John Stuart.[316] By Din-

[313] Dinwiddie to Trent, january 26, 1754, P.R.O., C.O., 5/14, 147-150; L.C. tr., 113-114; *Dinwiddie papers*, I, 56-57.

[314] William Johnson (1715-1774), Indian trader, interpreter, councillor, landowner, and military leader, was born in Ireland. He came to America about the time he reached his majority to manage his uncle's estates and settled in the Mohawk valley. He early became prominent. He won an ascendancy over the Iroquois never exceeded by any white man. The Mohawks adopted him and made him a sachem. His second and third wives were Mohawk women. He rendered valuable service to the English cause both in King George's war and in the final struggle, 1754-1763. His counsel was sought at the Albany congress of 1754, and by Braddock and Lord Loudoun. His greatest military success was his victory over Baron Dieskau, september 8, 1755, at Lake George. In 1756 he was made superintendent of Indian affairs for the northern colonies, and was thus a contemporary of Edmond Atkin and John Stuart, successively Indian superintendents for the southern colonies. He was knighted in 1755, made a colonel in 1756, and a major-general in 1772.

widdie the Indians were praised, the English extolled, and the French condemned according to the best usage of the time, after which he promised them all would soon be well. This fact was assured since he was sending Major Washington and Captain Trent to them with such assistance as would enable them to "deliver your selves from your enemies." [317] For diplomacy and subtle agitation, this letter stands unexcelled, probably unequalled.

A similar letter then followed to the Six Nations,[318] and finally one each to the Catawbas [319] and the Cherokees.[320] A year was a long time in the career of Robert Dinwiddie in America, and it had been a whole year since he had urged Colonel Thomas Cresap to supply him with detailed information about the "several nations of Indians . . . and . . . how to engage them to

315 Edmond Atkin, royal-appointed agent for Indian affairs for the southern colonies, Pennsylvania to Georgia. He was charged with regulation of the trade with the Indians, with their pacification, and with keeping them attached to the English interest. His salary was fixed at £200, his bond at £200. He was appointed in 1756. Lord Loudoun, military commander-in-chief, 1756-1758, was critical of Atkin's initiative. He was succeeded by Captain John Stuart. Atkin was at one time a merchant in Charleston and at one time a member of the governor's council. (The late John C. Parish, at the time of his death, was engaged in writing an account of Atkin. The best item to date on this superintendent is Professor Parish's paper read a few years ago before the American historical association and entitled, "Edmond Atkin, British superintendent of Indian affairs.")

316 John Stuart (c. 1700-1779), a Scot who emigrated to America in the 1740's, brought himself to the attention of the home government, and in 1762 succeeded Edmond Atkin as the superintendent of Indian affairs for the southern district. He was given a salary of £1000 with liberal allowances for Indian presents, an amount, however, which mounted rapidly until the Revolution. In due time, he induced the home government to name him a "member extraordinary" of each of the provincial councils from Virginia southward, with privilege therefore of sitting in each upper house whenever Indian affairs were under discussion. This move, in line with Dinwiddie's precedent, gave his position increased prestige.

317 Dinwiddie to Monacatoocha [n.d. 1754], *Dinwiddie papers*, I, 57.
318 Dinwiddie to the Six Nations [n.d. 1754], *ibid.*, I, 58.
319 Dinwiddie to the Catawbas, january 29, 1754, *ibid.*, I, 60.
320 Dinwiddie to the Cherokees, january 29, 1754, *ibid.*, I, 61.

the British interest." [321] In this Cresap had proved himself a good teacher and Dinwiddie an apt scholar, for
now the governor was able to talk with the Catawbas
in language which they well understood. He assured
this tribe that "with your assistance, the Cherokees,
the Chickesaws, the Indians on the Ohio, and the forces
from this dominion, we may be in a capacity to defeat
the unjust designs of the French and their Indians.
These tribes of Indians, called Chippeways, Ottaways,
and Arundacks, have by the perswasion and influence
of the French taken up the hatchet against us, but" –
and now what a handsome touch – "what are they but
children when compared to the brave Catawbas?"

He notified them that on "the 20th of may" – a date
so important in his estimation that he was almost beginning to reckon everything from it – he would meet
the Iroquois, the Twightwees, and other chiefs of Ohio
tribes at Winchester. To this place in the Shenandoah
valley, therefore, he invited them to dispatch two of
their chiefs to receive a "part of a present sent by your
father the king of Great Britain." But Robert Dinwiddie was a Scotchman and a practical realist. If his
letter, though written meticulously according to Indian
form, were left thus, he still would be in the dark as to
their actual intentions in the forthcoming conflict. With
this in mind he could not restrain an urgent after-
thought: "Pray send word how many of your warriors
will march to the Ohio," and a second P.S: "I desire you
will in my name desire the assistance of the Chickesaws,
and that they may send some warriors to join your nation to march to the Ohio." [322]

The governor had now done all that he could do until
the fourteenth of february when the general assembly

---

[321] Dinwiddie to Cresap, january 23, 1752, *ibid.*, 1, 18-19.
[322] Dinwiddie to the Catawbas, january 29, 1754, *ibid.*, 1, 60-61.

would convene. He deserved to win if for no other reason than for his prodigious efforts. No man ever studied the Indian problem and the Indian psychology more assiduously than he did. No official ever cultivated their friendship more eagerly and circumspectly. That he failed in part to gain their adherence now was not because of any mistake or neglect on his part, but because of conditions and circumstances over which he had little or no control. Braddock's defeat later showed how red men invariably went where success seemed more certain. Furthermore, the lack of any central Indian agency or jurisdiction at this time among the colonies was partly to blame. Each colony had its own Indian policy, and more, the Indian conferences frequently conflicted in time. But worse and most catastrophic of all was the unintelligent manner in which these natives were handled by the majority of the colonists. Dinwiddie alone of his time seems really to have realized the far-reaching consequences of this confused and haphazard approach to the Indian problem, but he was only one man and the cooperation he received from his fellow governors was almost negligible.

At last the significant day of february 14, 1754 arrived and Governor Robert Dinwiddie stood before his assembled council and house of burgesses. If he was the tired, sick, apprehensive man which all evidence seems to indicate, his words betrayed nothing of it.

"Nothing less than a very important concern," he told them, placatingly, "could have induced me to call you together again, after so short a recess. . . The dignity of the crown of Great Britain, the welfare of all the colonies on this continent and more especially of this dominion, engage me to have your advice and assistance in an affair of the greatest consequence."

Without further delay, he launched at once into

the heart of Washington's report from the west. The French, he told them, had erected a fort on a creek running into the Ohio and were preparing to build another on the river itself. They had two hundred and twenty canoes already made with many more "rough-hewed, to be made," in order to bring down the Ohio river early in the spring a number of their regular forces, some fifteen hundred, together with their friendly Indians, in order to build other forts on the Ohio, and that they proposed to make Logstown their headquarters. Furthermore, he went on, the French were seizing the goods of the English traders and sending the traders themselves as prisoners to Quebec, going so far as to inform Major Washington that their orders from the governor of Canada were not to permit any English subject to trade on the waters of the Ohio, but to seize such goods and take the men prisoners.

One such example the governor cited was the case of John Frazier. Frazier, though he escaped with his person, was deprived of his house which he had built and lived in for twelve years. When Major Washington complained to the French of this outrage, their officer is reported to have coolly observed, "that man was lucky that he made his escape, or he would have sent him prisoner to Canada."

This incident, looking at it carefully, seems to serve two purposes: first, it helps to fix the date of early English settlement in the Ohio country, and second — much more important — it seems to fasten on the French the onus of responsibility for the first overt act of aggression. Since this is the kind of action history charges against the French at Pickawillany in the Ohio country in 1751, coupled with the same kind of aggression for which they must be held responsible when they caused Ensign Ward to capitulate at the forks the next january,

it seems all the more likely that Washington's report to
Dinwiddie had not been exaggerated.

"These transactions," Dinwiddie declared, unequivo-
cally, to a startled assemblage, "are entirely inconsistent
with the treaties subsisting between the two crowns, and
contrary to my instructions from his majesty, whereby
I am directed to prevent any foreign power settling or
building any fortresses on his majesty's lands."

The Indians, he went on to recount, officered by the
French, were being turned loose on a helpless country-
side to murder, scalp, and torture men, women, and
children. Whole families were being slaughtered in cold
blood. Realistically, he paints for his audience a picture
of an "unhappy family! surrounded by a crowd of mis-
creants, dreadfully rushing on to perpetrate the most
savage barbarities, inexorable to the parent's intreaties,
insensible to the cries of the tender infant, basely determined to destroy, without provocation, those who
could not resist their violence." As though such words
might not be sufficient to arouse the legislators to action,
he continued the lurid picture: "Then you see the infant
torn from the unavailing struggles of the distracted
mother, the daughters ravished before the eyes of their
wretched parents; and then, with cruelty and insult,
butchered and scalped."

Yet, he warned his assembly they must not blame the
savages too much. They were but ignorant barbarians.
It was the French, the assembly was asked to remember,
who were "the abettors of these villanies" and the ones
against whom their rancor and indignation should rise.

"I assure you, gentlemen," he now concluded, "these
insults on our sovereign's protection and barbarities on
our fellow subjects, make deep impressions on my heart;
and I doubt not . . . you will enable me, by a full and

sufficient supply, to . . . secure the rights and assert the
honour and dignity of our sovereign; to drive away these
cruel and treacherous invaders of your properties, and
destroyers of your families, and thereby to gratify my
warmest wishes in establishing the security and prosperity of Virginia, on the most solid and permanent
foundations." [323]

Dinwiddie rested his case, and a good one it was. He
had appealed to his hearers on every point upon which
men have been vulnerable to war since time immemorial
– their honor, their safety, their freedom, the protection
of their homes and families, and finally a masterly touch,
the century-old hatred and distrust of the English for
the French. And he won. The pistole fee hatchet was
buried, and the combined burgesses and councillors
granted a liberal subsidy for carrying on the campaign.

"I prorogued our assembly this day," he wrote jubi-
lantly to Governor Sharpe of Maryland. ". . . they
have given £10,000 this money for the support of his
majesty's right to the lands on the Ohio in consequence
thereof I design immediatly to raise five or six companies of men." [324]

But his jubilation was short lived, as it is with most
men, and the day was not far off when he would suffer
the most acute disillusionment. The vision of a thousand
braves war-whooping across the mountains to aid their
"father," the king of Great Britain, would vanish like
frost before the rising sun. With herculean efforts he
turned to his fellow governors in an effort to rouse them
to a sense of their common danger, but with little
success. Jealousy over Indian control, bickering over

---

[323] *Journals of the house of burgesses* (1752-1755; 1756-1758), 175-176.
See also Draper manuscripts, 1JJ17-1JJ20.

[324] Dinwiddie to Sharpe, february 23, 1754, *Maryland archives*, VI, 39;
Dinwiddie papers, I, 80.

boundaries, quibbling about supplies, uncertainties of jurisdiction, all combined to defeat and strangle his most cherished plans.

No wonder the French felt themselves secure.

Appeals to Fellow Governors

Dinwiddie had appealed to the military, frontier, and social leaders of Virginia for aid in the coming test of strength. He had appealed to his Indian "brethren." He now turned to his fellow governors.

On january 29, 1754 he dictated seven separate and distinct personal letters to the seven governors of the most important British colonies, from Massachusetts to South Carolina. These stirring appeals for help went out to Sharpe of Maryland,[325] Glen of South Carolina,[326] Acting Governor Rowan of North Carolina,[327] Hamilton of Pennsylvania,[328] Belcher of New Jersey,[329] DeLancey of New York,[330] and Shirley of Massachusetts.[331]

[325] Dinwiddie to Sharpe, january 29, 1754, *Maryland archives*, VI, 33-34; *Dinwiddie papers*, I, 67-68.

[326] Dinwiddie to Glen, january 29, 1754, P.R.O., C.O., 5/14, 279-282; L.C. tr., 253-258; *Dinwiddie papers*, I, 61-63.

[327] Dinwiddie to Rowan, january 29, 1754, William L. Saunders, ed., *Colonial records of North Carolina* (Raleigh, 1886-1890), V, 172-174; *Dinwiddie papers*, I, 64-65. Matthew Rowan was acting governor of North Carolina in 1754. He was also president of the council. Rowan county, formed in 1753 from Anson county, was named in his honor.

[328] Dinwiddie to Hamilton, january 29, 1754, *Pennsylvania colonial records*, V, 714-715; *Dinwiddie papers*, I, 63-64.

[329] Dinwiddie to Belcher, january 29, 1754, *New Jersey archives*, 1st series, XVI, 444-445; *Dinwiddie papers*, I, 68-69. Jonathan Belcher (1681-1757), colonial-born governor of Massachusetts and New Hampshire (1730-1741) and of New Jersey (1746-1757). His father was a well-to-do Massachusetts merchant and member of that colony's council for many years. Like Dinwiddie he carried on a voluminous correspondence. He was aggressive, by some considered dictatorial. He is chiefly remembered for his interest in the founding of the College of New Jersey, now Princeton university.

[330] Dinwiddie to DeLancey, january 29, 1754, *New York colonial documents*, VI, 827-828; *Dinwiddie papers*, I, 65-66.

[331] Dinwiddie to Shirley, january 29, 1754, Emmet collection, no. 6215, New York public library (Colonial Williamsburg MSS.); *Dinwiddie papers*, I,

So far as we are able to discover there never had been before and there never was to be again during the colonial period such a widespread appeal from a single governor on the subject of cooperation. When the story of the successes and failures of cooperative efforts during the colonial period of American history is finally written, account will have to be taken of these attempts by Robert Dinwiddie of Virginia. Unwittingly, by so doing he helped prepare the American provincials for that unity of action without which the Revolution could never have been won.

In six of the seven letters is inserted one long paragraph almost verbatim. In this paragraph Dinwiddie reported on the following matters of interest to all officials: George Washington's reception by the French in the Lake Erie-Ohio region; the apparent preparations of the French for an invasion of that region in force; his own prompt measures to meet that emergency in calling out the militia; and his hopes from the forthcoming Virginia assembly, whose meeting he had pushed forward from april to february. He closed this section of his letter by a Macedonian call to his fellow

69-71. William Shirley (1694-1771) was educated for the law, which he practiced successfully in London for a decade, as well as in America. He came to Boston in 1731 and rose steadily, partly due to the patronage of the Duke of Newcastle but chiefly due to his own ability. He was made governor in 1741 and held that office until 1756. He gained much prestige for his share in the capture of Louisbourg in 1745. He was a major-general early in 1755 and after Braddock's defeat was made commander-in-chief of the military forces in America. He attended the governors' conference with Braddock at Alexandria and, as a result, was given command of the expedition against Niagara. It failed. A quarrel broke out between him and the new commander-in-chief, Lord Loudoun, the latter accusing him of incompetency. He was called to England early in 1756 but delayed his departure until october. He was later governor of the Bahamas for a short time but soon returned to Massachusetts to live until his death. In spite of the attacks of his enemies, he was honest, frank, courageous, ambitious, though somewhat tactless. He understood the whole colonial-imperial problem better than any governor save Dinwiddie and Pownall, his successor.

governors to come to his aid in what he significantly termed the "common cause."

In order that he himself "might be truly informed," as he explained in this lengthy paragraph, he had sent a messenger to the French commandant in the northwest to discover what steps the French had taken "on the Ohio prejudicial to his majesty's interest." It was no secret in Virginia, and certainly Dinwiddie made no attempt to hide the fact from Virginians, that the messenger was also authorized to find what steps the French were taking on the Ohio company's lands and prejudicial to the Ohio company's interests. The omission of any reference specifically to the Ohio company in any of these seven letters, even though Dinwiddie had mentioned the company in his letter to Lord Fairfax that same day, is perfectly understandable. The Fairfaxes were closely associated with Dinwiddie and with the Washingtons who were members of the Ohio company; there was every good reason therefore why he should feel free to speak of the company's interest on the Ohio. On the other hand, since Colonel James Patton of Augusta county was definitely not a member of the Ohio company but actually had his own land organization, as has already been mentioned; and since none of the seven governors, now communicated with, were members of either, the mention of the name of the Ohio company would not have served any useful purpose when harmony was so essential; it would even have been positively prejudicial. And anything "prejudicial," to use Dinwiddie's chosen word, might be suicidal. There is no evidence that the Virginia governor was guilty of duplicity; he merely was circumspect.

In most of the letters Dinwiddie was careful to give the name of his messenger, George Washington. Without contraction of spelling and with perfect grammar, he refers to him as "Major Washington (the gentleman whom I sent out)." [332]

Dinwiddie further epitomized Washington's report for each of the governors. He pointed out that the French had already built a fort on the Ohio, by which he meant French creek, a branch of the Allegheny, on which they had erected Fort Venango, the site of the present Franklin, Pennsylvania. This was in addition to the other two posts between that point and Lake Erie, namely, at Le Boeuf, where Waterford, Pennsylvania, now stands, and at Presqu' Isle, where the city of Erie has grown up. They had thus pointed their line of fortifications southward and directly towards the key locations at the forks, which both they and the English knew to be the gateway to the northwest. The Virginia governor was careful to emphasize, in consquence, that the French had "mounted eight pieces of cannon six-pounders" – whereas the English were supplied with only four-pounders. But worse than this, he had to report that the French had assembled a considerable quantity of materials which, they were very frank to inform Washington, they intended for the erection of other forts on the Ohio, more particularly at Logstown.

Logstown, the scene of the Indian conference two years before, was about eighteen miles west of the forks and present Pittsburgh, and is today marked by the nearby town of Economy. If Logstown was, as Dinwiddie reported, "destined for their chief residence," [333] the French later gave up the idea when they expelled Captain William Trent's force under Ensign Edward

332 Dinwiddie to Glen, january 29, 1754, P.R.O., C.O., 5/14, 279-282; L.C. tr., 253-258. This is the original letter sent and illustrates the point made. The printed Dinwiddie papers, I, 64, reproducing the governor's letter-book contractions, contains the amusing form, "Maj'r Washington (the gent. I sent)."

333 Dinwiddie to Glen, january 29, 1754, P.R.O., C.O., 5/14, 279-282; L.C. tr., 253-258; Dinwiddie papers, I, 61.

Ward [334] from the Ohio company-Virginia-British fort at the forks on april 17, 1754.[335] This site, which Washington had been quick to note in his journal as "extremely well situated for a fort," [336] was superior to the other in every respect. That it has proved to be successively the location not only for the fort just mentioned, but of Fort Duquesne, of Fort Pitt, and of the present great city of Pittsburgh is testimony to its strategic importance. The commanding view one gets today from the unobstructed location at the "point," out beyond the old Fort Pitt blockhouse, which is still standing, is well worth the time of any visitor to modern Pittsburgh. There the Allegheny, dark-green from the foliage on its banks along its attenuated course, joins the more cloudy and turbulent Monongahela as they form what the French most aptly styled "La Belle rivière."

Dinwiddie, in his letter to Glen, also quoted Washington as having reported that there were "220 canoes ready finished" and many more blocked out and that the French had stated they had expelled English traders because "the country had belonged to them" – which, unfortunately, was quite as much a fact as was the conflicting claim of the English.

The letter to Governor Glen calls for special mention. He had become governor of South Carolina while Dinwiddie was surveyor-general of customs and a member of Gooch's council in Virginia.[337] The new governor of Virginia therefore probably knew the southern execu-

[334] Edward Ward, an ensign (i.e., second-lieutenant) in the company of Captain William Trent. He was left in command of the Virginia-Ohio company storehouse-fort by Trent in the spring of 1754, during the latter's absence. He capitulated to the French on april 17, 1754.

[335] Ensign Ward's deposition, may 7, 1754, P.R.O., C.O., 5/14, 393-396; L.C. tr., 341-345.

[336] John C. Fitzpatrick, ed., *Writings of George Washington*, I, 23.

[337] James Glen was appointed governor in 1738; he held office, however, only from 1744 to 1756.

tive quite well. Considering the differences that soon
were to crop out between them, the following flattering
expression used by Dinwiddie was possibly intended to
have more point in the letter to Glen than to the other
governors. Dinwiddie said: "And it were superfluous
to advance many arguments with so discerning and sa-
gacious a servant of our master to prove the urgency that
presses every one of his majestys colonies to exert themselves on this occasion, and to vindicate the honour and
dignity of his crown, and justify his undoubted rights
against these invaders of the British property." He then
warned Glen that the French had "already engaged
three Indian nations, the Chipoways, Ottoways, and
Orundacks to take up arms against the English"; also
that from the best information obtained by Washington
they had "four forts on the Mississippi" besides "about
fourteen hundred men in garrison" at New Orleans.
Furthermore, "by means of the river Ovabaseck they
have a communication between Canada and the Mississippi, and some forts on the Oubask, to cover and protect this communication." Finally, he called Glen's
attention to the fact that the French had warned the Indians around the forks that they would return in force
in the spring, and had threatened them if they in the
meantime did not remain "entirely passive." It must be
admitted that the picture as Dinwiddie got it from his
major and passed on to the governors was indeed enough
to justify alarm for the "common cause" – that is, for the
English "common cause." For a man of Dinwiddie's
fidelity toward his majesty it is no wonder any failure
to cooperate fully would seem incomprehensible.

The next sentence used by Dinwiddie to Glen was
strictly personal. It does not occur in the communications to the other governors and is fair evidence that
already all had not been going well between the two

officials. It had to do with the perennial subject of Indians and Indian relations, a rock on which many a governor's political bark was wrecked during the colonial
era. Thus wrote Dinwiddie: "I duly observed what Mr.
President [William Bull,[338] president of the governor's
council in South Carolina] says on your being the
proper medium of my correspondence with the Catawbas and Cherokees." Both Dinwiddie and Glen were
touchy on the subject of all Indians; to make matters
worse, both men regarded these two tribes, because of
the overlapping of territorial jurisdiction, as the wards
of their respective provinces. Which is but another testimony to the grave responsibility that rests upon the
British crown for having repeatedly postponed in spite
of the continued urgings from the colonials the running
of provincial boundaries.

Dinwiddie attempted to conciliate Glen by explaining, even by pleading. This was no time to lose Glen's
support; hence he added: ". . . and if the urgency of
the present juncture did not perswade me to take the
more dispatchful method of sending directly to them
the necessary advices, I should think no way more eligible to apply to them, than thro so good hands, whose
concurrent influence might effectuate my desire, and I
promise myself, that your excellency will do me the
justice to believe, that this is the only motive, and not
the least intention of interfering with your government
in any degree, as I have no other inducement but the
prospect of dispatch in an affair that I consider as urgent
and of equal concern to all his majestys dominions on
the continent."

The Virginia governor went further in attempting

---

[338] William Bull (1683-1755), lieutenant-governor of South Carolina,
1738-1743. His father had been a member of the council and his son was
speaker of the house. The family also was interested in business, particularly
the Indian trade. Bull was succeeded as governor by James Glen.

to conciliate Glen than he had ever gone before, probably, and certainly was ever to go again with that official. But he was desperate for help on the Ohio and was willing to extend himself to be conciliatory. He continued: "I assure you sir, that I set a just value on the weight of your good offices which I am desirous to be favoured with, and that you would extend their influence to the Creeks and Chickasaws, that we may not leave an[y] assistance unemployed that we can obtain against his majesty's enemies." A long sentence indeed. But Dinwiddie was as earnest as his explanations were lengthy. The final sentence was a mixture of truth, diplomacy, and something approaching dissimulation: "Your friendly advice on the return of this express will be very agreeable. Wishing you health and happiness, I am most sincerely, your excellencys most obedient humble servant." [339]

Speed and action were of paramount importance with Dinwiddie. His urgent communication, dated january 29, 1754, which has just been analyzed and upon which Dinwiddie counted so heavily, never reached Glen's hands, so Glen later reported, until the last of february. Even then, Glen did not reply until march 14. He attributed his delay to the fact that Dinwiddie's messenger reportedly took sick en route to South Carolina. Glen had messengers of his own; just why he failed to use one of them at this critical time may never be known.

In his reply Glen reassured Dinwiddie that "this province will not be wanting in contributing a proportional assistance with the colonies." But Glen in reality was far from supporting Dinwiddie's program. In that very same sentence, he declared he felt it "incumbent" upon him, "on this occasion freely and candidly to speak

---

[339] Dinwiddie to Glen, january 29, 1754, P.R.O., C.O., 5/14, 279-282; L.C. tr., 253-258; *Dinwiddie papers*, I, 61-63.

my own sentiments." He then proceeded – and Glen was a good writer – to rehearse for Dinwiddie what Dinwiddie already knew, and what Glen knew he knew, for Dinwiddie himself already had told him. For instance, Glen re-echoed: "The French have, in time of peace, unjustly and contrary to treaty, invaded and possessed themselves of some parts of the British dominions, they have seized the effects belonging to the subjects of that crown and made prisoners of their persons, and in order to secure themselves in these usurped acquisitions they have built forts and are preparing to build more."

Glen in one breath urged immediate action, declaring that the French considered the British only a "rope of sand." But in the next breath he made immediate action impossible, by insisting that there first be launched a "union or association" of the colonies. Continued Glen: "Upon the whole, I am of [the] opinion, that the first step to be taken is to invite the other governments to an interview . . . and I am very hopeful that if you approve of this measure and with out loss of time [even though Glen's reply to Dinwiddie's letter of january 29 had consumed one month and a half], send off expresses, we may be in a condition to act with effect, perhaps early in the fall. . . This government will be ready but not till I hear that you have written to the other governors." [340]

It is now a known fact that the French did strike long before the fall – in fact, early in the spring, as Dinwid-

---

[340] Glen to Dinwiddie, march 14, 1754, P.R.O., C.O., 5/14, 295-298; L.C. tr., 271-276. The differences of opinion between Glen and Dinwiddie over Virginia-Carolina Indian relations hark back to an early period. They inherited a controversy that dates at least from the days of Alexander Spotswood, who complained of the actions of the Carolinians. See, e.g., Frederick Jackson Turner, "Character and influence of the Indian trade in Wisconsin," in *Early writings of Frederick Jackson Turner* (Madison, 1938), 101.

die had predicted they would do. Furthermore, he had done his best to hurry William Trent and George Washington forward with their "armies" of one hundred men each to meet them.

These things show either that Dinwiddie was far closer to the situation than Glen, or else that Glen never from the very first intended to help but that he covered up his dissimulation by this long letter of one thousand words on march 14, followed by another the same day of six hundred words – to which he even added a "P.S.," coaching Dinwiddie that he should not fail to "remember provisions is a prodigious article." [341]

If the letter just analyzed is a rare commentary on some of the factors that made for lack of colonial cooperation all through the colonial period, more especially during the critical days of 1754-1755, the second letter that Glen wrote Dinwiddie the same day, march 14, 1754, will, by comparison, beggar description. In this follow-up letter Glen gave Dinwiddie a real "intelligence test." In it even young George Washington did not escape Glen's counsel, which he distributed far and wide for the benefit of all who needed it. For example, Washington, who was under surveillance every moment he was present at the French fort and who is lucky to have escaped with his life, was told, through Glen's letter to Dinwiddie, that he "should have more minutely described it [the fort] . . . from salient angle to salient angle." This letter apparently was composed in all seriousness. Or was it?

Evidently Glen was in a writing mood. He was thoroughly stirred up. And well he might be. He had received in june 1753 an express from Dinwiddie, so he informed his assembly on march 5, 1754. The letter

---

341 Glen to Dinwiddie, march 14, 1754, P.R.O., C.O., 5/14, 299-302; L.C. tr., 277-280.

dealt with the French menace to the west. He declared
to them that he had answered it immediately. Also, in
november 1753 Dinwiddie had written him again on
the same subject – for Dinwiddie too had been in a writing mood. In Glen's address to his assembly he referred
to that communication from Dinwiddie as "another
letter from that gentleman." One can detect the note of
derision. But Dinwiddie got no answer from Glen himself, thanks to the vagaries of colonial correspondence.
The South Carolina governor explained to his legislators Dinwiddie was "in the Cherokee nation building
a fort. . . Within this three or four days a third express brought me another letter from him."

After all, these were only letters from a lieutenant-
governor to the northward who was apparently interfering in South Carolina's Indian preserves. Presently,
however, things took on a different complexion, when
Dinwiddie enclosed to him a "letter from the Earl of
Holderness [342] his majestys principal secretary of state
upon the same subject." This official communication
from England put an entirely new face upon the whole
matter. Holdernesse, as has already been seen, had made
Dinwiddie, not Glen, the intermediary in dispatching
his circular letter to the other governors, and that communication Glen did not dare treat lightly, much less
ignore. When Holdernesse's hand appeared, it will be
noted that Glen then, but not until then, brought the
matter of the French impasse before his two houses for
their consideration.

Even then, what he next told his assembled legislators
is amazing. It is a curious reflection on intercolonial

---

[342] Robert Darcy, fourth and last Earl of Holdernesse (1718-1778), succeeded to the title in 1721. He had some diplomatic experience—ambassador
to Venice, 1744-1746, and minister to Holland, 1749-1751. He succeeded the
Duke of Bedford as secretary of state for the southern department, june 18,
1751; for the northern department, march 23, 1754.

relations, but explains much otherwise inexplicable at the time. He frankly declared:

"I have ever looked upon it to be my duty and therefore I have made it my constant care to prevent your being unnecessarily allarmed, and tho the present unjust attack requires attention let it not give you any uneasie apprehensions for if a proper use be made of it I am so far from thinking that it will prove prejudicial to us that I am fully persuaded it will give peace and quiet to all the kings colonys for many years." [343]

One is tempted to speculate on the outcome of events, if Glen, in control of so important a colony, had taken the same cooperative point of view with Dinwiddie that Horatio Sharpe of Maryland and Arthur Dobbs [344] of North Carolina took.

Had Dinwiddie's entreaties prevailed with the other governors – particularly the governor of South Carolina – the French would not have gained their initial advantage; and if not their initial advantage, they would have lost their Indian support, in consequence of which the long and disastrous war would probably have been of short duration. The Roman cunctator himself never pursued a more Fabian policy than Glen advocated. The Virginia Rome might burn, while Glen, if he did not fiddle, would at least conduct a research investigation.

On april 15, in a lengthy rejoinder on a multitude of topics, Dinwiddie thanked Glen "for the care you have taken" in ordering the independent company, previously

343 Glen to the assembly, march 5, 1754, P.R.O., C.O., 5/14, 287-291; L.C. tr., 261-265. See also Report of committee of conference of South Carolina, march 30, 1754, P.R.O., C.O., 5/14, 291-294; L.C. tr., 267-269.

344 Arthur Dobbs (1689-1765), man of letters, landowner, legislator, and governor of North Carolina october 31, 1754 to march 28, 1765, was a native of County Antrim, Ireland. In 1745 Dobbs became co-owner of a tract of some 400,000 acres of land in North Carolina, and thus increasingly interested in the economic and political progress of that colony. Significantly, he was, as was the Virginia governor, a member of the Ohio company. Unquestionably he worked assiduously for what he regarded as the colony's best interests.

stationed in South Carolina, to Virginia, "which I daily expect tho not yet arrived." [345] Indeed it was not until may 10 that Dinwiddie was able to report to Glen that "your company is arrived after a very tedious passage, and this day are embarking on two sloops to carry them to Alexandria." Unhappily, they had arrived too late to help Trent at the forks. The capitulation there Dinwiddie had already detailed to Glen. Then Dinwiddie was forced to add: "The two companies from New York are not yet arrived, their delay is a very great loss to the expedition." [346] Even though Dinwiddie had written Glen on april 15 that he was "glad of the accounts you give" of the independent company, and even though they were almost as late as the two independent companies from New York, Dinwiddie dared not stir up another hornets' nest by even suggesting the slightest procrastination on Glen's part in getting his company up to Virginia. If he discerned what was in Dinwiddie's mind, Dinwiddie could not help that. Thus, in the hour of need, it began to look as though Dinwiddie's "fellow" governors, who seemed to prefer not to be their brother's keeper, were about to fail him. He watched while they slept.[347]

[345] Dinwiddie to Glen, april 15, 1754, P.R.O., C.O., 5/14, 485-488; L.C. tr., 439-445; *Dinwiddie papers*, I, 129. See also the interesting letter from Dinwiddie to Rowan [March 1754], *ibid.*, I, 91, explaining the curious error made by a London clerk regarding the whereabouts of the independent company; Dinwiddie to Glen, march 5, 1754, P.R.O., C.O., 5/14, 171-174; L.C. tr., 439-445; *Dinwiddie papers*, I, 90-91.

[346] Dinwiddie to Glen, may 10, 1754, *ibid.*, I, 168.

[347] If Dinwiddie had been the only official who apparently felt it necessary to take Glen to task, the controversy would have been one man's word against another's; but when the lords of trade take Glen to task, in two long communications separated by as much as a year, the situation assumes a serious aspect for the South Carolina governor. Though they sign the letters, according to the phraseology of the age, "your very loving friends," they do not mince words as they declare to him: ". . . you cannot but be sensible that the publick interest as well as your own character is very nearly concerned" (December 20, 1748, P.R.O., C.O., 5/402, L.C. tr.; december 1, 1749, P.R.O., C.O., 5/402, L.C. tr.).

Military Aspirations

"Now, sir, as his majesty is pleased to make me a military officer," wrote Robert Dinwiddie, civilian lieutenant-governor of Virginia, to John Hanbury, his trusted merchant friend in London, march 12, 1754, "please send for Scott, my taylor, to make me a proper suit of regimentals." [348]

What secret ambitions, what long smouldering aspirations, what cherished hopes toward the life military, may have been concealed in that curiously-worded letter from a man now reached sixty-one, a man who had truly been born and bred to a life of commerce, and who, so far as is known, had never concerned himself to learn even the rudiments of the military profession. Yet here he is ordering his "regimentals." That it was an ambition which lay close and deep in his heart is further borne out by a letter to his friend and agent, James Abercromby, in which letter, written october 23, 1754, he confided that he hoped to raise in the month of october ten companies of soldiers for the Ohio service and hoped to be found "worthy to be their colonel." He asked Abercromby to ascertain whether the home government would look favorably upon such a desired appointment, cited precedents that Abercromby could quote to the home authorities, and added significantly: "Please take some trouble in this." [349]

---

[348] Dinwiddie to John Hanbury, march 12, 1754, *Dinwiddie papers,* I, 104.

[349] Dinwiddie to Abercromby, october 23, 1754, *ibid.,* I, 376. Dinwiddie revealed himself only in his letters to James Abercromby, John Hanbury, and to the Earl of Halifax. One should read his letters to these men for comparison with the strictly official letters of the same date to, for instance, the lords of trade.

Dinwiddie further reminded Hanbury, in his "regimentals" letter above quoted, that his uniform should "be here by his majesty's birth day." Since a king's birthday was always observed in colonial Williamsburg with a special celebration, including a ball, the discharge of cannon, fireworks, and "entertainment" for the populace, it is evident that Dinwiddie intended to receive the colony's distinguished guests at the newly-completed governor's "palace" and himself be attired in his brandnew suit of "regimentals."

That letter is indeed so revealing that this section of it, given below in full, will be appreciated:

"I do not much like gayety in dress, but I conceive this necessary. I do not much care for lace on the coat, but a neat embroidered buttonhole, tho' you do not deal that way, I know you have a good taste, that I may shew my friend's fancy in that suit of cloths; a good laced hatt and two pair stockings, one silk, the other fine thread." To few persons, it may be said in passing, did he sign his letters as he did this one to Hanbury: "Dear friend, your affectionate humble servant." Not only were he and Hanbury close in their relationship, but on march 12, 1754 Dinwiddie was undoubtedly in a happy state of mind.

And why not? The capitulation of Fort Necessity and Braddock's defeat were still in the future. Those awful years of 1755-1757, when he stood like Leonidas, defending with a handful of men a three-hundred-mile frontier against a foe whose numbers seemed to be legion, were also still in the lap of destiny.[350] The announcement late in 1754 that his close friend, Governor Horatio Sharpe of Maryland, would be appointed, instead of himself, to command the combined 1754 expe-

---

350 Of course, Dinwiddie worked through trusted subordinates like George Washington. See Louis K. Koontz, "Washington on the frontier," *Virginia magazine of history and biography*, XXXVI (October 1928), 307-328.

dition to the Ohio, was as yet unknown to him. That the other colonies would prove so obdurate in coming to his aid in what he deemed so worthy an imperial program was undreamed of; and that his strong constitution would presently begin to give way under the unrelenting strain was totally unforeseen. On march 12, 1754 Dinwiddie surveyed from Williamsburg a future that must have looked roseate indeed.

That month of march was a busy one for the Virginia governor. His activities at this time are admirably summarized for us in a comprehensive letter written on march 1 to his personal friend and neighbor, Governor Sharpe. For example, he advised Sharpe that he had sent an "express," as colonial messengers were called, to the northern colonies to solicit aid from New England and New York for the approaching test of strength. He told Sharpe in his quaint way that "I am therefore in pain till I know what aid we may expect from them." He was also anxious to know what the Maryland assembly had voted to help him, though he was not apprehensive in the latter instance, since he felt Sharpe could always be counted upon. Hence he added: ". . . not doubting of your endeavours in soliciting the same." He reported further to Sharpe that Lord Holdernesse had just informed him that he had directed Governor James DeLancey of New York to send him "two of the independent companies there." They would be used to garrison the "forts I propose to erect at the forks of Monongahela" – meaning the Ohio. Reference to the independent companies that were to come from New York led Dinwiddie to call attention to a vital weakness in the imperial-colonial defensive mechanism in America: the inability of the regulars and the colonials to get on together. Dinwiddie's sentence to Sharpe read: ". . . but as new raised forces do not incline to mix with the regulars, I keep this as a secret [their going to the Ohio] till our forces are marched, and hope you will do the same." Here is a sad commentary upon the relationship at the time between these military representatives of two branches of the English-speaking people. It boded ill for the future.

Dinwiddie told Sharpe that he was having six companies of soldiers raised. These were to be at Alexandria by march 20. There his trusted commissary of supplies, Major John Carlyle, was to outfit "our small regiment" with wagons and "provisions for six months." [351] He already had sent out ten small cannon from the king's recent shipment to him.

The command of this little army had been a matter of concern to Dinwiddie. Not only did he feel personally responsible for its success but he was fully aware of the importance of selecting his subordinates wisely. He considered first Colonel James Innes, his close friend, a Scot then in the military service and at that time stationed with regulars in North Carolina. He considered George Washington, but George Washington regarded himself too young and not sufficiently experienced to accept the major responsibility. [352] Finally, his choice fell upon a man who had been under consideration from the very first, Joshua Fry, a professor of mathematics at the College of William and Mary. As Dinwiddie put it: "The command of the whole I have given to Colonel Joshua Fry, a man of good sense and an able mathematician." George Washington, with a lieutenant-colonelcy, was made second in command, though Dinwiddie does not refer to Washington in this letter to Sharpe. These two officers Dinwiddie felt he

---

351 Dinwiddie to Sharpe, march 1, 1754, *Dinwiddie papers*, I, 85-86.

352 Washington to Corbin, march 1754, John C. Fitzpatrick, ed., *Writings of George Washington*, I, 34; Louis K. Koontz, *Virginia frontier, 1754-1763*, 55.

could depend upon; for the rest, he wrote the Maryland governor that "we are in much distress for proper officers, but have taken all possible care of choosing the best we have, but," he added with keen insight, "not so well acquainted with the articles of war as I could wish."

Dinwiddie was a religious man, as his fast proclamation [353] and as his charges to the grand jury attest. He closed this informing letter with the observation that "as our cause is just, I hope for the protection of heaven."

If Dinwiddie were to be judged as to his military leadership by the instructions he prepared from time to time for his officers in the field his rating would be high. A fair sample of such is his "instructions to Joshua Fry, Esqr., colonel and commander-in-chief of the Virginia regiment," which he drew up and issued the first of march. He began by emphasizing the necessity of protecting the frontier settlements, by acting as long as possible strictly "on the defensive," but, if pushed to it, of rising to the occasion and not hesitating to "repell force by force." He acquainted Fry with what had been

[353] The proclamation, dated august 28, 1755, read as follows:

"WHEREAS we have but too much reason to fear, that our sins have justly provoked the Almighty to send down upon us his heavy judgements of war and famine; and as national repentence is the only remedy for national guilt, I have therefore thought fit to issue this proclamation, appointing wednesday the 24th of september to be religiously and devoutly observed as a general fast, for the solemn and public humiliation of ourselves before Almighty God, in order to supplicate His devine Majesty for the pardon of our sins, for averting those heavy judgments, and more particularly for the preservation of us from the hands of the enemies.

"AND I hereby strictly charge and require, that in all churches, where the ministers can possibly attend, devine service be performed, and a sermon be preached suitable to the occasion, and that on some preceding sunday they give notice of the said FAST and exhort their several congregations to a devout and religious observance of it" (*Virginia gazette*, september 12, 1755, quoted in the *Virginia magazine of history and biography*, xxv [January 1917], 16).

done already to get troops to Alexandria by the middle of april, of the supplies that he had ordered John Carlyle to furnish him, and of the cannon he had already sent out. All of this Fry of course knew about; but it is the part of a good commanding officer to acquaint his subordinates with the details on paper so that there may be no question about them. This Dinwiddie was doing in the "instructions." Dinwiddie had confidence in Fry, yet he thought proper to give him advice as to what should be kept uppermost in mind. Hence, he interposed in the instructions this observation: "Keep up a good command and regular discipline, inculcate morality and courage in your soldiers that they may answer the views on which they are raised." Not being an autocrat himself, Dinwiddie cautioned Fry to seek the counsel of others through courts martial: "You are to constitute a court martial of the chief of your officers, with whom you are to advise and consult on all affairs of consequence." [354] One of Dinwiddie's outstanding qualifications for military leadership was that he always first assured his subordinates of his confidence in them and then proceeded to leave emergencies in their hands.

Dinwiddie concluded his "instructions" thus: ". . . Sincerely recommending you to the protection of God . . . I heartily wish you farewell." It was indeed "farewell" that he bade his newly-commissioned officer. Fry not long afterward died as a result of a fall from his horse.[355] His second in command, George Washington, whom the governor originally considered for the chief place, now succeeded to it. There was indeed a destiny that shaped the ends for both Dinwiddie and George Washington.

Already by the middle of the month (march), how-

354 Instructions to Colonel Fry, march 1754, *Dinwiddie papers,* I, 88-90.
355 Louis K. Koontz, *Virginia frontier, 1754-1763,* 57.

ever, Dinwiddie, as his majesty's new "military officer," was having his usually imperturbable optimism put to the test. He unburdened his troubles on march 12 to Lord Holdernesse,[356] secretary of state, the lords of trade,[357] the Earl of Halifax,[358] John Hanbury,[359] and others. In a long letter to Lord Holdernesse, running to more than two thousand words, he detailed the colonial situation that confronted him in his new capacity as commander-in-chief of the forces that were being raised for the Ohio expedition. He acquainted that lord with the ten thousand pounds that the burgesses had finally voted late in february, only because he had prevailed upon them, he said, "with great application, many arguments, and with much difficulty." His own commission from his majesty, he reminded Holdernesse, had been "to raise the militia . . . to support his [majesty's] just right to the lands on the Ohio." The execution of it, however, as he pointed out, was quite another matter. He said he had consulted the council and "other persons of weight" in the colony and thereby found to his dismay that it would be impossible to force the militia to march to the Ohio, "as it remains uncertain [on their part] whether these lands are in this dominion, or belonging to Pensylvania." Here was a typical example of the baneful effects of the long-standing boundary disputes between colony and colony that too often paralyzed military operations at critical junctures. From this time on, Dinwiddie never ceased to urge the board of trade to order the line run between his colony and Pennsylvania. Yet it was as late as 1779 before the line,

---

[356] Dinwiddie to Holdernesse, march 12, 1754, P.R.O., C.O., 5/14, 165-168; L.C. tr., 125-134; *Dinwiddie papers,* I, 93-98.

[357] Dinwiddie to the lords of trade, march 12, 1754, P.R.O., C.O., 5/1328, 193-196; L.C. tr., 155-158; *Dinwiddie papers,* I, 98-99.

[358] Dinwiddie to the Earl of Halifax, march 12, 1754, *ibid.,* I, 100-101.

[359] Dinwiddie to John Hanbury, *op. cit.*

now one of the most famous in history, Mason and Dixon's, was extended westward "five degrees from the Delaware."

As a new commander-in-chief, Dinwiddie assured Holdernesse of his long-standing interest in the west. His vision as to the future of the country is clear. Thus he said: "The settling and securing the lands in the interior part of this large continent, particularly those on the back of this dominion has been much in my thoughts ever since my arrival at my government, and be assured, my lord, every thing in my power, in supporting the present expedition, shall be done with chearfulness." One of the reasons why Dinwiddie regarded the interior of the continent as so important, he told Holdernesse, was because the "skin and furr trade is to be conducted there to great advantage" – a subject that he was to stress time and again.

One of the statesmanlike acts of Dinwiddie's, and one fraught with consequences for the future, was his proclamation of february 19, 1754 as to western lands. As an "encouragement to the people to enlist with spirit," he informed Lord Holdernesse, he had granted "200,-000 acres of his majesty's lands on the Ohio; 15 years without paying quit rents. Copy of the proclamation I enclose you." [360] This emergency measure is worthy of study.

This grant by Dinwiddie overlapped, if it did not actually coincide with, the Ohio company's initial grant of identical size along the Ohio from the forks southwestward. Probably Dinwiddie felt that the Ohio company objective now had been merged in a larger imperial program; if, as is supposed, he regarded the Ohio company venture purely as an imperial advance guard, then it would be but natural that he should regard the

---

[360] Dinwiddie to Holdernesse, *op. cit.*

occupation of the same lands, with the quickest possible action, as justifiable on every ground. Not only that, but things had rapidly come to such a pass that it would be impossible for the Ohio company to carry out its original program, when he himself, representing the power of the largest colony, was finding himself taxed to the limit to accomplish the same end. As a member of that same company, he did not find his duty as a member at all incompatible with his duty to his sovereign and to Virginia. Hence his dramatic action on february 19.[361]

It was this land, as a result of Dinwiddie's emergency proclamation, that George Washington was to claim, and his soldiers were to claim, in the years to come.[362] Many of the soldiers, lacking faith in the grant or inclination to follow up their rights, sold their lands at a fair price to Washington, who thus came in time to possess vast holdings along the Ohio.[363]

"The reasons I went on," Dinwiddie explained to Holdernesse, "was to engage the people, that went on the expedition to remain there and make settlements; and [I] think it better to give that quantity to our people, than to give a quiet possession to the French of as many millions of acres, and I therefore hope, it will meet with his majesty's royal approbation." [364] Dinwiddie's actions customarily met with that "approbation."

One of the subjects that Dinwiddie discussed in this comprehensive letter to Holdernesse was the matter of

---

[361] Dinwiddie's proclamation, february 19, 1754, P.R.O., C.O., 5/1348, 334-336; L.C. tr., 211-212; Draper manuscripts, 1JJ20-1JJ22; Hening's *Statutes,* VII, 661-662.

[362] Washington to Governor Botetourt, october 5, 1770, P.R.O., C.O., 5/1348, 353-355; L.C. tr., 219-223; John C. Fitzpatrick, ed., *Writings of George Washington,* III, 11, 72; cf. *ibid.,* III, 26-29.

[363] For the most extensive study of these and other holdings, see Eugene E. Prussing, *Estate of George Washington, deceased* (Boston, 1927).

[364] Dinwiddie to Holdernesse, *op. cit.*

building forts. He and George Washington were to become co-partners in the work.[365] It ought perhaps to be explained that there were already erected or to be erected on the Virginia frontier, and indeed along all the frontiers, four distinct types of defenses: first, the fortified cabin; second, the blockhouse; third, the stockade; and finally, most important of all, the fort. The better-built log cabins on the frontier were strengthened with double doors, had portholes for the guns and cleared ground round about. The blockhouse was a two-story structure, with the upper story extending out over the lower, permitting the defenders to fire down upon their assailants. The stockade, or stockaded fort, was a blockhouse protected by a palisaded fence often surrounding it at some distance. The palisade itself was a series of posts planted in the ground, each post standing from eight to ten feet above the ground and having the upper end sharpened to a point for protection against scaling. Fort Necessity, as now restored in southwestern Pennsylvania, is an excellent example of this type of defense. The palisaded fence usually formed a rectangle, in which case blockhouses were often placed at each of the four corners of the enclosed area. One of the best illustrations of this type of defense is Fort Boone in Kentucky, which also has been restored. A unique feature about the roofs of the four blockhouses at the corners of the Fort Boone rectangle is that they slope inward.[366] Since this obviously would make it harder for

---

[365] The idea of frontier forts, even forts on the Ohio, in order to counteract the influence of the French forts there had been suggested by Dinwiddie to the lords of trade at least as early as december 10, 1752 (P.R.O., C.O., 5/1327, 531-536; L.C. tr., 415-424). Again on june 16, 1753 he had pointed out the "utility of building some forts upon the river Ohio in the western part of our colony of Virginia, for the security and protection of our subjects, and of the Indians in alliance with us" (See Lords of trade to Dinwiddie, august 28, 1753, P.R.O., C.O., 5/1344; L.C. tr.).

[366] A framed sketch of Fort Boone, showing the roof sloping inward, hangs

the Indians to set such a roof on fire with blazing arrows, while at the same time it permitted the besieged frontier men to lie on the roof and fire at their attackers, it is singular that the frontier defenses were not regularly so constructed. The finest example of the strongest type of frontier defense is Fort Frederick, completed in 1756. This fort still stands in western Maryland, a few hundred yards up from the Potomac river, and between Hancock and Hagerstown. It is of course rectangular in form, with a huge bastion at each of its four corners, permitting a cross-fire which would desolate a foe that might attempt to scale its seventeen-foot walls of Maryland sandstone. The walls were four feet wide at the base and two feet at the top. Each hinge on the gate weighed forty-two pounds. This fort occupies an acre and a half. It served its purpose during three wars, as many as seven hundred soldiers having occupied it at one time. The water supply came from three wells within the enclosure and they are still easily located. The one bastion that gradually fell into disrepair has been rebuilt. Here may be seen today, therefore, one of the most remarkable structures of the kind erected during the French and Indian war. It was built in 1756 through the efforts of Governor Horatio Sharpe of Maryland, with the moral support and encouragement of Governor Dinwiddie of Virginia.[367]

Fort-building was one of Dinwiddie's greatest interests and an activity of major importance for the colony of Virginia. In this he had the hearty cooperation of young George Washington, even though they occasionally differed as to the details of the defensive program.[368]

on the walls of the Filson club, Louisville, Kentucky. It was shown to me some years ago by the secretary, Mr. Otto Rothert.

[367] For a more detailed description of frontier forts see Louis K. Koontz, *Virginia frontier, 1754-1763*, 98-148.

[368] Louis K. Koontz, "Washington on the frontier," *Virginia magazine of history and biography*, XXXVI (October 1928), 307-328.

Among the problems inherent in such a program was that of making clear to the various boards and departments in England the peculiar needs of a colonial governor three thousand miles away, in a land whose geography those officials knew only imperfectly; and against a foe, the tactics of whom were totally different from those known in Europe. As early as march 7, 1753 – which was months before Washington was sent to the French – Dinwiddie had memorialized the crown, so the privy council reported, "representing the utility of building some forts upon the Ohio river in the western part of that colony for the security and protection of his majesty's subjects, and the Indians in alliance with his majesty, and proposing, that twenty or thirty cannon three pounders, may be forthwith sent from hence to place in the said forts." The board of trade, having been called on for advice, sought, in turn, the ordnance officials' counsel. They learned that the ordnance department thought "the application of the said governor for cannon be too early, in regard the forts are not yet erected." The board of trade was next asked "to consider the nature of the forts proposed to be erected." By the fifteenth of may the lords of trade were ready to report. In effect, they reported that in America there were different kinds of forts – all of them, moreover, differing from those in Europe. Thus they came to Dinwiddie's defense. They explained that if Dinwiddie had had in mind the building of such defenses as those on the continent of Europe which were always classed as "forts" and had applied for cannon and ordnance stores for such defenses "without transmitting regular plans, or any account of what progress was made in the building them, [it] would have been a very extraordinary proceeding." This, however, does not appear to be the case from anything in Dinwiddie's letter, they explain.

On the contrary, they "have reason to apprehend from the terms of the letter itself, as well as from the small size and number of the cannon required, (insufficient for regular forts of strength), ... are nothing more, than small wooden block-houses such as are usually erected in his majesty's colonys in America for the security of the Indians and the defense of his majestys subjects, transient traders amongst them." The board further went on record as understanding that Dinwiddie's request was for only thirty three-pound cannon; they therefore ". . . order the ordnance to prepare an estimate of 30 3-pounders with a proportion of stores for the forts." The ordnance department, in their turn, reported "that there are no three pounder ordnance in your majesty's stores proper for land service." They too, however, begin to cooperate by suggesting that, while they cannot supply three-pounders, they "can furnish the required number of four pounder ordnance." The estimate for these substitute pieces amounted to £1196/10/11.[369]

Thus did Dinwiddie's request run the gauntlet of official channels in London. He finally got from the crown the military stores that would be urgently needed one year later, when a series of crises in the Ohio west would have to be met in rapid succession.

Such were the forts about which Dinwiddie wrote in his long letter to Lord Holdernesse on march 12, exactly a year later. "When three or four forts are properly finished," he said, "I think fifty soldiers in each will be sufficient, and that will greatly encourage our

[369] Acts of the privy council, IV, 200-203; Office of ordnance to the lords of trade, april 17, 1753, P.R.O., C.O., 5/1327, 617-618; L.C. tr., 513-515; Lords of committee of council for plantation affairs to the lords of trade, april 19, 1753, P.R.O., C.O., 5/1327, 615-616; L.C. tr., 511-512; Lords of trade to the privy council, may 15, 1753, P.R.O., C.O., 5/211, 5-10; L.C. tr., 3-5. See also An account of the French forts from a deserter [1752], P.R.O., C.O., 5/1327, 567-570; L.C. tr.; cf. P.R.O., C.O., 5/1344, 1-5; L.C. tr., 120-124.

friendly Indians, to have a strong house to put their women and children in, when they go hunting, or to war, and at the same time prevent encroachments on his majesty's lands."

Dinwiddie's interest in securing the Indian to the English cause was second only to his interest in defense; in fact, the two were part and parcel of the same program. He had probably observed long before, during his earlier stay in Virginia, that the American Indian required a handling suited to the Indian himself. He appreciated that in any conflict between the English and the French, the Indian would probably hold the balance of power; and it was his far-sighted policy to maneuver the English into a position from which they could control this balance. He appreciated that the valuable fur trade depended upon Indian cooperation and he understood Indian psychology. For example, he knew that the Indian expected action and not delay. It was thus that he wrote Sharpe on march 3 urging vigorous action: ". . . if we do not make a push at this time, we shall loose all the Indians now in our friendship; the consequence thereof may prove fatal." [370]

"Presents" for the Indians, a device much employed by the French, was urged by Dinwiddie in his letters home as vigorously as the fort-building. As early as december 10, 1752, only a year after his coming to Virginia, and long before Trent's and Washington's reports reached him, he began agitation. The board of trade reported that they received a representation from Robert Dinwiddie, "proposing that a sum of money should be granted to be invested in goods for a present to the nation or tribe of the Twightwee Indians inhabiting the western parts of the said colony. . . That this nation or tribe . . . can bring into the field a larger number of

370 Dinwiddie to Sharpe, march 3 [1754], *Dinwiddie papers*, I, 105-106.

fighting men than any other tribe of Indians in those parts; that the securing them to the British interest will be of great utility and advantage, not only on account of the trade and commerce which may be carried on with them, but also on account of the security which, from an alliance with them, will be derived to your majesty's subjects, who may settle in the remote parts of this province; and that the most effectual way of gaining the friendship of those Indians will be by making them presents, as is proposed by your majesty's said lieutenant-governor." [371] Dinwiddie made a good case, because he had one. The commissioners of trade and plantations, otherwise known as the lords of trade, responded to such a plea. According to the minutes, they "therefore humbly propose to your majesty that a sum not exceeding £1000 should be applyed to this service out of your majesty's revenue of 21/ per hogshead upon tobacco, which revenue is appropriated to the contingent service of government, has frequently been applyed to that particular service, and is at present in such a state as very well to admit of this charge, it appearing from the receiver-general's account of the said revenue transmitted to us by Mr. Dinwiddie, that on the 25 of october last there was then in the treasurer's hands a ballance due to your majesty of nine thousand two hundred and fifty pounds eleven shillings and seven pence." [372]

These fort-building activities Dinwiddie described to Colonel William Fairfax, march 15, as "uphil work." If it had not been for such close associates as Colonel Fairfax on the council, and for others like him but who

---

[371] The lords of trade to the king, march 16, 1753, P.R.O., C.O., 5/1367, 24-26; L.C. tr., 14-15. As a matter of record it will be recalled that Dinwiddie had pointed out to the British government, even before he came over as governor, the importance of presents. "Friendship is chiefly secured by annual presents," he had written the lords of trade in august 1751 (P.R.O., C.O., 5/1327, 417; L.C. tr., 309-310).

[372] The lords of trade to the king, *op. cit.*

were not on it, Dinwiddie could hardly have stood the strain. He referred to Fairfax's communication as "your kind and friendly letter"; and revealing their close relationship, he went on to say: "If things had succeeded agreeable to your advice and mine, we should have been there [at the forks] before this time." The exactions of government were beginning to tell upon him. He wrote in the same letter: "I have been very much fatigued, but if I could accomplish what I have in view, I should not grudge any trouble." He was having great difficulty raising the necessary money to support his expedition under Colonel Fry. He and the council, he told Colonel Fairfax, who must still have been too ill to attend its meetings, were disappointed that the treasurer of the colony could not furnish the needed money.

The treasurer, John Robinson, who was also the speaker, may not have sufficiently forgotten the pistole dispute; at least it does not appear that he moved with special alacrity to procure Dinwiddie the funds he so sorely needed. However, Dinwiddie wrote Colonel Fairfax that the treasurer was unable to "borrow the money at Williamsburg or York, but that he had wrote by Mr. Washington to a gentleman at Fredericksburg to lend the money."

All this seems infinitesimally trivial to a later century where war chests of billions are underwritten, but the genius of Dinwiddie and of Washington throughout these years lies in the fact, of course, that proportionately to their means they were able to accomplish so much. To them might be applied the words used of Frederick the Great, "with little means he accomplished great ends."

As an evidence not only of the privations of this kind to which the governor was forced, but also of the place where his heart was, he stated to the colonel: "However, to give some life to the affair, I have borrowed £300, which I send you, to supply Colonel Washington with part, and the rest to Colonel Fry, and if you can borrow £300 more with you, it shall be paid at the court." He added, with meaning: "I wish it was in my power, I would advance the whole." He concluded this letter with a characteristic statement: "My philosophy is put on the rack to support myself under the disappointment, but patience is a virtue I must endeavour to exercise for some time." [373]

A letter dated march 15, 1754 from Dinwiddie to his youngest lieutenant-colonel in the service, George Washington, throws additional light upon the governor's qualifications to be a commander-in-chief of military forces in the literal and personal sense of the term. In this letter Dinwiddie shows that he was keeping in touch with the minutest details of the campaign. Although he had confidence in Washington, he did give him an unusual amount of advice; for instance, since the French were so early expected down the Ohio, "I think . . . it necessary," he wrote, "for you to march what soldiers you have enlisted, imediately to the Ohio, and escort some waggons, with the necessary provisions. . . Send a runner before you for intelligence, that you may not meet with any surprize. . . I entreat you to be diligent in your march; take what officers you see proper that are at Alexandria, and keep up a good discipline 'till Colonel Fry joins you." [374] All this may look like meddling in the details of a field campaign; but there is another angle to the picture. Washington, thirty-nine years younger than the governor, was as yet untried. As time went on, and as he acquitted himself creditably,

[373] Dinwiddie to Colonel William Fairfax, march 15 [1754], *Dinwiddie papers*, I, 108-109.

[374] Dinwiddie to Washington, march 15, 1754, *ibid.*, I, 106-107.

first with Jumonville, then at Fort Necessity, and finally
in defending the frontier, it will be found that Dinwiddie gradually placed greater and greater confidence in
him. Not only that, but the governor showed sound military wisdom in his unceasing caution not only to Washington, but to Fry as well, against being taken by surprise. He seemed to grasp instinctively the necessity of
guarding against it – a factor that, in the French and
Indian war, cost the English and the colonials more
heavily than any other. It was the essential element de-
termining success in Indian warfare. Yet it seemed a
lesson difficult for the young British officers, and sometimes even for the American, to learn. Therefore it is
worthy of note that George Washington, because of his
intuition, his long experience in the back country, or
the many admonitions from the governor, or because of
all three, was himself never caught with his forces in an
ambush. Yet Braddock, who ought to have profited by
what had been happening all along, was to be defeated
near the forks in 1755, chiefly because taken by "surprize." And again, as though experience were too hard
a teacher, Major James Grant,[375] three years later, in
leading an advance force for General John Forbes [376] in

---

[375] James Grant, army officer, with rank of major during the French and
Indian war. He served under General Forbes in the expedition against Fort
Duquesne. He led an advance detachment, fell into an ambuscade, was cap-
tured, and carried (with Major Andrew Lewis) to Canada. He was in time
released and in 1760-1761 campaigned successfully against the Cherokees.

[376] John Forbes (1710-1759), British officer who rose through long service
to brigadier-general in 1758. He was well thought of by Lord Loudoun. He
led the colonial forces from Pennsylvania, Maryland, Virginia, and North
Carolina with Indians and regulars against Fort Duquesne through the
summer and fall of 1758, himself so ill he had to be carried on an improvised
stretcher. His building of blockhouses—a step the efficacy of which Dinwiddie
and George Washington, and, to some extent, Pennsylvania, had already
demonstrated—along the route was a masterful move. It encouraged the
settlers and effectively discouraged the French and Indians. The building
of forts meant a Fabian policy; but it was wise strategy: Fort Duquesne was
a deserted post which Forbes took over on november 25, 1758.

the same locality fell into a similar trap. He too was
"surprized." Was it prevision that led Dinwiddie on
march 18 – three days after he had written Washington
a similar letter – to warn Fry in these words: ". . . I
desire you to send a runner or messenger before you,
that you may not be surprized by the enemy." [377]

In the above-mentioned letter to Washington are
found several evidences of the governor's willingness to
leave many matters to his young colonel's judgment. For
example, the latter's soldiers clamored for uniforms, having been theretofore clad only in their many varieties
of homemade garments. His confidence in Washington's
action in the matter – not to speak of his Scotch thrift –
are seen in his reply: "I have no objection to the soldiers
being in an uniform dress, on the head you propose, but
I am perswaded you have not time to get them made,
unless to be sent after you. In that case, care should be
taken of buying the cloth at the cheapest rate." [378] The
backwoodsmen who made up Washington's raw recruits
probably became insistent upon a new garb, the more
they saw and heard of the regulars attired in their
bright military dress. They were even willing to pay for
the new suits themselves, if they had to, as was the custom in the British army. As Dinwiddie explained, when
he wrote to Governor Sharpe: "In order to have them in
an uniform, they allow a deduction from their pay to
purchase a coat and breeches of red cloth." [379] Later on,
minor causes of friction occasionally arose between these
two men, Dinwiddie and Washington, both dominant
characters, yet, as will be seen, the tension did not last
long. This present letter to Washington closes with a
heartening word to the young officer, then probably in

---

[377] Dinwiddie to Fry, march 18 [1754], *Dinwiddie papers*, I, 109-111.
[378] Dinwiddie to Washington, march 15, 1754, *op. cit.*
[379] Dinwiddie to Sharpe, march 28, 1754, *ibid.*, I, 116.

the vicinity of Winchester, a town which Dinwiddie referred to as "far back on our frontiers." He closed with: "Pray God preserve you and grant success to our just designs. I am most sincerely, sir, your friend and humble servant."

Even though Joshua Fry was Washington's superior officer, and a colonel by Dinwiddie's creation, the governor felt it as incumbent upon him to give Fry generous counsel as he had Washington. On march 18 he cautioned him to "read over the articles of war, and select out of them such as you think proper for the regular discipline of your small regiment. After that, have them read at the head of each company that the soldiers may know the punishment they may expect on the breach of their duty." Being a man who put "duty" before almost every other consideration he expected the troops to do the same. All other things would then be given them.

This letter deals with supplies, commissions, warrants for money, and includes a goodly amount of counsel. In it there appears one line that reflects the army life on the colonial frontier: "The soldiers will want a little rum in their march, and some, according to the labour, when you come to the Ohio." Poor quartermaster John Carlyle must be able to supply everything for the little army, from tents to spirits, hence Dinwiddie continued: "You must therefore speak to Mr. Carlyle to send the quantity you may think proper."

Whether or not Dinwiddie kept, as a Williamsburg satirical writer of the time alleged he kept, "a little black ledger" [380] containing the names of his political enemies, he apparently preserved a very careful record of the qualifications and disqualifications regarding prospective young officers. He had these indexed in his

[380] See "Dinwiddianae" (Huntington library).

mind and passed them on from time to time to Fry and to Washington. To Fry he wrote on march 18: "As Captain Trent has a double company you cannot fix the lieutenant's till you come to the Ohio, and if you divide his company the eldest lieutenant has a right for a captain's commission; but as he is a Dutchman and canot speak good English, I think you [had] better prefer the next to him." And then: "Colonel Washington's brother must have a pair of colours, but not a lieutenant's commission as the lieutenants are already compleated." This latter because Washington had written Dinwiddie that he would be glad of a commission, if one were available, for his younger brother, John Augustine.[381] And finally: "One de Keyser [382] was mentioned by Colonel Fairfax for adjutant and quarter master." Dinwiddie added humorously: "I hear he is a dancing master and not acquainted with the exercise, if so, not eligible for that appointment."

One of the most serious problems that confronted the Virginia governor as military commander-in-chief was the disputes between the British and the Americans over rank. The regular officers, who claimed to hold their commissions from the king, usually refused to take orders from or serve under a provincial officer, even of higher rank. Such controversies at times almost paralyzed the service. To begin with, Dinwiddie had to select an officer to command the combined 1754 expedition to the Ohio. Such an officer must guarantee harmony. First in preference, as has been noticed, was Colonel James Innes; but Innes was not immediately

---

[381] John Augustine Washington (1736-1787), youngest and favorite brother of George Washington. He lived for a time at Mount Vernon and took care of it for his brother George during the latter's absence on the frontier. He was the father of Bushrod Washington, whom George Washington seemed to regard as his favorite nephew.

[382] Lehaynsius de Keyser was an ensign on the frontier.

available because on service in North Carolina with two independent companies. Innes was a Scotchman, had seen service under Governor Gooch in the Cartagena expedition, and seems to have been well known to Dinwiddie. Dinwiddie wrote him in unusual terms, march 23: "Dear James: Your kind letter of the 12th current I received by Mr. Ashe,[383] and I am very glad that I shall have the pleasure of seeing you at the head of a regiment of 750 men. I intended you the chief command of our forces, but the few now raised were to march directly to the Ohio, that [I] was obliged to commission the officers." The letter closed with expressions of attachment: "You know my regard and esteem for you. . . My wife, Lize, and the child, join me in sincere respects to you and Mrs. Innes." The expression, "Lize and the child" probably has reference to his older daughter, Elizabeth, now seventeen, and his younger daughter, Rebecca, three years her junior.

The military references in this letter are informative. Dinwiddie said to Innes: "The very thought you write me, occurred to me, and a month ago I wrote to [the] governors of New York and New England to make a faint towards Canada, to divert their sending the number of forces mentioned; whether they will put it in practice, I cannot say." The Virginia governor had had in mind all along a comprehensive program of colonial offensive and not one limited merely to the segment that Virginia regarded as her special responsibility. The word "dispatch" stood in Dinwiddie's regard only a little lower than "duty." He instinctively grasped another of the fundamental rules of warfare: seizing and holding the initiative. He wrote Innes: "Dispatch is absolutely necessary, and [I] hope you will bring your

---

383 John Ashe, officer in the North Carolina colonial militia and later brigadier-general.

forces by sea." His "P.S." carries for us valuable information regarding the equipment of the time, for it read: "His majesty sent 30 pieces of cannon, 4 pownders, with all necessary implements . . . no cowhorns or hand grenades here." [384]

Dinwiddie's relationship with Innes is a fair index to the governor's breadth of character. He wrote Innes in the friendly manner noted above; yet, when the occasion seemed to justify it, not a moment did he hesitate to criticize drastically his conduct. For instance he wrote on july 20: "The misfortune attending our expedition is entirely owing to the delay of your forces, and more particularly the two independent companies from New York." [385] A little later he wrote two letters regarding Innes, both interesting. In the one he criticized him for failure to answer his letters and look after certain other important details. Yet that same day he wrote a letter of recommendation to Braddock on behalf of Innes, but apparently without Innes's knowledge. On the whole, Dinwiddie made wise selections of his officers. He probably was right as to Innes's ability, though he differed with him at times and never hesitated frankly to tell him so. Dinwiddie had finally chosen Joshua Fry for the chief command when Innes was not available. After Fry's death, when Innes succeeded to the command, Washington wrote Dinwiddie regarding him: "I rejoice that I am likely to be happy under the command of an experienced officer and a man of sense, it is what I have ardently wished for." [386]

Captain James McKay,[387] in command of the troops

---

[384] Dinwiddie to Innes, march 23, 1754, *Dinwiddie papers,* I, 125-126.

[385] Dinwiddie to Innes, july 20, 1754, *ibid.,* I, 232.

[386] Washington to Dinwiddie, june 10, 1754, John C. Fitzpatrick, ed., *Writings of George Washington,* I, 74. Washington, on Fry's death, was made a colonel and held responsible for the troops from Virginia.

[387] James Mackay, Mackaye, or McKay, a native of Scotland, commanded

sent from South Carolina, was one of the regular officers whose presence on the frontier was an occasion for embarrassment for Dinwiddie. He declined to serve under Washington, who held only a colonial commission. Dinwiddie diplomatically decided that the only way he could settle the matter would be to place McKay immediately under his own command, since he himself was commander-in-chief. This was an intolerable situation in an emergency but was the best expedient the governor could hit upon for the time being. The governor appealed to Washington to get along with McKay as well as he could, for the sake of "unanimity"; and Washington replied that he could be depended upon, but he would "have been particularly obliged if your honour had declared whether he was under my command or independent of it." [388] The whole regrettable situation over rank, which long had irritated Washington, presently led to his resignation; but in due time his position was fully vindicated.

As was emphasized at the outset of this chapter, Dinwiddie had military aspirations. Whether he intended to take command personally in the field is not clear. The probabilities are that he did not intend to do so. It is rather difficult, however, to explain exactly what he had in mind when, on october 23, 1754, he wrote James Abercromby in London a very illuminating letter, already quoted in part: "I propose raising 10 companies of 100 men each . . . and if I am thought worthy to be their colonel, I shall be very glad, and am perswaded [this] will be very much agreeable to the officers and

an independent company of one hundred men from South Carolina. Apparently they came by boat to Alexandria and then marched to join Washington. Fitzpatrick succinctly states: "MacKaye was present at Fort Necessity and his name was appended to the articles of capitulation ahead of Washington's" (John C. Fitzpatrick, ed., *Diaries of George Washington, 1748-1799*, I, 81-82n).

388 Washington to Dinwiddie, june 10, 1754, *op. cit.*

soldiers. This I write to Sir Thomas Robinson, and you will soon find whether [it is] agreeable. There is the president [precedent] of the Carthagena expedition, and that to Canada." Dinwiddie referred to the ill-fated 1739 expedition participated in by Lieutenant-governor William Gooch of Virginia and to the attack of Governor William Shirley of Massachusetts upon Louisbourg in 1744. Regarding his colonelcy, attention has already been called to Dinwiddie's closing sentence in his letter to Abercromby: "Please take some trouble in this."

But disappointment was in store for the Virginia governor — whatever his military dreams. The redeeming feature is his reaction to that disappointment. By october 20 he had learned that Governor Horatio Sharpe of Maryland had been appointed to command the combined forces. Dinwiddie wrote in a letter to Captain Thomas Clark, of one of the independent companies from New York: ". . . I have received new instructions from Great Britain. . . Mr. Sharpe, the governor of Maryland has his majesty's commission to comand the forces on this expedition." He added: "He is to be with me in a few days, to consult a plan of operations." [389] Whatever chagrin Dinwiddie may have felt, he gave no indication of it. Not only was Sharpe his personal friend, but there was the royal mandate — and to that he had never failed to subordinate his own preferences. He did not fail now. In writing his patron, the Earl of Halifax, october 25, and referring to Sharpe's appointment, he interposed this significant comment: "I may venture to affirm that the greatest view I have, is to discharge the trust reposed in me, and the service left to my conduct, in such manner as to have his majesty's gracious approbation, and I shall continue, with assiduity, to

[389] Dinwiddie to Clark, october 20 [1754], *Dinwiddie papers,* I, 350.

perform my duty with integrity and spirit." [390] Here truly was the measure of the man.

Dinwiddie and Sharpe were such close friends that Sharpe's appointment as commander-in-chief of the expedition meant the carrying out of Dinwiddie's own cherished plans. The following "plan of military operations," which is known to have been drawn up after Dinwiddie learned of Sharpe's appointment, bears internal evidence of having been drawn up by Dinwiddie himself and then assented to by Dobbs and by Sharpe.

It reads, in part:

"In pursuance of their advice, and approbation of the scheme I propose, if possible, to assemble a thousand men, the independent companies included; and, unless the winter setts in too severely, very shortly I hope they will be able to carry the French fort, on the river Monongahela, at least, before it can be reinforced from Canada in the spring.

"This indeed, and building a fort, (which we think necessary) opposite to it, and an island in the Ohio, is all I can entertain very sanguine hopes of being able to execute, with so small a number of men as, I am affraid, will be under my direction, unless we are reinforced from home; as large detachments will be immediate[ly] necessary, and must be emploid in garrisoning those forts. . .

"And if we find there is the least prospect of succeeding therein; I will make an attempt, with our American strength, on the forts, which the French have built, near Lake Erie, up the river Buffaloe. And you will be pleased to assure his majesty, that nothing shall be wanting on my part to perform it." [391]

The foregoing pages paint a picture of the man whose

390 Dinwiddie to the Earl of Halifax, october 25 [1754], *ibid.*, I, 366.
391 Plan of operations, october 25, 1754, P.R.O., C.O., 5/14, 565-566; L.C. tr., 517-518; *Dinwiddie papers*, I, 351.

colorful letter, ordering a military wardrobe, opened this chapter. Tragically for Dinwiddie, it may be, he never had a chance to make use of those "regimentals" except in the capital city of Williamsburg. Surveying the data before us, to what extent did Dinwiddie seriously dream of a military career? What were his qualifications for such a rôle? To begin with, he already had been a successful businessman – as an exporter, and, in the customs service, as an inspector, collector, and surveyor-general. He was justified in feeling that he had been successful thus far also in politics, as a colonial executive. Is it not plausible that he should ask himself: "Why not a military leader?"

First, Dinwiddie had precedents in his favor. He must have been familiar with the accounts of the successful military leadership of such civilians as Cincinnatus, Jeanne d'Arc, and Cromwell. He already had cited to James Abercromby the precedents of William Gooch and William Shirley, governors respectively of Virginia and Massachusetts, who had had but little military experience to qualify them for the war-time appointments that they received.

Second, since he seems always to have been interested in the militia, in fort-building, and in studying the articles of war, it is significant that it had not been Spotswood, nor Gooch, but Robert Dinwiddie, who, with an eye to military advantages, had soon after his arrival as governor divided Virginia into four military districts and appointed an adjutant for each of them. George Washington was one of these new officers.

In the third place, the governor was, within an incredibly short time after his arrival in Virginia, adequately familiar with the internal machinery of the colony, with the Indian problem, and with the peculiar military needs of Virginia. In other words, he possessed another of the fundamentals of a successful military leader – to be thoroughly informed.

Fourth, he recognized the military necessity of a unified command "under a general officer," with a definite objective ahead in the campaign. In letter after letter he insisted on this point.

He always insisted, in the next place, on the adequacy of his soldier's commissary. Dinwiddie did not need to be prompted even by Governor Glen of South Carolina who, as has been noted, admonished him: "Remember provisions is a prodigious article." [392] Dinwiddie moved mountain-sized obstacles in order to clothe and shelter the men in the little army out on the frontier. Nothing so much as consideration for the comfort of the private soldier endears a commander to the rank and file of his followers.

Dinwiddie, in the sixth place, familiarized himself thoroughly with the topography of the country, with the strength as well as the weakness of the enemy, and the minutest military details. In this respect he even out-Loudouned Loudoun.

Seventh, he always appreciated the importance of the Indian alliance, because he realized that it might be – as it turned out to be – the decisive factor in some of the engagements and even some of the campaigns ahead. He had himself made a careful study of the Indian, his psychology, and his technique.

Eighth, he combined in proper proportion the care-taking, if not Fabian, qualities of a defensive commander with the military dispatch and technique of an offensive leader.

Furthermore, once he had appointed a subordinate to

392 Glen to Dinwiddie, march 14, 1754, P.R.O., C.O., 5/14, 299-302; L.C. tr., 277-280.

a responsibility, he extended him his confidence and gave him full rein; counselling him, to be sure, but always rewarding merit with as much alacrity as he punished disloyalty.

Finally, he had what every successful leader must have, a proper confidence in his own individual ability. Without self-confidence, a commander, particularly a new commander, is lost before he starts.

After all, who is to measure military success, and what is to be the criterion in doing so? What of the commander who keeps his eye fixed, as did Dinwiddie, on the distant goal rather than upon the zigzag route toward it? It may be said truthfully, both as regards the colonial wars and the later American revolution, that even George Washington, military genius that he was, usually lost his battles. But he won his campaigns.

This is the governor who, at one of his very first meetings with the Virginia assembly, showed his keen interest in things military, when he chose, from the many matters before him, to emphasize the subject of the militia. Said he, as his new audience must have sat in rapt attention:

"The season of the year, and your own private affairs, calling you to your respective counties, I desire to recommend to you, as far as your influence reaches, to see the laws in regard to the militia put in execution, by having the people duly mustered, and trained up in military discipline. We have an open and extensive country, without fortifications, so that the protection of our lives and estates depend chiefly (under God) on our militia."

Thus warned this eighteenth-century Scotch governor of Virginia in his peculiar way. He added in this message a further observation, attributed by some to George

Washington, when he continued: ". . . and it's the maxim of all wise nations, in time of peace, to prepare and provide against the exigencies of war." [393]

There are some who will say that these words were meant to apply only to an age that dealt with Indians, to an age that offered bounties for human scalps, and to an age that, for a period of two years, pursued "undeclared warfare"; but others will forever maintain that he spoke for eternity.

---

[393] *Journals of the house of burgesses* (1752-1755; 1756-1758), 99-100; *Dinwiddie papers,* I, 30.

Undeclared Warfare

On april 17, 1754 occurred an event – the first setback to Dinwiddie's determined stand – that might be regarded, in a sense, as the beginning of the French and Indian war.[394] It was that day which saw the capitulation to the French of Captain William Trent's English force at the forks.

This Virginia governor, erstwhile businessman, somehow possessed an uncanny appreciation of the military importance of the surprise factor in warfare. In practically every instruction he issued to his captains, majors, colonels, and county officers, he urged them to be ever on their guard. Accordingly, he had warned Captain William Trent to be on the alert in the Ohio country and so avoid being taken by surprise.[395] But a surprise was precisely what occurred. The collapse of the Trent project was a severe blow to him. The difficulties he had already encountered in sending Trent to the forks would have discouraged a less persistent man.

Recovering, however, from the shock of the capitulation, he determined to warn his countrymen, far and near, for the worst that might possibly happen. The long series of letters he prepared on may 10 to a wide circle of correspondents, in explanation of it all, must have taxed the energies even of his secretary, William Waller. He described the sorrowful story to the lords of trade, Lord Halifax, Lord Holdernesse, the lords of the treasury, and Earl Granville, as well as to Horace

---

[394] War was not formally declared until may 18, 1756.

[395] Dinwiddie to Trent, january 26, 1754, *Dinwiddie papers,* I, 55.

Walpole, Capel Hanbury, James Abercromby,[396] and
his fellow governors.[397] He explained to them that the
assembly, which was haggling over the pistole fee matter, refused to grant him any money. He then had consulted with the council, however, and on their advice
he had given Trent a commission, empowered him to
raise one hundred men, directed him to lead them to the
forks of the Ohio and there to "clear the ground, and
begin to erect a fort."

The governor had originally promised Trent that as
soon as he was able he would dispatch additional troops
to reinforce him. At last, on april 10, he ordered a detachment of one hundred fifty men, "under the command
of Colonel Washington," to Trent's support.[398] However, when Washington got within seventy-five miles of
the forks, as he later explained to Dinwiddie, he was
met by Trent's second in command, Ensign Edward
Ward.[399] Ward, according to Dinwiddie, revealed that
"the French, to the number of 1000 men, came down the
river Ohio, marched up to the fort, and summoned them
to surrender, and to march out with their guns and tools,
which they were obliged to do." The French, as is generally known, thereupon rebuilt what could have been

396 Dinwiddie to the lords of trade, may 10, 1754, P.R.O., C.O., 5/1328, 211-
214; L.C. tr., 167-172; Dinwiddie to Lord Halifax, may 10, 1754, *Dinwiddie
papers,* I, 162-163; Dinwiddie to Holdernesse, may 10, 1754, P.R.O., C.O., 5/14,
377-380; L.C. tr., 325-329; Dinwiddie to the lords of the treasury, may 10,
1754, *Dinwiddie papers,* I, 164; Dinwiddie to Earl Granville, may 10, 1754,
ibid., I, 166-167; Dinwiddie to Horace Walpole, may 10, 1754, *ibid.,* I, 165-
166; Dinwiddie to Capel Hanbury, may 10, 1754, *ibid.,* I, 153-155; Dinwiddie
to James Abercromby, may 10, 1754, *ibid.,* I, 156-157.

397 See, for example, Dinwiddie to Glen, may 10, 1754, *ibid.,* I, 167-168. He
also wrote to his titular chief, the Earl of Albemarle, june 18 [1754], *ibid.,*
I, 208-210.

398 Dinwiddie to the lords of trade, may 10, 1754, P.R.O., C.O., 5/1328, 211-
214; L.C. tr., 167-172; *Dinwiddie papers,* I, 161.

399 Washington to Dinwiddie, april 25, 1754, John C. Fitzpatrick, ed.,
Writings of George Washington, I, 40.

called the Ohio company-Virginia-British fort and renamed it Fort Duquesne.

Dinwiddie, highly indignant, informed the board: "I send you the ensign's account upon oath, with copy of the French commander's summons; which I conceive to be a most egregious violation of the treaties subsisting between the two crowns, to take possession of a fort begun in his majesty's name, and on his own undoubted lands." [400]

As a matter of record, the capitulation signed by Ensign Ward, april 16-17, 1754, is an interesting document. It is remarkable in that its phraseology is strikingly similar to the language of the message Washington himself had carried to the French commander, St. Pierre,[401] but a few months before for Dinwiddie.[402]

---

[400] Dinwiddie to the lords of trade, may 10, 1754, *op. cit.* Contrecoeur was acting strictly upon orders from home. See Minister to Duquesne, may 15, 1752 (Arch. Nat., Col., series F3, 14:30-32vo.; L.C. tr.): ". . . it appears that it was M. de la Jonquiere's idea to withdraw from the Ohio river the Indians who have been regarded for some time as rebels, or suspects, and without wishing even to destroy the freedom of their trade, it is necessary for you to settle two principal matters: first to make all possible efforts to drive the English from our land in these countries, and to prevent them from coming there to trade by seizing their merchandise and destroying their posts; second to make the Indians understand at the same time that it is not against them that we have come, that they shall have the freedom to go as much as they wish to trade with the English, but, that they will not be allowed to receive them in our lands." See also Jonquiere's order, dated may 29, 1750 (Arch. Nat., Col., series F3, 14:11-11vo.; L.C. tr.).

[401] Legardeur de St. Pierre, commandant of the French forces centering on Venango. He was superior to Joncaire, local commander. Both served under Marquis de Montcalm, governor of Canada (See John C. Fitzpatrick, ed., *Writings of George Washington*, I, 25-27). Fitzpatrick quotes J. G. Shea, as follows: "Legardeur de St. Pierre had just returned from an expedition toward the west when he was sent to succeed the dying Marin. He afterwards served under Dieskau and was killed in the 'bloody morning scout' just before the battle of Lake George (1755). His full name was Legardeur de St. Pierre de Repentigny" (*Ibid.*, I, 27n).

[402] Washington was commissioned by Dinwiddie on october 31 and left for the west on the same day. He returned to Williamsburg january 16 (See his account in John C. Fitzpatrick, ed., *Writings of George Washington*, I,

The Virginia governor, in that summons in the fall of
1753, had declared his "surprize" that the French were
erecting "fortresses" on "his majesty's dominions" in
violation of existing "treaties." These were Dinwiddie's
words:

"The lands upon the river Ohio, in the western parts
of the colony of Virginia, are so notoriously known to be
the property of the crown of Great Britain, that it is a
matter of equal concern and surprize to me, to hear that
a body of French forces are erecting fortresses, and
making settlements upon that river, within his majesty's
dominions."

"The many and repeated complaints I have received
of these acts of hostilities, lay me under the necessity
of sending . . . George Washington Esquire . . . to
complain to you of the encroachments thus made; and
of the injuries done to the subjects of Great Britain; in
open violation of the laws of nations, and the treaties
now subsisting between the two crowns." [403]

Contrecoeur,[404] the French commander to whom
Ward capitulated in april, with like justification had

22-30. See also John C. Fitzpatrick, ed., *Diaries of George Washington,
1748-1799*, I, 40-67). The governor was so impressed by Washington's report
that he ordered it printed immediately – almost to the young man's dismay,
for he had but a few hours, or at most overnight, in which to improve
its phraseology. He prefixed to it his apology, which he called his "Advertisement"; it is really an excellent discrimination between first-hand and
hearsay evidence. William Hunter, Williamsburg, was the printer. Copies
are extremely rare. A facsimile edition is being issued by Scholars facsimiles
and reprints, New York, with an introduction by Professor Randolph G.
Adams, librarian, Clements library.

[403] Dinwiddie to Legardeur de St. Pierre, october 31, 1753, P.R.O., C.O., 5/14,
117; L.C. tr., 103-105.

[404] "Captain Contrecoeur took possession of the unfinished English works
april 17, 1754. He completed them and named the fort Duquesne. By his orders Ensign Jumonville set off on his fatal reconnoissance, june 23d. Contrecoeur was in command of Fort Duquesne at the time of Braddock's defeat" (John C. Fitzpatrick, ed., *Diaries of George Washington, 1748-1799*, I,
75n).

then imitated Dinwiddie in word and phrase. He too, in turn, declared his own "surprise" that the English were erecting "fortresses" on the lands of the "king, my master . . . contrary to the last peace treaty." These, then, were Contrecoeur's words:

"Nothing can equal my surprise at seeing you attempt an establishment on the lands of the king my master, and that is the reason I am today, sir, deputizing the Seigneur Chevalier Le Mercier, captain of the Bombardier gunners, commandant of the Canadian artillery, to find out from you yourself, sir, by whose order you have come here to establish fortifications on the domain of the king, my master. This strategy seems to me to be so contrary to the last peace treaty concluded at Aix la Chapelle between his most christian majesty and the king of Great Britain, that I do not know to whom to impute such a usurpation, for it is an incontestable fact that the land situated along the Belle river [the Ohio] belongs to his most christian highness." [405]

Washington, immediately following Ward's capitulation, left Wills' creek, now Cumberland, Maryland, and journeyed toward Red Stone Old Fort [406] but fell back presently to the Great Meadows.[407] The Half-king

[405] See French draft of Captain Contrecoeur's summons to the British troops at Monongahela, april 16, 1754, P.R.O., C.O., 5/14, 389-392; L.C. tr., 337-345. See also *New York colonial documents,* VI, 841-842. Washington in his letter to Dinwiddie, april 25, 1754, gives the date of the capitulation as april 17 (John C. Fitzpatrick, ed., *Writings of George Washington,* I, 40). As late as march 17, 1755 the Duc de Mirepoix, French ambassador to England, could receive a memorandum which closed with: "It is only with the greatest regret that the king will see himself forced to give up the hope of a solid and durable peace, and France will always prefer to have England as an ally rather than an enemy." See Rouillé to Mirepoix, Affaires étrangères, correspondance politique, Angleterre (hereafter cited as A.E. Corr. Pol., Angl.), 438: 285-286; L.C. tr.

[406] Now identified as Brownsville, Pennsylvania. This was originally known also as Hangard, and Fort Burd.

[407] Not far from Uniontown, Pennsylvania.

and his Indian scouts, who were out reconnoitering for him, daily brought reports that parties of French and Indians were in the vicinity. Washington wrote Dinwiddie on may 27: ". . . this morning Mr. Gist [408] arrived from his place, where a detachment of 50 men was seen yesterday at noon, commanded by Monsieur La Force.[409] He afterwards saw their tracks within 5 miles of our camp." Thus, it was a matter only of days, if not hours, until these French parties would come into conflict either with the English Indians or with the Virginians. The only uncertain factors in the imminent clash were when and where.

Washington, in his letter of the twenty-seventh continued: "I imediately detached 75 men in pursuit of them, who, I hope, will overtake them before they get to Red Stone, where their canoes lie." He interposed a

[408] Christopher Gist (c.1706-1759), was surveyor and explorer of the Ohio lands for the Ohio company in 1750 and 1751, guide to Washington in his epochal journey to the French in 1753-1754, and soldier in the French and Indian war. His highest recommendation is the regard in which he was held by George Washington. He was with the latter at the Jumonville affair, at Fort Necessity, and in the Braddock campaign. He must have been well educated, judging by his mapping and surveying ability and the journal he kept. His courage, honesty, mentality, good judgment, and knowledge of frontier life evidently appealed to George Washington. His so-called "new settlement" was located about midway between the Monongahela and Youghiogheny rivers, where Mt. Braddock, Fayette county, Pennsylvania, now is. A testimonial letter from Edmond Atkin, superintendent of Indian affairs, to Governor Sharpe of Maryland, june 30, 1757, announcing that Gist would be appointed deputy Indian agent was included by both W. C. Ford (I, 443n) and by John C. Fitzpatrick (II, 43n), in their editions of George Washington's *Writings*.

[409] La Force, a French junior officer attached to the forces at Fort Duquesne. He was particularly successful in inciting the Indians along the frontiers. As Fitzpatrick points out, La Force is reported in the French translation of Washington's diary as having been active in apprehending deserters, so Washington learned from his own Indian scouts. Taken prisoner in the Jumonville affair, he was lodged in the gaol at Williamsburg, but with remarkable enterprise managed presently to escape. S. M. Hamilton says he carried a compass in his bold dash for freedom. He was recaptured in New Kent county, in spite of his ready offer of a generous bribe to his captor.

warning to Dinwiddie that he was positively obliged to have goods to give the Indians for services. "They all expect it and refuse to scout or do any thing without; saying these services are paid well by the French." [410] This was serious news for Dinwiddie, who was already having more than his share of troubles in raising funds to support his little army.

But worse troubles were in store: Washington was threatening to resign. And he would do it, he declared, unless the inequalities of rank and pay could be adjusted.[411] As Dinwiddie understood it, Washington was uneasy over the differences in pay; Washington promptly pointed out that it was the rank, rather than the pay, that irritated him.

It was a long communication that the governor received from George Washington from his military camp at the Great Meadows, and is dated may 29, 1754. *Mirabile dictu!* The young commander had just written more than twelve hundred words about "rank," "honor," and "volunteer service," without, up to that point in his letter, having given Dinwiddie so much as a hint that he had just fought one of the decisive conflicts of the times. In other words, it was none other than the day before, may 28, that he had met and vanquished Jumonville's force, at Half-king rock, where thus had been fired the shot that definitely set off the French and Indian war. It was what on both sides had long been feared – the overt act.

---

410 Washington to Dinwiddie, may 27, 1754, John C. Fitzpatrick, ed., *Writings of George Washington*, I, 54; *Dinwiddie papers*, I, 175.

411 Washington to Dinwiddie, may 29, 1754, John C. Fitzpatrick, ed., *Writings of George Washington*, I, 60; *Dinwiddie papers*, I, 176-180. See also Washington to Dinwiddie, may 18, 1754, John C. Fitzpatrick, ed., *Writings of George Washington*, I, 49-51; Dinwiddie to Washington, may 25, 1754, *Dinwiddie papers*, I, 171-174. Washington finally resigned in october 1754.

Staccato events had increased gradually in tempo to a climax. The French had planted their leaden plates as marks of ownership up and down the strategic watercourses in the Ohio country in 1749;[412] they had ousted English traders in 1752 from the Ohio trading-post known as Pickawillany;[413] they had turned out Ward and his fellow colonials at the forks in the spring of 1754, as has just been recounted; and they had forced back Frazier and other too-venturesome frontiersmen. From the English standpoint, these were definite acts of aggression. The French, on their side, alleged similar offense on the part of the English. But on none of these occasions had blood been shed. Now, however, on may 28, 1754 had come a different kind of action; and, unless something far out of the ordinary should happen, there would be no turning back.

"Now, sir, as I have answered your honour's letter," began Washington again, in the concluding part of his very long communication of may 29, "I shall beg leave to acquaint you with what has happened since I wrote by Mr. Gist." Almost nonchalantly, it would seem, after disposing of the matters of rank and honor, in the letter running to twenty-seven hundred words, the young Virginian then proceeded to acquaint Dinwiddie with his encounter with Jumonville – an encounter the consequences of which were to be among the most far-reaching in American history. Outstanding in importance though it is, it is not even referred to in most American histories.

Dinwiddie by summertime had reached Winchester,

---

412 See Céleron's journal, "Nouvelle prise de possession de l'Ohio," in Pierre Margry, ed., *Découvertes et établissement des français dans* . . . *l'Amérique septentrionale* (Paris, 1886), VI, 666-726; "Céleron's expedition down the Ohio," Wisconsin historical society *collections,* XVIII (1908), 36-58.

413 See William Trent's journal, june 21, 1752, P.R.O., C.O., 5/1327, 549-560; L.C. tr., 431-447; Dinwiddie to Captains Cresap and Trent, february 10, 1753, *Dinwiddie papers,* I, 22-23 and 22n.

always then referred to as "far out on our frontiers." He
finally had arrived there after his much-postponed endeavor to hold a conference with the long-overdue Indian chiefs. He wrote on june 1 his congratulations to
his youthful commander: ". . . I heartily congratulate
you, as it may give a testimony to the Indians that the
French are not invincible when fairly engaged with the
English. . . Pray God preserve you in all your proceedings and grant success to our arms." And he added,
in closing: "I remain, with great esteem." [414] Truly
nothing succeeded with Dinwiddie like success.

Following Washington's encounter with Jumonville,
Dinwiddie had more than his usual round of trials. He
had, for example, counted on Colonel Fry, his "man of
sense," to use "dispatch" and reach the vicinity of the
forks early. Weeks later, on may 4, he felt obliged to
write Fry: "You will allow me to be surprized on receiving your letter dated at Alexandria the 31st of april
last, when I perswaded myself you must be near Wills's
creek. . . It is a great misfortune that the active French
outdo us by their timely vigilance and application." [415]
Within the month, however, Dinwiddie was to learn of
Fry's death. On june 4 he wrote Lieutenant-colonel
Washington that "on the death of Colonel Fry, I have
thought it proper to send you the enclosed commission
to command the Virginia regiment, and another for
Major Muse, to be lieutenant-colonel." In this letter the
governor also acquainted Washington with the appointment of Colonel James Innes as "commander-in-chief
of all the forces"; and it is worth noting that the governor received Washington's hearty endorsement of his
choice.

Washington threatened resignation from the service

---

[414] Dinwiddie to Washington, june 1, 1754, *ibid.*, I, 186-187.

[415] Dinwiddie to Fry [May 4, 1754], *ibid.*, I, 147; see also Worthington C.
Ford, ed., *Writings of George Washington* (New York, 1889-1893), I, 97n.

over the question of whether royal appointees should outrank colonial officers of equal grade just when Dinwiddie felt he needed him most, and naturally the very frankest letters then passed between the two men. Nevertheless, these things did not obscure in their own minds – certainly never for long – the confidence each felt in the other. It is only in the minds of certain writers that it has been obscured. In the governor's letter of june 4, acquainting Washington with his promotion, Dinwiddie showed his genuine attitude: "You cannot believe the uneasiness and anxiety I have had for the tardiness of the detachment under Colonel Fry's command in not joining you some time since. Continue in good spirits, and prosecute your usual conduct and prudence, which must recommend you to the favor of his majesty and your country." Then he added the following line, full of meaning, and far too seldom quoted: "My friendship and respect I hope you do not doubt. I therefore remain with great truth, sir, your real friend." [416] Few indeed were the contemporaries to whom Robert Dinwiddie ever wrote in that vein.

Washington was evidently impressed by his governor's sincerity and good faith. He replied june 10. George Washington was likewise a voluminous letter-writer. The bound volumes of the Washington manuscripts in the Library of Congress reach the amazing total of four hundred seventy-two. But George Washington found his match in Robert Dinwiddie. Washington's reply on june 10 acknowledged Dinwiddie's three communications in four days. Then he wrote again two days later, in a vein which throws much light on the relations of the two men. In this long letter, chiefly in regard to rank, and running just short of twenty-five hundred words, he closed with: "Since I have spun a

---

416 Dinwiddie to Washington, june 4, 1754, *Dinwiddie papers*, I, 193-194.

letter to this enormous size, I must go a little further and beg your honour's patience to peruse it. . . I am, honorable sir, with the most sincere and unfeigned regard, your honour's most obedient and most humble servant. George Washington. [P.S.] The contents of this letter is a profound secret." [417]

In letter after letter to the officials in England and in those to fellow governors, Dinwiddie had reiterated his expectation of great accomplishments from the meeting with the Indian chiefs that he had long planned should take place in may 1754 at Winchester, a straggly settlement then regarded as out on the very outskirts of civilization. But his hopes must have begun to dim: first, Glen failed to give him cooperation on the Indian question;[418] then, other colonies proved too indifferent;[419] also, the Half-king sent the biblical excuse declaring that he must stay at home to protect his women and children. The melancholy result of it all Dinwiddie reported to Sir Thomas Robinson on june 18.[420]

Dinwiddie was still smarting from Ward's capitulation. He laid the failure to dislodge the French from the forks largely at the doors of the neighboring provinces.

[417] Washington to Dinwiddie, june 10, 1754, *ibid.*, I, 197-200; John C. Fitzpatrick, ed., *Writings of George Washington*, I, 84, where the date is given as june 12. See *ibid.*, I, 76n for explanation.

[418] Glen to Dinwiddie, june 21, 1753, P.R.O., C.O., 5/1327, 629-632; L.C. tr., 499-503; Glen's message to the assembly, march 5, 1754, P.R.O., C.O., 5/14, 287-290; L.C. tr., 261-265; Glen to Dinwiddie, march 14, 1754, P.R.O., C.O., 5/14, 295-297; L.C. tr., 271-276; Glen to Dinwiddie, march 14, 1754, P.R.O., C.O., 5/14, 299-302; L.C. tr., 277-280; Dinwiddie to Glen, august 5 [1754], *Dinwiddie papers*, I, 272-276.

[419] Dinwiddie to Hamilton, september 6, 1754, *Pennsylvania colonial records*, VI, 164; Sharpe to Baltimore, june 6, 1754, *Maryland archives*, VI, 67-68; Sharpe to Baltimore, august 8, 1754, *ibid.*, IV, 79-80; Plan of operations, october 25, 1754, P.R.O., C.O., 5/14, 565-566; L.C. tr., 517-518; Rowan to the lords of trade, march 19, 1754, William L. Saunders, ed., *Colonial records of North Carolina*, V, 109; *Gentlemen's magazine*, XXVII (May 1757), 195-197.

[420] Dinwiddie to Robinson, june 18, 1754, P.R.O., C.O., 5/14, 397-400; L.C. tr., 349-356; *Dinwiddie papers*, I, 201-202.

They had failed him in the hour of need. His letter to Lieutenant-governor James DeLancey of New York, june 20, 1754, reveals the Dinwiddie we are now coming to know. His resentment against a governor was never personal; it resulted only from his insistence that others should see eye to eye with him the imperial point of view. This letter to the New York governor is comprehensive; and it is typical of Dinwiddie's bitter feeling toward the governors, not toward Governor DeLancey as a man, nor toward Governor James Glen of South Carolina as a man, but toward whomsoever was to blame for the dilemma facing the British. One of his own paragraphs best tells that story. His scathing indictment of DeLancey and of New York, expressed in a syntax all its own, ran as follows: ". . . If your colony and the other neighbouring ones had granted proper supplies according to his majesty's commands, I think we should [have] be[en] able to dislodge the French from the fort, and cleared the Ohio river of these bad neighbours. Your two companies are at last arrived, after ten weeks daily expectation of them, but they are not agreeable to the order from home, which was to be two compleat companies which should have been drafted out of your four companies on so extraordinary duty, agreeable to the company from South Carolina, contrary to that, they are not compleat in numbers; many of them old that cannot undergo a march of 200 miles from Alexandria, and burthened with thirty women and children; and to compleat the whole, no provisions, which your former letters gave me reason to expect; no tents, which obliges me to make new tents; or any blankets, etc.; in short, much worse than new raised forces. As in duty bound by my orders, I am determined, with the few men I have, and the little money, to carry on the expedition with all the vigour our small forces will admit of. Suppose the French remained undisturbed on the Ohio, what will the consequence be to the British colonies on this continent? as undoubtedly they will make depredations on our present settlement, and you may bid farewell to the furr and skin trade. This dominion has very little trade with the Indians. I think yours is very considerable, but laying aside all these observations, they cannot shun to shew themselves good subjects by giving due obedience to the royal mandat[e]." [421]

Then came the capitulation at Fort Necessity, july 3-4. Dinwiddie at first was stunned. Not until july 24 did he recount to the lords of trade what had taken place in this first major engagement of the undeclared war.[422] But recovering from the shock, and with his back to the wall, his fighting instinct was aroused as never before. Thoroughly alarmed, he exerted himself far beyond his strength. Describing in detail Washington's capitulation, he wrote letters the selfsame day to Horatio Sharpe, to James Abercromby, to Secretary Robinson, to Henry Fox, secretary of war, to the Earl of Albemarle — one of his rare letters to that personage, to Earl Granville, to Lord Halifax, and to John and Capel Hanbury.[423]

---

[421] Dinwiddie to DeLancey, june 20, 1754, *ibid.*, I, 216-217.

[422] Dinwiddie to the lords of trade, july 24, 1754, P.R.O., C.O., 5/14, 419-422; L.C. tr., 367-375. For an interesting report of Washington's defeat at Fort Necessity, see the *Pennsylvania journal and weekly advertiser,* july 25, 1754, P.R.O., C.O., 5/14, 347 (North Carolina historical commission).

[423] Dinwiddie to Sharpe, july [24, 1754], *Dinwiddie papers,* I, 234-235; Dinwiddie to Abercromby, july [24, 1754], *ibid.,* I, 235-239; Dinwiddie to Robinson, july [24, 1754], *ibid.,* I, 243-244; Dinwiddie to Fox, july [24, 1754], *ibid.,* I, 244-246; Dinwiddie to Albemarle, july [24, 1754], *ibid.,* I, 247-248; Dinwiddie to Earl Granville, july [24, 1754], *ibid.,* I, 249-250; Dinwiddie to Halifax, july [24, 1754], *ibid.,* I, 250-252; Dinwiddie to John and Capel Hanbury, july [24, 1754], *ibid.,* I, 252-254.

From july 3-4, 1754, which marked Fort Necessity, to another memorable july date — and another setback for Dinwiddie, Braddock's defeat — was exactly a year, during which Dinwiddie redoubled his efforts in trying to concert measures of defense. George Washington, far from losing caste with Dinwiddie because of his capitulation, was warmly praised by the governor. The latter wrote his friend, Governor Sharpe, july 31:

"Colonel Washington's orders from me was by no means to attack the enemy till the whole forces were joined in a body, and they knew no intention of the enemy till the very morning they engaged." Washington, even on his own initiative, would hardly have attacked an overwhelming force; but since what he did had succeeded in the end, and since it accorded with Dinwiddie's general instructions, it pleased the governor. In consequence, in spite of everything, he took heart. After all, might not an ill military wind blow good for someone? That approximately was the old governor's attitude, for he added: ". . . if the misfortune attending our forces has roused the spirits of our neighbouring colonies, as you justly observe, [it] has done more than probably a victory would have effected." [424] By november Dinwiddie's own assembly had voted twenty thousand pounds more, without a rider. The governor began to feel that the Virginia burgesses were themselves getting a better perspective on this undeclared war.

The months preceding Braddock's arrival at the end of february 1755, as well as the months afterward, found Dinwiddie exerting himself beyond any man's ordinary strength. To the frontier counties he sent to purchase all the pork he could, and to North Carolina for three

---

424 Dinwiddie to Sharpe, july 31, 1754, *Maryland archives*, VI, 76-77; *Dinwiddie papers*, I, 258-259.

to four hundred pounds more; from Pennsylvania he took steps to engage six hundred thousand pounds of flour; from Boston he sought three hundred quintals of fish; and from North Carolina four or five barrels of rice. Other articles in proportion were ordered. His greatest difficulty was in securing horses and wagons, particularly carriages for the ordnance stores. Dinwiddie at times felt that his efforts were being nullified. He was particularly exercised over the clandestine shipments of foodstuffs from certain British colonies to the French "to support them," he protested to Sir Thomas Robinson, january 20, 1755, "in their horrid murders and barbarities." [425] This phase of the war will presently be discussed.

No wonder that when Braddock had been in America for some time he wrote back home that Governor Dinwiddie had cooperated to the fullest extent. And he went on to declare the Virginia governor was about the only person who had. This newly-discovered letter of commendation of a man who was so much misunderstood by his contemporaries from a man who seldom commended anyone is reported in the *Gentleman's magazine* for 1757. It is a testimonial worthy of being given here without serious abridgment:

"To Sir Thomas Robinson, Secretary of State.
"Williamsburgh, march 18 [1755]
"SIR: Immediately after my arrival, I forwarded letters to the different governors of this continent, to prevail on them to exert themselves in their respective governments towards obtaining supplies of men and money: recommending to them, to lock up their ports, so as to

---

[425] Dinwiddie to Robinson, january 20, 1755, P.R.O., C.O., 5/15, 285-288; L.C. tr., 182-184. For an example of the effect of the British blockade on the acute shortage of food among the French troops, see Bigot to his government, august 27, 1755 (Arch. Nat., Col., series F3, 14:134-138vo.; L.C. tr.).

render it impossible for the enemy to draw any provisions from us; which had been executed here by Governor Dinwiddie. The jealousy of the people, and the disunion of many colonies are such, that I almost despair of succeeding. Governor Dinwiddie has already obtained from his province twenty thousand pounds currency; and he hopes to obtain of the assembly a larger sum. North Carolina has granted eight thousand pounds; Maryland six thousand pounds; each the current coin of their respective governments. Though Pennsylvania is, without contradiction, the richest, and the most concerned in this expedition, yet it has supplied nothing hitherto . . . I think myself very happy in being associated with an officer of Mr. Keppel's [426] abilities and good dispositions, which appears by his readiness to enter into every measure that may be conducive to the success of this undertaking. – The justice which I must do Governor Dinwiddie, will not allow me to conclude this letter without acquainting you with the zeal which he has shewn, and the pains which he has taken, for the good of the service on this occasion; when I consider the faction which has prevailed over him in his government, I find he has succeeded beyond all hopes." [427]

426 Augustus Keppel (1725-1786), naval officer, was the second son of William Anne Keppel, second Earl of Albemarle. His squadron reached Virginia on february 20, 1755.

427 *Gentleman's magazine,* XXVII (May 1757), 195-196. Irritated over the delay in getting supplies, Braddock, later on, became critical even of Dinwiddie, among others, and unburdened himself two months later to Governor Morris as follows:

"Dear Morris: You will by the bearer, Mr. Peters, be informed of the situation I am in by the folly of Mr. Dinwiddie and the roguery of the assembly, and unless the road of communication from your province is opened and some contracts made in consequence of the power I have given, I must inevitably be starved. Sir John Sinclair (who by the by is ashamed of his having talked of you in the manner he did) has employed, by the advice of Governor Sharpe, a fellow at Conegachege, one Cressup, who has behaved in such a manner in relation to the Pennsylvania flower that if he had been a French commissioner,

Such a testimonial from Braddock about the governor's labors must have been sufficient recompense, Dinwiddie probably felt, for his strenuous campaign of preparation for the general. "These 12 months past I have been a perfect slave," he wrote James Abercromby on february 24, 1755, "and nothing [but] his majesty's commands, national service, and the good of these colonies could have prevailed on me to undergo such fatigue."

Braddock's objective, therefore, was Dinwiddie's. To regain the forks – with all it implied – for the Ohio company, for Virginia, for Britain, was in the governor's estimation the *ultima thule*. To William Allen of Philadelphia, who was endeavoring to fill his order on Pennsylvania for six hundred thousand pounds of flour for the expedition, Dinwiddie declared frankly, march 10, 1755: "If I live to see the French drove off the British lands and confined to their bounds in Canada, it will fully answer any trouble I have had about them." [428]

Victory at last appeared, as spring wore on, to be all but perched on Braddock's banner. Meanwhile, as has been indicated, the general's campaign dominated Dinwiddie's every waking hour through the close of 1754 and the early months of 1755. Even a cursory glance at the governor's voluminous correspondence during this time convinces one of this fact. "I am much engaged in facilitating affairs for the campaign," he had explained to Agent James Abercromby. And then he added, by

he could not have acted more for their interest. In short, in every instance but in my contract for the Pennsylvania waggons I have been deceived and met with nothing but lies and villainy. I hope, however, in spite of this we shall pass a merry Christmas together" (*Pennsylvania colonial records*, VI, 399-400).

To appreciate how inconsistent Braddock was, one has but to compare his complaining letter with Dinwiddie's to him, written the day before, may 23. Dinwiddie had extended him full cooperation.

[428] Dinwiddie to Allen, march 10, 1755, *Dinwiddie papers*, I, 524.

way of citing an example, "I have made a large purchase of provisions, horses, and waggons." Lesser matters dimmed into insignificance. The pistole fee was
no longer a nightmare and the Peyton Randolph episode
was rapidly fading into that haven of man's unpleasant
thoughts – the limbo of forgotten things. John Pownall,[429] secretary to the board of trade, had on december
26, 1754 expressed to Dinwiddie his "concern on the
uneasiness" that the latter had experienced in his administration as governor. There had been a time, indeed, when such things might have been a "concern" to
Dinwiddie; in march of 1755, however, he tossed them
off with a light heart. On the seventeenth of that month
he reassured Pownall: ". . . as the people are now sensible of their unjust clamour and complaints against me,
I excuse them, and we are now on good terms, and believe shall remain perfectly easy." And as to the man
who was once this thorn in the flesh, he could now write:
"I have restored Mr. Randolph to his office of attorney-
general, after his sending me a letter acknowledging his
errors and promise of a proper conduct for the future,
that now the pistole fee and all other grievances, unjustly complained of, cease."

Such times brought only temporary comfort, hence
he grasped whatever stray bits of it came his way. One
such instance that gave him great satisfaction was the
change in governors in South Carolina. That colony and
Virginia were more alike in many respects than any
two southern colonies – in wealth, population, creed,
and culture. But their governors cordially disliked each
other, with ill effects on imperial policy. Dinwiddie was
relieved therefore that Governor James Glen was being

429 "John Pownal, subsequently Sir John, was a brother of Thomas Pownal,
who was appointed successively to the government of New Jersey, Massachusetts, and South Carolina, and was a geographical and political writer of
distinction" (*Ibid.*, I, 338n).

replaced by one with whom he could work.[430] He wrote frankly to Abercromby: ". . . Mr. Littleton [431] is appointed to succeed Mr. Glen, and I suppose will soon be in Carolina, and I hope to keep up a proper correspondence. The other was so long in his letters and so dictatorial in style that I was quite weary in writing him." [432] In William Henry Lyttelton, Dinwiddie was not to be disappointed.

The assemblies in Virginia's neighboring colonies had not set the Old Dominion a good example, hence Dinwiddie confided to Abercromby: "But I dread success, as our neighboring colonies have been so indolent, refractory, and inconsistent with their own interest [433] and his majesty's commands as not to grant us any assistance, either in money, men, or provisions, except New York, about £3000 sterling; North Carolina, £6000, their money; Maryland the same sum; South Carolina and Pensylvania, not one farthing." A Dinwiddie cannot comprehend disloyalty; hence there followed this bitter sentence: "These neglects and disobedience to the royal mandate is inexcusable." [434]

---

[430] A main source of friction between Governor Glen and Governor Dinwiddie resulted from the proposed building of two forts in the Carolina back country near the Little Tennessee and the Tellicho. Both defenses were named Fort Loudoun. One was sponsored by Virginia, the other jointly by Virginia and South Carolina (See the Dinwiddie papers, P.R.O. *passim*, and the Plan and profile of Fort Loudoun by William De Brahm in the Huntington library).

[431] William Henry Lyttelton (1724-1808), brother of Sir George Lyttelton, was, as successor to James Glen, "governor of South Carolina 1755-1760, and subsequently of Jamaica; envoy extraordinary and minister to Portugal from Great Britain in 1766; made Baron Westcote july 31, 1776, and Lord Lyttelton august 13, 1794; died september 14, 1808" (*Dinwiddie papers*, II, 217n).

[432] Dinwiddie to Abercromby, march 17, 1755, *ibid.*, II, 3.

[433] Foreshadowing the events of two decades later.

[434] In fact, according to reports reaching the French court, the English colonists were so guilty of what Dinwiddie termed "neglects and disobedience to the royal mandate" that the "main purpose of the shipment of troops and munitions" to America was "to maintain law and order in the English colonies." As evidence, below is quoted a paragraph from hitherto unpub-

Dinwiddie thought in continental, imperial terms, never merely local. He therefore had ready upon Braddock's arrival a comprehensive plan of operations. This, he wrote Lord Halifax, march 17, 1755, he had submitted "freely to the general." [435] As will be seen presently, this was virtually the three-way plan of campaign finally embarked upon.

The whole spring of 1755 was devoted to solving the problems of supplying Braddock's army. Money, figures, statistics! Poor Dinwiddie. March 29, 1755, for instance, he wrote Thomas Walker, commissary, "to pay Colonel Innes £100, to pay Mr. Montour" for being interpreter. Businesslike, he added: "And take his receipt for the same." He could breathe easier, for, as he told Walker, "I think we now have provisions sufficient for the whole forces for 8 months, that I think you need not purchase any more." [436] With that amazing grasp of detail that was hardly exceeded even by his contemporaries, Benjamin Franklin and George Washington, he wrote hither and yon about "two chests of medicine" badly needed, "clothing," "flour" from Pennsylvania, "cash," "600 good fat cattle" "to be drove" from North

---

lished records in the Paris archives. The French court was writing its ambassador in London, practically at the time of Braddock's march, as follows:

"Ainsi, Monsieur, vous devez continuer á représenter la justice et la convenance d'un armistice, et employer les mêmes raisons dont vous avez déjà fait usage, pour démontrer la nécessité de cette convention préliminaire. L'Angleterre y doit avoir d'autant moins de répugnance qu'elle déclare positivement, que l'armement qu'elle a envoyé en Amèrique, n'a été fait pour offenser personne. M. le Duc de Newcastle et M. le Cher Robinson vous ont même confié que l'objet principal de ce transport de troupes et de munitions, étoit de maintenir l'ordre et la subordination dans les colonies Angloises. Plus nous croyons que ces deux ministres vous ont parlé de bonne foy; moins il nous est possible de concevoir sur quel motif peut être fondé le refus d'une suspension d'armes" (Rouillé to Mirepoix, february 3, 1755, A.E. Corr. Pol., Angl., 438:81-90vo.; L.C. tr.).

[435] Dinwiddie to Halifax, march 17, 1755, *Dinwiddie papers*, I, 527 (He wrote: "These are my sentiments, which I communicate to you only").

[436] Dinwiddie to Walker, march 29 [1755], *ibid.*, II, 12.

Carolina to Wills' creek on the Maryland-Virginia
border, "24 barrels of rice," "Irish beef," "500 small
arms, with slings, cartouch boxes, and bayonets, 10
drums and 15 halberts," "60 new tents from England,
and the same number made here" — all for the little
army. Meantime, from his Williamsburg supply he was
sending "500 arms to New Jersey, 400 last week to General Braddock," and 600 to Governor DeLancey of New
York. No wonder he wrote DeLancey that the Williamsburg magazine — the famous Powder Horn of the
Williamsburg restoration — was now, like the equally
famous cupboard, "quite bare." [437]

Typical of the Virginia governor's interest in the
commissary problems of Braddock's army are two most
enlightening letters,[438] written by him in may and june
1755. The first was to General Braddock, the second to
Major John Carlyle, the Virginia commissary appointed by Dinwiddie.

The Braddock campaign was in process of gettting
under way. Recommendations for positions here and
there were being sought and being given. Dinwiddie
himself was in a recommending mood. Colonel James
Innes,[439] John Rutherford, assistant to the new commissary, Thomas Walker, Colonel Adam Stephen,[440] and
George Washington were among those in Dinwiddie's
thoughts.[441]

[437] Ibid., II, 8-79, passim for typical examples.

[438] Dinwiddie to Braddock, may 23, 1755, ibid., II, 40-42; Dinwiddie to
Carlyle, june 28, 1755, ibid., II, 79-80.

[439] Dinwiddie to Innes, may 29, 1755, ibid., II, 7.

[440] "Adam Stephen succeeded to the command of Fort Cumberland with the
rank of lieutenant-colonel; commanded expedition to South Carolina against
the Creek Indians, and was later placed at the head of troops for defending
the frontiers of Virginia, with the rank of brigadier-general" (S. M. Hamilton, ed., Letters to Washington, I, 90n).

[441] Dinwiddie to Rutherford, april 12 [1755], Dinwiddie papers, II, 14;
Dinwiddie to Colonel Stephen, april 12, 1755, ibid., II, 13.

His recommendation of George Washington to General Braddock, even though the former had in october resigned his lieutenant-colonelcy over the question of rank, may have been one of the strongest reasons why Braddock sent Robert Orme [442] to the young Virginian with an invitation to join his staff as an aide. Later on Dinwiddie was to recommend Washington for preferment to Lord Loudoun, through Major-general Abercromby, soon after his arrival in America. At that time Dinwiddie declared he was convinced that had Braddock lived he would suitably have rewarded his young assistant. [443]

After all, this recommending habit was one of the many cardinal traits about Dinwiddie that make him stand out — the fact that he never failed to promote deserving persons. And when he did so, for example in the case of George Washington, he thereby laid the future United States forever in his debt.

March 29 (1755) found Dinwiddie in Alexandria. Cares of office at Williamsburg, if not forgotten, at least were almost a week's distance away. He was riding the crests once more, for he wrote with undisguised satisfaction to Governor Sharpe: "General Braddock, Commodore Keple, and myself came to this place on wednes-

---

[442] "Robert Orme, a lieutenant in the Coldstream guards; later, as captain, he accompanied Braddock to Virginia as his aide. He was wounded at the time of Braddock's defeat. His journal of the Braddock expedition was printed by the historical society of Pennsylvania in 1855" (John C. Fitzpatrick, ed., *Writings of George Washington*, I, 107n). See Jared Sparks, ed., *Writings of George Washington*, II, 71n, for Braddock's invitation through Orme to George Washington.

[443] Dinwiddie to Major-general James Abercromby, may 28, 1756, *Dinwiddie papers*, II, 425. In a letter to Washington on april 23, 1756 Dinwiddie gave definite encouragement: "Two generals are appointed for America — Lord Loudon and General Abercrombie — and it's thought they will bring over two battalions, but whether for this place or New York remains uncertain; but it's further said his majesty intends to send blank commissions for the Americans. If so, I doubt not you will be taken care of" (*Ibid.*, II, 388).

day night. The general reviews the forces on monday
and as soon as we hear Governor Shirley is on his way
to this place we propose to set off from this. The company that will be with us, are – the general, his aid de
camp, secretary and servants, the comodore, his secretary, your humble servant, his clerk and servant. I propose coming in my coach with the general and comodore
and I suppose the others will ride." [444]

Dinwiddie's regard for Braddock apparently was re-
ciprocated. They were working in close harmony. Typical of Braddock's and Dinwiddie's close relationship,
as of march 29, the governor wrote Colonel James Innes
that "he and I go to Annapolis to meet Governor Shirley
to settle the plan of operations." [445]

Life was by no means all humdrum with Dinwiddie.
A highlight in his career during these hectic days was
his presence at Alexandria, april 14, at the governors'
conference called by General Braddock.[446] History was
made, for weighty matters were settled there. The best
of contemporary evidence is Dinwiddie's description of
them in his letters to Sir Thomas Robinson, of course
to Lord Halifax, and to Governor Arthur Dobbs of
North Carolina, and all of them on april 30.

The plan of campaign, Dinwiddie reported to them,
had been unanimously agreed upon. One objective was
to attack the French on the Ohio; this was the task set
for Braddock, "with upwards of 3000 men." A second
objective was the fort at Niagara; and to this job were
assigned the two regiments under Governor William
Shirley and Sir William Pepperell. Finally, Crown
Point was to be attacked by "Colonel William Johnston

---

[444] Dinwiddie to Sharpe, march 29, 1755, *ibid.*, II, 5.

[445] Dinwiddie to Innes, march 29, 1755, *ibid.*, II, 7.

[446] Council held at Alexandria, april 14, 1755, P.R.O., C.O., 5/15, 623-626; L.C.
tr., 451-456.

with five thousand men, raised in the different colonies to the northward." [447]

Throughout the spring and early summer Dinwiddie continued to keep in touch with Braddock by letter, pinning his hopes on the day the general would come to grips with the foe. A fair indication of their relationship is Dinwiddie's letter to Braddock, dated june 3, 1755. It began: "Since writing my letter of yesterday's date I received your two letters of the 22d and 27th of may, but I observe Colonel Washington was not then arrived with [£]4000, which sum I hope will enable you to march. I have no doubt the French will surrender on sight of your forces." It concluded: "As Colonel Washington must be with you long before this, I hope he made you easy as to cash. My wife and two girls join me in wishing you health and success." [448]

After spending the month with Braddock in Alexandria, Dinwiddie had come out from that close association with the information for Agent Abercromby in London on june 6, that if Braddock were appointed to the governorship of Virginia to succeed Albemarle, the general desired him to be his lieutenant-governor. [449] Wrote Dinwiddie: "He and I live in great harmony, and I think him a very fine officer." [450] Here were loyalty and admiration even though Dinwiddie differed with Braddock as to many particulars of the campaign. For example, Dinwiddie urged speed, Braddock, long preparation; Dinwiddie, the maximum use of Indians, Braddock, the minimum; Dinwiddie, an adaptation by the regulars of the colonial troops' freedom of action, Brad-

447 Dinwiddie to Robinson, april 30, 1755, P.R.O., C.O., 5/15, 559-562; L.C. tr., 413-415; *Dinwiddie papers,* II, 15-16; Dinwiddie to Halifax, april 30, 1755, *ibid.,* II, 16-18; Dinwiddie to Dobbs, april 30, 1755, *ibid.,* II, 18-19.

448 Dinwiddie to Braddock, june 3 [1755], *ibid.,* II, 48-49.

449 Dinwiddie to Abercromby, june 6, 1755, *ibid.,* II, 57.

450 Dinwiddie to Abercromby, june 23, 1755, *ibid.,* II, 73.

dock, an insistence upon a good deal of "ceremony and formality" – even in the backwoods of Virginia and Pennsylvania; Dinwiddie, that the lighter troops should push forward and not be too hampered and retarded by the heavy artillery that had to be dragged up mountain after mountain over improvised roads, Braddock, that the entire army should proceed as one unit. Yet so positive was Dinwiddie of Braddock's success, in spite of those factors, that he thought Braddock "a very fine officer." In many respects he probably was. Socially, he would seem to have been a very likable man. There has been no criticism of him on this score even from his closest associates, his three aides – William Shirley, son of Governor Shirley, Robert Orme, and George Washington.

Finally on june 10 the last division of the army started for the Ohio.[451] Many interesting details are related in Dinwiddie's correspondence with the officials in England. Braddock had about three thousand men, according to the best figures at first available to Dinwiddie. He later reported them to be thirteen hundred men.[452] The general also started with one hundred fifty Indians under Half-king Monacatoocha.[453]

[451] Dinwiddie to the lords of the treasury, june 23 [1755], *ibid.*, II, 71.

[452] Dinwiddie to Dunbar, july 26, 1755, *ibid.*, II, 118. Braddock wrote to Sir Thomas Robinson on june 5, 1755: "I have at last collected the whole force with which I propose to march to the attack of Fort Duquesne, amounting to about two thousand effective men, eleven hundred of which number are Americans of the southern provinces, whose slothful and languid disposition renders them very unfit for military service. I have employed the properest officers to form and discipline them, and great pains has and shall be taken to make them as useful as possible" (P.R.O., C.O., 5/46, L.C. tr., 35-41). Bigot from Quebec reported, august 27, 1755, to his government that the English force had been 2000 men; and that the latter had been defeated, with a loss of 1500 men, by 250 Canadians and 600 to 700 Indians (Arch. Nat., Col., series F3, 14:134-138vo.; L.C. tr.).

[453] Dinwiddie to Robinson, june 23, 1755, P.R.O., C.O., 5/16, 29-32; L.C. tr., 23-25; *Dinwiddie papers*, II, 70.

While Indians in such military service were not on the regular payroll, nevertheless their alliance cost — cost the British government very many thousands of pounds sterling during the course of this long war. For instance, in the case of Monacatoocha, Dinwiddie informed Sir Thomas Robinson, june 6, 1755, exactly what at least one Indian payday alone cost: "I have sent to General Braddock a present for the Indians amounting to £599/2/3 in suitable goods." Here, at one throw, were several thousand dollars.[454]

Compared with Braddock, the French appeared to be hopelessly outnumbered. They seemed to have not above five hundred men, besides Indians, at their fort at the forks.[455] At least, this was according to "the best intelligence we have," Dinwiddie reported to Sir Thomas Robinson on june 6.[456] Either the English intelligence service was woefully inefficient or else the French rushed in strong new forces. At any rate, on june 23 he was writing Robinson that the "best intelligence" he could procure indicated the French had brought up seven hundred reinforcements, making twelve hundred all told. ". . . very few of them are regulars," Dinwiddie reported, "but [im]pressed men from their families."[457] A believer in the efficacy of sea power, he hoped that the several British squadrons would intercept any additional forces that might start out from Brest. Sea ascendancy was ultimately to prove a de-

---

[454] Dinwiddie to Robinson, june 6, 1755, P.R.O., C.O., 5/15, 585-586; L.C. tr., 432-434; *Dinwiddie papers*, II, 51.

[455] Fort Duquesne, which had been seized from Ensign Ward april 16-17, 1754.

[456] Dinwiddie to Robinson, june 6, 1755, P.R.O., C.O., 5/15, 584-586; L.C. tr., 432-434; *Dinwiddie papers*, II, 51.

[457] Dinwiddie to Robinson, june 23, 1755, P.R.O., C.O., 5/16, 29-32; L.C. tr., 23-25; *Dinwiddie papers*, II, 70. Cf. data attached to letter from Bigot to his government, august 6, 1755 (Arch. Nat., Col., series F3, 14:117, 118-118vo.; L.C. tr.).

cisive factor for the English [458] – but in june 1755 that time was not yet.

Dinwiddie held Braddock's second in command, Colonel Charles Dunbar, culpable for not attempting a move that often has changed the course of history. As Dinwiddie pointed out, Dunbar's troops had not even been engaged; furthermore, Dunbar still, after Braddock's defeat, had an army superior to the French; also he had sufficient munitions and food; and finally, the French were themselves in a state approaching panic, since they confidently expected Dunbar to strike. All these were advantages; there was but one fatal disadvantage, which, however, was the English army's ultimate undoing – namely, Dunbar's fear, fear of something that never happened. Therefore when the colonel precipitately retreated in august to Philadelphia, Dinwiddie charged with bitter irony that he had hastened into winter quarters in the month of august.

Immediately after Braddock's defeat, Dinwiddie wrote Dunbar a long, understanding letter. He apparently was certain Dunbar would try again against the French. He pledged him that if he would attempt to retrieve the loss, he would guarantee four hundred men and supplies.[459] To the amazement of the Virginia governor, Dunbar not only beat an ignominious retreat, but he also destroyed his ammunition and supplies, and had almost immediately thereafter to call upon the colonials for a great quantity of food.

Braddock's defeat more profoundly affected both Robert Dinwiddie and George Washington than any other single event during the critical years of the French

---

458 For evidence on the early successes of the English, see, for example, Dinwiddie to Boscawen, july 18, 1755, *Dinwiddie papers,* II, 105; Dinwiddie to Dobbs, september 2, 1756, *ibid.,* II, 494.

459 Dinwiddie to Dunbar, july 26, 1755, P.R.O., C.O., 5/16, 221-224; L.C. tr., 165-168; *Dinwiddie papers,* II, 118-120.

and Indian war. Yet its effect upon their lives seems never to have been fully appreciated. Braddock's road had been intended as a roadway to the west. It now became, instead, a road from the west. Dinwiddie made this clear.[460] Unexpected use was made of that highway. Braddock was dead; Washington was recuperating; the leaderless troops were demoralized; and Dunbar had gone to Philadelphia, into winter quarters in the summertime.

One thing Dinwiddie could do – and did do. He could call the Virginia assembly and lay the obligation for prompt action at their feet. No governor ever made a more stirring appeal for help. He pointed out that the roadway for the invader was now "laid open"; that a good part of Braddock's artillery was now in French hands; and that their lightning raids on the defenseless inhabitants were about to start up again. He told them he himself had already ordered out three companies of rangers in the three frontier counties. He begged them to improve the militia laws, to offer suitable rewards – as "our brethren of New England" have done – for scalps of the Indians, and to provide for a guard and a guardroom at the capitol.

Finally, he appealed to the burgesses on two points where they were most vulnerable. At one point, he rose to his oratorical height as he declared: "The natural bravery of our countrymen, if ever questioned, is now established beyond a doubt, by those Virginia forces, who purchased, with their lives, immortal glory to their country and themselves, on the banks of Monongahela."

The expense and burden that defense would cost them, he declared, would be borne in a worthy cause. It would be easy to bear because "it is to preserve to us, and our posterity, the most invaluable, and by all man-

---

[460] Dinwiddie to St. Clair, august 11, 1755, *ibid.*, II, 147-148.

kind esteemed, the most dear and most desirable of all human treasures, RELIGIOUS AND CIVIL LIBERTY." [461]

When the burgesses made their response to the governor, they re-echoed his praise of the British system and struck at the character of the government of their opponents. They concluded: ". . . we beg leave to assure your honor, that no endeavour on our part, shall be wanting to repel these cruel invaders of our properties; being fully convinced the people of Virginia will think no burthen too grevious, that shall be found necessary for the preservation of that which is so valuable and dear to them, their CIVIL AND RELIGIOUS LIBERTY." [462] The governor must have felt that the burgesses were getting a better perspective on events in the west.

Braddock's defeat, and its immediate aftermath, ends the first phase of this eighteenth-century "undeclared warfare."

[461] *Journals of the house of burgesses* (1752-1755; 1756-1758), 297-298; *Dinwiddie papers,* II, 134-136.

[462] *Journals of the house of burgesses* (1752-1755; 1756-1758), 299; *Dinwiddie papers,* II, 138.

Co-defender of the Frontier

Strong in defense, the English people have always tenaciously held on to their gains. Thus it was that after Dinwiddie had sought in vain to prevail on Colonel Dunbar at least to remain in the vicinity of the newly-exposed frontier, the governor himself rose to the occasion. William Shirley of Massachusetts was technically the commander-in-chief of all the colonial forces immediately after Braddock's death, but he was too far distant. The Virginia governor, therefore, having praised George Washington's valor on the field of Monongahela, turned to him who had so recently been Braddock's aide. Washington was but twenty-three. Dinwiddie, stating that he was "reposing especial trust in your loyalty, courage, and good conduct," lost no time in commissioning him, august 14, 1755, to be "colonel of the Virginia regiment and commander-in-chief of all the forces now raised and to be raised for the defense of this his majesty's colony." The governor's instructions the year before had been burdened with counsel. Now, full of confidence in his appointee, Dinwiddie's words read: "And you are hereby charged with full power and authority to act defensively or offensively, as you shall think for the good and wellfare of the service." [463] Thus, another time, opportunity knocked plainly at George Washington's door. One might well ask whether he, like Napoleon, created those circumstances; or did Dinwiddie place them squarely in his path?

[463] Dinwiddie's commission to Washington, august 14, 1755, *Dinwiddie papers*, II, 184.

The young colonel's instructions, as prepared by the old governor, so mirror the activities of the period that copious excerpts from them merit printing here: "Whereas the French have unjustly invaded his majesty's lands on the Ohio, and have sent flying parties of French and Indians, to robb, and murder our back settlers to the westward; which the legislature of this dominion having seriously taken into their consideration, and voted money for the protection of our frontiers, and for conducting the necessary expedition to drive the French from the Ohio: in consequence thereof, I have granted commissions for raising sixteen companies of men, to be formed into a regiment — the command of which regiment, together with the forces that now are, or may be employed in the country service, being given to you. . . As Winchester is the nighest place of rendezvous to the country which is exposed to the enemy, you are hereby required to make that your head quarters.

"The men to be regularly paid their full subsistance without any deductions; excepting two pence per month from each non-commissioned officer and private man, for the surgeon to purchase medicines; this money to be stoped by the pay-master, and to be paid to the surgeon quarterly; as also six pence per month from the drummers, to be paid to the drum major to repair the drums, and teach the drummers. You are hereby required to preserve good order and discipline among the officers and private men of the regiment under your command and to conform yourself in every respect to the rules and articles of war.

"You are to transmit to me weekly returns of the regiment and a return the first day of every month, with the variations that may have happened the preceding month. When any of the non-commissioned officers or private

Weekly Return of the first Company of the King's Reg.t

Officers present & fit to	1	Captain
	1	Lieutenant
		Ensign
Drum.r Rank & file	3	fitt for duty
		Sick
		Recruits
	1	fitt for duty
		Sick
	1	on party
	42	fitt for duty
	.	Sick
	.	Recruiting
	.	on party
since Last Return	42	Total Effective
	11	Wanting to Compleat
	.	Dead
	.	Discharged
	1	Deserted
	1	Entertained

Fort Dinwiddie
29.th Sept.r 1755 De P. Hog
John McNeill

men should happen to die, they are to be continued on the returns and rolls as effective men for twenty-eight days, to pay for his coffin, that the commander of the company may be no looser by his death.

"You are also impowered to purchase suitable goods for the Indians; and to offer them presents in such manner, and at such times as you shall think adviseable, either for attaining their interest, or promoting the service.

"As an aid de camp, and secretary are necessary to ease the duty of your command; I do hereby invest you with full power and authority to appoint and commission such person and persons as you shall think most adviseable – and as Mr. Dick has declared his intention of declining any further services as commissary; I also empower you to appoint a commissary in his room, together with an adjutant, quarter-master, and such other inferior officers as you shall find absolutely necessary to carry on the service with spirit and vigour.

"You are . . . in every respect, to conform yourself to the rules and articles of war herewith given you, for which I will see you justified in the just and due conformance thereto.

"I sincerely desire that you will inculcate morality and virtue among your men, to punish drunkenness and swearing. Wishing you health and recommending you to the protection of God, I am, sir, your friend and humble servant." [464]

As the governor had warned, Braddock's road instead of being a way to the west, only too soon would become a thoroughfare from the west for the invading red men. The technique of the enemy was to employ "flying parties" of fifteen to twenty Indians, each party led by a Frenchman. Innumerable bands of this size

---

[464] Dinwiddie's instructions to Washington, august 14, 1755, S. M. Hamilton, ed., *Letters to Washington*, I, 79-81; *Dinwiddie papers*, II, 184-186.

were organized from Fort Duquesne and dispatched
against the hapless borderers. The daring marauders
penetrated even to the Shenandoah valley. Their tactics
were to strike suddenly; and if that plan failed to resort
to subtler strategy. They would murder the inmates of
the cabins, scalp their victims, except a considerable
number carried into captivity, then burn the log house
with all its furnishings, save booty that could be carried
away.

Washington set about building a strong defensive post
in Winchester, then "far out on the frontiers." It was
named Fort Loudoun,[465] in honor of the new titular
governor of Virginia, who, however, was never to set
his foot in the Old Dominion. The scars of the old fort,
a most important rendezvous in its day, are still clearly
visible.

Dinwiddie's parting admonition to the new colonel
was his sincere desire that Washington would promote
morality and virtue among his men and punish drunkenness and profanity.[466]

Dinwiddie's postscript to it all – his "memorandum
for Colonel Washington" – is almost as interesting as
the preceding instructions. Not only must George Washington now start seeing to it that the pork and beef are
"trimmed and pickled," and that the meats are not stolen

---

465 This Fort Loudoun must not be confused with Fort Loudoun in Pennsylvania or with either of the two forts built in the Cherokee country of over-
mountain Carolina. One of the latter was built by Virginia and the other by
South Carolina and Virginia jointly.

466 That the new colonel lost no time in carrying out the instructions of
august 14, 1755 of his commander-in-chief is seen by the fact that the former
issued his own orders from Fort Cumberland, september 11, 1755, which read
in part as follows: "Any soldier who is guilty of any breach of the articles
of war, by swearing, getting drunk, or using obscene language, shall be se-
verly punished, without the benefit of a court martial" (John C. Fitzpatrick,
ed., *Writings of George Washington*, I, 179). See Washington's remarkable
general order to his Revolutionary army, deploring profanity (General orders,
august 3, 1776, John C. Fitzpatrick, ed., *Writings of George Washington*, v,
367).

while being salted, but he must practice economy: "You no doubt will have regard to a prudent frugality."

The governor had acted; George Washington was now about to swing into action; it was incumbent upon the assembly also to move. They did. The act they passed on march 8, 1756, providing for a string of forts along the frontiers, was undoubtedly a product of composite authorship. It read as follows:

"And whereas the frontiers of this colony are in a very defenceless situation, and openly exposed to the incursions and depredations of our cruel and savage enemies, who are daily destroying the lives and estates of the inhabitants of that part of the colony, and it is necessary that forts should be erected in those parts, to put a stop to those violent outrages of the enemy, and to protect the inhabitants in their lives and properties: be it further enacted, by the authority aforesaid, that a chain of forts shall be erected." [467]

From Braddock's defeat in july 1755 until Dinwiddie sailed from Virginia in january 1758, there was one absorbing thought in the Virginia governor's mind – the defense of the long-drawn-out, zigzagging, western frontier, the best defense of which, he time and again pointed out, was aggressive attack. In this long uphill struggle to protect the western border he had the constant collaboration of an important, nay, essential, man – young Washington. These years of trial, from the time he was twenty-three until he resigned in 1759 at twenty-seven, were years of preparation for his later, but scarcely greater, work. They brought out every fine quality George Washington possessed. Every problem he faced later on in the Revolution, he faced in miniature during these years on the frontier. Valley Forge, Lee's conduct at Monmouth, shortage of money, desertion of his men,

---

[467] Hening's *Statutes,* VII, 17-18.

calumny and criticism – all these he endured on the colonial frontier, twenty years before he was called upon to face them in the national service. The Virginia frontier could well be termed George Washington's West Point. As the account unfolds, through a reading of the Dinwiddie-Washington correspondence, it will be seen how impossible it would have been for either man to have done his work – certainly in the way it actually was done – without the aid of the other.

Two letters that passed between these men epitomize perfectly their relationship during this period.

Dinwiddie's youthful commander, with the rank of colonel, was out on the far-flung frontier, engaged in an uneven struggle with the bloodthirsty, war-whooping Indians and their daring French leaders. The sufferings of the people touched his heart. Below is the language in which the twenty-four-year-old Virginian poured out his very soul to his governor. Like a son to a father, he wrote him one of the most remarkable letters ever penned by one man to another:

"Your honor may see to what unhappy straits the distressed inhabitants as well as I, am reduced. I am too little acquainted, sir, with pathetic language, to attempt a description of the people's distresses, though I have a generous soul, sensible of wrongs, and swelling for redress. But what can I do? If bleeding, dying! would glut their insatiate revenge, I would be a willing offering to savage fury, and die by inches to save a people! I see their situation, know their danger, and participate their sufferings, without having it in my power to give them further relief, than uncertain promises. In short, I see inevitable destruction in so clear a light, that, unless vigorous measures are taken by the assembly, and speedy assistance sent from below, the poor inhabitants that are now in forts, must unavoidably fall, while the remainder of the country are flying before the barbarous foe. In fine, the melancholy situation of the people, the little prospect of assistance, the gross and scandalous abuses cast upon the officers in general, which is reflecting upon me in particular, for suffering misconducts of such extraordinary kinds, and the distant prospects, if any, that I can see, of gaining honor and reputation in the service, are motives which cause me to lament the hour, that gave me a commission, and would induce me, at any other time than this of imminent danger, to resign without one hesitating moment, a command, which I never expect to reap either honor or benefit from; but, on the contrary, have almost an absolute certainty of incurring displeasure below, while the murder of poor innocent babes and helpless families may be laid to my account here!

"The supplicating tears of the women, and moving petitions from the men, melt me into such deadly sorrow, that I solemnly declare, if I know my own mind, I could offer myself a willing sacrifice to the butchering enemy, provided that would contribute to the people's ease." [468]

It would have repaid any biographer of George Washington to have looked up Governor Dinwiddie's reply. The fact that the governor, sixty-three years of age and an ill man, wrote ten letters of appeal to county officials in ten different counties, all within the space of twelve hours, in response to Washington's plea, makes the governor's own reply equally remarkable. Like a father to a son, he wrote with undisguised anxiety as follows:

"Williamsburg, april 26th. 1756
"Sir: I received your letter by this express last night,

---

[468] Washington to Dinwiddie, april 22, 1756, John C. Fitzpatrick, ed., *Writings of George Washington*, I, 324-325.

and this morning laid all the letters before the house of burgesses and really it gives me very great uneasiness and concern to observe the dismal situation our back settlers are in – and when I consider the slowness of the house in raising men – I have sent expresses to the counties of Frederick, Fairfax, Prince William, Culpepper, Orange, Stafford, Spotsylvania, Caroline, Albemarle, and Louisa, ordering the commanding officers of each to march one half of their whole militia imediately to Winchester; and I shall send directly to Fredricksburg 40 barrels powder, 500 small arms, with shott and flints, to Commissary Walker who goes up from this to take the necessary care in distributing the same.

"I am excessively hurried with the above dispatches that I can write no more at present but recommending you to the protection of God I remain, sir, your most humble servant." [469]

The Indians were problem enough, but there were internal foes to combat as well. One of these, typical of the matters with which Washington and Dinwiddie had to cope, intruded itself into the midst of the frightful conditions on the frontier as pictured above by Colonel Washington – and demanded solution. Though the colonel's presence was urgently needed on the frontier, nevertheless, largely for his sake, the governor not only approved his absence but gave his blessing to a two months' leave that carried the young commander to Boston, and to potential greatness.

Distinct turning-points occur unmistakably in every man's life. One of these for George Washington took place between february 4 and march 23, 1756. This two-month period was occupied by his first trip to New England, and was profoundly to influence his life.

---

[469] Dinwiddie to Washington, april 26, 1756, S. M. Hamilton, ed., *Letters to Washington*, I, 232-233. Brock, in the *Dinwiddie papers* (II, 392) gives the date as april 28.

Equally important is the fact that it was Washington's old governor who made that journey possible; and this, too, notwithstanding the fact that he sometimes refused his young officer's requests for a few days' leave from the frontier. This time the governor not only granted his request; he also gave him letters of introduction and wished him Godspeed.

The facts briefly are these: George Washington had been chafing for upwards of two years under the galling inequalities in rank between colonial-appointed and royal-appointed army officers. Captains with a royal commission claimed precedence even over colonels with only a local commission. The situation had become so bad that he had actually resigned in october 1754. He was, therefore, in Braddock's campaign only by virtue of his position as the general's aide. He had, however, as has been seen, returned to the service on the frontier after Braddock's disastrous defeat; and in august 1755 Dinwiddie had made him a colonel and the commanding officer, as Innes had been. He and the governor worked shoulder to shoulder in defending the long attenuated frontiers. One of the important outposts was Fort Cumberland at Wills' creek by the Potomac. Though this fort had been built by Virginia, and was regarded, at least, by Dinwiddie as "a king's fort," it actually lay within the confines of Maryland. Here it was that one, a Captain John Dagworthy, assumed to command. He even went so far as to refuse to take orders from Colonel Washington. Governor Sharpe of Maryland, ordinarily very friendly to George Washington, felt obliged to support Dagworthy. Dinwiddie, ordinarily very friendly to Sharpe, felt obliged to support Washington. The stage was all set; trouble was inevitable. Dinwiddie stepped in at the psychological moment, as he had done so often before. He made it possible

for Washington to carry the controversy in person to
General William Shirley, governor of Massachusetts,
then in titular command throughout the colonies. His
mediation would be sought.

Washington wrote an interesting letter of appreciation to Dinwiddie for his permission to make the trip.
In it, like a modern executive, he laid out no end of
work for his junior officers to take care of during his
absence in the north. The first and the last paragraphs
of his letter read:

"Honorable sir: I can but return my very hearty
thanks for your kind condescension [470] in suffering me
to wait upon General Shirley, as I am very well assured
it was done with the intention to favor my suit. . .

"I have nothing particular to add, but to assure your
honour, that I shall use my utmost diligence in the prosecution of my journey and pretensions, and that I am,
etc." [471]

The conflict between the British and the colonials
over rank was symptomatic of the irritations which were
to multiply rapidly in the next two decades; Dinwiddie,
unconscious of the significance of his act, was willing to
make the grievance of this young man of twenty-four a
test case, by sending him in person to lay it before the
highest British military official in North America.

Already widely acclaimed as the "hero of Monongahela," Washington set out. The newspapers carried
accounts of his progress along the way.[472] Resplendent

---

470 See my chapter IV, in *Virginia frontier, 1754-1763,* for an appraisal of
the attitude of the two men toward each other.

471 Washington to Dinwiddie, february 2, 1756, John C. Fitzpatrick, ed.,
Writings of George Washington, I, 296-297.

472 Washington "left Alexandria on his journey to Boston, february 4. He
started on his return march 2. En route he passed through Philadelphia, New
York, New London, Newport, and Providence, visited the governors of Pennsylvania and New York, and spent several days in each of the principal
cities" (*Ibid.,* I, 297n).

in his colonel's uniform, seated on a fine horse, and accompanied by his aide, Captain George Mercer,[473] and two servants, George Bishop and John Alton, he must have made a striking impression everywhere. He did — if one may judge by the scraps of information that have filtered down. Other interesting things happened. In New York for example, he proudly recorded in his diary his patronage of the theater while there: "For treating ladies to ye Mm. [Microcosm] [£]1-8[s] New York my. [money]." [474]

When he arrived in Boston,[475] he of course presented his plea to General Shirley. Shirley was placed in a difficult position, nevertheless, his solution of the stalemate was a vindication of Washington's contention. These were his words that none could mistake:

"Governor Dinwiddie at the instance of Colonel Washington having referred to me concerning the right of command, between him and Captain Dagworthy, and desiring that I would determine it, I do therefore give it as my opinion that Captain Dagworthy who now acts under a commission from the governor of the province of Maryland, and where there are no regular troops joined, can only take rank as provincial captain and of course is under the command of all provincial field officers, and in case it shall happen, that Colonel Washington and Captain Dagworthy should join at Fort Cumberland, it is my orders that Colonel Washington should take the command." [476]

---

[473] George Mercer (1733-1784), was the son of John Mercer and was educated at William and Mary. He was a lieutenant, later a captain, on the frontier, serving with Washington.

[474] Washington's notes on journey to Boston, John C. Fitzpatrick, ed., *Writings of George Washington*, I, 298.

[475] "While in Boston Washington lodged at Cromwell's Head tavern on School street" (*Ibid.*, I, 299n).

[476] Shirley's order as to Washington, march 5, 1756, S. M. Hamilton, ed., *Letters to Washington*, I, 201. See also Charles H. Lincoln, ed., *Correspond-*

Jared Sparks, in his day the best-informed man in the United States on the subject of George Washington, has left this memorandum of the Virginian's stay in Boston among the New Englanders:

"He was well received, and much noticed, by General Shirley, with whom he continued ten days, mixing constantly in the society of the town, and attending with interest to the proceedings of the legislature of Massachusetts, then engaged in affairs of great moment respecting the requisite aids for promoting the grand scheme of military operations, recently agreed upon by a council of several governors assembled at New York. He also visited Castle William, and other objects worthy of a stranger's notice." [477]

This trip is an instance of the case in life, as so often happens, where the by-product eventually out-values the product. New Englanders came to know the young Virginian, as otherwise would not have been possible. The Virginian came to understand the New Englanders, as otherwise would hardly have been possible. These contacts were to prove to be of inestimable value. While in Boston, George Washington must have met John Adams, among others; and if he did, it is the essence of history. It was John Adams who later, in 1775, was to have much to do with nominating George Washington to be commander-in-chief of the Continental army.

ence of William Shirley, II, 412-413; John C. Fitzpatrick, ed., Writings of George Washington, I, 297n; Worthington C. Ford, ed., Writings of George Washington, I, 231n; Jared Sparks, ed., Writings of George Washington, I, 133n. This letter was given to Washington by Governor Shirley to deliver personally to Governor Sharpe on the colonel's way back to Virginia (See Maryland archives, VI, 380).

477 Jared Sparks, ed., Writings of George Washington, II, 132-133n. "Washington reached Philadelphia, on his homeward journey, march 14; passed through Chester, Pa., probably march 21; was at Annapolis, march 22; Dumfries, march 25; and Williamsburg, where he reported to Dinwiddie, march 30. He left Williamsburg for Winchester april 1 or 2" (John C. Fitzpatrick, ed., Writings of George Washington, I, 299n).

Would he have done so, had he and other New Englanders not come to know the hero of Monongahela back in
february and march, 1756? It is possible, but it is not
probable. As things transpired it was Robert Dinwiddie
who set the long train of events in motion.

Lord Loudoun and the Embargo

Lord Loudoun "appears to conduct his affairs with good sense and great secresy. Nothing perspires of his intentions." [478] In this choice language, penned on november 9, 1756, did Robert Dinwiddie characterize the man who had recently become his superior officer.

The appointment by the crown on march 17, 1756 of the ambitious military figure, John Campbell, fourth Earl of Loudoun,[479] as titular governor of Virginia,[480] upon the death of the inconspicuous and therefore agreeable holder of the sinecure, the Earl of Albemarle, was another turning-point in the fortunes of Robert Dinwiddie while in America. Next to the pistole fee controversy, Dinwiddie's relationship with Lord Loudoun, not only in the latter's capacity as commander-in-chief of the British forces in North America but also as titular

---

[478] Dinwiddie to Halifax, november 9, 1756, *Dinwiddie papers,* II, 544.

[479] John Campbell, fourth Earl of Loudoun (1705-1782), British army officer who rose to colonel in 1749 and major-general in 1755. In january 1756 he was selected not only as titular governor of Virginia (enjoying a double commission) but also commander-in-chief of all the crown's forces in North America. He did not reach New York, however, until july 23. The colonials did not rally to his banner, his plans miscarried, Fort Oswego and Fort William Henry fell under Montcalm, and by the close of 1757 the government had decided to recall him. Pitt's move was approved. Loudoun, like Dinwiddie, was another of the many Scots who rose to high government position in the British service in the eighteenth century. He died unmarried. See also the excellent study, Stanley M. Pargellis, *Lord Loudoun in North America* (New Haven: London, 1933), which, however, is not concerned, save in a few scattered references, with the Loudoun-Dinwiddie relationship.

[480] The lords of trade to Loudoun, march 17, 1756, P.R.O., C.O., 5/1367, 179-286; L.C. tr., 100-164. See also At the court of St. James, march 18, 1756, P.R.O., C.O., 5/1328, 527-531; L.C. tr., 395-397.

governor of Virginia, has been the source of greatest
misunderstanding about the Virginia lieutenant-governor. When he learned of Lord Loudoun's selection as
commander-in-chief of all the military forces in America as well as governor of Virginia, he wrote of it to his
close friend, the Earl of Halifax, on may 24, 1756, as
something "I am very glad of." [481] Nevertheless, Loudoun's appointment must have been somewhat of a disappointment for Dinwiddie; yet, loyal as he was to his
majesty, he gave no outward manifestation that such
was the case.

But the appointment of a full governor, at this stage
of affairs, cut directly across certain of Dinwiddie's personal plans and hopes. These rather secret hopes were
known at that time only to Dinwiddie's closest friends
but they are among the revelations that are now coming
to light. While these recent disclosures are not unfavor-
able to his reputation as an executive, they do reveal
more and more clearly his human side.

One reason for Dinwiddie's secret attitude toward the
appointment, and which, in truth, is no reflection upon
Lord Loudoun, is that the naming of any appointee – no
matter whom – to the sinecure of governor-in-chief
would have been, at that particular moment, an ill wind
financially for Dinwiddie. He hoped the king would
permit him, a commoner, to enjoy the full governorship's income, variously estimated to be from £2000 to
£3330, at least long enough partially to repay him for
his personal outlay during the past two years of struggle.[482] The naming of a full governor now meant the
end of that particular dream.

The second reason becomes more personal, with re-

481 Dinwiddie to Halifax, may 24, 1756, *Dinwiddie papers*, II, 418.
482 Dinwiddie to Abercromby, march 17, 1755, *ibid.*, II, 2-3. See also pages
201-235 above.

spect to Loudoun. The unambitious Earl of Albemarle, Dinwiddie's former nominal chief, was a man who had been content, like his predecessors, to remain in London or in the diplomatic service in Paris; he seems never to have contemplated coming to Virginia and seldom had concerned himself even to correspond with his lieutenant-governor, one of the rare occasions being the time when he wrote letters in Dinwiddie's behalf during the pistole fee controversy.[483] Such a person had made an ideal titular official. For such, however, Dinwiddie was exchanging what he termed a "noble man"; and this nobleman, while he already had been designated as commander-in-chief of Britain's military forces in North America, meant, it now appears, presently to become also resident, and actual, as well as titular, governor of Virginia.[484]

Evidently Dinwiddie suspected such a move on the new commander-in-chief's part, since on july 1, 1756, in his second letter to Loudoun, he asked him when he might expect him in Virginia, and, by inference, to preside in person over the colony. That Dinwiddie presumed Loudoun would make a stay of indefinite length in Virginia is seen from his offer to prepare the governor's palace in Williamsburg for him: "My lord, I shall be glad to know when I may expect the honor of seeing you here. I am to acquaint you that the government house is a very good one, but there are only three rooms besides the garrets and offices, seperate from the house. As I am sensible the house will be only sufficient for you and your attendants, if you will please let me know when you propose coming here, I shall

---

[483] Dinwiddie to Albemarle, june 18 [1754], *ibid.,* I, 208.

[484] Dinwiddie in his letter to Abercromby, june 6, 1755 states: "I observe by yours that some military noblemen are applying to succeed Lord Albemarle as general of this dominion, with proposal of residing here" (*Ibid.,* II, 57).

take care to have the house ready for your reception, and
rent a house for myself and family, which awaits your
answer." [485] That was july 1.

Dinwiddie's was a long wait. Not until september 22
did Loudoun reply to this offer of his lieutenant-governor to prepare suitable living quarters for him in Williamsburg. On that date he answered in a communication having to do chiefly with publishing his commission
in the press and with what date his salary [486] as governor
would begin. It proceeded in this non-committal fash-
ion: "As to my arrival within the dominions of Virginia,
it is impossible for me to say when his majesty's affairs
will permitt me in person to attend to the particular administration of the government of Virginia." [487] As it
turned out, Loudoun never set foot in Virginia, and the
correspondence on that point was for naught, except that
it served to keep Dinwiddie in suspense as to his chief's
plans and, consequently, in a state of uncertainty as to
his own. Hidden from Dinwiddie as the future was, this
letter from the governor-in-chief clearly indicated to

---

485 Dinwiddie to Loudoun, july 1, 1756, *ibid.*, II, 456.

486 The amount of the salary of Lord Loudoun, as titular governor of
Virginia, and payable (however he could get the money from perquisites) by
Dinwiddie, as lieutenant-governor, is as difficult to determine from their
nebulous agreement and infrequent correspondence as is the method by which
Dinwiddie could possibly raise the amount of salary he apparently agreed
to pay over to Loudoun's predecessor, the Earl of Albemarle. The latter
problem was discussed in a preceding chapter.

The fragments of documents throwing light on this puzzling question are
as follows: (a) The lords of trade on march 17, 1756 issued 114 instructions
to Lord Loudoun along with his commission. The 113th concerned his salary;
he was to receive "one full moiety of the salary and of all perquisites and
emoluments, whatsoever"; (b) seven items, as interesting as enigmatic, in
Lord Loudoun's notebooks, which indicate that his thoughts were much upon
this moot subject; (c) a series of letters exchanged on the subject between
Dinwiddie and Loudoun; some of the letters are in the *Dinwiddie papers,*
others are in the Huntington library; (d) several of Lord Loudoun's bills of
exchange, which are in the same library.

487 Loudoun to Dinwiddie, september 22, 1756, Loudoun papers, LO 1880
(Huntington library).

the lieutenant-governor that he himself, unless he should resign or secure a leave of absence, would otherwise be placed in an intolerable position, one different from any ever occupied heretofore by a lieutenant-governor of Virginia.

Thirdly and finally, Dinwiddie himself certainly had, at one time, legitimate military aspirations. He was apparently at first encouraged by the home government to believe he might become commander-in-chief of more than merely the Virginia forces. After having been finally passed over in favor of Governor Horatio Sharpe of Maryland, Dinwiddie showed on the surface no trace of resentment, because he probably never inwardly experienced it; for Sharpe was essentially a civilian, a fellow executive, and his close personal friend; besides, Sharpe customarily sought his neighbor Dinwiddie's counsel as a matter of course.[488] Governor William Shirley of Massachusetts, who in turn superseded Sharpe as commander-in-chief, was also essentially a civilian, and, in point of miles from Dinwiddie, very distant. His presence would never become embarrassing. As compared with Sharpe or Shirley, however, Loudoun was a surprise choice so far as Dinwiddie was concerned. For one thing, he was a career military figure, who probably would seldom seek counsel from a lay military leader such as his lieutenant-governor. Not only that, but Dinwiddie was an ill man for several years. He mentioned frequently his fatigue. After Loudoun's arrival he complained of a "paralitic disorder" [489] and

---

[488] Sharpe to Dinwiddie, march 7, 1756, *Maryland archives*, VI, 350.

[489] Dinwiddie to General Abercromby, october 6, 1756, *Dinwiddie papers*, II, 527. See also Dinwiddie to the Earl of Halifax, september 24, 1756, P.R.O., C.O., 5/1329, 29-32; L.C. tr., 19-21; *Dinwiddie papers*, II, 520. While Dinwiddie's paralysis distinctly shows in his handwriting at this time, nevertheless he pressed this matter of ill health largely, it would seem, to escape what he feared would become an intolerable situation with Loudoun also residing in

even more persistently than before appealed to the home authorities for a leave of absence.[490]

The impression the histories of the period leave on the reader is that Dinwiddie and Loudoun were at loggerheads with each other; that this situation gradually was aggravated and came to a climax when Dinwiddie lifted Loudoun's embargo from Virginia ports,[491] and that thereafter the two men were estranged. This impression is unfair to Dinwiddie; it is unfair even to Loudoun. That may be true, but it is only partial truth. The whole truth is completely at variance with the common impression; the fact is Loudoun, when he finally closed his correspondence on this point with his lieutenant-governor, wrote him that while he had indeed at the time been incensed at his removal of the embargo, that unpleasant affair was now all over and buried.[492] And Loudoun made no reservations whatever.

The differences between these two Scots, John Campbell and Robert Dinwiddie, both men loyal – as either interpreted loyalty – to his majesty's service, came to the surface, therefore, over the embargo Loudoun laid on colonial shipping, or what Braddock had called "locking up the ports" – a device occasionally employed by nations from time immemorial.

Soon after his arrival in America Lord Loudoun put a stop to all outbound shipping from Virginia.[493] That action, however, was not the first of this kind during the war. It was none other than Dinwiddie, since he had

Virginia. Dinwiddie, after his return to London in 1758, lived on until 1770, certainly with his mental faculties quite unimpaired.

490 Dinwiddie to Abercromby, january 4, 1757, *ibid.*, II, 580.

491 Dinwiddie to Loudoun, may 6, 1757, *ibid.*, II, 618.

492 Loudoun to Dinwiddie, september 9, 1757, Loudoun papers, LO 4432 (Huntington library).

493 Loudoun to Sharpe, august 20, 1756, *Maryland archives,* LII, 593-594. Mr. Philip O. Proctor, M.A., has kindly verified the citations in this chapter to the *Maryland archives* and to the *Pennsylvania colonial records* and has contributed additional citations to these sources.

studied the effects of illicit trade for many years prior
to becoming governor, who had laid and enforced an
embargo on Virginia produce early in 1755,[494] approximately a year before Loudoun's action. Evidently there
was no conflict over principle between the two men. The
lieutenant-governor seems to have been the first of the
colonial executives to suggest a truly comprehensive
program of embargoes, central control of authority, and
a prohibition that would be general in its operation
over all the colonies. At the time Dinwiddie had placed
his own restriction on the shipping he had explicitly
stated his reasons. He held that the provisions which
were reaching the French on the Ohio and which enabled them to conduct "their unjust invasions" were
coming to the enemy through New York and Pennsylvania and other colonies to the northward.[495] To Governor James DeLancey of New York he expressed his
views frankly enough, january 14, 1755.[496] It was a serious indictment. He had put his finger upon vital points
of weakness in Britain's commercial system and suggested appropriate remedies. He had pointed out to Sir
Thomas Robinson and to the lords of trade that it was
essential to keep the British and colonial troops properly supplied while out on the exposed Ohio frontier.
This safeguarding could not be guaranteed, he showed,
unless there were prohibited all shipment of indispensable foodstuffs, like flour, pork, beef, and bacon, from the
English mainland colonies to the French sugar islands
(even by way of Cape Breton), where they eventually
were exchanged for sugar and molasses. Besides, if those
articles must be had by any of the colonies from New

---

[494] Dinwiddie to the lords of trade, march 17, 1755, P.R.O., C.O., 5/1328,
351-352; L.C. tr., 293-295; *Dinwiddie papers*, I, 526-527.

[495] Dinwiddie to Robinson, january 20, 1755, P.R.O., C.O., 5/15, 285-287; L.C.
tr., 182-184.

[496] Dinwiddie to DeLancey, january 14, 1755, *Dinwiddie papers*, I, 456-457.

England to Georgia, they could be procured quite as readily from the British, as from the French, sugar islands; moreover, the former were suffering from a serious dearth of legitimate trade. Dinwiddie had advocated adding foodstuffs to the English government's list of enumerated articles; they would then have to be transported exclusively in British-owned or colonial-owned vessels and exclusively to British territory. Furthermore, he would require every shipper to give bond that he would carry his cargo solely to British territory, and in due time to return a certificate from the consignee as a token of performance. The shipper would thus cancel or take up his bond. Foreshadowing the rule of 1856, he quoted precedents to show that embargoes were effective only when enforced.

He had written with cogent reasoning to Sir Thomas Robinson, january 20, 1755. One excerpt stands out: "The feeding our enemies may in some cases be deemed a Christian duty; but surely these enemies that commit the most barbarous cruelties and unjust actions, can have no pretentions to be fed, to support them in their horrid murders and barbarities. I shall write the lords of trade on this subject . . . but the lucrative dastardly views of some traders have no restraint." [497]

The letter to the lords of trade, which Dinwiddie had promised Robinson he would write, was prepared within twenty-four hours thereafter. Two excerpts from it should be quoted: "Many vessells with flour, bread, pork, beef, etc. from the British colonies, proceed to Lewisburg, formerly called Cape Briton, where they are received with great marks of favour, when they barter their provisions for rum, sugar, and molasses, the produce of the French sugar islands; much to the prejudice of our sugar plantations; and from Lewisburg the

---

[497] Dinwiddie to Robinson, january 20, 1755, *op. cit.*

provisions are sent to Quebeck, and from thence dispersed to their forces and forts down the river Ohio."

Such illicit traffic was so reprehensible to Dinwiddie that he castigated in vigorous language those who were responsible: "This trade is carried on by people not properly to be termed British subjects, who from lucrative views for their own advantage do not consider the pernicious consequence of feeding their enemies, that have committed the most barbarous cruelties and have in view the conquest of all his majesty's empire on this continent; I cannot think of this unjustifiable trade, but with great abhorrence."

Dinwiddie, always respectful, summed up the justification for this long discourse on the subject: "My lords . . . you may think the concern and trouble I am under, in providing provisions for our forces; when the French are supplied with these necessaries from the very people they are invading." [498]

Presently, in Dinwiddie's estimation, the time for action arrived, even though he exonerated Virginia from being one of the offenders. Rather than appear to show partiality for his own province by allowing her ports to remain open, he would cause Virginia to lead the way and close her own ports, as an example to the other colonies worthy of emulation. He therefore wrote the lords of trade on march 17, 1755: "I have laid an embargo on provisions, as a precedent for the other colonies, to prevent the French being supplied therewith; though I verily believe there is none carried from this colony." He added: "The general [Braddock] has wrote to the different colonies to lay an embargo likewise on provisions." [499] The general wrote from Williamsburg,

---

[498] Dinwiddie to the lords of trade, january 20, 1755, P.R.O., C.O., 5/1328, 315-318; L.C. tr., 253-257; *Dinwiddie papers*, I, 475-477.

[499] Dinwiddie to the lords of trade, march 17, 1755, P.R.O., C.O., 5/1328, 351-352; L.C. tr., 293-295; *Dinwiddie papers*, I, 526-527.

march 18, 1755, to Secretary Robinson in London in corroboration of his action and of Dinwiddie's.[500]

Between february 8 and july 8, 1755 all of the colonies from Massachusetts to Maryland imposed one or another type of embargo, doubtless most of them influenced by the recommendation from Braddock – not to speak of Virginia's example.[501] Shirley of Massachusetts, DeLancey of New York, Belcher of New Jersey, Morris[502] of Pennsylvania, Sharpe of Maryland, and Dinwiddie of Virginia kept messenger expresses busy with their correspondence reporting the progress of the prohibition. The embargoes at this time, differing from those to be imposed presently by Loudoun, were mainly in restraint of trade with the enemy, particularly in foodstuffs.

Two other problems descended upon the Virginia lieutenant-governor's shoulders at a most inopportune time, in the summer and fall of 1755. And neither of these problems – short crops of grain and some thousands of uninvited guests suddenly dumped upon him – was of his own creation. Result: another embargo. To the well-intentioned Governor Charles Lawrence[503] of Nova Scotia, he protested vigorously in his letter of december 1755:

---

500 Braddock to Robinson, march 18, 1755, P.R.O., C.O., 5/46, L.C. tr., 1-10.

501 Dinwiddie to the lords of trade, march 17, 1755, *op. cit.*

502 Robert Hunter Morris (c. 1700-1764), son of Lewis Morris, was born at Morrisonia, New York. He served on the council of New Jersey, and then as its chief justice, while his father was governor of that province. He accepted the governorship of Pennsylvania in october 1754. He resigned in august 1756.

503 Charles Lawrence (1709-1760), British army officer. He accompanied the army to Halifax in 1749, became soon a member of the council, lieutenant-governor in 1754, and governor in 1756. See Dinwiddie to Lawrence, december 1755, *Dinwiddie papers*, II, 293-294; see, curiously, the attitude of Henry Fox toward Dinwiddie in this matter. Henry Fox (1705-1774) succeeded Sir Thomas Robinson as secretary of state for the southern department. Fox to Dinwiddie, august 14, 1756, Loudoun papers, LO 1489 (Huntington library).

"I received your six letters of same tenor and date the
11th of august, by six different sloops, with French
neutrals. I wish you had given me previous notice of
your coming, that I might have been better prepared to
receive them. It was a surprize to me to have above 5000
people sent to this dominion so late in the year, and more
so, as our crops are very short from the drought of last
sumer, which occasioned my laying an embargo on all
provisions, prohibiting any to be exported."

Three attempts to set up an effective embargo marked
the year 1756. First came the joint action of the so-called
"bread provinces" of New York, Pennsylvania, and
New Jersey, imposed upon the recommendation of De-
Lancey's successor, Sir Charles Hardy,[504] governor of
New York. This tri-colony embargo was in force during the summer of 1756, in fact until august 20, when it
was taken off Pennsylvania's trade by that colony's new
governor, William Denny.[505]

These early embargoes were not imposed simultaneously, a fact that made them partial failures. Thus the
very day that saw Denny lift the Pennsylvania embargo
witnessed also Loudoun's imposition of another, the second of the year.[506] It was to run the same gauntlet its
predecessors had and to fare as well: it was carried out
only by Loudoun's loyal lieutenant-governor, while it
was flaunted elsewhere. The third and last embargo during 1756 resulted from the lords of trade's circular letter

---

[504] Charles Hardy (d. 1780), naval officer, son of a lord of the admiralty
of the same name. He attained the rank of admiral and like his father was
knighted. He was governor of Newfoundland, 1744 and governor of New
York, 1755-1757.

[505] At a council held at Philadelphia, august 20, 1756, *Pennsylvania colonial
records,* VII, 221. William Denny (1709-1765), was lieutenant-governor of
Pennsylvania from august 20, 1756 to october 1759. He was Cambridge-edu-
cated, travelled in Europe, and all his life maintained cultural associations
in England. He had some military experience, beginning in 1743.

[506] Loudoun to Sharpe, august 20, 1756, *op. cit.*

to the governors.[507] It met with varying success, from a declaration of cooperation on the part of Sir Charles Hardy of New York in his letter to the lords of trade on december 28,[508] to the petition of the Pennsylvania assembly placed before Governor Denny. That assembly instead of acceding to its governor's request prayed him for dispensation from the embargo's provisions so far as they applied to neutral trade.[509]

The august 20 embargo of the new commander-in-chief, Lord Loudoun, met resistance from Virginia's neighbor, Maryland. From Albany Loudoun wrote Sharpe to prohibit the exportation of all foodstuffs "as I do not know how soon I may want all that the colonies can furnish." [510] But the members of the Maryland lower house thought their colony already had a sufficiently rigid law and unanimously refused Sharpe's and Loudoun's request of them to comply.

Loudoun's first embargo, that of august 20, 1756, aimed at two objectives: to keep English foodstuffs from reaching the French and to assure that an unfailing supply of such articles reached the English. His letter from Albany to Governor Sharpe, august 20, if

507 Circular letter from the lords of trade to the governors, october 9, 1756, *Maryland archives,* XXXI, 183.

508 Hardy to the lords of trade, december 28, 1756, *New York colonial documents,* VII, 215.

509 Denny to the assembly, january 13, 1757, *Pennsylvania colonial records,* VII, 387-388; G. E. Reed, ed., *Pennsylvania archives,* 4th series (Harrisburg, 1900), II, 772. See also Assembly to Denny, february 22, 1757, *Pennsylvania colonial records,* VII, 420.

510 Loudoun to Sharpe, august 20, 1756, *op. cit.* Immediately upon receipt of Loudoun's urgent instructions, Sharpe, on september 24, 1756 (*Maryland archives,* LII, 589-590), addressed both houses of his legislature. On september 18 the Maryland house went on record as follows: "On motion, that a bill be brought in, to lay an embargo on all provisions, resolved unanimously, that as there is an act of assembly of this province, which sufficiently prohibits the exportation of grain, provision, etc. to any of the French islands or territories, that there is not an immediate occasion to lay an embargo on provisions" (*Ibid.,* LII, 602).

taken alone, might readily, however unintentionally, leave the impression that the king had given orders solely to him as the new commander-in-chief. As a matter of fact, Dinwiddie had already suggested such a procedure when he wrote Loudoun on july 1, 1756: "We have six months ago [early in 1756] prohibited the exportation of all kinds of provisions here, but to our own colonies, and then to give bond, with security to produce a certificate of their being landed there." Then he added this statesmanlike observation: "If this was general over all the colonies on this continent, I am convinced the enemy would be in great want of provisions." [511] To Dinwiddie's consternation he presently learned that the embargo, so strongly urged on august 20 by Loudoun, had, so he understood, been removed in New York. Hence he frankly wrote Loudoun:

"I have laid prohibition on the exportation of all manner of provisions, but I observe the prohibition is taken off at New York, which surprised me, and I conceive it will not answer the intention of the crown, if it is not general in all the colonies. . . I begg pardon, I was going out of my sphere, but my sincere regard for your lordship and success to our affairs against the comon enemy, makes me a little sanguine." [512] Dinwiddie appears to have had no response from Loudoun as to his attitude toward the embargo, even though it had been in effect as more or less of an experiment for some months. Meantime the Virginians clamored for an opening of their ports. They declared that since the prohibition was off in all the northern colonies, partiality really had been shown other colonies by Lord Loudoun and Virginia discriminated against. They were reversing what was precisely the same argument that Loudoun

[511] Dinwiddie to Loudoun, july 1, 1756, *Dinwiddie papers*, II, 456.
[512] Dinwiddie to Loudoun, september 8, 1756, *ibid.*, II, 498-499.

himself was presently to use when he charged that Dinwiddie, by raising the embargo, had made it appear that he (Loudoun) was showing partiality towards Virginia.

The Virginia council had been consulted and advised removal. All these factors, reported Dinwiddie, influenced him to save Virginia's forty thousand bushels of Indian corn:

"The prohibition on exportation of provisions from this [colony] was much complained of as all the northern colonies have taken off that restriction and as we had upwards of 40,000 bushels of Indian corn of former year's crop on hand, the council thought it advisable to take off the prohibition otherwise that corn would have been a total loss, and I am perswaded your excellency will think if the prohibition is not general in all the colonies, it will not answer the design proposed in preventing any supplies to our enemies, and if the northern colonies lay the prohibition so absolutely necessary at this time, it shall be immediately laid here, as the power of doing so is lodged with the governor and council. I therefore pray your direction herein." [513]

It is incomprehensible why Loudoun should have permitted himself to appear so indifferent to an acute economic crisis in an important colony like Virginia. Notwithstanding Dinwiddie's repeated inquiries about the embargo, the governor-in-chief failed to enlighten his lieutenant-governor. In a fairly long letter to Dinwiddie on october 25, 1756 he discussed odds and ends — from the royal American regiment and the problems of recruiting officers to "a very good post . . . near Colonel Cresshops [Cresap's]" and his disapproval of George Washington's abandonment of Fort Cumberland on the exposed frontier. These things were important, to be sure, but so was the embargo; and it was

---

[513] Dinwiddie to Loudoun, october 6, 1756, *ibid.*, II, 525.

unfair to throw on to Dinwiddie's shoulders the entire responsibility for the decision as to the time for lifting it, unless Loudoun were prepared to support him in whatever decision he might make.

Thus, about midway in the letter just analyzed, there was devoted to Dinwiddie's pressing questions regarding the embargo, only this one sentence by Loudoun: "As to the embargo, I shall not enter on that subject at present, as I left your letter at Albany, and shall answer it as soon as I return." [514] Viewing the matter of correspondence dispassionately, the case for Loudoun as an efficient officer looks none too promising. For example, the governor-in-chief did not communicate at all with Dinwiddie, the latter later pointed out, between october 25, 1756 and the following january 8.

Laissez-faire was not an unwise policy for any titular governor to adopt when he had a zealous deputy like Dinwiddie; but Loudoun's failure to keep in closer touch with the colony over which he nominally presided – even though he never so much as set foot in it – is difficult to explain to his credit. His greater failure, however, was that of failing to keep Dinwiddie constantly advised of military developments at the north. Little wonder is it that the lieutenant-governor should write to the Earl of Halifax on november 9, 1756: "I have not heard from Lord Loudoun for upwards of a month. He appears to conduct his affairs with good sense and great secrecy. Nothing perspires of his intentions." [515] It was not that Loudoun lacked time to write;

---

[514] Loudoun to Dinwiddie, october 25, 1756, Loudoun papers, LO 2087 (Huntington library).

[515] Dinwiddie to Halifax, november 9, 1756, *Dinwiddie papers*, II, 544. Dinwiddie complained on the same date to Henry Fox, Lord Walpole, and the lords of trade that Loudoun had not written him for "upwards of a month" (*Ibid.*, II, 538-545). See also Dinwiddie to Abercromby, january 4, 1757, *ibid.*, II, 579.

as will be seen presently, the ironical fact is that he was, meanwhile, engaged in much letter-writing – involving a bitter controversy – with Governor Shirley of Massachusetts.

But the time finally came when Loudoun did write Dinwiddie, on january 8,[516] and again on february 28, 1757.[517] These letters are remembered chiefly for the light they throw on Dinwiddie's reiterated questions as to the continuance of the embargo. Loudoun's letters had comments on such matters as Dinwiddie's health and the "impracticability of the roads in some parts of the county," [518] but not a syllable about the embargo.

On april 8, 1757 Dinwiddie once more inquired of Loudoun when the prohibition, particularly as it affected Virginia tobacco, might be lifted.[519] Still not one word came back from Loudoun until april 24. Then, at the close of his letter of that date, he continued to plead that he was not yet ready to commit himself, as he began with the same four words used the preceding october 25: "As to the embargo, I hope very soon to be able, to write to you that I have no further use for it; in the mean time I hope to be able, to return most if not all of the men we pressed in Virginia, as I hope to man the transports without them; and I hope the country will see, that I shall on every occasion avoid giving the trade any distress when the carrying of the service does not make it absolutely necessary." [520]

Loudoun's term "very soon" should, on the contrary, have read, "not very soon." Whether intentionally or

516 Loudoun to Dinwiddie, january 8, 1757, Loudoun papers, LO 2652 (Huntington library).
517 Loudoun to Dinwiddie, february 28, 1757, *ibid.*, LO 2940.
518 *Ibid.*
519 Dinwiddie to Loudoun, april 8, 1757, *Dinwiddie papers,* II, 608. See also Dinwiddie to Loudoun, april 6, 1757, *ibid.*, II, 606.
520 Loudoun to Dinwiddie, april 24, 1757, Loudoun papers, LO 3447 (Huntington library).

otherwise, he continued to keep Dinwiddie in the dark for months at a time. On january 4, 1757 Dinwiddie confided to James Abercromby, agent: "I have not a line from Lord Loudoun since the 25th of october, so that his plan of operations for [the] next campaign will be better known with you than they are here, as nothing perspires. He is very secret in his whole transactions." Still attempting to live up to his principle of loyalty, Dinwiddie added, ". . . which is perfectly right."

Sympathy is felt instinctively for the tired lieutenant-governor as one reads toward the close of that letter: "I am still in a badd state of health, and greatly reduced. I did not care to write for leave to go home without Lord Loudoun's aprobation. I have wrote him strongly on that subject, but as yet have received no answer, and it is very uncertain whether he comes here this winter, and I hope my friends at home will not find fault with my intention, as my health requires it." [521]

On march 2, 1757 Loudoun suddenly issued a drastic order, by circular letter, to all the governors. Two important excerpts read:

"As you must be sensible of the necessity of secrecy, in operations of this nature, I cannot doubt, that you will excuse my not laying the plan before you.

"This measure I see necessary to recommend to Virginia, and all the governments northward of it, that his majestys services may not be disappointed, of a supply of such ships or vessels, as may be necessary for carrying this important service into execution, so essential to the welbeing of his majestys colonies.

". . . An embargo has this day taken place in the port and ports of this province." [522]

---

[521] Dinwiddie to Abercromby, january 4, 1757, *Dinwiddie papers,* II, 579-580.

[522] For one of these letters, see Loudoun to Sharpe, march 2, 1757, *Maryland archives,* VI, 532.

It is evident from this circular that this embargo of Loudoun's was different from all preceding embargoes: it was designed primarily to provide a sufficient number of merchant ships to transport his troops to the attack on Louisbourg. Dinwiddie's reaction to the circular is best seen in his cooperation. The lieutenant-governor, though in poor health, had meantime planned to reach Philadelphia in time for the conference of governors called by Loudoun. Loudoun was delayed and Dinwiddie wrote back to Virginia an illuminating letter, march 5, 1757, addressed to a member of his council, John Blair:

"Lord Loudoun has thought it absolutely necessary for his majesty's service to lay an embargo on all shipping in these northern colonies, and by the enclosed copy of his letters to me you will observe he has desired it to be laid in Virginia. It took place in this port last night, and Governor Sharpe sends an express to Maryland to the same purpose. You are to see who of the councell you can, and communicate the same to them. And enclosed I send letters to the collectors and naval officers of each district on that subject, which, after you have seen the gentlemen of the councill, you are to forward to them and publish them in our weekly paper. Lord Loudoun is to be here next wednesday, when I hope he will soon dispatch us, for I am very weary of the place, and want to return home. I think that embargo cannot be of long duration, I fancy great prejudice to trade, and on his lordship's arrival here I shall endeavour to have it taken of[f]." [523]

Sir Charles Hardy apparently differed with Dinwiddie as to the duration of the prohibition on shipping, for Loudoun has recorded in his microscopic handwriting in his notebook for march 9, 1757: "Sir Charles

[523] Dinwiddie to Blair, march 5, 1757, *Dinwiddie papers*, II, 596.

Hardy advises that the embargo should not be taken of[f] till the service is compleated." [524]

Light is thrown on the subject by quoting here one of Loudoun's typical entries regarding the embargo:

"Som[e] letters from the governor and a messag[e] from the assembly to throw of[f] the embargo as layed on in the provinces to the northward

"I approved that it was layed on in Virginia and Boston and all the provinces between that at Boston they had [   ] on for a limited time I had aquanted them that it must continue there till it was taken of[f] the whole.

"That I had applied to the governors to lay on the embargo that if they had not done it I must order them to lay on vessels of war in ev[er]y port to have enforsed it for the service and safty of the publick could not stope" [525]

Maryland shippers and other commercial men also were smarting under the imposed ban, hence Loudoun in New York wrote Governor Sharpe of Maryland on april 30 that he hoped "soon" to lift it.[526]

Dinwiddie on may 2, 1757 wrote Lord Loudoun: "At present we have no king's ships here. Many merchant ships loaded, and in daily expectation of the embargo being taken off, which I shall be glad of your lordship's orders so to do." [527]

On the following day, may 3, 1757, the Virginia house of burgesses took Loudoun's trade ban "under their most serious consideration." They drew up that same day a solemn resolution, which signified unmistakably that they were starting to perfect their technique of public

---

[524] Loudoun's memorandum book, Huntington manuscripts, 1717 (vol. 3), 9 (Huntington library).

[525] *Ibid.*, 47.

[526] Loudoun to Sharpe, april 30, 1757, *Maryland archives,* VI, 545-546.

[527] Dinwiddie to Loudoun, may 2, 1757, *Dinwiddie papers,* II, 617.

protest – a powerful weapon in England and in America even in the eighteenth century. They called Loudoun's attention to their high taxes, to their bumper crops of grain that were thus prevented from reaching less fortunate parts of the empire, and to their tobacco crop frozen in the warehouses, for tobacco was currency in Virginia. This resolve is worth quoting:

"RESOLVED, that an humble address be presented to his honor the governor, to acquaint him that this house taking under their most serious consideration the load of heavy taxes which the people of this colony must necessarily sustain for carrying on the present war, which they are desirous to prosecute with a becoming vigor and resolution, and reflecting on the great and insuperable inconveniences which must attend the raising of supplies from a total stagnation of our trade, occasioned by the present embargo, whereby not only the very large quantities of grain this colony is able to spare, in this year of great plenty, to relieve the distresses of our fellow-subjects in other parts of his majesty's dominions, must unavoidably perish and be lost, but also the greatest part of our tobacco, the only commodity by which we can gain credit in Great-Britain, must remain unexported, and the people be thereby rendered incapable of paying their taxes: we think it our indispensable duty to beseech your honor in the most humble and earnest manner to take off the said embargo." [528]

The pressure was becoming greater and greater. Dinwiddie made a strong argument out of all these factors and wrote Loudoun another letter, four days after his earlier entreaty:

"Enclosed I trouble you with a resolve of our house

---

[528] *Journals of the house of burgesses* (1752-1755; 1756-1758), 448. See also preface, xxix.

of burgesses in regard to the embargo, on which I called the council, to advise with thereon. They are unanimous in their opinion of the absolute necessity of taking off the embargo, otherwise the people will not be able to pay their taxes, and as your lordship thinks soon of giving orders thereon, I hope you will not take it amiss on the pressing solicitations of councill, house of burgesses, and petitions from numbers of people all over the dominion, that I give my assent for taking off the embargo, which I propose to do next week." [529]

Despite the distance intervening, some of the noise from all this agitation in Virginia ought to have reached the commander-in-chief's ears. But it did not. Loudoun on may 5 sent another circular to the governors, but it contained not a word regarding the embargo. [530]

The widespread effects of this shipping prohibition inspired an account of that subject in particular, and other subjects generally, in the London publication, *Gentleman's magazine,* for july 1757. Under the caption "American affairs" and the date "Philadelphia, may 5," appeared an illuminating cross-section of the progress of the war. It begins:

"A general embargo was laid the beginning of march on all vessels throughout the provinces from Nova Scotia to North Carolina, which is still to continue for some time, and is much felt here, as it puts an almost entire stop to business. The intent was to procure about 10,000 tons of shipping for the transportation of soldiers, provisions, stores, artillery, etc. Above 8000 tons are now assembled at New York, whence the principal embarkation is intended. With these lie the transports that came from Cork last winter, which are refitted,

---

[529] Dinwiddie to Loudoun, may 6, 1757, *Dinwiddie papers,* II, 618.

[530] Circular to southern governors from Lord Loudoun, may 5, 1757, P.R.O., C.O., 5/48; L.C. tr., 379-384.

and ready for the same purpose, all which carry, at one ton and a half per man, about 8000 soldiers. There is also an embarkation to be made here of 450 men of the first battalion of royal Americans; being ordered for South Carolina. The rest of the shipping taken up by the government are transporting provisions to New York and Carolina. This embargo was also designed to procure seamen, the privateers having swept away such numbers. . . The assembly of Virginia have passed a bill for giving £80,000 for the king's service." [531]

Sharpe's colonists of Maryland put just as much pressure on him, as the Virginians had done on Dinwiddie, in order to force him to lift the ban on shipping. He appeased them for a time, but only for a time, for they "renewed their sollicitations." What made them so insistent, Sharpe told Loudoun, was their knowledge that "30 vessels had been permitted to clear and sail from Virginia since the beginning of that month." More convincing yet to the Maryland governor, apparently, was a paper that fell into his hands, an authenticated copy of a port order sent out for the Virginia lieutenant-governor, upon advice of his council.

That was too much for the Marylanders. And it was too much even for Sharpe, friend of Dinwiddie though he was. Did he not have his own colonial constituents to consider? He therefore informed Loudoun that since he was persuaded his lordship did not "desire to distress the trade of this province more than that of Virginia (the staple whereof is the same as ours)" he therefore flattered himself that Loudoun would not disapprove of his action in lifting the ban. [532]

Sharpe's letter to Loudoun was dated june 4. Loudoun wrote Sharpe on the fifth, which, since it was the next

---

[531] *Gentleman's magazine*, XXVII (July 1757), 336.
[532] Sharpe to Loudoun, june 4, 1757, *Maryland archives*, IX, 19.

day, could not of course have been a reply. Sharpe had informed Loudoun he had just removed the embargo, and Loudoun had informed Sharpe that he was not to remove it, until seven days after his (Loudoun's) fleet had sailed for its French objective. "And," he added, "it will not be taken off here [New York] any sooner." [533] So much for another illustration of the tardiness of colonial correspondence.

On june 17, 1757, from on board the "Sutherland" at Sandy Hook, Loudoun unburdened himself to William Pitt regarding Dinwiddie's alleged stab in the back:

"And Lieutenant-governor Dinwiddie, as I am informed, and have reason to believe, has broke the concert made with the other provinces, of keeping on the embargo; and without my knowledge or consent, has taken it off in Virginia, on the 8th of may. This never came to my knowledge till the 19th, the day before we sailed, that I received a letter from Governor Sharpe, with a copy of the order of the council, dated may 5th to the collector of the customs, granting liberty for ships to sail on the 8th. By this, Mr. Dinwiddie has broke through the concert I have made, and been endeavoring to establish among the provinces. By his suffering ships to sail, they may fall into the hands of the French squadron, in their cross from the cape to the northward, from whom they may get intelligence of this embarkation, which it does not appear, by all we can learn from the prisoners, that they had before; and to me personally, it is surely, as cruel an action as it was possible for one man to do another; for from my having the honor, to be governor of that dominion, it will be believed, that the lieutenant-governor would not have taken it upon himself, without my concurrence; which is doing all that lay in his power, to give me the appearance of partiality,

---

533 Loudoun to Sharpe, june 5, 1757, *ibid.*, IX, 20.

which, whilst they see it in that light, must diminish that weight, the kings commander-in-chief ought to have." [534]

Loudoun reminded Sharpe in his june 5 communication that the embargo was "absolutely necessary" in order "to prevent the enemy from having intelligence of our motion, from any ships they might take." [535] With his reputation as commander-in-chief somewhat in the balance, Loudoun had set his heart upon military success in the present campaign. Surprise he regarded as one of his vital weapons. Hence it is natural that Dinwiddie's action seemed to him to strike him a blow where he felt himself particularly vulnerable. If a nemesis seemed to follow any official's best intentions more than Loudoun's, it was Dinwiddie's.

Loudoun was not in possession of all the facts in the case; certainly he did not realize how devastating to harmony between himself and Virginia's officials had been the inability of the lieutenant-governor, though he had been writing urgent letters to his superior officer, to get any replies from his military commander-in-chief and his chief governor. One is therefore somewhat prepared for Loudoun's immediate reaction to Dinwiddie's embargo-lifting, a reaction that Loudoun set down in his revealing little book under date of june 18, 1757. Interestingly enough, Loudoun referred to Dinwiddie never as governor, which, strictly speaking, he was not, but always as "Lieutenant-governor Dinwiddie," as noted below:

"Writ to Lieutenant-governor Dinwiddie acquainting him with the information I had of the p[r]oseeding of his councel as to the embargo, my opinion of it, and the nomberles bad consequences it must have both in giving intellege[nce] to the enemy, the breech of union

---

534 Loudoun to William Pitt, june 17, 1757, P.R.O., C.O., 5/48, L.C. tr., 397-407.
535 Loudoun to Sharpe, june 5, 1757, *Maryland archives,* IX, 20.

among the colonies, and the appe[a]rance of parshality
it gives to the kings commander-in-chief from whence
he may easily guess how that must appear to me personaly" [536]

Loudoun's letter to Dinwiddie the same day that he
made his letter book notation is too important here to
abridge:

"On board his majesty's ship Sutherland
June 18th 1757

"SIR: I have just now received an application from
Mary Land for liberty for ships in certain situations to
depart, in which letter Governor Sharpe acquaints me
that on the 2d instant one of the merchants that were applying for liberty to sail, presented to him an authentick
copy of an order that had been sent to the port officers
of Virginia by the clerk of the council, which was dated
the 5th day of may, and was contained in the following
words 'The governor having thought proper by the
advice of the council to discontinue the embargo, I
hereby acquaint you, that you are permitted to clear
out any vessels from your district after the eight of this
instant, upon taking bond with security and a certificate
as usual.'

"I cannot avoid on this occasion acquainting you that
this measure of yours seems to me very extraordinary,
and inconsistant with what has passed between you and
me, both in letters and on the conversations we had together at Philadelphia.

"It seems to me a measure which by it's consequences
is likely to give the enemy information of the motions of
his majesty's forces in this country and by that enable
them to prevent a junction of them, for carrying on the
service, and by that defeat the operation, and render

---

[536] Loudoun's memorandum book, Huntington manuscripts, 1717 (vol. 4),
11 (Huntington library).

useless the whole preparations, and very great expence both of the mother country and of the colonys for this campaign, and this at a time when a French squadron was in those seas, who saild northward from the cape may 4th and I have reason to believe those are not the only French vessels may get intelligence destructive to the service, if they fall into their hands.

"This proceeding has likewise another very bad consequence as it breaks in to the concert with the other provinces, and destroys that confidence which is so necessary for the good of the whole and for carrying on the publick service.

"And you must forgive me to acquaint you if I look on it as extremely prejudicial to the service by endeavouring to deminish the credit of the person the king has thought proper to intrust with the management of the war in this country by giving him that air of partiality so very improper for any man in that station from whence you must judge of the light it appears in to me personaly." [537]

Four days later, in a letter dated "from on board the Sutherland at sea june 22d 1757," Loudoun wrote to Cumberland a letter that tells much. Besides valuable military information about the campaign and references to the problems of insuring the receipt of correspondence, it contains a lengthy condemnation of Dinwiddie.

Loudoun was seasick, which did not improve his mind or his temper. As he said: ". . . I hope your royal highness will make some allowance for my being at sea, where I am never well, and my head always muddy, and not able to write one sentence to an end, and get through a letter only by perserverance."

Having in a paragraph of four hundred sixty-five

---

[537] Loudoun to Dinwiddie, june 18, 1757, Loudoun papers, LO 3851 (Huntington library).

words justified the principle of an embargo, the commander-in-chief opened up against his lieutenant-governor with all the ammunition at his command. He attacked him in what he regarded his most vulnerable spot – where men have always attacked men – the pocketbook. Dinwiddie had lifted the embargo for personal gain, held Loudoun, and with the hope of getting all he could before he left America.

In fairness to both parties, this section of Loudoun's letter should not be mutilated by abridgment. It was a bitter arraignment: "I have likewise mentioned in my publick letter Lieutenant-governor Dinwiddie's conduct, which is in my opinion very strong. As he is a man of sense, I can account for it no other way but that, as he has desired leave to resign, he has done this for money, and is determined to get all he can in any shape before he goes.

"I shall not be able to write to my Lord Halifax by this packet, but will begin to write to him on the state of the colonies as soon as this is gone, that it may be ready for the next opportunity. In my last I recommended Lieutenant-colonel John Young [538] to him, for a successor to Mr. Dinwiddie, in case his lordship had no better man in his view. He is one I am sure money will have no influence on, or he must change strangely before it has. If Mr. Dinwiddie's behaviour appears in the same light it does to me, I should think superseding him, in place of giving him leave to retire, would have a good effect." [539]

[538] "Lieutenant-colonel John Young was severely wounded at the fall of Fort William Henry, august 9, 1757. It is stated in the Abercromby correspondence, previously referred to, that so confident was Young of his appointment that he had sent to the colony 'a post-chaise for his use'" (*Dinwiddie papers*, II, 602n).

[539] Loudoun to Cumberland, june 22, 1757, Stanley M. Pargellis, ed., *Military affairs in North America, 1748-1765* (New York: London, 1936), 375-377.

In his condemnation of Dinwiddie Loudoun received aid and comfort from the above-mentioned John Young who, rumor had it, would succeed Dinwiddie as lieutenant-governor. Loudoun thought so, Dinwiddie thought so, and apparently Young thought so. Loudoun and Dinwiddie were agreed that Young was a good man for the place. Dinwiddie went out of his way to write home in commendation of Young, and he appeared sincerely interested in his appointment.[540] How far his attitude was based upon personal knowledge of Young's qualifications and how far it was influenced by his desire to support Loudoun's expressed choice is not known. He even reached the point where he began to count on Young's taking over certain personal equipment he had bought for the palace in Williamsburg — non-standing furniture, the Virginians called it.[541]

It is now known that Colonel Young, far from reciprocating Dinwiddie's sentiments, was one of those partially responsible for Loudoun's growing resentment against Dinwiddie. An entry, months later, in Loudoun's own notebook, headed "Governor Dinwiddies reasons for taking of[f] the embargo," is sufficient evidence:

"Albany november 14t[h] 1757 monday. Frost. "Dinwiddie – talking with John Young about Dinwiddies behaveiour about the embargo and of the order he has rece[i]ved to go home now without any reason notted to me from the ministry whether this is done out of favour to him or on my representation of him from the Hook by which if it is meerits or a ponishment the use it would be of is lost.

"Colonel John Young informes me that he has heard tho not certain of the truth that Mr. Dinwiddie has been for sometime past been concerned in privat tread [trade]

---

540 Dinwiddie to William Pitt, march 22, 1757, *Dinwiddie papers*, II, 599; Dinwiddie to Abercromby, march 22, 1757, *ibid.*, II, 601-602.

541 Dinwiddie to Young, july 9, 1757, *ibid.*, II, 667.

and that it is suspected that even before he took of[f] the embargo in Virginea that he allowed shipes to sail in which he had privat tread which made a clammor and occasioned the embargo being taken off.

"Tis sade [said] that during the embargo a vessal saild from Virginea with a cargo of the vallew of £200 currence and has since brought into New York and layed in Beverly Robinson [542] 50 pippes [pipes] of madera wine in return." [543]

Loudoun closed that extraordinary entry for november 14 with a "Quere: What cargo did she car[r]y and to what market to bring such a return in which at £50 the pippe the price at New York shall amount to £2500." [544]

Colonel Young was not the only individual who fanned the suspicion dangerously smouldering in Loudoun's mind. According to another long entry in Loudoun's notebook a Mr. Byrd gave him information, that someone else had given him, regarding Dinwiddie. It would be damaging to Dinwiddie's reputation if true. Let the uncensored entry tell its own story:

"Albany november 16t[h] 1757
Wednesday Soft [balmy?]

"Mr. Bird teles me that by a letter he has had from Virginea he is informed that the counsel tooke of[f] the embargo on an appli[cation] from Mr. Dinwiddie the lieutenant-governor and that several of them thought it a very wrong measure at the time.

---

[542] Beverly Robinson (d. 1792), son of Speaker John Robinson of the house of burgesses (not John Robinson sr., member of the council; Brock is in error in *Dinwiddie papers,* II, 686-687n). He moved to New York. He not only acquired wealth but married into the Philipse family. As John C. Fitzpatrick states, he "adhered to the crown in the Revolutionary war, and is remembered principally for his connection with Arnold's treason" (*Writings of George Washington,* I, 299n).

[543] Loudoun's memorandum book, Huntington manuscripts, 1717 (vol. 2), leaf 21v.

[544] *Ibid.*

"He furder teles me that he has feard that he allowed several shipes and vessals to sail before the embargo was taken of[f] and that it was believed he was deeply concerned in the cargoes that tis hard to be sure of the [   ] it concerned as he manages all that by Mr. Hunter the contractors agent and Mr. Rolston his clark

"That furder Mr. Dinwiddie has been greatly blamed in former embargoes for allowing shipes to sail that it was always believed he had cargoes in those shipes." [545]

Meantime, Dinwiddie lost no time in replying promptly and fully to Loudoun's charges in his letter of june 18. What Dinwiddie alleged to be the facts is completely at variance with Young's, Byrd's, and Loudoun's statements and allegations. Dinwiddie wrote Loudoun on july 9, 1757:

"Your letter of the 18th [june] gives me much concern. On your desire I wrote to all the officers of the customs to see the embargo on shipping be properly put in force. I wrote to your lordship the 6th of may,[546] and enclosed you an address from the house of burgesses of their uneasiness on account of the embargo, and that they were determined to vote no supplies unless the embargo was taken off. I advised with the councill, who were unanimous on the necessity to comply with their request. There were then upwards of 50,000 bushels of wheat on board of ships, bound for Great Brittain and Ireland, which was likely to perish if that indulgence was not granted; and the legislature were further going into a dispute of the legality in laying the embargo, which I endeavoured to prevent, and thought it more eligible to take off the embargo than to admit of any dispute of your power in ordering it; at the same time to be prevented from complying with your orders

---

[545] *Ibid.*, leaf 21v and 23r.
[546] See Dinwiddie to Loudoun, may 6, 1757, *op. cit.*

in raising men, since they appeared determined not to vote any money for the service till that was complyed with. For these reasons I hope your lordship will excuse my doing an affair quite contrary to my private inclination."

Dinwiddie advanced two more arguments: "At the same time it was then noticed the embargo was taken off in New England, and that I never received an answer to the letter I wrote you on that subject of the 16th of may, which gave me room to believe your lordship approved of the step I had taken."

As to Loudoun's charge of favoritism toward Virginia, and that Dinwiddie's action would tend to diminish Loudoun's prestige, he said: "It gives me greatest concern that you write it was endeavouring to diminish the credit of the person the king was pleased to entrust with the management of the warr in this country, by giving him that air of partiality so very improper for any man in that station. Give me leave, my lord, there is not a person on the continent that will more chearfully support your person and authority, and obey your comands more readily than myself; and that of your lordship's partiality must be quite out of the question, as the stepp taken was without your knowledge, and the supporting his majesty's service made it absolutely necessary to do it."

The clinching argument followed: "I have a letter from Lord Holderness, directing me, without any regard to the embargo to order every vessel loaded with grain, etc., for Britain, Ireland, and the British plantations, to be cleared outwards, giving bond and security for delivering their cargoes at the places cleared out for." And finally: "I hope, for the reasons given you above, you won't retain a dislike to my conduct on this head, as the necessity of his majesty's affairs in this collony obliged me to this stepp, and I shall be uneasy till I have a line from you excusing me thereon." [547]

Dinwiddie was oblivious of the correspondence and conversation, current during the summer of 1757, between Young and Loudoun as to his supposed culpability. On the same day, july 9, that he penned that long letter to Loudoun in an effort to clear himself, he wrote also to Colonel Young: "By the desire of his excellency, the Earl of Loudoun, I give you the trouble of the enclosed pacquet, to be forwarded to him. I hope this will meet you in good health. I have not as yet one letter from home in regard to my resignation of the government. I observe the pacquet by which the first letters were to go, did not sail from New York till the beginning of june, but as I wrote by other opportunitys, I am in hopes soon to have an agreeable answer, and that you are to succeed me. As the people here know of my intentions of going home, I have been applied to for the sale of my negroes and household furniture, but I have rejected selling till I hear from you, as I am of opinion you incline, if you succeed me, to purchase these things that you will want on such occasion. The delay of the forces from Brittain must give Lord Loudoun great uneasiness, as the frequent changes of the ministry, and the intestine divisions at home must give our enemies great advantage over us. We are at present threatened with a number of French and Indians from Fort Du Quesne. The regiments in this government's pay are augmented to 1000 men, which with Colonel Stanwix's half batalion and the provincials of Pensylvania and Maryland, I conceive will be sufficient to repell any force they are able to bring against us." He began his final paragraph with a now familiar refrain: "Entirely in the dark as to Lord Loudoun's motions, I shall be

[547] Dinwiddie to Loudoun, july 9, 1757, *Dinwiddie papers*, II, 664-665.

obliged if you will favor me with any news with you.
With sincere wishes for your health, I remain with due
regard." [548] The finding of Young's letter bringing that
much-sought "news," if he ever replied to Dinwiddie,
would make entertaining reading.

And this is where the Dinwiddie-Loudoun relationship has been left, up to this time, by historians. Far
from this being the conclusion of the whole matter, it
is submitted here, on the contrary, that a portion of a
letter written by Loudoun to Dinwiddie from New
York on september 9 is by all odds the most important
in the entire series. It is a revelation of Loudoun's
changed attitude toward Dinwiddie. Apparently it has
never before been noticed, let alone quoted. It is two
brief paragraphs in the midst of a letter which Loudoun
wrote Dinwiddie regarding a number of military matters. These two paragraphs, which are the high point of
the entire series of letters between the two officials, have
to do, of course, with the embargo:

"As to what I writ in relation to the embargo, you
will not be surprised at it, when I have informed you,
that I had expresses from many different provinces,
convayed to me by merchants, who all came to sollicit
relief at a very critical time, just when I was ready to
sail, and when I knew of a fleet of the enemy's being in
those seas, able in half an hour to demolish the whole
embarkation, if by any of those ships they had got intelligence of us, and every one insinuating the partiality
showed by me on this occasion to the dominion of Virginia, and no account of this transaction being arrived
from you.

"As to the embargo being taken off in New England,
previous to your doing it, I have never heard it before,
but I will own that those governments did never keep

---

[548] Dinwiddie to Young, july 9, 1757, *ibid.*, II, 666-667.

it well; for several of their small smuggling vessells got out during the whole time of it; for which they have payed; for we have taken several of them on their return from St. Eustatia, and which have been condemned and sold. – The truth is I was extremely hurt at the time, but it is now all over, and I have forgot it." [549] Here – to Lord Loudoun's credit – is the key to the ultimate relationship between the two men.

Dinwiddie was not the only colonial governor who aroused Loudoun's ire. Had he been, certain inferences might follow. In truth, the letters that passed between Loudoun and Dinwiddie are mild reading compared with those exchanged during a bitter dispute carried on by Loudoun, practically at the same time, with Major-general William Shirley, governor of Massachusetts. This latter controversy is referred to here only because of the collateral light it throws upon Loudoun's relationship with Dinwiddie.

This unfortunate altercation between Loudoun and Shirley seesawed back and forth; Shirley wrote Fox on september 5, enclosing a letter dated august 29 he had received from Loudoun, and which he declared was an "extraordinary attack his lordship hath thought fit to make upon me." [550] Loudoun followed suit on september 13 by communicating his charges against Shirley to the committee of war at Boston.[551] Not to be outdone, Shirley promptly, two days thereafter, forwarded to Fox an extract from Loudoun's letter containing the charges.[552] But one day later, september 16, he sent Fox additional data to refute the contention that he had been

[549] Loudoun to Dinwiddie, september 9, 1757, Loudoun papers, LO 4432 (Huntington library).

[550] Shirley to Fox, september 5, 1756, P.R.O., C.O., 5/46; L.C. tr., 557-559.

[551] Loudoun to the committee of war at Boston, september 13, 1756, P.R.O., C.O., 5/46; L.C. tr., 635.

[552] Shirley to Fox, september 15, 1756, P.R.O., C.O., 5/46; L.C. tr., 583-587.

responsible for the failure of provisions at Oswego.[553]
Who shall judge among these veterans in his majesty's
service?

Loudoun apparently had gained little through his
embargo; he reaped chiefly criticism. Furthermore, he
had so aroused the "apprehensions" of the Massachusetts people because of his views as to the quartering and
billeting of soldiers that the council and house of representatives on december 16, 1757 [554] framed a message to
Shirley's successor, Thomas Pownall,[555] about it. Next,
Loudoun had failed in his military plans – whatever,
whoever the cause. And, finally, by incurring the ill-will
of Shirley he was laying up added trouble for himself.

[553] Shirley to Fox, september 16, 1756, P.R.O., C.O., 5/46; L.C. tr., 637-653.

[554] The council and house of representatives to Governor Pownall, december 16, 1757:

"Our apprehensions of the extent of the act of parliament so far as it relates to quarters and billeting differ from those of his lordship. . .

"We beg leave further to observe, and we doubt not your excellency will
think it a proper occasion. That the inhabitants of this province are intitled
to the natural rights of English born subjects; that by the royal charter
the powers and privileges of civil government are granted to them, that the
enjoyment of these rights, these powers and privileges is their support under
all their burdens and pressure, this will animate and encourage them to resist
to the last breath a cruel invading enemy, the loss or hazard of these enjoy-
ments from any other cause naturally tends to deject and dispirit them"
(P.R.O., C.O., 5/513, 481-483; L.C. tr., 655-658).

[555] Thomas Pownall (1722-1805), born and educated in England, early
became interested in the colonies and imperial problems. Soon after leaving
college he entered the service of the board of trade, where his brother John
was secretary. In 1753 he came to New York with Sir Danvers Osborn, the
new governor. Osborn committed suicide. Pownall remained to study colonial
conditions. He attended the Albany congress and presented a recommendation. He returned to England in 1756, discussed with officials the American
scene, and returned to the colonies with Loudoun as a kind of special secretary. Again he returned to England (presenting Loudoun's case against
Shirley) ; and again, in due time, back to America, now as governor of Massachusetts. He arrived august 3, 1757. His three years as governor were profit-
ably spent in continuing his investigation of the entire colonial system. The
fruits of this interest are embodied in his valuable work, *Administration of
the colonies,* which ran through many editions. He was a man of ability,
versatility, and vision.

In short, he had suggested the advisability of having certain officials removed, one of them being Robert Dinwiddie. Instead, the cumulative effect of the increasing number of representations at home against him eventually would bear fruit – his own recall by Pitt in 1758.

Such, briefly, is a hectic chapter not only in Robert Dinwiddie's career in America, but in the American career of Robert Dinwiddie's second titular chief, the man who conducted his affairs with such "great secresy that nothing perspired."

To summarize: Even though Loudoun's appointment must have meant Dinwiddie's disappointment, the two might have worked together harmoniously during the months of their official relationship in America, had Loudoun deigned to answer Dinwiddie's letters. Dinwiddie's forte was letter-writing. Loudoun's silence, especially in such a juncture, seemed to him incomprehensible. This was a personal matter.

In pinning so much faith on an embargo, Loudoun was relying upon an uncertain quantity; for no concomitant of war is more difficult to handle than an embargo. Fair examples are the trade prohibitions during the American Revolution, the War of 1812, the War between the States, and the world wars of the twentieth century.

Whether or not Dinwiddie was among those officials who during their term of office still continued to carry on private business – which under the peculiar circumstances of his day would be entirely natural – there is no direct evidence that the Virginia lieutenant-governor lifted the embargo because it affected his own purse. The truth is that he had good grounds for removing it, in view of the example set by New England, in view of the petitions of the house of burgesses, and in view of the peculiar attitude of Lord Loudoun on the whole episode. Loudoun finally replied to Dinwiddie's two urgent inquiries about the embargo. But though he eventually wrote of it, he did so, however, only after almost interminable delay, from october 26 to april 24. Even then his replies concerning it were mere sentences in otherwise long letters and were almost parenthetically thrown in. In the first letter he excused himself on the ground that he had left Dinwiddie's letter somewhere else and therefore could not answer it; in the second one he said he hoped soon to be able to write that he would have no further use for an embargo. The commander-in-chief had made a grave military mistake by not keeping his ranking associates, like his own lieutenant-governor, informed of developments.

In the next place, Loudoun was quarreling with others – not alone with Dinwiddie. These quarrels, plus delays in prosecuting the war, finally led, not to Dinwiddie's recall, but to his own.

His notebooks, kept in his peculiar microscopic handwriting and showing a meticulous interest in even the smallest minutiae of his campaigns, clearly reveal an overweening love of detail. One is tempted to apply to him the characterization of a certain American president by one of his biographers, who declared: "He confused insistence upon a detail with fidelity to a principle."

Loudoun was irritated with problems which were all but unsolvable; he was impatient and Dinwiddie was ill, and their differences were accentuated by distance. They did not maintain close contact and long delays bred suspicion.

Finally, new light is cast on the ultimate relationship of the two men over the matter of the embargo. Instead of the embargo marking a final bitter climax and a definite break between them, as has hitherto been held by historians, quite the opposite is true. Loudoun's own enlightening sentence – and his last to Dinwiddie regarding the embargo – will bear repeating: "The truth is I was extremely hurt at the time, but it is now all over, and I have forgot it." [556] That Loudoun was man enough

---

[556] In the exchange of communications the last extended letter from Dinwiddie to Loudoun, dated december 24, 1757, is so typical of the problems facing Dinwiddie up to the very last, in his relations with his titular governor, and at the same time answers so many other questions about Dinwiddie's attitude toward Virginia, that it is here given in full:

"Right honorable: I have not been honored with a line from your lordship for some time; and as I am disappointed of a king's ship to accomodate myself and family home, I have taken my passage in the Baltimore, Captain Crookshanks, and I expect to leave this in ten days.

"As your lordship did not incline to pay my contracts made in General Braddock's time, and as some of them I am engaged to pay – as also 151/18/10 for transporting Captain Wray's company from this to the head of the bay, which was by Colonel Stanwix's order, and I desired Colonel Hunter to procure a vessell for that service, and being refused payment he applied to me, and I thought myself obliged to pay him. After settling the whole there will be a ballance due from me, which I shall leave with Colonel Hunter, to be applied as your lordship may direct; and when the account is finally settled I shall trouble you with a letter and his obligation to be accountable to your lordship.

"The enclosed letter from the council I am desired to forward you, which I do by this express; it chiefly relates to the £50,000 granted by parliament to the two Carolinas and this dominion and we believe left to your lordship in proportion to the services each of these colonies have done for his majesty and the common cause and no doubt your lordship will distribute that sum in an equal manner agreeable to the merits of each different colony.

"As I am going to leave this government, I think it my indespensable duty to acquaint your lordship that this colony has raised upwards of £200,000 for his majesty's service, and kept in pay a regiment ever since the commencement of hostilities, which I am convinced is attended with above three times the charge and expence of the other two colonies mentioned in the grant by parliament – the money and credit sent me has chiefly been expended in General Braddock's time, and in presents etc. to the Indians and the accounts have been transmitted to the treasury.

"The legislature readily obeyed your orders in sending forces to South Carolina, with powder and lead from the magazine; – in short, my lord, I must do the country the justice to say, that they have been more ready than any of the others in supporting the common cause, and I doubt not you will readily agree that they are intitled to a greater share of that generous donation, and they are very glad that it's left to your lordship's distribution.

"The country is now much in debt, and wants many necessaries for the

Right Honble   Williamsburg Decr 24th 1757

I have not been honor'd with a Line from Your Lordship for some Time; & as I am disappointed of a King's Ship to accomodate myself & Family Home, I have taken my Passage in the Baltimore Capt. Crookshanks, & I expect to leave this in ten days.

As Your Lordship did not incline to pay my Contracts made in Genl. Braddock's Time, & as some of them I am engag'd to pay — as also 151..18..10 for transporting Capt. Wray's Company from this to the Head of the Bay, which was by Col^o. Stanwix's Order, & I desir'd Col^o. Hunter to procure a Vessell for that Service, & being refused Payment he applied to me, & I tho^t. myself obliged to pay him — After settling the whole there will be a Ball^a. due from me, which I shall leave with Col^o. Hunter, to be applied as Your Lordship may direct; & when the Acc^t. is finally settled I shall trouble You with a Letter & his Obligation to be accountable to Y^r Lordship.

The enclos'd Letter from the Council I am desir'd to forward You, which I do by this Express, it chiefly relates to the 50,000£ granted by Parliament to the two Carolinas & this Dominion & we believe left to Your Lordship in Proportion to the Services each of these Colonies have done for his Majesty & the Common Cause & no doubt Your Lordship will distribute that Sum in an equal Manner agreeable to the Merits of each different Colony.

The Country is now much in Debt, & wants many Necessaries for the Public Service from Home, & they have great Dependance on this Money to qualify them to make the proper & necessary Supplies; & I hope You will excuse my writing so fully on this Affair, which is done as my Duty & that Regard I have for this Dominion.

I am surpriz'd I do not hear of Col^o. Young's appointment, as my Private Letters from Home assure me he will succeed; & it wou'd have been Pleasure to me & Service to him if I had a few Hours Conversation with him before I left this.

If the great Hurry & multiplicity of Your Affairs will allow You Time, to honor me with a Letter to London, it will be very agreeable to

Your Excellency's
most obed^t. hble Servant
Robt. Dinwiddie

Earl of Loudoun

FACSIMILE OF DINWIDDIE'S LETTER TO THE EARL OF LOUDOUN
[First and last paragraphs only; reduced to about one-half size of original]

thus to recognize the validity of Dinwiddie's position in regard to the embargo and had the courage to write that sentence is certainly to his credit.

public service from home, and they have great dependance on this money to qualify them to make the proper and necessary supplies; and I hope you will excuse my writing so fully on this affair, which is done as my duty and the regard I have for this dominion.

"I am surprized I do not hear of Colonel Young's appointment, as my private letters from home assure me he will succeed; and it would have been [a] pleasure to me and [a] service to him if I had a few hours conversation with him before I left this.

"If the great hurry and multiplicity of your affairs will allow you time to honor me with a letter to London, it will be very agreeable to

"Your excellency's most obedient humble servant"

(Loudoun papers, LO 5082 [Huntington library]).

Place in History

Dinwiddie, ill and worn out, begged to be allowed to return to England for his health. He left Virginia january 12, 1758 of his own volition.

The city fathers of Williamsburg ought by that date to have had some measure of the man. He had not only lived his seven years as governor in Williamsburg in close association with the local authorities, but he had also spent many years in their midst while a member of Governor Gooch's council. And now in 1758, since the chances were many that he would never return to America, there was every reason for them to come forward with the unvarnished truth if they held anything against him. If he had become *persona non grata* in Virginia, as historians have almost universally maintained, they surely would have adopted toward him a frigid silence or taken advantage of the occasion to vent their spleen against him. Did they seize the opportunity to do so? Quite the contrary. On the eve of his embarkation for London the corporate authorities of the city of Williamsburg voiced an address "to the Honorable Robert Dinwiddie, Esquire, his majesty's lieutenant-governor and commander-in-chief of the colony and dominion of Virginia:

"MAY IT PLEASE YOUR HONOR: We, his majesty's most loyal and affectionate subjects, the mayor, recorder, aldermen, and commonalty of the city of Williamsburg, in common council assembled, beg leave to return your honor our unfeigned acknowledgements for the great care and assiduity with which you have transacted the public affairs during your administration in this colony.

"The inhumanities daily perpetrated on our frontier inhabitants by a cruel and insidious enemy, and the successful attempts of our fleets and armies, justly excite in us the most interesting concern, but a steady confidence in his majesty's wisdom and the hopes of conciliating the favour of that being who presides over the most powerful legions, revive our declining spirits, and create in us the warmest expectations to see in his majesty's reign, that happy age restored wherein the British standards were displayed with glory and virtue, and liberty inspired the breast of every Briton.

"Permit us, sir, in a more particular manner, to return your honor our thanks for the kind regard you have shown to the interest and welfare of this city, and to request that you would be pleased to think this corporation an object worthy of your further patronage and protection, and at the same time to assure you that we do, with the greatest sincerity, wish your honor and family an agreeable voiage to England, and that you may there enjoy every felicity which reason can suggest or your prudence require." [557]

After his return to England Dinwiddie's interest in the welfare of Virginia continued unabated. He served the colony of Virginia up to the time of his death.[558] From London he wrote to Richard Corbin in Virginia a letter that is typical. He called attention to the fifty thousand pounds which had been granted by parliament [559] to reimburse Virginia and her two southern

---

[557] Address of the corporation of Williamsburg to Dinwiddie [January 1758], *Dinwiddie papers,* II, 724-725.

[558] Dinwiddie lived more than a decade after his return to England, until july 27, 1770. Death thus came in his seventy-eighth year.

[559] Parliament set aside £50,000 as partial reimbursement to the colonies, this action being influenced by Dinwiddie's strong representation to the home government as to the just claim on the part of Virginia and her neighbors.

neighbors for their expenditures during the war and which was ready for distribution. He stated he intended to apply for the division – that is, at least for Virginia's share. He added, recalling the charges of his detractors: "I hope my character is above their reach to hurt me, and their endeavours shall not prevent my doing everything in my power for the service of Virginia, as I shall always have a sincere regard for the collony in general, and many worthy friends in particular."

In substantiation of his contact with his old friends in the New World, another illuminating paragraph in the Corbin letter attests:

"I've ordered Messrs. Hanbury to send you a cheese and some porter, which I fear you have not received, as you do not mention it. I shall desire Messrs. Buchanan [560] to send you a chest of lemmons, which I begg your acceptance of. My health continues but very poorly, tho' I have travelled upwards of 1300 miles this summer. My paralisise complaint continues, and effects my spirit a little. Your son dined with me before he went to Cambridge. He is truly a sober, well-behaved young gentleman. . . I shall do everything in my power, but it will be necessary on the death of our friend, Mr. Buchanan, to have a merchant to assist me. I believe Messrs. Hanbury's will be the most proper. It will be time enough on a vacancy, for there is no possibility of procuring a reversion, and some time hence will be time enough for your son. I hope Mr. Foukier [Fauquier] gives good satisfaction to the people. He

---

[560] "John Buchanan, colonel of militia of Augusta county, was the son of Colonel James and Jane (Sayers) Buchanan, of Northumberland county, Pennsylvania (from whom also, the late President James Buchanan is said to have descended). He married Margaret, daughter of Colonel James Patton, was associated with him in all of his exploring expeditions, and was a man of of courage, energy, and ability. The town of Buchanan, Virginia, was named in his honor" (*Dinwiddie papers,* I, 268n).

is a very good-natured gentleman, and has a good interest here. Pray, when you see him present my kind respects. I am sorry for the great trouble you have in my affairs. I can only say that I shall be glad on all occasions to serve you and yours. My wife and two girls join me in sincere respects to your lady and pretty family, and I am, with great truth, worthy sir, your most obedient and much obliged humble servant." [561]

It is interesting to note his mention of his successor, Francis Fauquier. He was appointed to his position in february 1758 and arrived in Virginia the following june 5.[562] John Blair, president of the Virginia council, was in the meantime acting governor. Not always are comparisons odious. Here is a case in point. Blair wrote to the board of trade, june 20, 1758, regarding the new governor, Fauquier, that he hoped the incoming official and his family would "all prove publick blessings to this country, and make up our loss in his predecessor." [563] It is significant that Blair referred to Dinwiddie's leaving Virginia as a loss, and that after Dinwiddie's return to England, John Blair jr., while a law student in England, was at times a guest of the former governor; in fact, Brock calls him a protégé.[564]

Another fragment that shows something of the attitude of the British toward Dinwiddie's accomplishments may be noted. Whatever may be the traditionally-thought-of reception of a prophet in his home country,

---

[561] Dinwiddie to Corbin, november 1758, *ibid.*, II, 722-723.

[562] John Blair, in a letter to the lords of trade dated Williamsburg, june 20, 1758, stated that Fauquier arrived june 5, 1758. His letter also furnishes verification, if it were needed, that Dinwiddie left on january 12 (P.R.O., C.O., 5/1329, 161-166; L.C. tr., 121-127). *Journals of the house of burgesses* (1752-1755; 1756-1758), xxix, gives the date of Fauquier's arrival as june 7.

[563] Blair to the lords of trade, june 20, 1758, P.R.O., C.O., 5/1329, 161-166; L.C. tr., 121-127.

[564] *Dinwiddie papers*, I, xvi note. Brock, who is authority on this point, states that Colonel Richard Corbin's son was also a guest of the former governor while he was in London.

Robert Dinwiddie, returned favorite son, was honored by his fellow Scots, october 4, 1758, by being presented with a "burgess ticket," together with the "freedom of the burgh of Dumfries." [565]

While epitaphs on tombstones are not necessarily conclusive historical evidence, they are at least evidence. The following inscription on the tablet erected to the memory of Robert Dinwiddie is to be found in the parish church of Clifton, Bristol, England:

In this church are deposited the remains of Robert Dinwiddie Esqr. formerly governor of Virginia, who deceased july 27th, 1770, in the 78th year of his age.

The annals of that country will testify with what judgement, activity, and zeal, he exerted himself in the publick cause, when the whole North American continent was involved in a French and Indian war.

His rectitude of conduct in his government, and integrity in other publick employments, add a lustre to his character, which was revered while he lived,

And will be held in estimation whilst his name survives.

His more private virtues and the amiable social qualities he possessed

Were the hapiness of his numerous friends and relations

Many of whom shared his bounty

All lament his loss.

As his happy dispositions for domestic life

Were best known to his affectionate wife and daughters,

They have erected this monument

To the memory of his conjugal and paternal love, which they will ever cherish and revere

With what piety and tenderness he so greatly merited

Farewell blest shade! no more with grief opprest

Propitious angels guide thee to thy rest! [566]

---

[565] *Ibid.,* vii note. Furthermore there is on record a certificate, bearing date of september 5, 1758, which admitted Dinwiddie's younger daughter, Rebecca, "to the privileges of a burgess of the town of Renfrew, Scotland" (*Ibid.,* ix note).

[566] This inscription was kindly copied for me by Mr. James A. Dinwiddie

It is curious that, contrary to so much factual evidence, Dinwiddie has been so long pictured as an avaricious, arrogant, inefficient, fussy individual.[567]

This may have arisen partly because a man with vision and ambition for his country as a whole, rather than mere personal aggrandizement, is bound to incur current ill-will. This immediate estimate often is erroneous,

Wilson of 3 Mount Terrace, Taunton, Somerset, England, enclosed in his letter of march 7, 1938.

[567] The following examples will illustrate the point:

"Dinwiddie continued in office until january 1758, when he sailed for England, unregretted by the people of his province and certainly by Washington. Jealousy of the young officer on the part of the governor, and an irritating exercise of authority over him, met with proud and even angry protests in return, made official dealings between the two anything but pleasant. Dinwiddie was both fussy and inefficient, always magnifying his official position and asserting the rights of the prerogative, though doing it in a most unimpressive manner. His style of writing makes one think that he was a sort of improved edition of John Usher, who afflicted New Hampshire so long" (H. L. Osgood, *American colonies in the eighteenth century* [New York, 1924], IV, 430).

"He was in continual conflict with the colonial legislature, which persistently refused to vote adequate funds for carrying on the war, and in consequence he advocated the imposition of an arbitrary poll tax by parliament. This, combined with his arrogance, his avarice, and his indecision, made him unpopular, and led to his recall in 1758" (*New international encyclopaedia*, 2nd edition, VII, 38).

"He arrived in the colony in 1752. He was rapacious, and unscrupulous in the accumulation of wealth. Owing to his exaction of enormous fees authorized by the board of trade for the issue of patents for lands, he gained the ill-will of the people of Virginia, and when he called for money to enable him to oppose the encroachments of the French, the house of burgesses paid no attention to his expressed wishes. . . Worn out with trouble and age, he left Virginia under a cloud caused by a charge made by his enemies that he had appropriated to his own use £20,000 transmitted to him for compensation to the Virginians for money expended by them in the public service. He died at Clifton, England, august 1, 1770" (*Harper's encyclopaedia of United States history*, III, 117-118).

"Dinwiddie . . . governor of Virginia (1752-1757). Under his regime the first attempt was made to seize Fort Duquesne and other French forts. . . He was recalled in 1758" (Funk & Wagnalls, *New standard encyclopedia*, IX, 213).

"Dinwiddie's administration was marked by a constant wrangle with the assembly [house of burgesses?] over money matters" (*Encyclopaedia britannica*, 14th edition, VII, 392).

and is of value only when checked against ultimate achievement.

Thus the terms which seem to be damning may in light of another century really be sincerest praise.

Yes, he was arrogant – against persons and forces which he felt were detrimental to the colony or to Britain's interests. Avaricious for colonial expansion and wealth – yes, very – but not for purely personal gain.

Any charge of inefficiency must be carefully scrutinized. Any man will fail at certain points, being human, but if he stubbornly fights for and carries his main objectives, these minor ineffectualities do not call for indictment. And Dinwiddie was nothing if not stubborn and aggressive in his fight for western colonization and expansion. This was the crux of the bickering and recrimination between him and others, and between him and the legislature. But results show it was a cause worth a querulous man's stubbornness.

Any disparagement of his conduct toward, and relationship to, Washington is based on purest fiction.[568] That they disagreed somewhat was inevitable. Both men were ill much of the time, both were strong-willed and aggressive. It was but natural that diversity of procedure might cause argument. The net result of their relationship was respect and confidence.

Also the charge that he was recalled to England is simply not fact, as his letters amply attest. He had long begged to be relieved of the burden of his office owing to failing health. Numerous letters show the regard held for him here and abroad.

Hence from this total misconception there gradually

---

[568] Jared Sparks, notwithstanding the credit that rightly belongs to him for the early editing of George Washington's *Writings* and for the painstaking researches that Herbert B. Adams in his two-volume life of Sparks so properly commends, is largely responsible for this erroneous conception of the relationship between the two men.

emerges the real man. He was possessed of a lifelong devotion to the crown and almost as long to Virginia. He was fiery and irritating and exacting, but withal for a cause. His determination to hold the Ohio valley against the French changed the course of colonial history.

It was because of the inadequacy of funds [569] allowed him by the provincial legislature to carry on his program of defense that he advocated the arbitrary poll tax by parliament. This, in turn, contributed to his unpopularity and the hue and cry of avarice, on the part of a faction in the lower house. Such a cry is part of the price of success paid by men of achievement even in our own day.

A great deal of quoted material has been employed in this characterization. Since it is largely composed of actual letters written by and to Dinwiddie, the statements confirmed or discredited by them should stand squarely on their own feet. Owing to the hitherto distorted conceptions of his character and actions, it has seemed justifiable to present in their own quaint phraseology and content these communications as indisputable evidence.

Among others, five persons stand out as influences upon that youth who was later to become the Father of his Country. One thinks instinctively of Mary Ball Washington, his mother; of Lawrence Washington, George's half-brother, fourteen years his senior; of Sally Fairfax, George Washington's relative by marriage, his close neighbor, his youthful critic, and the wife of his best friend; of Lord Fairfax, his early patron; and, finally, of his sponsor, who, in a sense, was

---

[569] Not only were the funds inadequate but the burgesses set up a finance committee to supervise the expenditures of the monies after they were appropriated.

his discoverer, Robert Dinwiddie, lieutenant-governor
of Virginia. And of these five persons who powerfully
influenced George Washington's career, Robert Dinwiddie's rôle was unique. Therefore, America's debt to
him is great.[570] It would not be facetious and quite within the bounds of truth, because of this influence upon
young George Washington and upon the early and
growing west, to term Robert Dinwiddie the Grand-
father of his Country.

---

[570] An epitome of Dinwiddie's place in American history appears in Louis
K. Koontz, "Robert Dinwiddie: a chapter in the American colonial frontier,"
Pacific historical review, v (December 1936), 359-367.

Bibliography

MANUSCRIPT SOURCES

England

BRITISH MUSEUM: Additional manuscripts.

Contain a volume (6865 items) of material covering the French and English disputes over the Ohio region, a conflict in which Dinwiddie was much interested.

PUBLIC RECORD OFFICE: Colonial office papers.

C.O. 5:13-20 (Original documents. 1742-1762. Correspondence with colonial governors, chiefly military).

Of value in regard to the French danger in the Ohio valley and Dinwiddie's connection with it.

C.O. 5:211-215 (Entry books. 1753-1763. Secretary's dispatches).

Pertains to the correspondence between Holdernesse and Dinwiddie regarding the situation in the Ohio valley.

C.O. 5:1308-1334 (Virginia. 1691-1774. Original papers, letters, and enclosures to the original board of trade, from the governors, Edmund Andros to Lord Dunmore).

The source of a vast amount of hitherto unexploited Dinwiddie material.

C.O. 5:1337-1338 (Virginia. 1694-1753. Letters from the governors, Alexander Spotswood to Robert Dinwiddie, to the secretary of state).

Includes a number of letters of Dinwiddie on the Ohio situation.

C.O. 5:1344 (Virginia. 1722-1780, 1783. Miscellaneous).

Includes several Dinwiddie letters.

C.O. 5:1358-1369 (Virginia. 1689-1774. Entry books).

Pertains to the board of trade's approval of Dinwiddie's Indian and land policies (1753).

A large proportion of the above-mentioned materials (through the medium of photofilm, photo-enlargements, photostats, and transcripts) are available in the manuscript division of the Library of congress.

France

AFFAIRES ÉTRANGERES. Correspondance politique, Angleterre.

—— Memoires et documents, Angleterre.

Volume 25 of this series includes numerous documents relating to the French claims to the Ohio valley and clearly shows the problems with which Dinwiddie was confronted in his efforts to prevent the French from limiting the English colonies to the region east of the Alleghenies.

ARCHIVES NATIONALES. Ministère des colonies.

Series F contains material relative to the French activities in the Ohio country which eventually led Dinwiddie to send George Washington on his historic mission to the French.

United States

CLEMENTS library (Ann Arbor, Michigan).

Shelburne papers.

Contains, for example, reports from the governors to the board of trade.

HUNTINGTON library (San Marino, California).

Abercromby papers.

Both those of the general and of the agent are included.

Brock collection.

This collection, originally brought together in Richmond, Virginia by R. A. Brock, contains a great quantity of papers of importance to a study of Dinwiddie.

Dinwiddianae

Anonymous satirical poem dealing with problems arising out of Dinwiddie's administration.

Loudoun papers.

Contain numerous important letters between Dinwiddie and various influential figures in England. Particularly interesting are the notebooks kept by Lord Loudoun, titular governor of Virginia. His handwriting is often illegible, chiefly because his penned characters are almost microscopic in size.

MASSACHUSETTS HISTORICAL SOCIETY (Boston).

Parkman collection.

Five volumes cover Dinwiddie letters between 1751 and 1755, copied from the Dinwiddie letter books in London in 1880. Most of these are included in the *Dinwiddie papers*.

NEW YORK PUBLIC LIBRARY.

Chalmers papers.

Includes valuable material pertaining to the problems arising out of illegal settlements in the Ohio valley.

PENNSYLVANIA HISTORICAL SOCIETY (Philadelphia).

Etting collection, Ohio company papers.

Volume I contains much material on problems arising out of English and French conflict on the Ohio.

SOUTH CAROLINA STATE ARCHIVES. Historical commission of South Carolina (Columbia).

Indian book (1750-1757).

Volumes II-V relate to Indian affairs in South Carolina, chiefly, but include some material on the Iroquois, Cherokees, and Catawbas, and the relations of the English with the Six Nations.

VIRGINIA HISTORICAL SOCIETY (Richmond).

A rich collection which contains, for instance, John Blair's diary. Many of the documents have been printed in the *Virginia magazine of history and biography.*

WILLIAM AND MARY COLLEGE LIBRARY (Williamsburg, Virginia).

Contains nearly complete file of the indispensable *Virginia gazette.* Many items of great value in the manuscript division have been printed in the *William and Mary college quarterly historical magazine.*

WILLIAMSBURG RESTORATION (Williamsburg, Virginia). Colonial Williamsburg, inc., division of research and education.

Contains many thousands of items, bearing directly or indirectly upon Dinwiddie.

WISCONSIN STATE HISTORICAL SOCIETY (Madison).

Draper manuscripts.

Preston papers (QQ) (6 volumes).

Contain much data upon the early phases of the French and Indian war on the Virginia frontier.

Newspaper extracts (JJ) (4 volumes).

Maryland gazette is of particular value.

PRINTED SOURCES

DINWIDDIE PAPERS. Official records of Robert Dinwiddie, lieutenant-governor of the colony of Virginia, 1751-1758, edited by R[obert] A[lonzo] Brock. Vols. III and IV of the Virginia historical society collections, n.s. (Richmond, 1883-1884) 2 vols.

An extensive, but by no means complete, collection of his official correspondence as lieutenant-governor, compiled from letter books still in the possession of the society.

ENGLAND. Acts of the privy council, colonial series, edited by W. L. Grant, James Munro, and Sir Almeric W. Fitzroy (Hereford, 1908- —).

GENTLEMAN'S MAGAZINE (London, 1731-1907).

Valuable corroborative and interpretative matter appears in the issues for 1751-1755.

GIST, CHRISTOPHER. Journals with historical, geographical and ethnological notes . . . , edited by William M. Darlington (Pittsburgh, 1893).

JOHNSON, SIR WILLIAM. Papers, edited by James Sullivan and Alexander C. Flick (Albany, 1921-1933) 8 vols.

Valuable for Johnson's activities among the Indians.

JOURNAL OF THE COMMISSIONERS for trade and plantations (London, 1920- —).

Indispensable for the pre-governorship period of Dinwiddie.

MARGRY, PIERRE, editor. Découvertes et établissements des français, dans l'ouest et dans le sud de l'Amérique septentrionale (1614-1754), mémoires et documents originaux (Paris, 1876-1886) 6 vols.

Includes Céleron's journal during the expedition down the Ohio river in 1749.

MARYLAND ARCHIVES.

Correspondence of Governor Horatio Sharpe, 1753-1771, edited by William Hand Browne (Baltimore, 1888-1911) 4 vols.

Proceedings of the council of Maryland, 1636-1770, edited by William Hand Browne (Baltimore, 1885-1912) 11 vols.

Proceedings and acts of the general assembly of Maryland, 1637-1761, edited by William Hand Browne, et. al. (Baltimore, 1883- —).

NEW JERSEY. Documents relating to the colonial history, edited by William A. Whitehead, Frederick W. Ricord, and William Nelson (Trenton, 1880- —) 1st series, 28 vols.

NEW YORK. Documents relative to the colonial history, edited by E. B. O'Callaghan and B. Fernow, J. R. Broadhead, collector (Albany, 1853-1887) 15 vols.

—— Documentary history, edited by E. B. O'Callaghan (Albany, 1850-1851) 4 vols.

NORTH CAROLINA. Colonial records, edited by William L. Saunders (Raleigh, 1886-1890) 10 vols.

Includes material on North Carolina's reaction to the dangers of French encroachments.

PARGELLIS, STANLEY McCRORY, editor. Military affairs in North America, 1748-1765 . . . (New York, 1936).

Contains some choice material pertaining to the Dinwiddie-Loudoun controversy.

PEASE, THEODORE CALVIN, editor. Anglo-french boundary disputes in the west, 1749-1763 (Collections of the Illinois state historical library, XXVII, French series, II) (Springfield, 1936).

Indispensable for a general study of the rivalry between the English and French for control of the Ohio valley.

PENNSYLVANIA. Minutes of the provincial council, from the organization to the termination of the proprietary government [March 10, 1683 to september 27, 1775] (Harrisburg, 1831-1840. Reprinted, Harrisburg, 1851-1853. Vols. I-III reprinted, Philadelphia, 1852) 10 vols.

Comprise the first ten volumes of *Pennsylvania colonial records,* by which name they are commonly cited.

—— Pennsylvania archives, edited by Samuel Hazard, 1st series, 12 vols. (Philadelphia, 1852-1856).

Provide a complete picture of the American colonial frontier during the eighteenth century.

—— PENNSYLVANIA archives, edited by G. E. Reed (Papers of the governors) 4th series, 12 vols. (Harrisburg, 1900-1902).

SHARPE, HORATIO. Correspondence (see Maryland).

SHIRLEY, WILLIAM, governor of Massachusetts and military commander in America. Correspondence, 1731-1760, edited by Charles Henry Lincoln (New York, 1912) 2 vols.

STATE OF THE BRITISH and French colonies in North America, with respect to number of people, forces, forts, Indians, trade, and other advantages (London, 1755).

> The publisher sent a copy of this item to Robert Dinwiddie, who, on february 24, 1756, wrote him in acknowledgement and stated his objections to the views contained in the pamphlet (*Dinwiddie papers,* II, 349).

SUMMERS, LEWIS PRESTON, editor. Annals of southwest Virginia, 1769-1800 (Abingdon, 1929).

VIRGINIA. Calendar of state papers and other manuscripts preserved in the capitol at Richmond, edited by W. P. Palmer, S. McRae, R. Colston, and H. W. Flournoy (Richmond, 1875-1893) 11 vols.
> Volume I covers the period from 1652-1781.

—— Executive journals of the council of colonial Virginia, edited by H. R. McIlwaine (Richmond, 1925-1930) 4 vols.

—— Legislative journals of the council of colonial Virginia, edited by H. R. McIlwaine (Richmond, 1918-1919) 3 vols.

—— Journals of the house of burgesses of Virginia, 1619-1776 (title varies), edited by J. P. Kennedy and H. R. McIlwaine (Richmond, 1905-1915) 13 vols.

—— Statutes at large; being a collection of all the laws of Virginia from the first session of the legislature in 1619, edited by W. W. Hening (Richmond, 1819-1823) 13 vols.
> Contains important information on Virginia and by no means so restricted in scope as the title might indicate.

WASHINGTON, GEORGE. Journal of my journey over the mountains; while surveying for Lord Thomas Fairfax, baron of Cameron, in the Northern Neck of Virginia, beyond the Blue Ridge in 1747-8, edited by Joseph Meredith Toner (Albany, Munsell, 1892).

—— Journal of Colonel George Washington, commanding a detachment of Virginia troops, sent by Robert Dinwiddie, lieutenant-governor of Virginia, across the Alleghany mountains, in 1754, to build forts at the head of the Ohio, edited by Joseph Meredith Toner (Albany, Munsell, 1893).

WASHINGTON, GEORGE, Diaries, 1748-1799, edited by John C. Fitzpatrick (New York, 1925) 4 vols.

—— Letters to Washington and accompanying papers, edited by Stanislaus Murray Hamilton (Boston, 1898-1902) 5 vols.

—— Writings of George Washington, edited by Jared Sparks (Boston, 1834-1837) 12 vols.

—— Writings of George Washington, edited by Worthington Chauncey Ford (New York, 1889-1893) 14 vols.

—— Writings of George Washington, from original manuscript sources, 1745-1799, edited by John C. Fitzpatrick (Washington, D.C., 1931-——).

The most complete and scholarly collection yet made available.

Index